W9-BLT-493

INSIGHT GUIDE
Wales

Discovery
CHANNEL

APA PUBLICATIONS
Part of the Langenscheidt Publishing Group
L

ABOUT THIS BOOK

Editorial

Edited by
Brian Bell
Updated by
Roger Thomas

Distribution

UK & Ireland
GeoCenter International Ltd
The Viables Centre, Harrow Way
Basingstoke, Hants RG22 4BJ
Fax: (44) 1256-817988

United States
Langenscheidt Publishers, Inc.
46–35 54th Road, Maspeth, NY 11378
Fax: (1) 718 784-0640

Canada
Thomas Allen & Son Ltd
390 Steelcase Road East
Markham, Ontario L34 1G2
Fax: (1) 905 475 6747

Australia
Universal Press
1 Waterloo Road
Macquarie Park, NSW 2113
Fax: (61) 2 9888 9074

New Zealand
Hema Maps New Zealand Ltd (HNZ)
Unit D, 24 Ra ORA Drive
East Tamaki, Auckland
Fax: (64) 9 273 6479

Worldwide
Apa Publications GmbH & Co. Verlag KG (Singapore branch)
38 Joo Koon Road, Singapore 628990
Tel: (65) 865-1600. Fax: (65) 861-6438

Printing

Insight Print Services (Pte) Ltd
38 Joo Koon Road, Singapore 628990
Tel: (65) 865-1600. Fax: (65) 861-6438

First Edition 1989
Third Edition 2001

CONTACTING THE EDITORS

We would appreciate it if readers would alert us to errors or outdated information by writing to:

Insight Guides, P.O. Box 7910, London SE1 1WE, England.
Fax: (44 20) 7403-0290.
insight@apaguide.demon.co.uk

www.insightguides.com

This guidebook combines the interests and enthusiasms of two of the world's best known information providers: Insight Guides, whose range of titles has set the standard for visual travel guides since 1970, and Discovery Channel, the world's premier source of nonfiction television programming.

The editors of Insight Guides provide both practical advice and general understanding about a destination's history, culture, institutions and people. Discovery Channel and its Web site, www.discovery.com, help millions of viewers explore their world from the comfort of their own home and also encourage them to explore it first hand.

How to use this book

This fully updated edition of *Insight Guide: Wales* is carefully structured to convey an understanding of the country and its culture as well as to guide readers through its wide range of sights and activities:

◆ The **Features** section covers the history and culture of Wales in a series of lively, informative essays by experts.

◆ The main **Places** section gives a detailed guide to all the sights and areas worth visiting. Places of special interest are coordinated by number with the maps.

◆ The **Travel Tips** listings section is filled with facts on travel, hotels, restaurants, shops and more. Information may be located quickly by using the index on the back cover flap (which also serves as a bookmark).

The contributors

This edition of *Insight Guide: Wales* has been restructured and thoroughly updated by one of the book's original authors, **Roger Thomas**. A prolific writer on travel, history and the outdoors, Thomas lives in Crickhowell in the Brecon Beacons National Park, and was assisted in this project by his son, **Huw**, who lives in Cardiff.

Thomas likes to get off the beaten track with the help of his mountain bike, and also likes to get away from the stereotypes that so often characterise writing about Wales. "Defining Welshness isn't easy," he says. "Wales isn't defined by flat caps and male voice choirs. The deeper you look, the more complicated it gets. There are Welsh speakers and English speakers, suspicious North Walians and garrulous South Walians, eisteddfod lovers and eisteddfod haters, traditional farming communities and the aspirational middle-classes, avid readers of the *Western Mail* and those who turn their TV aerials eastwards to pick up all the English stations."

In updating the book, Thomas relied heavily on the work of contributors to previous editions. The essay on the Welsh Character was written by **Dannie Abse**, who has been described at various times in his life as a Jewish Welshman, a radio broadcaster, a doctor practising in London's Soho, and one of Britain's leading poets. He is especially fond of Ogmore-by-Sea, in Glamorgan, "where I can walk under the seagulls and blown skies and think about Wales and the people of Wales and their unfathomable strangeness."

A contingent of top journalists experienced in covering Wales for Britain's national media provided most of the original text, much of which survives in this edition. They included **Anthony Moreton**, **Ena Kendall**, **Frank Barrett**, **Tony Heath**, **Paul Gogarty** and **James Lewis**. Other chapters were provided by **Marcus Brooke**, **Stuart Ridsdale**, **Mike Mockler**, **Brian Bell** and **Diane Fisher**. The history section was written by **Sara Jackson**, and the original Travel Tips information came from **Emyr Griffith**.

The book was proofread and indexed by **Penny Phenix**.

Map Legend

— —	State Boundary
- - - -	Region Boundary
— • —	National Park/Reserve
- - - -	Ferry Route
✈ ✈	Airport: International/ Regional
🚌	Bus Station
ℹ	Tourist Information
✉	Post Office
✝ ✝	Church/Ruins
✝	Monastery
☪	Mosque
✡	Synagogue
♜ ♜	Castle/Ruins
🏛	Mansion/Stately home
∴	Archaeological Site
∩	Cave
🗿	Statue/Monument
★	Place of Interest

The main places of interest in the Places section are coordinated by number with a full-colour map (e.g. ❶), and a symbol at the top of every right-hand page tells you where to find the map.

CONTENTS

Maps

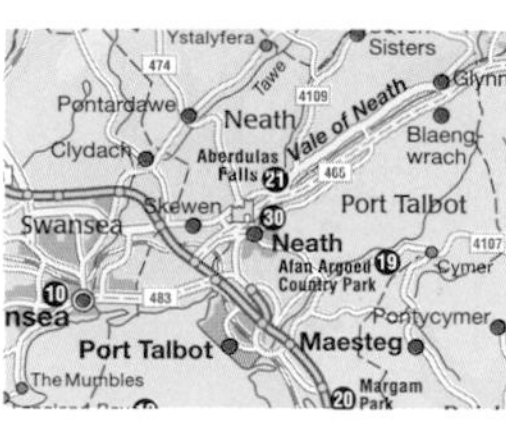

Introduction

History

Features

Llangorse Lake, Brecon Beacons.

Information panels

Travel Tips

◆ **Full Travel Tips index is on page 273**

Places

8

30/6
30/6

DAVIES
DAVIES

Western Mail
SPO
WALES . . . WAL

SEASIDE AND SUMMITS

Wales's appeal lies partly in its distinctive character and partly in the variety of its outdoor pursuits

The principality of Wales, the mountainous land which points to the Irish Sea, is little more than 135 miles (216 km) long and at one part less than 35 miles (56 km) wide. The border runs from the mouth of the Dee in Liverpool Bay in the north to the mouth of the Wye on the Severn estuary in the south. It roughly follows the lines of the dyke built to contain the Celts by Offa, the powerful Anglo-Saxon king of Mercia from 757 to 796.

This 168-mile (269-km) frontier earthwork provides walkers with an introduction to Wales (a good place to start is Knighton, at about the halfway mark). Some 300 years after Offa, the Normans drove the Welsh further into the hills, establishing the Marches and the powerful Marcher Lordships along the border.

Traditionally, Wales is a melodic land of green hills and welcoming valleys, of Welshcakes, crumbling castles, poets and song. It has sweeping sandy beaches and dramatic coves, sheep for shawls, lamb for the pot and ponies for trekking over hills. It is less populous than England, though its accessibility from southern, central and northern parts of the country make it a popular holiday haunt.

From London the M4, skirting Bristol, crosses the second Severn Bridge, opened in 1996, and plunges immediately into Wales, following the industrial south coast past Newport, the capital at Cardiff, and Swansea towards the cliffs and beaches of Pembrokeshire. Halfway up the M5 between Bristol and Birmingham, at junction 8, the M50 leads west to the pretty town of Ross-on-Wye, where it meets the A40 from Gloucester, which crosses the border at Monmouth and dives between the Black Mountains and Brecon Beacons before heading back down to the Pembrokeshire coast.

Mid-Wales can also be approached from the M50 or from the M54 which leaves the M6 at junction 10A just north of Birmingham. The A5 takes the road on to Shrewsbury, from which you can head across the border at Welshpool and make your way down to Aberystwyth, the town of the University of Wales on Cardigan Bay.

North Wales is distinctly different from the south. The great crags and gullies of Snowdonia have long attracted hikers, rock-climbers and mountaineers. Equally deserving, though less well publicised, is the region's glorious coastline, stretching north from the Dovey estuary round the Llŷn Peninsula and Anglesey to the River Conwy and on to the the resorts of Colwyn Bay, Rhyl and Prestatyn. Nowhere else in Britain are high mountains and quality seaside found in such close proximity. ❑

PRECEDING PAGES: shepherding the flock; Vale of Rheidol Railway; farmhouse cheese, cellar-matured for six years; John Hughes's Grogg Shop, Pontypridd.
LEFT: bed-and-breakfast farmhouse, Rhayader.

W&LLR
GUARD

THE WELSH CHARACTER

The English have long followed Shakespeare in caricaturing the Welsh. Here, leading Welsh poet Dannie Abse separates myth from truth

Most tourists returning home from Wales report that the Welsh are a friendly people. Not only is there – as the song goes – "a welcome in the hillsides" but the locals appear to be particularly anxious to please: so much so that sometimes they may tell the enquiring visitor what he or she wishes most to hear rather than the truth, the whole truth and nothing but the truth.

Supposing you halt your car at some country crossroads hoping that you are well on your way to, say, Llanberis. (*Llan* is the Welsh, by the way, for "church" or "parish".) You wind down the window in order to ask that short-statured Welshman who happens to be standing conveniently nearby if you are near your destination. "Only 10 miles to go," he will say smiling pleasantly. "You'll be by there in 20 minutes easy." You thank him and you drive on. An hour later you realise that there are such things as Welsh miles (in the same way that there are Irish miles) and that the smiling rustic denizen was only trying to please by giving you good news.

Ebullient and emotional

This trait of friendliness and the wish to please the Welsh would recognise in themselves. In the Welsh national newspaper, the *Western Mail*, one correspondent, Hilda Evans, wrote: "We are warmhearted, ebullient, inquisitive, emotional, extrovert. Our blood is mixed. There is hardly a coloured face amongst us but Irish, Welsh, Spanish and English – also I believe Italian – have interbred. We are the people of the Welsh valleys. We shock the staid English: we overwhelm them with our kindness and generosity and they frequently consider us inferior."

Inferior? It is doubtful whether these days the English do look down on the South Walians. Perhaps they used to. Nowadays, it is the North Welsh who look down on the mixed-blood South Welsh. "They're Arabs down there," they say without intending any particular racial hostility but acutely mindful of the fact that most people in industrial South Wales often do not speak the old language. And both the South and the North look askance at the West Walians, especially those who happen to come from Cardiganshire where, it is said, Welsh generosity has gone into reverse.

"He's a Cardi," the rest of the Welsh nation remark, meaning that, while this person from Cardigan may be friendly, he's also sly and clever and oleaginous and stingy. "He's a Cardi. He's got short arms and deep pockets. After you've talked to 'im, you 'ave to count your teeth." This, of course, is pure slander. The reputation of Cardis is as inaccurate as the Irish being thought stupid or the Scots being considered mean.

LEFT: guard at Welshpool and Llanfair Railway.
RIGHT: a traditional quarry worker.

The Welsh, like many minority nations, do have a need to define their national character, to emphasise their differences – the problem comes when trying to come up with a definitive definition of "Welshness".

Over the past 30 years there has been, in Wales, a marked acceleration of cultural changes. Old traditions have faded or are fading, religion is holed and the once crowded chapels emptier, the coalmines closed down, the population forced to be mobile. But Wales – and the notion of Welshness, albeit in its many and varied guises - is not on a downward spiral. Far from it. There is a new self-confidence in the Wales of the 21st century. In the arts and commerce, Wales is making waves. "Cool Cymru" might be a fanciful invention, an ultimately unconvincing provincial response to the metropolitan snobbery of London. But it does

contain more than a grain of truth. There's an air of optimism in certain part of Wales. A new breed of rock bands, singers, actors and writers is gaining national and international recognition. They are not defined by their Welshness, but they are proud of their roots.

But what a tangled web this business of roots can be. One thing in Wales that hasn't changed a great deal over the years, decades, centuries, millennia (at least since Offa put his dyke across the border in the 8th century) is its populace's inability to agree amongst themselves on anything save the shape of a rugby ball. The Welsh are past masters in the art of internecine conflict. It's a trait which was certainly evident in medieval times, when the chronicler Giraldus Cambrensis, on his travels through Wales, noted : "If they would be inseparable, they would be insuperable."

THE LANGUAGE

Only one in five Welsh people speak the language, but efforts to encourage its use are working.

The new National Assembly, Wales's first home-bred political forum since the 15th century, hasn't cured a propensity to indulge in introspective arguments about exactly who is and who isn't truly Welsh. At the extreme poles, we have die-hard Welsh speakers who refuse to accept the claims to "Welshness" made by their monoglot English-speaking fellow countrymen. Many of the latter take huge offence at this while displaying little interest in – and hurling much derision at – traditional culture and attitudes.

In between these two extremes we have all shades of opinion - which is why it is dangerous to make a stand on the shifting ground of the Welsh character.

The bald facts are these. Around 20 percent of the nation understands Welsh. In cultural terms, the language is enjoying something of a renaissance. Young people are speaking it proudly; it's highly visible everywhere on road signs and fascia boards; it now helps a great deal if you can speak Welsh when you're applying for a job in certain government organisations, quangos and some parts of the Welsh media; and in Cardiff there has grown up a Welsh-speaking middle class which aspires to the clout yielded by London's opinion-formers. There are some trends here which might start to become slightly worrying if you happen to be one of the 80 percent of the population who doesn't speak Welsh.

Reinventing history

The Welsh in their new self-consciousness – not only the Welsh-speaking community – have tended to re-invent their history. In school youngsters are told about Welsh legendary heroes – of Cunedda the Burner, of Hywel Dda and his four bitter sons, of Llywelyn the Great and Llywelyn the Last and, most of all, of Owain Glyndŵr, Prince of Wales and national hero who, in 1401, called upon his men to "free the Welsh people from the slavery of their English enemies."

The Welsh once were a people "taut for war" against the English but they were defeated. And according to the nationalist poet, R.S. Thomas:

There is no present in Wales,
And no future;

There is only the past,
Brittle with relics,
Wind bitten towers and castles
With sham ghosts;
Mouldering quarries and mines;
And an impotent people,
Sick with inbreeding,
Worrying the carcase of an old song.

Those like R.S. Thomas lament the passing of the old ways, the old religion, the old language, the righteous orators that spoke the word, scriptural or political, intensely and thrillingly. They have gone, they say, for the most part, those gesturing figures in pulpit or wild-eyed on soapbox, gone into the photographic plates of a Welsh social history book or into the remembering imagination of poets.

This is half true; but the discerning visitor will still meet their sons and grandsons, their daughters and granddaughters and recognise through them that certain Welsh national traits are not completely soluble. Like others, the Welsh are a perdurable people.

If the Welsh themselves, whatever their individual complexion, are aware that they are a nation with a deep sense of their past, English visitors, too, have commented on how they have apprehended the ubiquitous spirit of history while in Wales. For instance, before World War I, Edward Thomas, who took a walking tour through Wales, spoke of "phantoms following phantoms in a phantom land – a gleam of spears, a murmur of arrows, a shout of victory, a fair face, a scream of torture, a song, the form of some conqueror and pursuer of English kings."

Earlier still, in the 19th century, Matthew Arnold, finding himself in Llandudno, remarked that Wales is "where the past still lives, where every place has its tradition, every name its poetry, and where the people, the genuine people, still know this past, this tradition." So, as a Welsh school textbook suggests, "The torch of history in Wales is handed on from age to age."

The English are aware also of other Welsh characteristics, not least Welsh talkativeness. It is not so long ago that the trains leaving from Paddington to South Wales consisted of separate carriages – that is, they were not open-planned. Then, half a dozen strangers would look out of the window, or suck their mints, or read their newspapers, but they would not speak to each other. It was not the "done" English thing. The English are happy with few words and even fewer gestures and like to keep strangers at a comfortable distance from them-

LEFT: chambermaid at Llandudno.
ABOVE: sheep farmers at Builth Wells market.

selves. And in a train leaving England for Wales, who knows who is not English?

Only when the train had passed through the Severn Tunnel, only when the passengers felt themselves to be safely in Wales, only then would the carriage suddenly hum with conversation. As Rudyard Kipling wrote: "The Celt goes talking from Llanberis to Kirkwall, but the English, ah the English, don't say a word at all!" The Welsh love talking and they love those who talk well.

Why are the Welsh such eloquent talkers? They have always bred colourful trade union leaders like Arthur Horner, who could electrify a crowd of strike-bound miners. Up and down the land there have been unforgettable soapbox preachers. "I have heard most London preachers," wrote Caradoc Evans, "but I have heard few who can outdo the preachers of my boyhood."

Caradoc Evans, a Cardi and once the most reviled man in Wales because of his criticism of the Welsh nation, softened when he spoke of certain Welsh preachers. "Before theatres and picture palaces, churches and chapels were places of entertainment – entertainment that refreshed the soul and fortified man in his pilgrimage. There might have been in the pulpit more loose-livers than saints, but the biggest sinner could preach and the newest priest could recite the collect and prayers of the Common Prayer Book in a good, wholesome voice."

Then there have been fine political orators like David Lloyd George in the early years of the 20th century, Aneurin Bevan in the postwar years, and Neil Kinnock in the 1980s, all famous for the lovely gift of the gab, for true Welsh *hwyl.* The Welsh gift for articulate cadence is rooted in the fact that Welshmen and women are, for the most part, a non-conformist Old Testament people and in their childhood they early caught the accents and dignity of biblical English.

Innocent lies

Sometimes the natural verbal exuberance of the Welsh develops into a comic exaggeration – comic, that is, to Englishmen and other foreigners. Of Iolo Morgannwg, renowned 18th-century Welsh hero, rogue, forger, poet, antiquary, it was said that he could see seven sails where there was but one. And many a Welsh hero, before and after him, has had a similar multiplying imagination.

When Shakespeare portrayed Owain Glyndŵr he made that Prince tell such innocent lies that those who overheard him could only laugh. Glyndŵr boasted: "At my birth, the front of heaven was full of fiery shapes. The goats ran from the mountains, and the herds were strangely clamorous to the frighted fields. These signs have mark'd me extraordinary; and all the courses of my life do show I am not in the roll of common men!" When Glyndŵr swanked to Hotspur, the Earl of Northumberland's son, "I can call spirits from the vasty deep," Hotspur replied tartly, "So can any man; but will they come?" Shakespeare invites us gently, even affectionately, to laugh at Welsh hyperbole.

In our time, English poets such as Robert Graves and Michael Burn have comically continued this tradition. In *Welsh Incident*, Robert Graves makes a solemn Welshman tell of wondrous things that came out from the sea at Criccieth with accurate humour, and Michael Burn, writing his *Welsh Love Letter*, sighs:

Were all the streams of Gwynedd
In one great river joined
Dwyfer, Dwyryd,
Glaslyn, Ogwen,
And Mawddach in flood
And all in between us
I'd swim them
All!
To reach you,
O, how I love you

Were all the forts of Gwynedd
In one great fortress linked
Caer and castle
Criccieth, Harlech,
Conwy, Caernarfon,
And all in flames
I'd jump them jump them
All!
To reach you,
O, how I love you!

See you Saturday
If it's not raining

Welsh humour

Have the Welsh themselves a sense of humour? Visitors may be misled by the ponderous and solemn manner of Welshmen when they are trying to be formal or when articulating small complaints: "Sir, members of our choir feel very strongly about the nature of the posters advertising our concert on behalf of the Powys Wildlife Trust. Why should David Evans and others be allowed an Esquire after their names when William Price has no such appellation?"

But the Welsh do have a sense of comedy and can laugh at themselves. It is true that Welsh comedy often relies on the joke or the narrative going "over the top" into farce. The stories of Rhys Davies press into pure farce and novelist Gwyn Thomas (known in Wales as Gwyn the Mouth) regularly delivered wonderfully farcical epigrams.

So if those who live in Wales are carried away by the power and excitement of words and by old-time rhetoric, there are home-bred comedians and critics ready and willing to record and mock it all.

Thus Dylan Thomas describes how, when he was a boy, he heard his older cousin, Gwilym, praying: "O God, Thou art everywhere all the time, in the dew of the morning, in the frost of the evening, in the field and the town, in the preacher and the sinner, in the sparrow and big buzzard. Thou canst see everything, right down deep in our hearts; thou canst see us when the sun has gone; thou canst see us when there aren't any stars, in the gravy blackness, in the deep, deep, deep pit; thou canst see and spy and watch us all the time, in the little black corners, in the big cowboys' prairies, under the blankets when we're snoring fast, in the terrible shadows, pitch black, pitch black; thou canst see everything we do, in the night and the day and the night, everything, everything; thou canst see all the time. O God, mun, you're like a bloody cat."

Wales, then, is the Land of Speech as much as it is the Land of Song. Not that the latter is merely a commercial tourist invention, as one can soon learn by visiting the Millennium Stadium (a prosaic name indeed for the new arena that has taken over from the hallowed Cardiff Arms Park) at an international rugby match. The standing crowds sing the National Anthem, *Land of my Fathers*, in Welsh as if they have been rehearsing it for years. And in one sense they have. They sing it with such a martial melancholy that the listener is reminded how "in every dirge there sleeps a battle-march".

Equally memorable and surprising encounters are not hard to come by, anywhere in the country. Sooner or later, if you are willing – for you cannot be alone in Wales for long except on top of a mountain – something thrilling is bound to happen: a song or a seagull flying through a rainbow, or just a signpost (bilingual) pointing backward towards a dark legend. ❑

LEFT: old-style elegance at Llandrindod Wells Victorian Festival.

RIGHT: modern Welsh magic at the Museum of Welsh Life, St Fagans, Cardiff.

CAMBRIAE TYPUS
Auctore
HUMFREDO LHUYDO
Denbigiense Cambrobritano.
HIBERNIAE PARS
Dublin
OCCIDENS.
Mona insula. L.
Anglesey. A.
Mon. B.
VERGIVIUM SIVE HIBERNICUM MARE
MOR WERIDH, Britannis,
THE YRISHE OCEANE, Anglis.
L. A. B. litterę, vocabulis adiectę, notant illud esse Latinum, Anglicum, aut Britannicum, quod est incolarum.
Lhyn.
Aberdaron
Demetia.
Ceretica
DE HEN
Cantrema
Rosia
OCTOPITARUM PROM.
Scala Miliarium Anglicorum.
10
20
30
40
50
60

Aliquod Regionum huius tractus synonÿma, prout Latinè, Britannicè & Anglicè etiamnum appellantur.
Cambria, L.
Cambrÿ, B.
Wales, A.
Ceretica, L.
Ceredigion B.
Cardigan, A.
Venedotia, L.
Gwÿnedhia, B.
Northwales, A.
Pouisia, L.
Powijs, B.
Demetia, L.
Dÿfet, B.
Westwales, A.
Dehenbart, B.
Sutwales, A.
ANGLIAE PARS olim LHOEGRIAE appellata
Cum Priuilegio
ORIENS.
Lÿrpol.
Waringthon
Merse flu.
Frodshau
Ciuitas legionum L.
Caer Lheon B.
Chester A.
Holt
Maylor
Gwayn.
Whÿtchurch
Prÿce
Drayÿthon
Hodnet
Ymwÿthig. B.
Shreusburÿ A.
Salopia L.
Neuport
Tongne
Shÿfnal
Bolÿngal
Enfild
Kÿnford
Brangonia olim, nunc Vigornia L.
Caerfrangô B.
Worcestre, A.
Teuksburi
Claudia, & Glouernia L.
Caer Glosi, et Caer Loÿw B.
Glocestre, A.
Danica sylua.
Dean forest.
Veuta Belgarum L.
Caer oder yn nant bathon B.
Brightstowe A.
DOTIA.
Ceri
Arwyÿdh.
Cedewen.
Melienydh
Elfel.
VI
SIA.
Euas.
Rei
nuc.
ARTIA.
Gwent.
Si
luria.

Decisive Dates

500–100 BC: The Celts settle in Wales.
AD 43: The Romans, under Emperor Claudius, invade Britain. By AD 78, Wales has been conquered.
340: Defences are built against Irish raiders who eventually make permanent settlements in Wales.
410: After nearly four centuries of occupation, the Romans withdraw from Britain and the Dark Ages begin. Saxon invasions increase in frequency.
500: The Saxons are defeated at Mount Badon, the battle possibly won by the legendary Arthur (of Round Table fame). But this victory is short-lived and the Saxons continue to settle in Britain.

500–550: The Age of Saints. Celtic saints wander through Wales preaching Christianity and converting others to the faith. To the east, the Anglo-Saxons remain pagan.
784: Offa of Mercia, a powerful Saxon king, builds Offa's Dyke, giving Wales an eastern boundary.
878: Rhodri Mawr, the most notable figure in Welsh history before the arrival of the Normans, is slain. The first Welsh ruler to succeed in uniting most of Wales under his overlordship, his reign also coincides with increasing Viking attacks on Wales.
927: Under the pressure of Viking attack, the Welsh kings submit to the English as over-king.
1039: Gruffydd ap Llywelyn, the last of the Welsh high-kings, takes to the throne, achieving a short but successful rule over Wales as a whole.
1063: Earl Harold, the future king of England, drives an army into Wales, Llywelyn is killed by his own men and England's ascendancy reaffirmed.
1066: The Norman Conquest of England. Harold is killed at Hastings and the Norman Lords Marcher are established along the Welsh borderlands.
1141: When Henry I of England dies, Wales experiences a resurgence, strongest under the two Llywelyns of Gwynedd. Local culture flourishes, territory is reclaimed and Wales moves towards unity.
1176: First eisteddfod held at Cardigan.
1267: Llywelyn II extracts from England the Treaty of Montgomery and is recognised as Prince of Wales, with overlordship of all other Welsh princes and barons.
1282: The Welsh resurgence ends as Llywelyn II is killed and Wales falls before Edward I's advance. By the Statute of Rhuddlan (1284), Wales becomes an English principality; in future the eldest son of the English king is designated Prince of Wales. Edward begins building castles in Wales.
1301: Edward's son becomes Prince of Wales.
1349: The Black Death sweeps Wales, claiming casualties of up to 40 percent.
1400: Owain Glyndŵr leads revolt against England, the whole of Wales behind him.
1410: Glyndŵr disappears and the rebellion is humiliatingly suppressed by Henry IV and his son.
1455: The Wars of the Roses break out in England, the Yorkists and the Lancastrians struggling for the throne.
1485: Henry Tudor, of Welsh descent and with Wales behind him, wins the Battle of Bosworth and is crowned King of England. This establishes Welsh lineage on the English throne and marks the end of the Wars of the Roses.
1536: First Act of Union. Henry VIII enacts the complete political and legal union of Wales with England, whose shire system is extended to Wales.
1588: First publication of the Bible in Welsh.
1642: Civil War breaks out in England. The restoration in 1660 of Charles II is welcomed by Wales.
1660: The Bardic Order is in decay, suffering from loss of patronage and the influence of Humanism.
1718: Printing presses are introduced to Wales and the number of books printed in the Welsh language rises sharply.
1735: The Methodist Revival begins.
1795: The Iron Industry becomes well established in South Wales.
1789: First "modern" eisteddfod held at Corwen.

1811: Methodists break with the Church of England. Wales becomes a "non-conformist nation".
1831: The Merthyr uprising: debt-stricken workers riot, ransacking the local debtors' court and raiding the town for sequestered goods. Troops are called in, leaving behind them two dozen townspeople dead. Throughout the decade, "Scotch Cattle" raids abound as miners take action against blacklegs and get their revenge on unpopular managers.
1839: The first of the Rebecca Riots. Turnpike gates are smashed in rural areas, the locals objecting to the high tolls exacted from them.
1843: Hugh Owen, in his *Letter to the Welsh People*, calls for better education, seeing it as an essential pre-requisite to Welsh prosperity.
1850s: Coalmining in the Rhondda rapidly develops, the South Wales coalfield becoming one of the most important in the world.
1868: Liberal political supremacy is established in Wales, the Liberals holding 21 Welsh seats.
1872: The University College at Aberystwyth is founded, followed by colleges at Bangor, Cardiff, and later, Swansea.
1881: The Welsh Sunday Closing Act is passed, keeping pubs shut on the Sabbath.
1891: The Tithe Act transfers payment of tithes to the Anglican Church from resentful non-conformist tenants to the landlords.
1895: The National Trust acquires its first property in Britain at Dinas Oleu, Barmouth.
1906: The General Election brings sweeping Liberal victories in Wales.
1908: David Lloyd George becomes Chancellor of the Exchequer.
1914: Dylan Thomas, poet and author of the radio play *Under Milk Wood,* is born in Swansea.
1920: Anglican Church In Wales is disestablished.
1921: For the first time, a decline in the number of Welsh speakers is recorded.
1922: Lloyd George, in office since 1916, steps down as Prime Minister; Liberal fortunes dwindle.
1925: Plaid Cymru, a nationalist party, is founded.
1930: Depression deepens over the South Wales coalfield, with jobless as high as 30 percent.
1939: The outbreak of World War II serves to pull Wales out of economic depression.
1950: With the assistance of government schemes, limited prosperity returns to Wales.
1955: Cardiff is declared the official capital.
1962: The Welsh Language Society is founded.

PRECEDING PAGES: Wales when it was Cambria.
LEFT: charm. **RIGHT:** traditional Welsh doll.

1964: The first Secretary of State for Wales is appointed to British Cabinet.
1966: In a local by-election, the first Plaid Cymru candidate is elected to Parliament. Plaid Cymru emerges as threat to Labour, but Labour re-establishes ascendancy in the 1970 General Election.
1967: The Welsh Language Act allows the use of Welsh in legal proceedings and on official forms.
1979: In a general referendum, the Welsh vote to reject devolution. Only 13 percent vote in favour.
1981: Only 19 percent of the population speaks Welsh, a census shows.
1982: A new TV channel, S4C, begins transmitting programmes in Welsh at peak times.

1987: Wales becomes the most popular location in Britain for overseas investors.
1988: The ambitious development of Cardiff's docks, a 10 to 15-year project, gets under way.
1997: With only one in two people bothering to vote in an independence referendum, limited devolution is endorsed by a margin of just 0.6 percent.
1998: Parliament passes the Government of Wales Act setting up the National Assembly for Wales.
1999: Elections for first National Assembly are held. Labour has a majority and Alun Michael, Tony Blair's (but not Wales's) preferred candidate is elected First Secretary.
2000: Alun Michael resigns. Rhodri Morgan, the people's choice, takes over as First Secretary. ❑

BEGINNINGS

First came the Celts, then the Romans, the Saxons and the Normans. It's no wonder Wales has so many imposing castles

Tacitus famously described the spectacle beheld by the Roman legionaries as they prepared to cross the Menai Strait and invade Anglesey: "The enemy lined the shore with a dense, armed mass. Among them were black-robed women with dishevelled hair, like Furies brandishing torches. Close by stood Druids, raising their hands to heaven and screaming dreadful curses." This depiction of the Celtic people is one that has always appealed to the popular imagination, fascinated by the Druid as the possible possessor of some secret, esoteric knowledge.

We know little of the Celts and what knowledge we have is derived largely from the Roman invaders who provided highly subjective and often appalled accounts of an energetic and war-like people whose religion involved human sacrifice.

It was with the arrival of the Celts (500–100 BC) from their homeland along the Rhine that Wales began to evolve a distinct culture of its own. Before this – and right up to the end of the Bronze Age – it had been the recipient of waves of different cultural influence. Even today's Welshman believes it is his Celtic ancestry that sets him apart from the more sedate, matter-of-fact Englishman, providing him with a whole range of romantic characteristics: eloquence, a fiery personality, a richly fertile imagination.

The Roman invasion

In AD 43 Emperor Claudius launched a full-scale invasion of Britain, bringing Wales under the influence of yet another people. Despite fierce opposition from the Welsh tribes who, under Caractacus, helped maintain British resistance along the border for eight years, the conquest of Wales was achieved by AD 78. Although some tribes such as the Silures in southeast Wales were moved out of their hill-forts into towns, many of the smaller groups continued their traditional way of life. But four centuries of Roman occupation was bound to leave its mark.

LEFT: Pentre Ifan's ancient burial chamber.
RIGHT: a Roman incursion restaged at Merthyr Tydfil.

A network of forts and roads held down the Welsh tribes, Chester and Caerleon serving as the major garrison towns. Roman civilisation, although it took deeper root in the southern and eastern lowlands where towns with columned temples, baths and piped water were built, also left its mark in the mountainous regions. Copper was mined on Parys Mountain, Anglesey, and gold in the southern foothills of the Cambrian Mountains. However rugged the landscape, the Romans imposed straight roads.

Despite Roman countermeasures, the 4th century brought increasing pressure from new invaders as barbarian tribes descended on Britain. The Saxons raided England's east coast, and the Irish – who had not been conquered by the Romans – raided Wales. As official defences weakened, the Irish made permanent settlements in Wales, in particular in the northwest and southwest. Even today, the name "Irishmen's huts" is given to any group of round and ruined huts that nestle on a headland or hillside.

After the Romans withdrew in AD 410, Britain slipped into the Dark Ages. During this unchronicled period, the Welsh language and the notion of Wales as a separate place began to emerge. Saxon tribes swept across southern Britain, their advance checked momentarily by the British victory in AD 500 at Mount Badon. Speculation runs whether Badon was won by the legendary Welsh hero, Arthur himself. Nonetheless the Saxons continued pushing westwards and northwards, isolating the Celts of Wales and allowing Wales to emerge as a territorial unit.

The indigenous people took a conscious pride in the one thing they felt marked them off from their Saxon enemies: their Christianity. Although the pagan Anglo-Saxons were largely converted in the 7th and 8th centuries by missionaries from Rome, Christianity had survived in some Welsh regions from the Roman period, while in others it was reintroduced from Gaul.

In the "Age of the Saints", a period stretching from the end of the 5th century to the early 6th, Celtic saints, either alone or with a band of followers, travelled through Wales preaching and converting others to the faith, establishing churches and monasteries as they did so. The Anglo-Saxons to the east they left well alone.

LATIN LEGACY

The Romans bequeathed many words to Welsh, including *pont* for bridge and *ffenestr* for window.

As the 6th century dissolved into the 7th, the Anglo-Saxons resumed their gnawing expansion, driving the Welsh towards the foothills of the central mountains. By the 8th century, Mercia was one of the most powerful kingdoms in southern Britain. It was at this time that Offa, the greatest of all Mercian kings constructed "Offa's Dyke", a boundary marking the frontier between the Celtic Welsh and the Germanic Mercians *(see page 104)*. Wales had for the first time acquired an eastern frontier, and one not greatly differing from the present national boundary.

The Wales of this period was splintered and disunited, a country of squabbling princes constantly at war with one another. Out of this confusion rose Rhodri Mawr, ruler of Gwynedd. In the face of an increasingly serious Viking menace, he used opportunistic marriages as a tool for forging the bardic dream of a united Wales able to safeguard Welsh social and cultural traditions. But he was killed in AD 878, with Welsh unity still unattained.

Quarelling princes

The English kingdoms, in contrast, were becoming united. After Alfred's death in 901, Wessex became increasingly stronger, Wales increasingly fragmented. After a brief period of stability under Hywel Dda (Howell the Good), Rhodri's grandson, Wales again sank into a century of political instability. No one ruler was able to unite Wales, despite the recurring and destructive invasions of Norsemen who raided monasteries and farmland alike. Welsh princes, with no vision of national cohesion, continued to divide the country and quarrel amongst themselves until the coming of Gruffydd ap Llywelyn (1039–63), who succeeded in uniting Wales under one king. Engaging himself in constant warfare, not only along the border but in Wales too, he extended his rule into every corner of Wales. His success was short-lived. Earl Harold, England's future king, drove an army into Wales, and in 1063 – in what was becoming a Welsh royal tradition – Llywelyn was killed by his own men.

Just three years later, Harold himself lay dead on the battlefield at Hastings, as the English in turn fell before the invading Normans. This victory provided no relief for the Welsh, for the triumph of William the Conqueror was to change Wales as violently as it changed England.

The Normans

Because Llywelyn's defeat had returned the country to the local rule of warring princes, Wales was in no position to face the Norman threat. Although William the Conqueror had no plans for the outright conquest of Wales, he set up powerful Norman barons along the Welsh borderlands in order to secure the flanks of his new kingdom. These were the Lords Marcher, who immediately began the attack of Welsh lands around them, dispossessing their rulers.

The rights of the Lords Marcher, far exceeding those of their fellows in England, were almost regal in their extent. As William was obliged to turn a blind eye to such accumulating power, these barons, commanding bands of trained knights on horseback, advanced on Wales.

When William was succeeded by his son in 1085, the power of the Lords Marcher increased even faster. The little kingdom of South Wales suffered the greatest. The Normans advanced through the region as far westwards as Pembroke. But, although they held and colonised the lowlands of South and Mid-Wales, the north and the uplands remained largely Welsh.

As the Normans advanced, they built castles and fortifications. The original motte-and-bailey castles made of earth and wood were later replaced by those whose ruins are still liberally scattered across the Welsh landscape. The Norman dominated areas became strongly feudal (a system alien to the existing Welsh system of landholding), with the castle as the centre of administration, and the lord surrounded by holdings of his vassals who were bound to him by duties of military service in exchange for land. Under the castle's protection and encouraged by the lord's granting of both charter and guaranteed trading rights, towns such as Cardiff and Swansea sprang up.

Under the spreading influence of the Normans the Church was also transformed, its structure reorganised first into diocese, then into deaneries and parishes. The changes introduced were welcome, renewing the Welsh Church's vigour and bringing it into closer contact with a reformed papacy. However, the death of Henry I in 1142 led to new disruption as disputes broke out over the succession. Wales, as it was so often to do, took advantage of England's weakness. ❑

LEFT: ancient kingship remembered at Conwy Castle.
ABOVE: Caerphilly Castle, mysterious at dawn.

BEATI PACIFICI
REGERE IMPERIO POPULOS
JAMES I.
KING of GREAT BRITAIN
FRANCE and IRELAND
Defender of the Faith &c.
Paulus Vansomer p.
An Original Painting in the Palace of Hampton Court.
G. Vertue Sculp.

ENGLAND'S TAKEOVER

Conflict with England ended when a king of Welsh descent came to the English throne. But soon political union was to undermine Wales's culture

The period following Henry I's death in 1135 became known as the Welsh resurgence. Lands were recovered, the arts and scholarship flourished, monasteries became centres of learning, and princes encouraged the bards, giving them an established position and duties at court.

So rose the Welsh tradition of the great bards, this "second generation" ranking with those of the 6th and 7th centuries. Precious folk legends were collected and preserved, including *The Mabinogion*, the great medieval collection of Welsh prose. In around 1136 the Welsh historian Geoffrey of Monmouth wrote his *History of the Kings of Britain*, an engaging – though highly unreliable – work which was later revealed to be more fiction than fact.

The resurgence went much deeper than politics and strife. In the mid-14th century, as Wales was grappling with the social problems that followed yet another military defeat, lyrical, naturalist and love poetry flourished as never before and Wales produced its finest early poet, Dafydd ap Gwilym.

A feudal state

This cultural flowering was strongest under the greatest and last princes of Gwynedd, the two Llywelyns. Llywelyn ap Iorwerth (Llywelyn the Great, 1194–1240) and Llywelyn ap Gruffydd (Llywelyn the Last, *circa* 1246–82) were accomplished military commanders who learnt much from their Anglo-Norman foes. They absorbed Welsh territories to unite large parts of the country and formed a feudal state guarded by stone castles. Laws were codified and taxation systemised. As a matter of policy, the Llywelyns arranged marriages with both the English royal family and the powerful Lords Marcher.

It soon became evident to the English crown that the threat posed by this new and strengthening neighbour could no longer be tolerated. Llywelyn I had contended with a relatively weak English king, Henry III, and Llywelyn II achieved his greatest success when England was divided by the barons. England had needed peace at all costs and so, by the treaty of Montgomery (1267) Llywelyn had gained control of nearly all of Wales and was recognised by Henry as Prince of Wales with overlordship of

all other Welsh barons and princes. But, with the accession of Edward I, Llywelyn was confronted with the most powerful of English medieval monarchs – and one determined to subdue Wales.

When Llywelyn II was killed in 1282 in the middle of the second of Edward I's Welsh Wars, the Welsh defence was quickly overcome. To secure his conquest, Edward built a chain of castles at Rhuddlan, Conwy, Beaumaris, Caernarfon and Harlech, all on defensible water sites, so that they could if necessary be supplied by sea.

The Statute of Rhuddlan (1284) reinforced the Treaty of Aberconwy, imposed on a chastened

LEFT: James I, the first Stuart king (reigned 1603–25).
RIGHT: a warrior looks out from Conwy Castle.

Wales by Edward in 1277. Wales was henceforth to be an English principality, and in future it would be the eldest son of the English monarch who would carry the title Prince of Wales. In 1301 Edward's son became the first such prince to be invested. The statute established five new shires on the English model and strengthened the grip of Canterbury over the Church of Wales.

Some Welshmen and princely families, seeing the Llywelyns' policy not as an assertion of Welsh independence but as a threat to freedom

and a heavy financial burden, had almost welcomed Edward I's settlement. So did others who benefited by the conquest from increased contact with the outside world brought about by entering service with the royal armies in France or the administration of the Crown. But the peace imposed was short-lived; resentments ran too high, dissatisfactions too deep.

The last revolt

The Wales of 1282 was not united with England and there had been no intention of its being an equal partner. Indeed, much of the administration lay in English hands and England seized control of trade. Discontent centred on the subordinated Welsh position, on galloping social changes and on memories of what might have been. In 1349 this discontent was exacerbated by plague when the Black Death swept Wales as it had swept the rest of Europe. Four people in 10 were said to have died.

IMPERIAL CASTLES

It took 500 tradesmen imported from England and 1,500 semi-skilled labourers to build Conwy Castle in 1283–87.

The stage was set for uprising and rebellion, and with the accession to the English throne of Henry IV, a Lancastrian and a usurper, revolt could be justified. All that was required was a leader. He appeared in the form of Owain Glyndŵr, born in 1344 of noble Welsh lineage. The rather ignominious trigger for a widespread rebellion was a private territorial dispute between Glyndŵr and a Marcher lord.

Glyndŵr's campaign began in 1400 in northeast Wales. He then consolidated his hold on the southwest and established a base in the northwest in the mountain core of Gwynedd. From this base, Glyndŵr attempted to carry out reforms and create national institutions, including two universities, to give him the trained administrators his new state would need. His efforts to give to Wales the attributes of 15th-century nationhood ran to the holding of parliaments in Machynlleth, Harlech and Dolgellau.

Second-class citizens

England retaliated with devastating success. The crisis of his reign over, Henry IV and his son Prince Henry (whose military talents were to ensure him victory at Agincourt) could turn their attention to Wales. By 1410 Glyndŵr had disappeared, the last rebellion had died.

Defeat this time involved humiliation. The lands of the rebels were seized by the king, who imposed severe fines. Most importantly, the Welsh became second-class citizens: they were not allowed to bear arms or to be appointed to public office; no Englishman could be tried by a Welshman or have evidence given against him by a Welshman. Intermarriage was forbidden. In the border towns, the Welsh were denied citizenship.

But history has the knack of conjuring up the most unexpected volte-face. In just over half a century, a Welshman – no less – was to sit on the English throne. It happened as a consequence of England becoming embroiled in the internecine blood-bath of the Wars of the Roses as the House of York and the House of Lancaster tussled for power. After the prolonged turmoil was over, the only surviving claimant to the throne was Henry Tudor, born in Wales, whose grandfather had been of pure Welsh stock. To the delight of the Welsh, a Welsh dynasty sat on the throne of England in fulfilment of centuries of bardic prophecy. When Henry landed in Wales in 1485, the bards hailed him as the new Arthur. Henry met the English forces led by Richard III at Bosworth, where Richard was betrayed and killed in battle. Henry was crowned Henry VII, King of England, inaugurating the Tudor dynasty. Shakespeare, chronicling the Tudor line, was to portray Richard as an evil, scheming hunchback in his popular melodrama *Richard III.*

Henry VII rewarded his followers generously: Welshmen entered local positions of power on a large scale and were made welcome at his court. Something resembling a job rush from Wales to London began. Henry introduced few reforms in Wales, however, and it was left to his successor Henry VIII to institute that drastic solution to the Welsh problem: the complete union, political and legal, of Wales with England.

LEFT: detail from a stained-glass window in Ruthin Castle's banqueting hall; Welsh hero Owain Glyndŵr.
ABOVE: the Tudors imposed their own art and imagery.

London supreme

The Acts of Union of 1536 and 1542 have often been seen as the beginning of the end for true Welsh independence. They undermined the Welsh language by proscribing it for many official and almost all legal purposes. They introduced English law and led to a widening social division between the anglicised Welsh gentry and the ordinary people. The former, who had been the mainstay of Welsh higher culture, increasingly entered English educational institutions and Inns of Court in English towns and cities.

The Acts of Union are also seen as initiating a rapid decline of Welsh cultural life, replacing it with a London-based culture. Administratively, Wales was abolished as a separate entity. Crucially, the ancient system of nomenclature disappeared. English lawyers found the Welsh *ap* (son of) confusing and so the ap Hywels became Powells and the anglicisation of surnames extended to all levels of society.

The Acts, however, are subject to conflicting historical interpretation. At last, Welshmen had equality with Englishmen before the law. The new legal and administrative arrangements brought a stable and peaceful life, which in turn opened up opportunities for individual advancement and financial gain. At Henry VIII's accession, Wales had been in turmoil and lawlessness prevalent. The new shires, the chief units of administrative and legal control, were given boundaries that remained barely changed until the 1970s.

With Union came reformation of the church. Again there was little protest as the old religious structure was systematically smashed and the Dissolution of the Monasteries began. Monasticism had long since lost its hold on people and the Welsh did not feel strongly about the question of papal supremacy. Indeed, most of them were glad to be rid of the financial burdens this distant figure imposed.

RELIGIOUS SWINGS

The Puritans promoted Nonconformism in Wales, but this was suppressed when the monarchy was restored. Freedom of worship was finally permitted in 1689.

Under the Tudors, Wales – although still not rich by comparison with England – enjoyed a degree of prosperity. The period saw an increase in the population, the development of coal and lead mining and the growth of trade. Almost every sector of the Welsh economy found an outlet in a new and much larger market.

The Welsh transferred the loyalty felt towards the Tudors to England's next dynasty, the Stuarts, who took over the throne in 1603. When civil war broke out in England in 1642, many of the Welsh remained Royalist. They tried to remain aloof from the tumult of the times, and the ruling Puritans, despite their reforming zeal, had little success in imposing their values on the Welsh peasantry. Wales generally welcomed the restoration of the monarchy in 1660, when Charles II came to the throne.

Crisis in culture

By the 18th century the cultural separation of the two layers of Welsh society was complete. The upper, anglicised layer looked to England for its standards of social behaviour, literature, speech and religion; but in the years after the Civil War even the lower, Welsh-speaking strata was to undergo a profound change. The bards had been central to the Welsh social structure in a manner that had no parallel in English society. Welsh high culture, poetry and music had been oral, the bard its guardian. They were also the historians, genealogists and musicians. But under Elizabeth I's rule in the late 16th century, Welsh literary culture suddenly seemed narrow, reactionary, even barbaric, and the bards were urged to modernise their art. By 1660 the bardic order was in decay.

A few diligent scholars attempted to bridge the gap between the new and the old learning. Although Welsh was excluded from state administration, it returned as the language of Anglican liturgy in Welsh churches. The use of Welsh in the churches played a crucial role in both preserving the language and spreading religious zeal. In 1567 the Prayer Book and New Testament were translated into Welsh, with the whole Bible following in 1588.

The power of print

As the vigour of the ancient traditions of music, history and literature declined, a new, serious, pious book-reading public arose, and the old oral culture was replaced by a printed culture. The culture was not of literature and learning but of piety and devotion. Between 1660 and 1750 the stream of Anglican tracts in Welsh became a flood.

Before the 18th century had run its course, three revolutions were to have struck Wales. The cultural revolution opened the doors for the Methodists and a religious revolution, while at the same time industrial revolution wrenched the Wales of history into the Wales of today. ❑

LEFT: Henry VIII and Jane Seymour, one of his six wives, portrayed in Cardiff Castle.

Welsh Fights Back

Driving into Wales on any major road supplies a painless and instant introduction to the Welsh language. The road signs are in Welsh as well as English and even the dimmest of linguists can scarcely fail to take on board sooner or later that *milltir* means miles, *lôn* lane and *toiledau* exactly what you would expect.

Welsh is now widely in evidence all over the country, *de rigueur* from railway stations to post offices, gas companies to water authorities, banks to supermarkets. Cities and towns carry their Welsh names as a matter of course: Cardiff/*Caerdydd*, Swansea/*Abertawe*, Newport/*Casnewydd*, Abergavenny/*Y Fenni*. A heavily subsidised Welsh TV channel, S4C, backs up the language and creates a market for actors, writers and film producers working in Welsh. Its most popular soap opera, *Pobol y Cwm* (People of the Valleys) has been running for 20 years and is watched by half of all Welsh speakers.

The language's most remarkable quality must surely be its powers of survival. Living in the closest possible relationship with English, one of the most powerful and all-pervading languages on earth, the miracle is that it was not swallowed without trace centuries ago. Yet, according to one recent census, 508,000 people (17.9 percent) speak Welsh. That's a far cry, admittedly, from the million who spoke it in 1900, but it's holding its own better than Scots or even Irish Gaelic.

The most hopeful sign is that there has been a slight upturn in the number of those speaking Welsh who are under 14. In recent years, there has been a notable surge of interest in the language, not least in anglicised South Wales where a significant number of parents want their children educated entirely through the medium of Welsh.

The Welsh equivalents of the Irish *Gaeltacht*, its language strongholds, are the north and west. Just as Welsh seems poised for recovery, a growing threat presents itself in these areas. Historically, in South Wales, the hold of the language was broken by the Industrial Revolution and the massive influx of immigrant workers from England and Ireland. Contemporary trends are also, it is argued, diluting the Welsh-speaking pool, as the old pattern of life in the north and west of Wales is being changed through a wave of immigration. In the past few decades, the relatively cheap and empty acres of west Wales, along with farmsteads left vacant as properties amalgamated, became a spiritual klondike for seekers after an alternative way of life, largely people coming from the big English cities.

In the north, second homes are seen as a major threat in previously homogeneous Welsh villages. Many incomers make strenuous efforts to learn Welsh, but a learned language must invariably be second best to a mother tongue.

For many Welsh people, the fate of the language, compounded by immigration, adds up to a sensitive, not to say explosive, issue. But as that distinguished Welshman, Sir Ifor Williams, once put it, "the people of England and Wales are formed of the same racial ingredients, although not necessarily in the same proportions: the same is true of Christmas cake and Christmas pudding, only one has been baked and the other boiled."

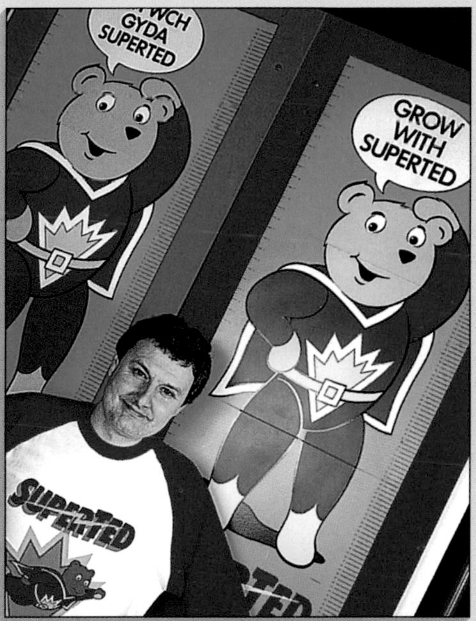

RIGHT: Welsh mascots have to be bilingual.

Welsh is not easy to learn, but it holds the key to a rich literature going back through the hymns and folk ballads of the 18th century and medieval storytelling to the age of bards in the 6th century, and the odes and elegies of Taliesin and Aneirin.

They were writing in the earliest British language – Welsh, which with Cornish belongs to the Brythonic branch of Celtic speech – and references to Catraeth (Catterick) show that their Britain went far beyond present-day Wales. In a sense, therefore, Welsh belongs to the whole of Britain. ❑

METHODISM AND MINING

Two great revolutions permanently changed the face of Wales in the 18th and 19th centuries. One was spiritual, the other industrial

The decay of the old oral culture left a void into which stepped the forces that moulded the Wales of non-conformist chapels, preachers, miners' choirs and pubs that stayed closed on Sundays.

The fervent wave of Methodism that swept Wales began in earnest in 1735 with the conversion of the charismatic religious leader Hywel Harris, but previous movements heralded this "religious revolution". The Society for the Promotion of Christian Knowledge (SPCK) had been active during the reign of Queen Anne, but more crucial were the efforts of Griffith Jones, vicar of Llanddowror in southwest Wales. He organised a system of preachers travelling from parish to parish, spending three months in each, where they taught the illiterate to read.

Although Jones was concerned not with education as such but with the spread of religion, he played a vital role in making Wales literate – and, what's more, literate in Welsh. By the end of the 18th century, most people had attained some degree of literacy in their own language, and this aided the rapid spread of Methodism.

Comparisons with Calvinism

Welsh Methodism originated independently from English Methodism and remained closer to Calvinism than Wesleyanism. The established Church soon came to be seen as the church for the English and the gentry, while the chapel held the loyalty of the people. In 1811 the Methodists severed their connection with the Church of England to become a separate denomination – a break that was to have unexpectedly serious consequences for the latter.

And so Wales became a "nonconformist nation", Methodism and nonconformity reflected in a radical political tradition and representing the "Welsh way of life". The level to which religion influenced politics is illustrated in the 1881 Sunday Closing Act, prohibiting the Sunday opening of pubs – an Act that remained enforced in parts of Wales until the early 1980s. Chapels sprang up everywhere, the accompanying choral singing turning Wales into the "Land of Song". After two decades of concern over diminished spirituality and increased materialism and one decade of zealous activity on behalf of the Methodists, Methodism in Wales peaked in the great spiritual revival of 1904–05.

How did the Methodists manage to achieve such overwhelming success in Wales compared to the much more modest following they attracted in England? They appeared at a time of vacuum in Welsh culture and used new methods to reach parts of the population other religions had failed to reach. They depended on the power of the spoken word, employing eloquence that could induce a degree of frenzy in congregations. To further Methodism's appeal to the people, hymns were often set to versions of popular folk songs or even hits from the English theatre.

LEFT: traditional Welsh costume.
RIGHT: Wales's oldest chapel, at St Govan's Head.

But there were also negative reasons for its startling success. In England there was deep-rooted Anglicanism to contend with, a powerful force at that time. Wales, in contrast, lacked an established church, and had few other rivals for the people's interest – no great commercial and business activity, no sophisticated aristocratic life nor energetic political centre.

Renaissance and romanticism

The Revival gave the Welsh a new respect and strengthened the position of the Welsh language. Although it filled a gap, it couldn't appeal to the intellectuals who were also looking for a new order; instead, they attempted a national revival by restoring Wales's ancient history and literature.

By far the greatest number of poems written in Welsh in the 18th century were hymns – the vehicle of Methodist revival. A mini-Renaissance was under way, with London Welshmen playing a leading role as London Welsh societies flourished.

In his passion to restore the glories of the Welsh past, Iolo Morgannwg, at the heart of the Welsh Renaissance, had no qualms about inventing new ones. Iolo, the "Purveyor of Instant and Ancient Culture", founded the Gorsedd of the Bards and largely inspired the ceremonial rituals of today's National Eisteddfod.

In their patriotic fervour, the Welsh also sought to resurrect past heroes. A clamour rose up around Prince Madoc, who was believed to have sailed to and discovered North America in 1170. In a report of the discovery of a tribe of Welsh-speaking Indians, lay the opportunity to prove the claim beyond doubt. Amid great enthusiasm and anticipation, one John Evans sailed up the Missouri to find them. The Madocs, when discovered, were undeniably Red Indian, but possessed as keen a knowledge of Welsh as an Australian Aborigine.

It was, however, neither the cultural revolution nor the religious revolution that was to have the most enduring effect on Welsh society, broadening horizons while ensuring the steady infiltration of the English language and the corresponding decline of the Welsh. These changes were to be wreaked by the transformation of the Welsh economy from an agrarian to an industrial base.

THE BIRTH OF THE EISTEDDFOD

As part of Wales's spiritual realignment, the Druids were romanticised and placed at the forefront of Welsh history. Although in today's popular mythology, the Druids are associated with Stonehenge, they were Celtic priests who arrived much later. They met in sacred groves, and there is evidence that they made human sacrifices.

In the 18th century, the eisteddfod – a folk festival and cultural gathering which can be traced back to medieval Wales – was revived. Welsh authors arranged publication of new editions of ancient texts of dictionaries and grammars. After 1718 printing presses appeared and the number of books printed in Welsh soared.

Revolution to riot

Industrialism in Wales developed as a result of the use in iron smelting of coal and coke in place of charcoal. Parts of Wales were rich in both coal and iron. In the south the most rapid industrial growth occurred in the 1790s as the number of iron works along the northern outcrop of the South Wales coalfield multiplied. By 1796 the iron industry of southeast Wales, with its growing coal dependency, had outstripped Shropshire and Staffordshire to produce 40 percent of Britain's pig iron.

Communication networks were vastly improved. In 1804 Trevithick's steam locomotive made its first run alongside the Welsh canals. Roads were improved by the establishment of road trusts, and, in one of the age's greatest engineering feats, Thomas Telford constructed a road – the A5 – that ran through the wilds of Snowdonia to extend across the Menai Strait by means of a suspension bridge.

But while one face of Wales underwent industrialisation, different pressures bubbled in the rural areas. The great population explosion struck Wales a blow as it struck the rest of Europe. At the first census, taken in 1801, Wales had a population of 587,000; by 1921 the figure was 2.6 million – almost five times as many over three and a half generations.

The result was an increase of poverty in the lower sections of society. The old system of parish relief broke down, its provisions quite inadequate to cope with the swelling populace and the conditions prevailing after 1815.

Wales between 1815 and 1848 was a country of social unrest and riot. The Napoleonic Wars had brought some prosperity to the richer farmers, but with peace and the reopening of trade with the continent, prices tumbled. Victory over the French also entailed the iron works losing their best customers, the army and navy, and a spate of enclosures only aggravated the seething discontent.

LEFT: old skills displayed at Celtica, Machynlleth.
ABOVE: slate quarrying became a major industry in North Wales.

King Coal

Between 1846 and 1914, 43 million Europeans emigrated to the United States. Yet Wales, from the 1890s until 1914, was the only country apart from the USA to register net immigration. By the 1880s the South Wales coal empire was all-pervasive. Mining towns and villages developed a unique, intensive culture, with their choral singing, demands for education, and later, fervent loyalty to the local rugby team. From 1850 the southeast sucked in people from the rest of Wales and beyond until nearly four-fifths of the Welsh population was lodged in this increasingly English-speaking region.

But the miners of South Wales worked in appalling conditions and before long their resistance, like that of the farmers, took on a violent aspect.

The 1830s was a decade of "Scotch Cattle" power in the eastern valleys of South Wales. In a campaign against blacklegs, unpopular managers, profiteers and the like, raiders came from the next valley, unrecognisable in women's clothes, animal skins and with blackened faces, the leader wearing horns on his head. The

Scotch Cattle approached at night amidst much lowing and horn blowing and embarked upon a ritualistic smashing-up of windows and furniture and roughing up of occupants.

South Wales's most serious outbreak of violence took place in Merthyr Tydfil, in 1831. Merthyr was the biggest town in Wales, born with the recent industrialism and having no deep roots in the past. In 1831 agitation for the Reform Bill was at its height, along with renewed protests against the system whereby workers had to take wages in part in goods supplied by the coal or iron owners. The town, plunged into a debt crisis by the recession of

1829, rose up in May 1831, sacking the local debtors' court and ransacking the district for sequestered goods. Troops were called in, incensing the protesters, who attacked them. The soldiers opened fire and left two dozen dead.

It took two pitched battles before order was reimposed, but the newly militant working-class consciousness was to last for over a decade. It was only with the doomed Chartist attack made on Newport in 1839 that this working-class militancy began to give way to the working-class Liberalism that was to be, for so many decades the leading force in Welsh politics.

Rioting was by no means confined to industrialised areas. The Highways Act of 1835 placed road improvement in the hands of road trusts that advanced the money and made their profit from toll gates set up along the road. In poor areas the trusts would increase their revenue by increasing the number of gates, and long journeys made by farmers thus became cripplingly expensive.

The Rebecca Riots

The first attack on a turnpike gate occurred in May 1839 in Pembrokeshire. It was demolished by a party of men with blackened faces and wearing women's clothes. These attacks are known as the "Rebecca Riots", as the leaders were addressed as Rebecca, the justification for their actions found in Genesis: "and they blessed Rebecca and said unto her, let thy seed possess the gates of those which hate them".

A major campaign begun in 1843 led to gates being cleared from a large expanse of south-west Wales. Before long, the Daughters of Rebecca began to extend their targets beyond the destruction of toll gates alone: in Carmarthen the hated workhouse was attacked.

Stirred in part by the supportive coverage given by *The Times*, government commissioners began in 1843 to investigate the all too evident grievances. The resulting report was sympathetic to many of the farmers' aims and the government acted quickly. The trusts were unified, tolls made uniform and even, in some instances, reduced. The Enclosure Act made any enclosure dependent on an initial public enquiry and the 1847 Poor Law Board began making the Poor Law more humane.

It was, however, the ever-expanding coalfields that were really to relieve the pressure by absorbing the rural population explosion.

The radical tradition

Wales in the 19th century was a melting pot of a variety of movements and developments, affecting different sections of the populace. In North Wales the people remained primarily concerned with religion, as the Methodists firmly established themselves. During this period the gulf between the nonconformist Welsh-speaking countryside and the anglicised industrial areas became entrenched, creating a division that remains today.

The latter half of the 19th century also saw Wales gain a new sense of political direction, a sense of "Welshness". By this time 80 percent of the principality belonged to a chapel and by 1891 the Liberals were in control, their power based on opposing landlords and rallying the support of the anti-established church. It was the nonconformist and chapel aspect that was to give to Welsh Liberalism its individuality, generating "Welsh Radicalism" (as opposed to English Liberalism) and giving direction to the new Welsh nationalism.

Welsh nonconformity reveals its power in many ways. Numerous government Bills were introduced to lift the disabilities of the nonconformists and to disestablish the Anglican Church (the Church in Wales was disestablished in 1920, and the first Archbishop of Wales was elected). The 1881 Welsh Closing Act typifies the fusion of nonconformity and politics. Tenant farmers refused to pay tithes to the Church of England, so the 1891 Tithe Act transferred payment from tenant to landlord.

A sense of Welshness and of national direction flourished even further after the government's publication in 1847 of the controversial "Blue Books", a survey into the state of education in Wales, an area in desperate need of attention. The conclusions drawn – that the Welsh language was a "barrier to the moral progress" of the people, and that Welsh country women were universally unchaste – caused widespread outrage. A united nonconformist front was formed, and popular leaders achieved success as they spread political awareness amongst the common people, providing them with a single, coherent philosophy.

VICTORIAN VALUES

The railway boom of the mid-19th century speeded the movement of coal, and engineering technology was used to build a suspension bridge over the Menai Strait.

Hugh Owen, in his Letter to the Welsh People (1843), called on them to organise primary schools and apply for Privy Council Grants (which had long been available to them), to take all action to further the cause of education. He dedicated 40 years to the creation of such schools and training colleges, to establishing a National Eisteddfod and to equipping a Welsh middle-class with grammar schools and universities. Owen prepared the way for a new prosperous and respectable Wales.

In 1872 the University College at Aberystwyth was founded, subscriptions provided even by those from the most rural of areas with the lowest of incomes. In the 1890s colleges at Bangor and Cardiff were also estab-

LEFT: the Menai Bridge, one of Thomas Telford's lasting achievements. **ABOVE:** friends bringing wedding presents to a 19th-century "bidding".

lished. This sense of national mission grew to such an extent that by the 1880s and 1890s many were pressing for Home Rule.

The nationalist party, Cymru Fydd (Young Wales), accordingly flourished, but nationalism was not particularly popular in the great centres of power in southeast Wales, the anglicised towns and cities, and the movement died a decisive death.

The Great War

Welsh Liberalism began enjoying its golden years. The party scored sweeping victories in Wales in the 1906 election, disestablished the

Church in 1920, and saw the rise of the Welsh radical, David Lloyd George, to become first Chancellor of the Exchequer, then Prime Minister of Britain. His success encouraged optimism and pride in nationhood, especially in the rural communities that had put such faith in the benefits of education.

Lloyd George remained Prime Minister from 1916 until 1922, heading a coalition government; but, by the end of his term, the political climate in Wales had changed. World War I had a dramatic impact on Welsh life and religion, and cleared the stage for the triumph of the Labour party. The Liberals feared both Labour's rise and the increasing militancy and violence of the industrial areas, of which the Tonypandy Riots of 1910 are a chilling example.

Liberal optimism had belonged to a period of economic prosperity; Welsh speakers had been on the increase and chapel membership had never been so high. But after 1918 the optimism vanished. The nonconformists, under the influence of rural depopulation, industrial slump and the advance of the English language, experienced decline and loss of faith.

The Chapel, which had served the villages and hamlets, found it hard to adapt to the new society with its open communities, mobile population and scattered families. The spread of mass media entertainment only served to weaken the Chapel as the centre of cultural life. (On the other hand, the Anglican Church proved much more successful in attracting the English immigrants who arrived in Wales in increasing numbers after 1945.)

In the face of the international concerns of the world after 1918, Welsh Radicalism suddenly appeared irrelevant. Britain had now to face the real cost of the war and, when Lloyd George stepped down from office in 1922, the Liberals' fortunes fell with him. In the coalfields, Labour's dominance was absolute by the 1930s. The Welsh economy depended so much on export that the collapse of the coal trade, with the turn to oil and consequent pit closures, crippled it. Strikes erupted, but in an economy of falling demand they could achieve little.

Mining's legacy

In 1913 South Wales produced almost one-third of world coal exports. More than a quarter of a million men (41,000 in the Rhondda alone) worked in 485 Welsh collieries. South Wales was coal. In the 1880s and 1890s no-one had been concerned that South Wales's total dependence on heavy industry and on export made it impossible for secondary or spin-off industries to develop as an economic insurance policy in the narrow valleys.

In fact, the region had never been properly industrialised at all. And so the Depression of the 1930s, whose effects were worst in the heavy industry that formed the basis of the Welsh economy, came to hang heavily and seemingly irremovably over the mining communities. ❑

Left: Victoriana, popular with collectors, on display in a Hay-on-Wye shop window.

Princes of Wales

Not for nothing is Wales officially known as a principality. It is a land once ruled by warrior princes, whose memories live on in the names of counties and towns as well as in the first names of many of its more patriotic citizens. Charles, heir to the British throne and the present Prince of Wales, is a modern-minded prince who went to university at Aberystwyth and did a crash course in Welsh. But some critics claim that his heart is really in Scotland and that he has never devoted enough time to Wales.

There are some who do not recognise his title. His ceremonial investiture in Caernarfon Castle in 1969 attracted people with lapel badges proclaiming "No Englishman is Prince of Wales" and much time was spent, before the great day, scrubbing off wall slogans declaring that "Llywelyn Lives", a reference to the native medieval rulers of Wales.

There were principalities in Wales before the Norman Conquest in 1066, ruled by the families of Gwynedd, Powys, Dyfed, Ceredigion (Cardigan), Brycheiniog (Brecon) and Morgannwg (Glamorgan). They were engaged in quarrels for supremacy but the Welsh were united, after a fashion, by Gruffydd ap Llywelyn, just before the Conquest.

From then on, Wales was to be regarded as a danger and English earls were encouraged to extend their territories into Wales from border cities such as Chester, Shrewsbury and Hereford. They made considerable inroads, though without subjugating the people, and it fell to a new generation of princes to try to drive them back out.

The 12th-century skirmishes between the Welsh princes – Owain Gwynedd, Rhys ap Gruffydd and Owain Cyfeiliog of Powys – are best recorded by Giraldus Cambrensis (Gerald of Wales), the son of a Norman settler who became a noted scholar and churchman and wrote of his tour through Wales in 1188 while seeking recruits for the Crusades.

In this period there arose Llywelyn ap Iorwerth, later to become Llywelyn the Great, Prince of Gwynedd, and the most powerful ruler in Wales since the Norman invasion. But it was his grandson, Llywelyn the Last, who embarked on the biggest campaign to drive back the English. He was joined by his brother, Dafydd.

Edward I retaliated and Dafydd was executed and Llywelyn killed in a skirmish at Cilmeri, near Builth Wells. Thus ended the great princely dynasty. In an effort to placate the Welsh, who were still mounting minor rebellions, Edward revived the title of Prince of Wales and conferred it on his son, who had reportedly been born in Caernarfon.

The next attempt to establish an independent Wales was mounted by Owain Glyndŵr (Owen Glendower), a descendant of the princes of Powys and Deheubarth, who sought alliances with the Scots and Irish and negotiated with the French. Declared Prince of Wales, he held parliaments – at Machynlleth, Dolgellau and Harlech – and went on to appoint bishops, to demand the independence of the Welsh Church, and to plan the building of two Welsh universities. But his rising also failed and, although twice offered a pardon by Henry V, Glyndŵr, the last Welsh Prince of Wales, was forced into outlawry and died ignominiously in some hiding place which was never discovered.

RIGHT: Prince Charles is invested as Prince of Wales by the Queen at Caernarfon Castle in 1969.

So, in the face of the small minority of nationalists who still raise their glasses to Llywelyn and Glyndŵr, the tradition established by Edward I lives on with the ceremonial princes of today.

Edward VIII, later Duke of Windsor, who was invested Prince of Wales in 1911, was respected in South Wales, where he seemed genuinely shocked by the poverty he witnessed during his visit to the coal-mining areas in the depression of 1936. ❑

THE DEVOLUTION DRAMA

As more and more English people bought cheap second homes in Wales, calls arose for the principality to exert greater control over its own affairs

Although a few areas of Welsh industry – such as Swansea, with its oil refining interests – were less badly hit by the Depression, disaster faced the coalmining heartlands and the eastern valleys in the 1930s. The tide of immigration turned to one of emigration.

The Welsh fled to the English Midlands and the Southeast, areas which still possessed an expanding light industry. And, as the industrial areas turned increasingly towards Labour, and the Liberals retreated to the Welsh-speaking areas, the gap widened between north and south, between industrial and rural Wales.

Government commissioners were appointed to rehabilitate Britain's worst hit areas, one being South Wales. Reduced rents, rates and taxes were introduced to encourage new industries. Retraining schemes aimed to give workers the skills required in growth areas of the country, and grants and loans were offered to assist workers and their families to move elsewhere.

World War II

It was the outbreak of World War II that really pulled Wales out of depression. Once again, the metal industries had a market; munitions factories sprang up on or by coalfields. Crucially, the new industry provided employment for women, who until then had been unemployed or forced to find work in England. The war created a new workforce, skilled in factory operation, and left behind old munitions factories as available floor space for light industry. When peace returned in 1945, the government started a major programme encouraging new industry into Wales, once again by means of grants and low-interest loans.

As demand for steel expanded, the Abbey Plant at Port Talbot becoming the largest in Europe. New enterprises started up on a scale unknown in Wales and government investment in roads, motorways and new towns contributed to economic expansion.

Trade unionism provided a cohesive force, not only protecting workers' rights but also producing strong bonds of loyalty among workers. The movement gave birth to many leading politicians, the most celebrated being Aneurin Bevan, universally known as "Nye" Bevan. The Member of Parliament for Ebbw Vale from 1929 until his death in 1960, he was the life and soul of Britain's postwar Labour government and, as Minister of Health, launched the pioneering National Health Service.

By the mid-1950s Wales had achieved nearly full employment, but the 1960s brought more pit closures. Between 1947 and 1974, 150 collieries closed; in 1960, 106,000 men worked in the South Wales coalfields, compared with the handful today who work the few surviving private mines (the National Coal Board's mines have all closed). The steel industry met with the same fate a decade or so later. The decline

LEFT: Aneurin Bevan, a great Welsh orator and a major force in the Labour Party until his death in 1960.
RIGHT: Japanese factories created much-needed new jobs in the Valleys in the 1980s.

in the British car industry, coupled with rising supplies from the United States, Germany and Japan, led to more redundancies.

By 1966 most of Wales was classified a "Development Area", receiving direct government assistance. Although diversification had cushioned the fall, the recession of the 1970s proved Wales to be still far more vulnerable to economic slump than many parts of England.

The Japanese arrive

The quest to strengthen and stabilise the Welsh economy goes on. The flow of new companies and government incentives has made Wales the most favoured location in Britain for overseas investors, attracting the largest number of Japanese investors and substantial amounts of American funds. Thousands of new jobs have been created, particularly in the high-tech and white-collar industries which have sprung up around Cardiff and Newport on the "M4 Corridor".

The ambition to develop Cardiff into a significant financial and administrative centre is being achieved with the relocation of major institutions – including American banks – here. This is in no small measure due to the new image being forged for the city with the realisation of the Cardiff Bay redevelopment, the largest of its kind in Europe. Nearly 3,000 acres (1,200 hectares) of old dockland are being redeveloped as part a 10- to 15-year project to create in the Welsh capital "a city for the future".

Likewise, the old industrial valleys are the focus of new initiatives – though here, the challenge of rejuvenating former mining areas suffering from old housing, high unemployment, poor roads and industrial dereliction is, if anything, greater than reviving Cardiff's notorious "Tiger Bay" waterfront. If Wales has an "inner city problem", it is located not in Cardiff but in parts of the industrial valleys.

Tourism, displaying the highest profile of the new Welsh industries, provides the most jobs and brings to Wales well over £1,000 million a year. However, only 3 percent of foreigners visiting Britain come to Wales for an overnight stay. Welsh tourism is facing up to the huge challenge of taking on London, Stratford-upon-Avon and the Cotswolds in an attempt to increase this figure – particularly the element which applies to the much courted "big-spending Americans" – by improving the image of Wales overseas. New hotels (especially in Cardiff) and the endorsement of international celebrities such as Sir Anthony Hopkins and Tom Jones may well begin to overcome the outdated image from which Wales suffers as a place of coalmines and ladies in tall hats.

The face of Welsh tourism is changing. As more English people go abroad for their holidays, Wales has tried to compete by offering short breaks and activity holidays. The development of narrow-gauge railways has been heavily promoted, South Wales has heritage parks, West Wales has a major theme park, North Wales has Llechwedd Slate Caverns. Activity holiday providers specialise in everything from guided walks to mountain biking, pony trekking to canoeing.

But economic change and development have put predictable pressures on the fabric of Welsh society – in particular, the language question.

The mobility offered by railways in the 19th century and the increased exposure to English in the 20th century through the mass media made Welsh more vulnerable than ever. The depression of the 1930s had driven Welsh speakers out to anglicised coastal areas and even to England, and the prosperity of the 1950s brought in non-Welsh-speaking immigrants.

Language and nationalism

A pattern developed: as the standard of living rose, so the number of Welsh speakers fell. By 1961 only a quarter of the population spoke Welsh. Even great literary figures no longer used it as a medium. Dylan Thomas, the Welsh poet, was a master of language – the *English* language. A product of an Anglo-Welsh background, growing up in Swansea, he could speak no Welsh. Although his love of Wales permeated some of his finest poems, his sentiments were expressed in English.

Those who saw the language and Welshness threatened in the postwar world could only resent Thomas's growing reputation. Perhaps the best-known Welshman internationally since Lloyd George, he was not Welsh-speaking, and to some he therefore represented not Welsh achievement in literature but the relentless anglicisation of Welsh literary culture. The threat to the Welsh language and the resulting tension fuelled every movement in Welsh politics.

In 1925 Plaid Cymru, the Welsh nationalist party, had been founded by the merger of two groups of intellectuals headed by the poet Saunders Lewis. Their main objective was to ward off threats to Welsh language and culture; almost as a by-product of this, they advocated self-government for Wales. Although abounding in intellectual talent, the party had little political know-how. It attracted distinguished figures concerned at the erosion of the native culture, but found little support outside the limited circle of writers and university teachers.

Its pacifist members were outraged when, disregarding general protest, the government constructed a bombing range in Llŷn, in the heart of a deeply Welsh farming community. In September 1936 Saunders Lewis and two other leaders of Plaid Cymru set fire to the construction hut at the new aerodrome at Penrhos. They gave themselves up and Plaid Cymru gained its first martyrs. Such a gesture and any public interest in Welsh nationalist activity were, however, soon eclipsed by the more urgent concern of World War II itself.

Then, in 1962 Saunders Lewis came out of retirement to broadcast on BBC Wales his views on "The Fall of the Language". He called for the use of "revolutionary methods" to preserve the language, proclaiming its preservation as being central to the survival of Wales itself. Out of this broadcast grew the Welsh Language Society.

Immediately a campaign began to blot out

LEFT: a statue at Blaenafon Big Pit celebrates Welsh miners, whose jobs vanished in the 1980s.
RIGHT: the poet Dylan Thomas, giving a reading.

The English Invaders

Rural depopulation, a hurt as debilitating as inner city decay, is not unique to Wales. Neither is the cheque-book stampede to snap up houses and farms which otherwise would end up derelict reminders of a past age. But in Wales there is a difference: the language spoken by a fifth of the principality's 2½ million people.

Inevitably, an influx of monoglot English speakers dilutes local communities whose mother tongue is still Welsh. Second-home owners who seek to impose the standards of metropolitan England on essentially uncomplicated villages get short shrift – not to mention short change. Fortunately most newcomers are sensitive to cultural differences. Lions and lambs lie happily side by side, though it is not always clear who is cast in which role.

That's not to say that there has been no resentment. In the early 1980s a fanatical (but small) group of arsonists attacked some second homes in Wales. The arguments still rage. After all, the injection of outside cash is not to be sneezed at. Without subventions from England – and elsewhere – many communities would be reduced to isolated enclaves of the elderly, unable to maintain acceptable standards of housing and social care. Fresh faces mean that local skills are retained and the village shop is better able, with swollen summer takings, to weather the long winter. On the downside is the inevitable anglicisation of community life.

About 20,000 dwellings in Wales are officially listed by local authorities as second homes. Perhaps another 10,000 come into that category – those "winter lets", houses rented out by absent home owners from October to Easter. In some districts – certain villages in Snowdonia, for example – the concentration is particularly high.

Part-time residents form one strand in the tangled skein of the English invasion. Permanent settlement is another, less discussed until roaring property prices in the more prosperous parts of Britain sent many eager buyers hurrying to Wales. The rush got under way in 1988 after the Government dramatically cut taxes paid by high earners.

At the height of the boom, the equivalent of a £150,000 house in southeast England might have cost £50,000 in Wales, leaving the £100,000 balance to provide a steady income without the traumas of city life.

The controversy continued for much of the 1990s as house prices – especially in London and the Southeast – continued to soar. Paddocks where rogue sheep once grazed are being turned into manicured gardens. There are rows about long-established rights-of-way. White plastic garden furniture is beginning to sprout in Snowdonia. There are frequent plastic gnome alerts.

The invasion has its positive side. New skills are brought in. The Welsh, notoriously laid back when it comes to business, are finding that it is possible to be an entrepreneur without behaving like some rapacious robber baron. Capital is being invested in craft industries which otherwise would have simply muddled along. And returnees – Welsh people who spent years in the fleshpots of London or Manchester – are finding a welcome when, to quote a song of great sentiment, they "come home again to Wales".

The north coast resorts have special significance in the Anglo-Welsh mix. The retired increasingly populate Llandudno, Rhyl, Colwyn Bay, Prestatyn and lesser-known locales. The density of blue rinses and walking sticks is such that a 20-mile (30-km) stretch of that bracing seaboard is known in Wales as the Costa Geriatrica. Older armies, arriving without the fuss surrounding the cash-rich younger cadres, may yet command the greatest attention. ❑

LEFT: the traditional Welsh cottage, luring the English.

English words on road signs, and slogans were emblazoned demanding a separate TV channel for Wales. Sit-ins in the studios of the BBC and HTV were staged. A few members even perpetrated bomb explosions in public buildings, and attacked aqueducts bringing water to England from Wales.

The activities of the society were effective. In 1967 the Welsh Language Act allowed the use of Welsh in legal proceedings and on official forms. In 1972 the Government accepted the Bowen Report recommending bilingual road signs. In 1982 a new TV channel began transmitting programmes in Welsh at peak hours.

Britain's Labour Party, whose position in Wales, strengthened by the 1930s Depression, had appeared so stable, suddenly found itself in the 1960s under threat from the nationalists. The climax of Labour's ascendancy came in the 1966 general election, when it won 32 out of 36 Welsh constituencies. It had expanded its appeal from the hardcore working-class vote across the whole spectrum of Welsh society, replacing the Liberals as the "national" party of Wales.

Then, in the 1966 Carmarthen by-election, the president of Plaid Cymru, Gwynfor Evans, was elected into parliament with a sensational 17 percent voting swing against Labour. Plaid Cymru, which had never been taken seriously and had remained a small and struggling group, emerged as a real threat.

ABOVE: politician Gwynfor Evans, who helped make Plaid Cymru a party to be reckoned with in the 1960s.

The devolution debate

With the approaching depression of the mid-1970s, Labour looked for all the support it could muster, and was prepared to make concessions to both Scottish and Welsh nationalist feeling. Both were offered their own assemblies. On 1 March 1979, St David's Day, the Welsh voted by referendum whether they wanted such a measure of self-government.

The result was a decisive "No". Only 13 percent of votes supported this very modest degree of devolution. Welsh-speaking Wales feared perpetual domination by the anglicised South. Plaid Cymru worried that such an assembly would create a permanent Labour majority. Others anticipated increased bureaucracy.

But the real fear was simple enough. It was that political devolution would be economically destructive, that the Welsh would lose their new prosperity. Wales therefore opted for security – with the rest of Britain.

In the 1979 general election Wales also swung harder towards the Conservatives than any region in Britain apart from London. To some, this breaking with decades of political tradition of Welsh radicalism is yet further proof of the relentless anglicisation of Wales.

This anglicisation has been furthered as English buyers acquire "second homes" in Wales – cottages ripe for renovation, available as a result of rural depopulation. This trend has also served to push up property prices in some parts of Wales, so fuelling local resentment. Retired couples come from England to settle in the north and west of Wales.

The concern is that this can only serve to further dilute the language. In the Welsh heartland, 80 to 90 percent of the population speak Welsh, but such areas are fragmented by towns, holiday areas and a wedge of English speakers across Mid-Wales. In the anglo areas the number of Welsh speakers falls to 20 percent and, in some cases, to below 10 percent.

The response of a Welsh nationalist minority was to start burning unoccupied English-owned second homes. The campaign spread to London, with extremists planting firebombs in the premises of estate agents who sold such properties. It was, however, a short-lived campaign; nowadays, an uneasy truce exists in areas where sentiments run deep.

Government policy has been to discriminate positively in favour of the language. Welsh-language schools exist in most areas, and the language is used widely on TV and radio. Indeed, the official backing for Welsh has been energetic enough to arouse the resentment of monoglot English speakers, who consider themselves just as Welsh as anyone else. After all, four-fifths of the Welsh people can speak *only* English, and there is bitterness that Welsh language speakers are allocated too many of the limited resources available, that there is too much TV in Welsh at peak viewing periods, that attention is being diverted from more pressing social and economic issues.

A new referendum

When the Labour Party returned to power in Westminster in 1997, after a gap of 18 years, it won 30 of the 36 seats in Wales and immediately revived the question of devolution. In a referendum, Scotland voted clearly, though not overwhelmingly, for its own assembly. But the Welsh were still cautious. Only half those eligible bothered to vote and just over half of those said "Yes". So the 60 delegates who would initiate Wales's National Assembly in Cardiff in 1999 would be inaugurating an institution endorsed by just over one in four of their fellow citizens. Crucially, it would have no tax-raising powers and would therefore be condemned by its opponents as being a mere talking shop, a toothless dragon. Was such an expensive luxury really necessary, critics asked, at a time when a severe downturn in Asia's economies threatened the buoyancy of foreign investment in Wales?

Once again, voters had divided along the traditional lines: north versus south, Welsh speakers versus English speakers, cities versus the rural heartland. A common identity seemed as elusive as ever.

Strangely enough, increasing tourism may prove an ally rather than an enemy. Many of the new tourist attractions strongly emphasise the language and its place in Wales's cultural identity. A wider understanding has been forged outside Wales of the principality's "otherness" and certainly there is little danger of encountering a repetition of the infamous index entry that once appeared in the *Encyclopaedia Britannica*: "For Wales, see England". ❑

LEFT: tourists flock to picturesque Betws-y-Coed.

The Japanese Influx

The economy of Wales, long associated with trades such as coal mining and steel making, has changed. As these traditional "smoke-stack" industries have declined, Wales in recent times has been particularly successful in attracting overseas investors who take advantage of tempting start-up packages or wish to add Britain or Europe to their portfolio. Now, in place of many of the long established industries, Wales is home to enterprises ranging from electronics through biotechnology to food production with investors from as far afield as Japan, Canada and Italy.

The benefits to Wales from this inward investment are considerable. Between 1983 and 1998, over 1,370 foreign companies invested in Wales, creating and safeguarding 175,000 jobs, particularly in areas where the decline in old industries had resulted in serious unemployment problems.

Why has Wales – a country perceived in some circles to be an also-ran in the race to keep up with the 21st century – become such a favoured destination for foreign investors? Paradoxically, its historic problems have given it certain contemporary advantages. The price of setting up and running businesses in Wales compares very favourably with other parts of the world, due to low telecommunication costs, a good infrastructure and the availability of government grants. Alongside these factors is a large and flexible workforce, which has proven itself ready to adapt to new working practices.

These qualities, of course, have been trumpeted worldwide by the Welsh Development Agency (WDA) with considerable success. A glance at the list of diverse international companies that have set up in Wales makes surprising reading to those who see Wales as a rural backwater. From America there are Ford and General Electric, manufacturing car parts and aerospace technology respectively. The Italian tyre firm Pirelli also has premises here, along with the German automotive company Bosch Siemens.

The Japanese have a massive presence, with large companies such as Sony, Matsushita and Hoya Lens manufacturing everything from television sets to ophthalmic glass. In world terms, Wales – with more than 50 Japanese companies based here – is beaten only by the United States when it comes to Japanese investment, a striking fact when one remembers that the first Japanese company, Takiron, arrived only in 1972.

RIGHT: a familiar presence in many Welsh schools.

Four of the world's top six electronics manufacturers are established in Wales, while over 150 companies, including leading multinationals, are engaged in the construction of automotive components. The relatively new boom in "call centre" business is another strong sector, alongside other white-collar industries such as financial services.

But it's not all work. Closer economic links to other cultures bring closer social links, perhaps best typified by the Japanese. The large expatriate Japanese population in Wales has shown remarkable enthusiasm for the Welsh way of life. The

Welsh passion for rugby is one which is shared by the Japanese and the tradition of male voice choirs has also captured their imagination, a choir from the industrial city of Fujisawa recently undertaking a tour of Wales. In Tokyo there is even the Clwb Hiraeth, or Homesickness Club, where workers returning to the land of the rising sun can find a reminder of their days in the land of song.

The Welsh have reciprocated by proving to be adaptable to new ideas. In the Japanese factories everyone wears the same uniform, calls each other by their first names and shares canteens and car parks. They even all belong to the same trade union, quite an achievement in a country with such strong traditional ties to the Labour movement. ❑

THE HERITAGE BUSINESS

Could former coal miners transform themselves into congenial tourist guides? Such post-industrial notions did not go down too well in the Valleys

"We'll keep a welcome in the hillsides," runs the opening line of that maudlin Welsh song beloved by male voice choirs. But its sentiments of a warm, open-hearted welcome offered by the close-knit mining communities of the Valleys are now something of an anachronism. You may still be able to find large, cheerful miners waiting to greet you when you "come on home to Wales", but these days they work at the Big Pit Mining Museum, Blaenafon, where tourism has replaced the hard graft of coalmining.

Is Wales becoming nothing more than "a nation of museum attendants?" asked Swansea academic Hywel Francis in 1981 in an article in the Welsh magazine *Arcade*. "My Orwellian nightmare," he wrote, "is a big black sign at the Severn Bridge: You are now entering a protected industrial relic. Pay £5 to view this disappearing society."

The good old, bad old days

To be fair to Wales, "Theme Park Britain" is a charge that can be levied on all parts of the UK, from the twee – and ultimately spurious – Englishness of the perfect Cotswold village to the unashamed flaunting of tartan and bagpipes by the Scots. And it's a phenomenon that is spreading worldwide, from the fake folklore of ceremonies staged specially for tour groups to the bizarre themed hotels of Las Vegas.

Industrial history plays a significant role in Wales's own heritage business. The country has its fair share of "living history" museums which recreate the past in an easily digestible way. The concept took root in Wales with the opening in the early 1970s of the Llechwedd Slate Caverns at Blaenau Ffestiniog, followed by the slate museum at Llyn Padarn near Llanberis. Both attractions at least have the pedigree of being, in previous incarnations, bona fide industrial sites, as opposed to out-and-out fakes specially created for the tourist market. At Llechwedd and Llanberis they discovered a new meaning to the old adage: "Where there's muck, there's money." The idea rapidly spread.

PRECEDING PAGES: the traditional tourist image of the Welsh wool spinner. **LEFT:** history revived at St Fagans Museum of Welsh Life.
RIGHT: a slate rockman, now a museum piece.

In the 1980s, the development of the Rhondda Heritage Park on the site of the old

Lewis Merthyr Colliery near Pontypridd, raised the possibility that soon there would be more mining museums than mines in South Wales – a situation that, at the start of the 21st century, now exists in the former industrial Valleys. The Rhondda Heritage Park plan contained a particular irony: it was at this colliery in 1983 that the miners held a stay-down strike which presaged the subsequent national strike held to save jobs. (A further irony is that the man who led that first strike became an advisor on the plans to turn the colliery into a museum.)

In his book *The Heritage Industry*, Robert Hewison highlighted the dangers of industrial museums which recreate the past in a way which we would like it to have been, rather than the way it really was. The Rhondda Heritage Park is typical of many large-scale British heritage parks which include a "cast" of characters in period costume. In many of these parks such employees were recruited at government expense through job creation schemes: the unemployed of today paid to pretend to be the employed of the 1920s.

For these "museums" the temptation is to "sanitise" the past: trim out the nasty bits, omit the poverty, the hunger and the strikes – to see life as a cinema newsreel film of the 1930s and 1940s, where the working classes are always irrepressibly cheerful, despite all the dreadful odds.

The Museum of Welsh Life at St Fagans, near Cardiff, is an agreeably arranged repository of buildings and artefacts mostly of pre-industrial Wales – what Hywel Francis describes as the "Cymric Merrie England": "Welsh dance, costume, barns, crafts, coracles, carts and idyllic sterilised whitewashed cottages". Now the museum is absorbing the era of industry, placing the life of the collier beside that of the coracle maker. There is a Miners' Institute here, brought from the Ogmore Valley and reassembled brick-by-brick, and a row of tiny cottages where the ironworkers of Merthyr Tydfil once lived. As far as Wales is concerned, the industrial worker and rural craftsman are both now part of history.

But what of the financial argument: the claim that the packaging of industrial heritage in this way generates prosperity? The Valleys of South Wales now house a number of attractions based on industrial heritage. These bring in lots of visitors, although it's fair to say that the benefit to the area as a whole is limited since there are few hotels and restaurants. Great claims were made in the 1970s and '80s for the reviving effects of tourism in the Valleys. Strategy documents were drawn up, fantasy job creation figures were quoted, publicity campaigns were launched. While there are examples of modest success, the Valleys have not become a mainstream tourist destination; it was optimistic in the extreme to expect them to capture the imagination of the mass market.

The Big Pit

Blaenafon is the home of the Big Pit Mining Museum, the first – and most famous – of the Valleys' industrial heritage attractions. In the 19th century, Blaenafon was one of the more prosperous towns in South Wales, with an ironworks and coalmine. Today, the closed-down stores and general look of the town are a depressing reminder that its days of economic vitality have departed.

In the 1980s, the town counted on tourism to safeguard its fragile existence. The main local colliery, Big Pit, reopened as a mining museum – for the first time allowing tourists kitted out with hard hats and miner's lamps to travel down a mineshaft to see what life was really like for workers underground.

In financial terms, Big Pit has been moderately successful. With job creation labour, a further project was launched to turn Blaenafon's old ironworks into another "industrial heritage" attraction. It shows that the town played a pivotal role in the Industrial Revolution both in pioneering manufacturing techniques and, later, in trade unionism. The Chartists' movement for workers' rights grew up around Blaenafon: from here in 1839 they marched on Newport with hopes of insurrection. But for the residents of Blaenafon, tourism is seen to have been a false dawn: the promises of prosperity are unfulfilled. People call at the museum, but then travel on to somewhere else – often to nearby Abergavenny which in style is more like a typical English market town than anything you are likely to find in Wales.

The Big Pit museum itself succeeds largely on attracting school parties, many of whom are working on school history projects about the Industrial Revolution. The men who provide you with hard hats and lamps, and who lead the tours underground, are ex-miners. The museum – and the guides – don't "sanitise" history here: these, after all, are real miners, not people on a job creation scheme pretending to be miners. They talk of how women and children worked below ground, the hard physical back-breaking labour of hewing coal, the pit ponies that stayed in the dark for 50 weeks of the year.

THE END OF PROGRESS

What worries many critics is that the relentless "museumising" of the Rhondda and other areas of South Wales implies that normal life has now reached a full stop.

It's shocking, and very moving: but is it good box office? How long before the marketing men, in order to "maximise revenue", demand more of a showbusiness style?

One of the ex-miners at the museum admitted that his work as a guide wasn't much of a job. "I'm glad I've got a job but it isn't real work. Coal mining was hard but there was a sense of doing something: and there were good times with your pals." He looked up towards the pithead baths, which now house a cafeteria: "This isn't right."

In another part of the Valleys the past from a different era has been recreated. Llancaiach Fawr near Gelligaer in the Rhymney Valley is a Tudor manor house – a rare survivor within Wales – that has been refurbished with great attention to historic accuracy. But it's not just the historic fabric of the house that's on display. Llancaiach Fawr is billed as "living history", and, for the most part, it lives up to the hype. Once over the threshold, visitors are greeted by actors in period costume, speaking in the style of the 17th century. The house sets out to recreate the time of the Civil War and a visit by King Charles to Llancaiach Fawr, though we are assured that events enacted are based on a yearly calendar so that, unless you come on the same day every year, you won't see the same thing twice.

It's all carried out with great enthusiasm. It's impossible to trip up the costumed servants, who remain "in character" throughout, refusing even to recognise friends and neighbours. All the world, it seems, is a stage. ❑

LEFT AND ABOVE: locals who would once have worked in factories now demonstrate crafts or conduct tours.

WELSH HEROES

The Welsh love words. Not surprisingly, therefore, they have produced their fair share of poets, novelists, politicians, actors, and pop singers

A land beneath which men burrowed tirelessly for coal and on which others perform fearless feats with the oval ball is guaranteed to supply an abundance of heroes. Some observers will not be shifted from the view that the gladiatorial figures in red jerseys (hopefully running rings round an English XV at Cardiff's Millennium Stadium) are the greatest and bravest in Wales. The reverential glee which greets these men (capped, not medalled, for their country) when they take the field at Cardiff is peculiarly Welsh.

The hero count in Wales is high and hundreds with legitimate claims queue to join the roll of honour. Some heroes are self-selecting: the Welsh soldiers who in 1879 defended Rorke's Drift against the Zulu Impi, winning 11 Victoria Crosses (Britain's highest gallantry award) in the process, for example; or the mines rescue teams who went into the inferno after Gresford Colliery blew apart in 1936 to try to find survivors.

But, after much deliberation and not a little argument, Wales plumps for the political and cultural giants as the best, the bravest and boldest – men and women whose lives deeply affect the nation's psyche to this day.

Champion of the underdog

Before politics was taken over by image makers and presentational gurus, Aneurin Bevan (popularly known as Nye Bevan and pictured on page 44) towered over British parliamentary proceedings. He died in 1960, a gifted life cut short at 63. A monument to Nye, who began as a miner, stands at Waun-y-Pound, an unexceptional hilltop near his home town of Tredegar, a mining community in the eastern Valleys now sadly reduced by contractions in the coal industry. No huge likeness carved by some great sculptor stands on the windswept hill. Instead, there are now four large monoliths. Three represent Ebbw Vale, Rhymney and Tredegar, the towns comprising the Ebbw Vale constituency he represented for 31 years; the fourth is bigger, representing Bevan himself.

Radical, rebel, bon viveur, scourge of conservatism, champion of the underdog: Bevan was all these. But he is best remembered for the creation of Britain's National Health Service, the forerunner of which was the ponderously named Tredegar Workmen's Medical Aid Society. The British Medical Association, the doctors' trade union, took its medicine manfully after first opposing "socialised medicine"; today the BMA is among the stoutest defenders of a health service which puts care above cash.

LEFT: David Lloyd George and his wife camping in 1913. **RIGHT:** the opera singer Adelina Patti.

The Welsh wizard

David Lloyd George would be rated by some a greater Welsh figure than Nye Bevan. True, he achieved the ultimate in British politics, becoming Prime Minister in 1916 and holding power through the flush of victory in 1918, after which the Liberal world began to come apart. His guile amply demonstrated Welsh cunning. His notorious womanising won envy, admiration and loathing. Quite a catalogue for a man born, strangely enough, in Manchester at the height of Lancashire's textile boom. He was brought up in the tiny village of Llanystumdwy in North Wales under the tutelage of his uncle Richard Lloyd, a cobbler and chapel elder. When he died, he was buried there in a simple grave – at least, simple for a world-renowned statesman – by the River Dwyfor. A nearby museum of Lloyd George memorabilia is much visited.

His flamboyance was legendary. Flowing hair, voluminous cape, generous moustache and overwhelming charm captivated everyone.

Women adored him and his sexual exploits were the subject of much gossip and secret envy. He neglected his Welsh wife and favoured English company between the sheets. Political honours were auctioned to swell party funds, company shareholdings were acquired in dubious circumstances. It hardly seemed to alter Lloyd George's popularity one bit.

A pyrotechnic poet

One of Wales's more recent heroes, the poet Dylan Thomas, evokes similar feelings of ambivalence. He also provokes equally fierce defences of a life and talent which rose like a rocket and ended with the big bang of an alcoholic in a hotel room in America. Thomas started out as a journalist on the local paper in Swansea. Tradesmen rather than professionals, journalists have been known to develop strong tastes. His were for words, beer and whisky. His words remain as stimulating as the spirits which consumed him. Remembered for impromptu recitations in London's Soho pubs as well as for the exquisitely honed lines of *Under Milk Wood*, he was as flamboyant as Bevan and as captivating as Lloyd George.

He worked mostly at Laugharne on the Carmarthenshire coast. From the wooden shed near his home, known as the Boathouse, he looked out over the Taf Estuary, a swelling river at high water and a vast expanse of mud flats when the tide drained away. He was a regular at Brown's Hotel in the sleepy little town's main street.

The Boathouse has become a major tourist attraction, full of Dylan Thomas memorabilia. Photographs of the poet, a cigarette characteristically stuck in the corner of his mouth, are on display. A video recounts his life. Dylan Thomas postcards sell briskly.

Thomas had enemies among the Welsh-speaking literati who were envious of his magic and scornful of his inability to converse in their tongue. But he is counted one of the 20th century's literary giants, a wizard with words whose place in the Welsh hall of fame is secure.

Destination Hollywood

Richard Burton was another of Wales's most revered figures. Arguably he can be rated one of the world's greatest classical actors, although he rarely achieved his potential. The son of a miner, he was born Richard Jenkins at Pontrhydyfen, a village which in a sense he never left, even though he travelled far and wide and was feted like a king. Love of his home patch marked him out as a true Welshman.

A sensitive, perceptive school teacher, Philip Burton, took the young Jenkins under his wing and "Richard Burton" emerged. The name change was more than symbolic. His mentor fostered the young Richard, whose father became addicted to that popular Welsh drug, alcohol.

Richard Burton was a man of great appetite and passion, and his marriage to Elizabeth Taylor was an epic which generated immense public interest. In the end he came home again to South Wales for that final embrace of his native soil. The funeral attracted the world's press but the importance of its actual location was not universally understood. Burton never lost his Welshness despite all the worldly seduction which attended his brilliant career on stage, on film and off the set. He never let go of the simple Welsh beliefs in the virtues of work and commitment – and drinking, an activity at which he rivalled Dylan Thomas. That addiction, however, and his unrelenting love of women, took second place to a love of words.

Another Welsh actor who could have gone the same way as Burton is Anthony Hopkins, who was brought up in Port Talbot a stone's throw from Pontrhydyfen. A committed drinker in his youth, this Oscar-winning performer gave up the booze entirely, a move which helped him to become one of Hollywood's most bankable stars. Despite a background in theatre, Hopkins professes no particular love for the stage and it is in movies such as *The Silence of the Lambs* in which he is most comfortable. Unlike Burton, Hopkins is no Welsh patriot; although he once donated £1 million to the conservation of Snowdonia and received a knighthood from the Queen, he lives in the US and took American citizenship. The Welsh actress Catherine Zeta Jones went one step further in 2000 by marrying into Hollywood royalty in the shape of Michael Douglas.

Voices that made millions

Wales has always embraced people of other lands and other cultures. New arrivals with panache and individuality are especially welcomed in South Wales, itself a hotch-potch of nations. Until the discovery of coal and iron, the Valleys were silent places, peopled only by farmers. Internationalism in the shape of workers from many lands changed that.

One person from far away who vividly stamped her imprint on Wales was Adelina Patti, a great and glamorous opera singer. Judged by the composer Verdi the finest soprano of her time, she was born in Madrid in 1843 of Italian parents and led a fabulously successful life, captivating audiences across the globe. In 1886 Adelina Patti – Madame Patti, as she was known – bought the the impressive Craig-y-Nos (Rock of the Night) Castle in the upper Swansea Valley and lived there until her death in 1919.

Two Welsh actors who wowed Hollywood: Richard Burton (**LEFT**) and Anthony Hopkins.

Nowadays, Wales has its own indigenous opera sensation in Bryn Terfel. Rising from a rural background in the Welsh-speaking foothills of Snowdonia, Terfel has become one of the biggest international stars in opera. Steeped in Welsh choral tradition, Terfel's fortunes really took off after winning the Leider Prize at the 1989 Cardiff Singer of the World Competition.

Another Welshman who has used the power of song to transcend his humble beginnings is Tom Jones. Born Thomas John Woodward into a working-class family in Treforest, South Wales, he learnt his trade in working men's clubs and pubs before his charisma and roaring voice catapulted him to stardom and regular bookings in Las Vegas nightclubs. Cardiff's Shirley Bassey also made a big noise internationally with songs such as *Goldfinger*.

Wherever you travel in Wales, you hear of other heroes. The novelist Kate Roberts and the trenchant dramatist Saunders Lewis wrote in Welsh and are widely revered among the 500,000 who speak "the language of heaven".

In the industrial valleys, Will Paynter, a charismatic orator and miners' leader, and the socialist Keir Hardie, a Scot who was MP for Merthyr Tydfil from 1900 to 1915 and is remembered for his championing of the unemployed, are names to conjure with. ❑

REAL SEA MINE

THE CHAPELS

The Land of Song needed its rehearsal rooms, and these were provided by a 19th-century explosion of church building

From Llangollen to Llanelli, from Colwyn Bay to Cardiff, the chapels punctuate the landscape. Few villages are too small to have their four-square Bethel or Bethania, their Siloh, Soar or Saron. Whatever the elusive "Welsh way of life" may be, the chapels have played a crucial part in it.

Architectural gems are rare. The founders of Welsh Nonconformity despised outward show – that was for the Anglicans and Roman Catholics. All that was needed was four walls and a roof, hard wooden pews, a pulpit and, perhaps most important of all, an organ or harmonium. Most date from the mid-1800s, by which time the Church of England had come to be seen – and rejected – by the Welsh as representative of the landowners, Toryism and Englishness. The next 70 years – the golden age of Nonconformism – was also the great age of chapel-building, by the Calvinistic Methodists, and Wesleyans particularly, but also by the Baptists, Congregationalists, Presbyterians and other, smaller sects.

Standing room only

A religious census in 1951, a pretty slap-dash affair, showed that, if seating capacity was any guide, Wales was far and away the most religious part of the British Isles. Its churches and chapels had seating for three-quarters of the population. In some areas, indeed, notably the counties of Breconshire and Merioneth, there were actually more seats than people.

The golden age of Nonconformity was carried forward by the great pulpit orators and itinerant preachers, often of humble origin and little formal education, who preached to vast congregations out of doors. With the kind of mass appeal that evangelists such as Billy Graham have exercised, they created the climate for three great religious revivals which swept Wales in 1840, 1859 and 1904. The last of these was the most emotional and saw large-scale conversions reckoned to swell chapel membership by 90,000.

LEFT: an outdoor hymn service.
RIGHT: a church at Criccieth.

By World War I, the total number of chapelgoers was estimated to be more than 500,000. Nothing like that number now attends regular worship, but the chapels cling on tenaciously with impoverished congregations. And still there is no better singing in Wales.

It was the chapels that gave Wales its *hwyl* (pronounced *who-ill*), a word which has no precise English equivalent but expresses a mixture of extrovert fervour and emotion. This found its outlet in the singing of hymns, some with dozens of verses.

Although it was fire and brimstone from the pulpit, the congregations could, did, and still do, let rip with the stirring hymns. Day-long prayer meetings, too, were outlets for bursts of impassioned oratory which many of today's theatrical giants would find hard to equal. As Trevor Fishlock observed wryly in his perceptive book, *Wales and the Welsh*: "In terms of sheer prayer hours, Wales must have a handsome credit balance in heaven!"

The chapels were the birthplace of the great male voice and mixed choirs which, before the end of the 19th century, had made Wales, in the popular parlance, the "Land of Song". Those same chapels, ironically, nearly put paid to the harp which, for no reason that would bear intelligent scrutiny, was labelled "the devil's instrument". The playing of it declined dramatically, though perhaps only in public.

Condemnation came easily to the hell-fire preachers. In its extreme form, it occasionally resulted in the ritual drumming out of chapel of some hapless servant girl who had got herself in the family way; and the man responsible, too, if he could be found.

Cruel sanctions could also be imposed on illegitimate children if they were found out. And there are still elderly chapel folk who will say, as in the tones of the fundamental revivalist preachers, "We're not here to enjoy ourselves."

The influence of the Nonconformist chapels on the Wales of today is something for future historians to quarrel about. Certainly there are many who argue that their puritanism and fundamentalism stifled debate on progressive ideas such as Darwinian biology; that they generated tensions and subconscious feelings of guilt and sinfulness, particularly in sexual matters.

Equally clearly, the chapels offered hope and a sense of community for poor, isolated and ill-educated communities. Also, without doubt, the fervour of Nonconformity in Wales saved the threatened Welsh language, and the chapels are still an important ally in its ongoing fight for survival.

A Parson's Pleasures

A graphic account of the life of a country parson in Wales in the 19th century is contained in the diaries of Francis Kilvert, an Englishman who was rector of Clyro in Powys from 1865 to 1872.

The imminent doom of the Welsh language had been prophesied from the time of the Act of Union in 1536, which made English the language of administration and of the courts. Though the fears were exaggerated, the bias in favour of English language and culture grew inexorably. This was partly because of English immigration and Welsh emigration, and partly because the Welsh were persuaded that the surest route to material advancement and the good things in life lay through learning the language and ways of England.

But the language survived, in no small measure because of Bishop William Morgan, who translated the Bible into Welsh. There were the beautiful words of the Welsh Bible, published in

1588, and read in the home and in the pulpit every Sunday. God himself, it appeared, was indeed Welsh. And Bishop Morgan's Bible was, more importantly perhaps, read in the Sunday School, where many of today's older Welsh speakers first learned the language at a time when it was not widely taught in schools.

Always on Sunday

The Sunday Schools, which had been going since the late 1700s, did not even have to be held in chapels: they could be convened in barns or farmhouses. One of the founders of the Sunday School movement, Thomas Charles, even set up a society in London to raise money to print New Testaments in Welsh. The teachers were unpaid and the only qualification that was demanded of them was the ability to read.

The pupils, adults as well as children, recited and sang what they had learned at Sunday School and thus acquired a limited sort of education when no other was available. Urdd Gobaith Cymru, the still-vigorous Welsh national youth organisation, also had its origin in the chapels and, through its annual eisteddfod, camps and other activities, continues to give young people a chance to preserve and rejoice in their Welshness.

The Welsh preacher-poet also continues to thrive and is often to be found chaired or crowned at the National Eisteddfod of Wales and at the scores of smaller, one-day chapel eisteddfodau which often carry on far into the night, particularly in North Wales.

From chapels to colleges

It was the chapels, too, which were responsible for the creation in 1872 of the University College at Aberystwyth, known as the "college by the sea" and the first higher education institution to be established in Wales apart from the Anglican college at Lampeter, in West Wales.

Aberystwyth's first Professor of Music was hymn writer Joseph Parry, vividly described in Jack Jones's novel, *Off to Philadelphia in the Morning*. And since there were, at that time, no Welsh orchestras or concert halls, or even any great tradition of orchestral music, most other composers found their main outlet in the composition of hymns. The hymns are still sung, as lustily as ever, though the number of singers has dwindled. Even in the 1920s chapel membership remained at about 400,000. Figures are hard to come by, but the total now is likely to be nearer 200,000.

The dramatic decline in the number of Welsh speakers since 1920 has played its part. The emigration associated with the Depression of the 1920s and 1930s dealt a further blow. Cultural influences from the other side of Offa's Dyke provided alternatives to chapel-going. The geographical and cultural isolation of so many Welsh communities was further broken down by newspapers, books, cinema, radio and TV.

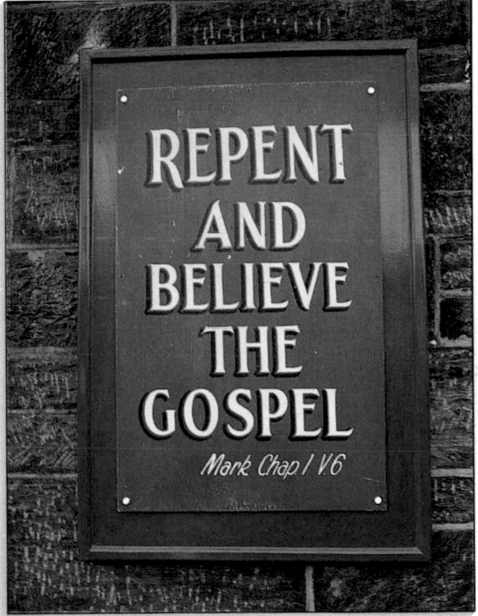

In the more industrialised and anglicised areas especially, the kind of Sabbatarianism which was the hallmark of the chapel now counts for little or nothing. Licensing laws have been liberalised, making the "dry" Sunday in Wales a thing of the past.

Old animosities between the Church in Wales – created by the Disestablishment of the Church of England – have mostly given way to a new spirit of ecumenism. Chapels have combined, and theological colleges have closed. But the chapel buildings remain. They played a crucial part in creating the principality of today, and Wales would not be Wales without them. ❑

LEFT: the chapels nurtured many great choirs.
RIGHT: exhortation at Ffestiniog Railway Station.

ANATOMY OF AN EISTEDDFOD

These cultural gatherings help determine what it means to be Welsh, so fierce arguments – always popular in Wales – are guaranteed

One of the world's most spectacular cultural gatherings? An excuse for a week of maudlin sentimentality? The occasion for celebrating a way of life essentially Welsh and totally separate from other parts of the United Kingdom? The Royal National Eisteddfod of Wales has been called all these things and many more.

But first, a necessary word about Welsh words. An eisteddfod is a public meeting at which contests in literature and music are held. Poetry and singing predominate. Hundreds of eisteddfodau (Welsh plurals take *au*, not *s*) take place every year in towns and villages throughout Wales. Some of the smaller gatherings are as highly regarded for their cultural content as the National – the eisteddfod at Llangwm, a remote village a few miles off the A5 trunk road near Bala in the north, is one such star in the Welsh firmament.

Eisteddfodau for all

There's an eisteddfod for pensioners, one for South Wales miners, another for the Urdd (the Welsh League of Youth). Most schools enter the lists. Not everyone understands the language – only 500,000 of Wales's 2.8 million people speak Welsh – but the spirit is widely shared.

The National is simply the star at the top of the pyramid. There the honours are the greatest. The ambitions and the strivings of every competitor in a sprawling network of eisteddfodau focus on the National – perhaps to be awarded the Bardic Crown or the Bardic Chair, the two highest honours in a land where achievement in things cultural is highly valued.

Much of what goes on at the National does not require the visitor to know the language. Arts and crafts competitions, music and ceremony stand unaided. But a lot does. It takes something of a mental gymnast to comprehend the precise rules of Welsh poetry and the intricate patterns of penillion singing. More popular forms are widely known, even beyond Wales – few Welsh men and women admit to being unable to sing the national anthem, even though they don't understand the words.

The language of the eisteddfod field (the *maes*) is Welsh. That doesn't mean that other tongues are not heard; far from it. To help non-Welsh speakers, there are free hand-held receivers through which an English commentary can be picked up.

PRECEDING PAGES: a National Eisteddfod.
LEFT: the National is the most important eisteddfod.
RIGHT: dancing at an international gathering.

Welsh is the language spoken in the main pavilion where the major events are staged with boundless brilliance. The building seats upward of 5,000. On the huge stage the bards in their ceremonial robes stare out across the footlights; the cuter members of the audience play "spot the bard" – a game in all conscience difficult enough in the cavernous surroundings and one made even harder by the costumes' ability to make every bard look alike.

They are there for the big ceremonies, the

Crowning and the Chairing. Two events of more intense theatricality are hard to imagine. As with Hollywood's Oscars, the winners are not supposed, in theory, to know in advance. A name is called out, a spotlight sweeps the audience and lights on the successful competitor who is then led on to the stage amid thunderous applause. Curiously, the winner invariably seems to be wearing a neat suit.

In a kingdom not as united as its title supposes, the National offers scope for social and political comment. The chaired Bard at the 1988 festival caused controversy for attacking nuclear power in his winning ode. Elwyn

Edwards, a careful man, took the opportunity to point his literary finger at Trawsfynydd nuclear power station, an incongruous pile in the middle of the Snowdonia National Park, blaming it for cancer cases in his home area. Revealingly, the Central Electricity Generating Board reacted angrily. Trawsfynydd is now closed. Was the bard able to summon up the druidic powers of his ancestors?

Outside the main pavilion hundreds of stalls promoting everything from Welsh lamb and Celtic fashions to wood carving and harp repairing, line up like some eastern bazaar. Fat cats such as the Wales Tourist Board inhabit huge glossy stands. In a remote corner, tiny tents extol the virtues of fringe causes. It's an engaging mix of the self-important and the grass roots, the professional presence of the big organisations contrasting with the improvised, home-made appearance of the amateur exhibitors. But the whole show doesn't come cheap. The National is now big business, costing over £2 million to stage, aided by grants of more than a quarter of a million pounds from Government funds.

The National is peripatetic, a restless culture fest which roams around Wales without settling in a permanent home. It comes to rest for a week every August, one year in the north, the next in the south. The cycle is as predictable as the rising of the sun: a different location each year and a new set of insoluble traffic problems for a different set of perspiring policemen.

Rows about the need for a permanent location occur with equally predictable regularity. The Royal Welsh Agricultural Society's splendid show ground at Builth Wells is slap in the middle of Wales and would be a happy choice. Monotonously, the National's governing body votes for the open road, citing the need to involve local communities. It is a well-founded argument – as proved by the heroic fund-raising undertaken in the chosen areas.

Partners with Mammon

Commercial sponsors, including financial institutions and industrial companies, have increasingly come to the aid of the National. Their influence is certain to grow and perhaps the day will come when logos will be emblazoned on the bards' robes.

If that does happen, it will follow to its logical conclusion the canny footwork of a certain Iolo Morgannwg, the bardic name of Edward Williams, an 18th-century Glamorgan stonemason whose influence on the festival persists to this day. Although the first eisteddfod is believed to have been held at Cardigan more than 800 years ago, the cunning Iolo invented the Gorsedd of Bards (the Bardic Circle) and forged documents to support the story he was the sole surviving member of the ancient Druids.

Today Wales is littered with circles of Gorsedd stones – each marking the place where an eisteddfod has been held. Williams stage-managed the first Gorsedd ceremony at which bardic "degrees" were awarded on 21 June 1792, choosing Primrose Hill in north London as the site for an event which contributes much to the National's colourful pageantry.

Youth is finally being allowed its place in the eisteddfod. Rock and folk music, through the medium of Welsh, have helped to revive the language. But as recently as 1979 it was considered unacceptable, and eisteddfod officials pulled the plug on an impromptu rock concert which drew hundreds away from the conventional pursuits. Now a rock pavilion is officially sanctioned.

LAND OF THEIR FATHERS

A moving moment at the National is the welcoming ceremony for Welsh people from abroad. Dozens of countries are represented, even a Welsh community in Patagonia.

A word of warning for the thirsty eisteddfod-goer. Alcohol is banned from the *maes* and the beer tents so much a part of other Welsh events – agricultural shows, festivals and sports meetings – are notable by their absence. This is good news for the public houses and restaurants which stock up in advance, only to be drunk dry in a matter of days; bad news on a hot day when approved-of lemonade tastes tepid. Thirst for spectacle however, overrides all other appetites and the National's rich diversity satisfies most tastes.

Quite separate from the National is the Llangollen International Eisteddfod, held every July in that tranquil North Wales town of 3,500 people. Staged in a field between the River Dee and the Llangollen Canal, which connects to the waterways of the English Midlands, it is a celebration of nations speaking – or rather singing, dancing and making music – to one another.

It was first held soon after the guns fell silent in 1945. Europe was a wreck and the festival sought in a tentative way to heal wounds that were not visible, to bridge gaps opened up by six years of bloody conflict. Half a century on, its success is beyond dispute. Singers, dancers, instrumentalists, orchestras and choirs from all over the world converge on Llangollen for a week of entente cordiale. It was here in 1955 that the 19-year-old Luciano Pavarotti, a member of the prize-winning Modena Choir, was so enthralled at hearing Tito Gobbi perform that he decided on a career in opera. Forty years later, in 1995, he returned to perform at the eisteddfod's closing concert.

The events are competitive, of course. Swedish choirs contest with Canadians and dancers from the Ukraine try to outdo Morris

LEFT: an important function of the eisteddfod is to keep alive traditional Welsh music.
ABOVE: dressed for an eisteddfod at Llangollen.

Men from Shropshire, a few steps across the English border. But all is secondary to the spirit of kinship between nations.

Llangollen is a pretty town blessed with one of Wales's most convivial wine bars and some picturesque riverside paths. Quiet it is not during eisteddfod week. Singing, dancing and fraternising go on continuously. For 12 hours a day on the field – and much longer in the town itself – the atmosphere is electric. Fiesta time in rural Wales brings New Orleans and Catalonia to the green hills, Ankara and Argentina to the friendly pubs and cafés. National costumes, brilliant hair styles and complexions of every hue combine with the picture postcard setting to produce a photographer's dream.

The International is given to scoring some noteworthy "firsts": groups from the People's Republic of China and the Soviet Union were first seen in Britain at Llangollen. It precedes the National by a couple of weeks, giving enthusiastic eisteddfod goers just enough time to catch their cultural breath.

Extreme opinions

Some believe the two are rivals, competitors in a cultural league where everyone claims the sweetest music, the deftest footwork and the catchiest tunes. A minority of old National supporters regard the International as an upstart which ignores Welsh, "the language of heaven", and threatens to dilute an ancient culture. An equally small group describes the National as an anachronism set in sentimental cement and fixing Welsh in a permanent linguistic ghetto. Neither analysis stands the acid test: a visit.

Complementary rather than competitive, they stand for different values springing from a shared base. The National carries a strong and compelling emotional appeal. Every Welsh woman, every Welsh man defines Welshness in a personal way, but their support for the National is today virtually total. An ancient institution, even allowing for Iolo Morgannwg's antics, it continues to stir the blood of Celts and others. It commands respect for people living in a part of the United Kingdom which considers itself different from neighbouring England. Not better, just different.

The International is a coming together of people scattered across the globe, people whose forebears fought each other in the name of who knows what. An affirmation of friendship is always welcome. Every July the Llangollen festival provides just that, cultural glasnost ahead of more recent political thaws. ❑

ABOVE: ancient rites rehearsed at a National Eisteddfod.

Welsh Choirs

All Welshmen sing like angels. That's what all Welshmen like to think, anyway. Put any two together and within minutes they'll have a sing-song going. Put 100 of them together and you'll have one of the world's great choirs pounding out one of the world's great melodies, anything from Bach's Oratario to Joseph Parry's Myfanwy. Although there are very good ladies' and mixed choirs, it is the male voice choir that is the best-known part of the Welsh musical tradition. The great choirs – the Morriston Orpheus, the Pendyrus, the Treorchy, the Rhos, the Pontardulais and the Llanelli among them – are carrying on a tradition that goes back a century or more and is inextricably interwoven with Welsh cultural life.

Giraldus Cambrensis, the great Welsh cleric who travelled the country in the Middle Ages, noted how the people sang in harmony. For centuries, that love of music was expressed in Welsh harp tunes, in simple unaccompanied singing and in penillion singing, an improvisatory art form unique to Wales.

Choral music came with the arrival of industrialisation and nonconformity. The nonconformist revival in the 18th and 19th centuries was a people's religion. The church was for the toffs, and ordinary people turned to the chapels with their strong emphasis on preaching and hymn singing. Love of music was also inculcated by the popularity of tonic sol-fa, a method of reading music without the traditional notation.

Many theories are invariably aired when it comes to explaining why the Welsh are so musical. One is based on the language, and the supposition that Welsh men and women open their mouths fully when they speak. The voice therefore comes from an open throat, which gives purer vowel sounds reminiscent of Italians. The Welsh also seem able to project the voice, in contrast to the southern English who speak between their teeth, hardly opening their mouths.

Given this aptitude combined with a cultural association that placed great importance not just on music but on Welsh music expressed in hymns, it was hardly surprising that choirs were formed.

The first of the big male voice choirs was probably formed in Ebenezer chapel, Trecynon, a suburb of Aberdare, in about 1849. Others quickly followed. But the great growth occurred in the last quarter of the 19th century, in the heyday of Victorian industrialisation in Wales. By then, the male voice choirs had become very large indeed – up to 150 strong. They were even going to London to perform before royalty – in Britain, the ultimate accolade.

Few of those Victorian choirs have survived. Recently a population with more money to spend and new ways in which to spend it found choir practice increasingly irksome. As attendances at chapels and Sunday schools declined, so did the choir tradition. But Welsh people never lost their ability to sing, as anyone who has watched a rugger international at Cardiff or attended one of the "festivals of a thousand voices" in London's Royal Albert Hall will testify. And in the late 1960s a new wave of enthusiasm for choral singing broke through. New choirs were formed, and the old ones were given a further lease of life. More choirs were created than at any time in the previous 100 years.

RIGHT: rehearsing with gusto.

Wales is not just about male voice choirs, though, and the tradition of musicality has been kept alive by the choral societies, the mixed choirs in which the sopranos and altos find a place alongside those lovely basses, baritones and tenors.

The latter, for some reason, are in short supply. "Where have all the tenors gone?" is a standard cry of choral music directors. Where indeed? Perhaps some of them have taken off for Sweden, which has developed an excellent choral tradition for small, balanced choirs. ❑

RUGBY: A WELSH RELIGION

Although modern rugby football is essentially an English invention, the Welsh have embraced the game with a remarkable passion

Twice a year on winter Saturday afternoons, come rain or shine or apocalypse, more than 70,000 people cram themselves into the Millennium Stadium in Cardiff. The occasion is the Big Match: the International. It's the day all Wales has been awaiting for. Wales is facing one of five teams at rugby: England, Ireland, France, Scotland or the recent entrants to the competition, Italy.

The atmosphere builds up through the morning. By the early afternoon the city is awash with red-bedecked fans who have arrived from Llanwonno, Llandudno and Llancayo by coach, car and other carriage to support "the boys". Red scarves and red hats are worn; giant green leeks, usually cardboard cutouts but often the real thing, are carried; white and green flags with the red dragon superimposed are waved; echoing the warrior tribes of old, faces are painted in the national colours.

Stadium for a new millennium

Cardiff is unique not just because rugby has reached the status of a quasi-religion in Wales but because the Millennium Stadium is bang in the centre of the city. Where the Murrayfield stadium is a good couple of miles from Princes Street in Edinburgh and Twickenham might just as well be on the south coast for all they know about it in London's Piccadilly, the Millennium Stadium on Westgate Street is literally as well as metaphorically a stone's throw from St Mary Street, the city's posh shopping centre.

Until the Millennium Stadium replaced the old Cardiff Arms Park, the experience of watching the game could be uncomfortable. With about half the crowd without a seat and at the mercy of Wales's capricious weather, those getting wet had to comfort themselves with the knowledge that as many again would gladly swap places with them. The act of attending a game is now a far more civilised affair in a new stadium that provides seating for all of its 72,500 occupants and also offers greater shelter from the elements.

Rugby is played everywhere in Wales. Any piece of land will do to sprout the H-shaped posts. It doesn't have to be rectangular and in a country like Wales it won't necessarily be flat. Every boy who has ever played rugby will tell

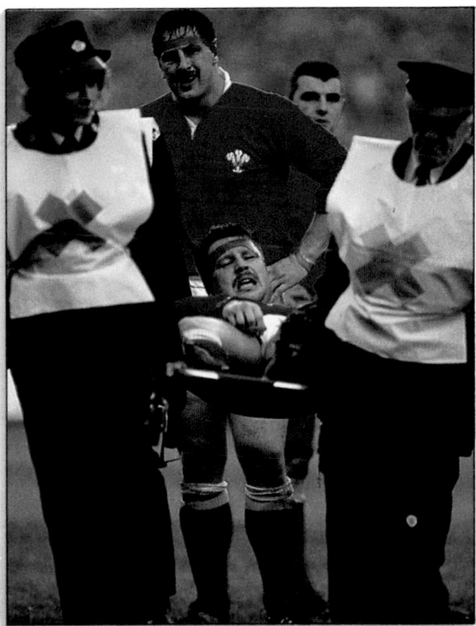

of grounds precariously perched on the edge of cliffs or so steeply angled that you need mountaineering gear to score a try.

Water plays an important role in Welsh rugby. The Taff, which before it was cleaned up made the Danube look like drinking water, runs just outside the west end of the Millennium Stadium (there's even an attractive new riverside walkway for promenading fans). But beer plays an even more important role. Post-match bacchanalia fuelled by a few pints puts all the heavenly choirs combined to shame.

The other seminal influence on the game is music. Music is the very soul of Wales; there have been eminent individual singers such as

LEFT: tense moment in an international match.
RIGHT: it's a game that's played vigorously.

Madame Adelina Patti and Sir Geraint Evans, but music finds its greatest expression in great choirs like the Morriston Orpheus, the Pendyrus and the Treorchy Male Voice. Every Welshman – especially every Welshman with a few beers inside him – imagines he is the lead tenor in the choir.

The unevenness of tone induced by alcoholic stimulation is, however, negated by mass. The sound of over 70,000 voices belting it out louder than Shirley Bassey ever imagined possible always has a stimulating effect on the 15 men on the pitch wearing the red jerseys. Englishmen have been known to go faint at the sound, New Zealanders have been known to travel half way across the world to hear it.

The greatest of the songs is *Mae'r Hen Wlad fy Nhadau*, the national anthem. This is only sung once, at the start. *Sospan Fach*, Little Saucepan, the "national anthem" of Llanelli, and two hymns, *Cwm Rhondda* (known to most English speakers for its opening words "Guide me O Thou Great Jehovah" and its chorus of "Bread of Heaven") and *Calon Lan* are great favourites.

One of the three will originate somewhere in the crowd. The refrain will be taken up and the tune will move around the great amphitheatre, urging on "the boys" to even greater effort. Strong men have been known to request *Calon Lan* sung by the stadium's "choir" as the one tune they would take with them to BBC Radio's mythical land of Desert Island Discs.

The cohesive strength of the crowd and the unresolved nit-picking over the name of the Millennium Stadium highlight two contrasting sides to the Welsh character: the enthusiastic bonding in the face of a common enemy perversely coupled with an inexhaustible talent for and internecine warfare. Any sane person would have ensured that Cardiff Arms Park – the spiritual home of rugby – would survive at least in name with the coming of the new stadium. Instead, there emerged the prosaic Millennium Stadium, which joins all the other "Millennium" projects destined, as the 21st century rolls on, to have an increasingly dated ring to them.

Nothing, of course, is straightforward – especially in the convoluted world of committees and local politics. Strictly speaking, the old Arms Park was not the Arms Park at all. It was the Welsh National Ground. The real Arms Park was next door and still exists in the lee of the massive Millennium Stadium. It's where the Cardiff rugby club plays, and it became the official Arms Park as a result of a complex history involving the Welsh Rugby Union and the Cardiff Athletic Club. The world at large shunned such pedantry: as far as rugby fans from Aberystwyth to Auckland were concerned, Wales played on the hallowed turf of the Arms Park – and still do.

Stadiums with attitude

So some call the new ground the Arms Park, some the Millennium Stadium, and there is even talk of selling the name to a corporate sponsor in an effort to raise funds. But the stadium is only the apex of where it all happens. Rugby is everywhere. Any pantheon dedicated to the game would include names such as Rodney Parade in Newport, St Helens in Swansea, Sardis Road in Pontypridd and Stradey Park in Llanelli. Especially Stradey. Stradey is the home of all that is Welsh in rugby. Down there they don't go in for a lot of English nonsense. The scoreboard gives the names of the teams in Welsh; the crowd speaks Welsh, their first language.

At Newport's Rodney Parade the crowd is very anglicised – hardly surprising as the town is almost in England. It's neither as anglicised nor as witty as the new Cardiff ground, where the sheepskin coats and peaked caps could almost reflect the crowd at the Harlequins' ground in London, university men all.

At St Helens there's the whiff of the sea in Swansea Bay just across the road, but it is in Pontypridd, Pontypool, Newbridge and Maesteg that one really feels in the heart of a Welsh crowd. Once they would have been miners. Now the pits have gone and the men are probably employed in Bridgend or Cardiff assembling television sets and video recorders for the Japanese.

The players themselves are much the same as ever, gods in different sizes. The greatest gods are men like Cliff Morgan who in the late 1940s and early 1950s was to rugby what Dennis Compton was to cricket, a buccaneering genius. Or Onllwyn Brace, who brought distinction to the scrum-half job when all he was expected to do was feed the great men outside him. Billy Cleaver with the fair mop of hair and Merve the Swerve, Mervyn Davies, the back-row forward who led Wales through one of their golden eras in the 1970s when nothing was impossible. Gareth Edwards and Barry John are other giants from this golden era.

After a bleak period when it seemed that Wales would never match feats such as their mythic victory over a previously unbeaten New Zealand side in 1905, Welsh international rugby is beginning to show signs of recovery. The team is becoming more assured under the management of New Zealander Graham Henry, and it received a huge boost when it beat England and South Africa in 1999. Now the squad boasts players such as Neil Jenkins, who has taken his place in the pantheon of Welsh rugby heroes by becoming the highest scoring player in game's history. ❑

No Holds Barred

Rugby's predecessor, the ancient Welsh sport of *cnapan*, was played across fields by up to 1,500 naked men fighting to get a wooden ball into the opponents' territory.

LEFT: Wales takes on Scotland.
ABOVE: fans at a world cup match in Cardiff.

The World Comes to Wales

Perhaps the biggest thing to have happened to Welsh rugby in recent years has been the 1999 World Cup. Hosted in Cardiff's magnificent new stadium, this event brought together the finest rugby-playing nations in the world and, despite the Welsh team's disappointing performance, firmly placed Wales back on the rugby map. Due to the many competing teams, the event was spread over other parts of Britain and Europe, but it was in Cardiff that the competition really came alive. As fans from the far-flung reaches of the globe mingled in the pubs and streets surrounding the stadium, Wales proved that the country was still fluent in the ancient language of rugby.

THE FOOD REVOLUTION

Once upon a time there wasn't much worth mentioning except for lamb, cheese and puréed seaweed. But tastes are changing

Wales, which used to be regarded as a gastronomic wilderness, has been responding to tourism's demands for better food: there are now plenty of good places to eat – both modestly and not so modestly. Local people's expectations have been growing, too: the number of pubs serving good bar meals is growing, and more adventurous fast food turns up in small towns and villages, which have their Chinese and Thai take-aways.

It was not always so. A growing appreciation of good food within Wales together with the influences of tourism have changed the menu dramatically. Technical colleges and catering establishments are bringing on chefs of high calibre, who are quickly snapped up by discerning restaurateurs. Talented chefs from outside Wales – often attracted by the lower start-up costs when establishing their own businesses – are creating a climate of healthy competition and helping to raise standards generally.

Fighting the flab

Basics, like steak and chips, chicken and chips, fish and chips, sausage and chips are, of course, obtainable everywhere from Cardiff to Caernarfon. Note that repetitive addition: chips. Thereby hangs a tale, a cautionary one. Wales has been swamped with healthy eating publicity aimed at cutting down obesity, heart disease and other problems stemming from unsuitable diets, and government campaigns to encourage heathy eating are having an effect. Cuts of meat have become leaner and the chips are cooked in sunflower oil. Lard is out, unsaturated fats in.

The traditional Sunday joint – the equivalent of beef in England – is succulent Welsh lamb. The farmers of Wales have managed to produce a meat which is comparatively fat-free. With a registered sheep population exceeding 10 million, there are enough lamb chops and shoulders of mutton in the offing to last for ever.

Another traditional meal – now something of a culinary cliché – is cawl. One of Wales's most nourishing and sustaining dishes, this simple soup is well laced with bite-sized chunks of vegetables and lamb. Follow that with a few slices of bread made of locally milled flour topped with Caws Aberteifi (a tasty cheese made in Cardigan) and you will feel replete.

Then there's the famous – or infamous – laverbread. It's not a bread at all. Black and gooey, it's a puréed seaweed mixed with oatmeal, a concoction not to everyone's taste. Found mainly in South Wales, it is usually eaten at breakfast with bacon and eggs or as a starter to a main course.

Cockles, gathered on the shores of Gower, a peninsula nosing into the Bristol Channel near Swansea, and in the Dee Estuary in the north, are another Welsh tradition. The air sung by another Celt – Molly Malone of Dublin, who wheeled her barrow through streets broad and narrow, crying cockles and mussels, alive alive-o – has no Welsh counterpart, but cockle pie (cockles,

LEFT: the traditional butcher, an endangered species. **RIGHT:** a warming broth in winter.

bacon and spring onions under a pastry roof) strikes a happy chord.

Wales, like Scotland, has its salmon. Sewin, a pink-skinned sea trout, is equally popular, and as much sought after as Conwy salmon. Trout taken from Trawsfynydd Lake are said to be the fattest in the land; not everyone cares to eat them because the lake supplied cooling water to the nuclear power station, now decommissioned, which sits alongside it.

For a between-meals snack, welshcakes are favourite. Flat scone-like cakes the diameter of a tea cup, baked with sultanas and currants, they can be eaten plain or buttered, hot or cold.

Even before this recent trend, there were cosmopolitan influences at work. For a land reckoned to be somewhat insular, Wales has a remarkable diversity of eating places. Italians settled in the Valleys of the south generations ago, and have established a niche in the catering trade. Cafés run by Rabiottis and Sidolis stand alongside others with "Evans" and "Jones" above the door. Latins and Celts fuse, marry and combine to produce a lively society dishing up interesting food.

The capital city, Cardiff, caters for all tastes. There are long-standing authentic Chinese restaurants here (as opposed to the pale imita-

So much for the traditional side to Welsh cooking. In the past 15 years or so, there has been a marked trend amongst the more adventurous chefs to give traditional dishes a modern twist, or to use traditional ingredients to prepare a more modern, lighter style of cuisine. This trend has been welcomed by Taste of Wales, an organisation created to encourage the use of fresh, local produce in contemporary and traditional ways and to raise levels of quality throughout the industry. The new style of Welsh cuisine includes such taste ticklers as chicken on tagliatelle with tarragon sauce and deep-fried leeks, or seabass with confit fennel, Swiss chard, salsify chips and vanilla sauce.

tions you see in most places). The city's cosmopolitan atmosphere is reflected in its range of restaurants – everything from Italian to wholefood, French to traditional Welsh.

Chefs with style

Twenty or 30 years ago it would have been easy to list the good places to eat in Wales within the confines of this chapter. Nowadays, it's not possible. There are so many good chefs working in Wales that they deserve a separate review. They oversee the kitchens of all kinds of establishments, from upmarket country house hotels where you can expect to pay a considerable amount for a meal (though far less than a comparable restaurant in London), to humble country pubs which serve excellent value, cleverly created bar meals which have nothing in common with the "chicken and chips" formula. Ask locally – everyone knows where to find the best places to eat. You may also find a copy of the free *Dining Out in Wales* booklet, produced by Taste of Wales, helpful.

THE HARD STUFF

Although it can't compete with Scotland and Ireland, Wales does distil some drinkable whisky. You can also find a few Welsh wines, though they're nothing special.

Farmhouse cheeses

Welsh cheeses have staged something of a renaissance in recent times. As one respected food writer remarked when encountering a cheeseboard at a country house hotel, "[It] was quite remarkable. It was entirely Welsh in origin yet managed eight cheeses quite separate in character… I'm told that one French inspector for a well-known guide remarked that it was better than anything he'd come across in France in the last three months."

Wales has been well known for cheese in the past. There's the white, crumbly, and much-imitated Caerphilly cheese, for example. Welsh Rarebit, the once-popular dish of roasted cheese, is nowadays quite hard to come by. Wales's new "cheesy" reputation has been inspired by small, farm-based producers determined to return cheese-making to its traditional roots. In a revolt against blandness and mass-production, they began producing distinctive cheeses which sell – much in the way of fine wines – on the strength of their label. There's the award-winning Caws Cenarth, for example, from near Newcastle Emlyn in West Wales, which makes traditional Caerphilly cheese and has outlets as far afield as Harrods and Fortnum & Mason. Other cheeses widely available include the brie-style Pencarreg, from Lampeter, and Llanboidy from Pembrokeshire, a traditional hard-pressed mature farmhouse cheese.

There are many small producers scattered throughout Wales, especially in the west and along the Teifi Valley. You'll find their produce on the menus of good hotels and restaurants.

It has taken Wales some time to come in from the cold in matters gastronomic and the journey has yet to be completed in some parts, but the demand for good food combined with cheerful service is recognised and increasingly met – with or without chips. ❑

LEFT: shoppers in a Swansea market.
ABOVE: a bed-and-breakfast farmhouse at Rhayader.

17

GREAT LITTLE TRAINS

Wales's narrow-gauge railways have a wide appeal, not least because they run through some of the country's most spectacular scenery

Lovers of steam who visit Wales are in for a rare treat: around a dozen narrow-gauge steam railway lines. These were not designed for the edification of tourists or even the transportation of passengers – some were built to transport slate from mountain quarries to seaports. After falling into disuse around the middle of the 20th century, they were resuscitated by enthusiasts who formed railway preservation societies.

What makes a railway narrow gauge? The term applies to any track between 1ft 6in (450mm) and 3ft 6in (1,050mm) wide. Lines more than 3ft 6in are sub-standard gauge; lines less than 1ft 6in are miniature; standard gauge as used by today's rail services is 4ft 8½in (1.4 metres). The attractions of the "little trains", other than the steam, are their intimate size and their leisurely progress which gives passengers a grand opportunity to enjoy the scenery.

Preserving the past

Britain's very first railway preservation society was formed in Wales in 1950 to save the Talyllyn Railway. Opened in 1865, it is the only "little train" with a record of continuous service. The Talyllyn has its headquarters at Tywyn in the heart of Cardigan Bay. From here, a slightly more than 7-mile (12-km), 2ft 3in (67mm) track runs inland following the river valley through spectacular scenery, much of which is within the Snowdonia National Park. At Dolgoch station the line crosses an impressive viaduct and walks from the station will take you to Dolgoch Waterfalls.

The Talyllyn's rolling stock includes the Talyllyn, a steam locomotive built in 1864. The society's Narrow-gauge Railway Museum at Tywyn Wharf station has the best collection of narrow-gauge relics in Britain. These include engines from Britain, Ireland and France.

North of Tywyn, and still on Cardigan Bay, stands Porthmadog, the home of two preserved narrow-gauge railways. The Ffestiniog line originally opened in 1836 with horse-drawn rolling stock which brought slate from the mines at Blaenau Ffestiniog to the port of Porthmadog. It had a maximum gradient of 1 in 70 which permitted laden wagons to free-wheel from quarry to port.

In 1860, the Ffestiniog became the first steam-powered narrow-gauge railway in the world: visitors came from far and wide to view this engineering marvel. Then the line began to carry passengers as well as slate. In 1951 a preservation society was formed to save the Ffestiniong which had stopped operating. Volunteers rushed forward and by 1955 the railway had started up again. Today it's a great success.

The Ffestiniog's 2-ft (600-mm) track runs for almost 14 miles (22 km) through oak forests and past luxuriant rhododendrons through what is claimed to be the most scenic narrow-gauge route in Wales. As the train proceeds, the valley

PRECEDING PAGES: Porthmadog railway station.
LEFT: the narrow-gauge Brecon Mountain Railway.
RIGHT: the scenic Cambrian Coast line.

unfolds and reveals superb views of Snowdonia National Park.

The Ffestiniog's oldest locomotives are from 1863, but the line is even better known for its double-ended articulated engines which were built in the society's workshop. Yet there is a disappointment for purists: the Ffestiniog has converted all its locomotives from coal to oil firing because of the risk of forest fires.

The Welsh Highland Railway, Porthmadog's second narrow-gauge line, was formerly the longest narrow-gauge railway in Wales. Its 2-ft (600-mm) track opened in 1923 but was, from its inception, doomed to failure, having started

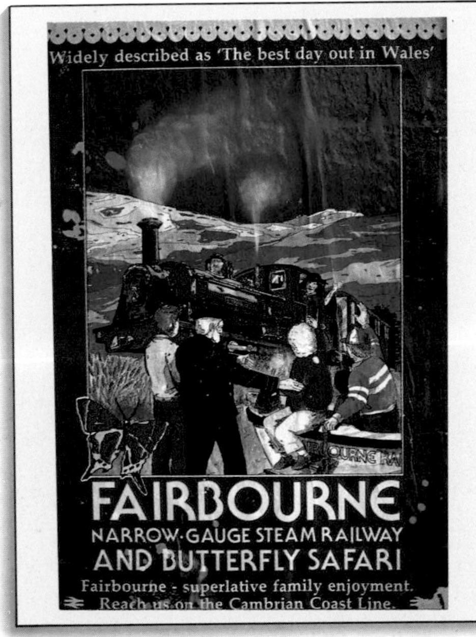

too late to enjoy any real chance of industrial survival. However, after the success of the Ffestiniog, the future looks bright for the Welsh Highland whose current 1-mile (1.5-km) route is exceptionally scenic.

The Welsh Highland originally ran through the foothills of Snowdonia to the North Wales coast. In recent years there have been successful attempts to reinstate part of the northern section. A separate narrow-gauge company, Rheilffordd Eryri/Welsh Highland Railway (Caernarfon), runs trains on a 2-ft (600-mm), 7-mile (12-km) track from Caernarfon to Waunfawr. The long-term objective is to reinstate the line all the way to Porthmadog.

On the coast, between Porthmadog and Tywyn and running for about 2 miles (3 km) above a magnificent sandy beach and so close to the waves of Cardigan Bay that you fear it will get its feet wet, is the Fairbourne Railway. The line, originally horse-drawn, was built to carry materials for the building of Fairbourne village.

The Fairbourne is actually a miniature rather than a narrow-gauge railway, with a track 15in (375mm) wide. It operates with replicas of famous narrow-gauge locomotives hauling period-style wooden coaches. Yet the Fairbourne is possibly the most functional of all "little railways", carrying local people as well as tourists from Fairbourne to the ferry which crosses the Mawddach Estuary to Barmouth.

The Vale of Rheidol Railway has its headquarters at Aberystwyth. The track – almost 12 miles (19 km) long – was opened in 1902 for the purpose of transporting lead and timber and passengers, and has a 2-ft (600-mm) gauge. Yet, in spite of this narrow gauge the tiny locomotives are more than 8ft (2 metres) wide and each weighs just over 25 tons.

The Devil's Bridge

The one-hour journey is spectacular, especially the final third where, as the veteran steam locomotives snort their way up steep gradients, around tight bends and on ledges overhanging precipitous drops, you look back to where you were 10 minutes before. Finally, the track passes through a deep rock-cutting to end at the "Devil's Bridge" terminus, at an altitude of 679ft (204 metres). Actually, there are three bridges, one above the other. According to legend, the lowest was built by the devil who claimed as payment the first soul to cross. The village dog was sent over.

Close to the border with England is the Welshpool and Llanfair Light Railway. This line, often called the "Farmers' Line", was built in the early 20th century to carry passengers and their products to the market towns of Welshpool and Llanfair. The route winds its way through a rich mosaic of pastoral and wooded hill country, climbing steep gradients over a switchback 8-mile (13-km) route between the Severn and Banwy valleys. At one stage the train puffs and puffs and puffs its way up a 1 in 30 gradient.

The line, which has a gauge of 2ft 6in (750 mm), was re-opened by enthusiasts in 1963 after having been closed down in 1956. The society prides itself on the international flavour of its rolling stock and locomotives and you will have the opportunity to travel in vintage coaches from Austria or comfortable modern ones from Sierra Leone while being pulled by a locomotive from Germany or from a sugar plantation in the West Indies.

Back in the Snowdonia National Park is the somewhat different Snowdon Mountain Railway which departs from Llanberis. This is Britain's only rack-and-pinion railway – which means, in brief, that the drive of the locomotive is through rack pinions on the rails and that its wheels merely serve to carry its weight.

Since its inception, nearly 100 years ago, the Snowdon Mountain Railway has been strictly a passenger operation and has never needed to be rescued by preservation societies and their like. The line is so popular that advance booking is advisable in July, August and September. Trains do not run in severe weather or when the wind is high. It takes almost one hour to ride the 5 miles (8 km) of 2ft 8in (800mm) track which runs to within 66ft (19 metres) of the summit of Mount Snowdon. Gradients are as steep as 1 in 5½.

On a clear day the unfolding views are unsurpassed, rivalled only by those enjoyed by walkers who decide to make it to the 3,560-ft (1,085-metre) summit under their own steam. The trip is exciting and not for those of a nervous disposition.

Some timid passengers were on board when the railway opened on Easter Monday, 1896. Engine No. 1, the Ladas, fell into a ravine. Two passengers who wrongly anticipated that the coaches would also fall leapt for safety: one of them died in the attempt. The company has operated without a No. 1 engine ever since and has never had another accident.

Around the lakes

Narrow-gauge enthusiasts should not dash off when they return to Llanberis but should make their way across town to Gilfach Ddu station and the Llanberis Lake Railway. This line has been scavenged from two companies which, for nearly a century, served the Dinorwig slate quarries. The track bed is from one and the rolling stock is from another. The 2-mile (3-km) track, dwarfed by mountains which are reflected in the lake, runs along the edge of Llyn (lake) Padarn. It has a 2-ft (600-mm) gauge. On a clear day visitors can enjoy superb views of Snowdon.

The Bala Lake Railway is another lakeside railway in the Snowdonia National Park. It runs for nearly 5 miles (8 km) between Bala and Llanuwchllyn along lovely Llyn Tegid, the largest natural lake in Wales.

Southern routes

Although North and central Wales have the lion's share of the little railways, there are also a few in the south and west. The Brecon Mountain Railway runs into the foothills of the Brecon Beacons from Merthyr Tydfil. The Teifi Valley Railway operates from Henllan near Newcastle Emlyn. The Gwili Railway (a standard-gauge line) runs through a wooded valley from Bronwydd near Carmarthen. There's also a standard-gauge line at Llangollen in North Wales.

A word of warning: with one or two exceptions, preserved railways do not run during the winter and, for the remainder of the year, schedules are varied and irregular. Check before starting on your trip. Some lines, on occasion, substitute diesel for steam locomotives.

Railway enthusiasts visiting Wales need not

LEFT: a poster from the past.
RIGHT: Porthmadog station on the Ffestiniog line.

confine themselves to travelling on preserved lines. Some of the most glorious countryside is traversed by tracks of the ordinary passenger services which can also whisk the steam enthusiast from one preserved line to another.

The so-called Cambrian Coaster is a good example. The sea is rarely out of sight on this breathtaking 58-mile (93-km) passenger line between Machynlleth and Pwllheli, with the train speeding alongside golden beaches, through windswept dune-land and, on one dramatic stretch, clinging to steep cliffs.

En route, the track crosses three river estuaries, the highlight being the half-mile-long Barmouth timber trestle bridge spanning the Mawddach Estuary. Look out also for Harlech and Criccieth castles and the Italianate village of Portmeirion. Those with steam withdrawal symptoms will break their journey at Tywyn, Fairbourne and/or Porthmadog from which narrow-gauge steam trains depart.

Everyday rail routes

Other scenic standard passenger routes are the 83-mile (133-km) trip from Chester to Holyhead; the 121-mile (195-km) journey from Shrewsbury via Llanelli to Swansea on the aptly named "Heart of Wales" line; the 81-mile (130-km) journey from Shrewsbury to Aberystwyth and the 28-mile (45-km) run from Llandudno Junction to Blaenau Ffestiniog. The last two provide the opportunity to join narrow-gauge steam railways: the Vale of Rheidol at Aberystwyth and the Ffestiniog at Blaenau Ffestiniog.

Travelling on the everyday passenger services rather than on preserved lines provides the visitor with the chance to meet locals rather than other tourists. Although the stiff upper-lipped Brit, commuting for the umpteenth year on the Basingstoke to London line, may never yield more than a courteous nod of the head and a curt "Good morning", the Welsh housewife travelling between Llanwrtyd and Llandrindod Wells for her weekly shopping will be delighted to chat with you.

Your cup – not to mention your glass – may well run over if you travel on the Chester–Holyhead line, for here you will be entertained not only by the Welsh and possibly the English but also the Irish. (Holyhead is the terminal for a ferry service to the Irish Republic.) ❑

RIGHT: a "great little train" at Morfa Harlech.

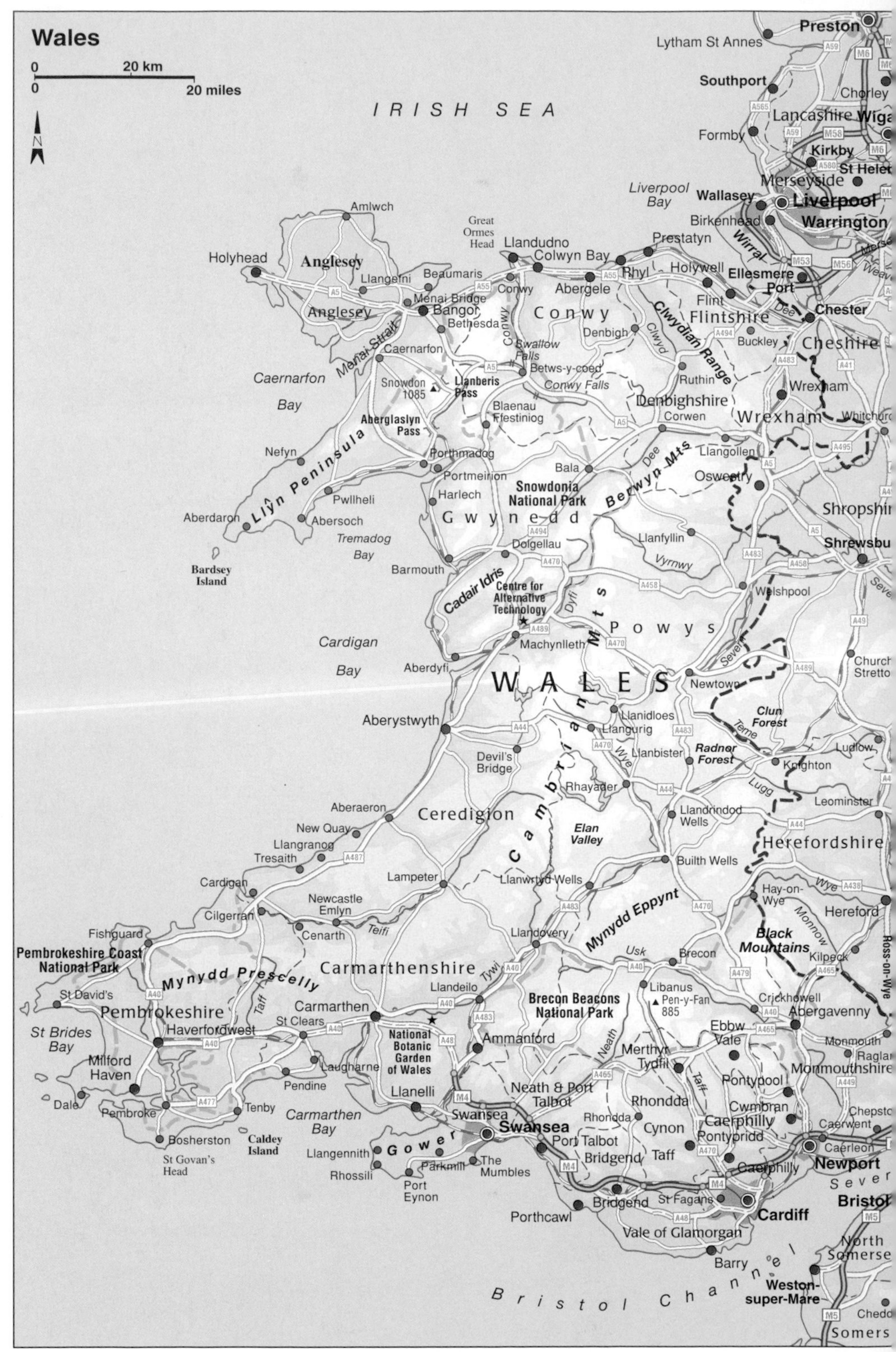

Wales
0 20 km
0 20 miles
N
IRISH SEA
Liverpool Bay
Preston
Lytham St Annes
Southport
Chorley
Lancashire
Formby
Kirkby
Merseyside
Wallasey
Liverpool
Birkenhead
Warrington
Wirral
Prestatyn
Holywell
Ellesmere Port
Chester
Flint
Flintshire
Cheshire
Buckley
Amlwch
Holyhead
Anglesey
Llangefni
Beaumaris
Menai Bridge
Bangor
Great Ormes Head
Llandudno
Colwyn Bay
Rhyl
Abergele
Conwy
Bethesda
Denbigh
Clwydian Range
Clwyd
Menai Strait
Caernarfon
Caernarfon Bay
Snowdon 1085
Llanberis Pass
Swallow Falls
Betws-y-coed
Conwy Falls
Ruthin
Denbighshire
Wrexham
Blaenau Ffestiniog
Aberglaslyn Pass
Corwen
Llangollen
Nefyn
Llŷn Peninsula
Porthmadog
Portmeirion
Bala
Oswestry
Berwyn Mts
Dee
Pwllheli
Abersoch
Aberdaron
Harlech
Snowdonia National Park
Gwynedd
Shropshire
Tremadog Bay
Bardsey Island
Dolgellau
Llanfyllin
Vyrnwy
Shrewsbury
Barmouth
Cadair Idris
Centre for Alternative Technology
Welshpool
Dyfi
Cardigan Bay
Machynlleth
Powys
Aberdyfi
Severn
WALES
Newtown
Church Stretton
Clun Forest
Aberystwyth
Llanidloes
Llangurig
Cambrian Mts
Teme
Devil's Bridge
Llanbister
Radnor Forest
Knighton
Ludlow
Wye
Rhayader
Lugg
Leominster
Aberaeron
Ceredigion
New Quay
Llangranog
Tresaith
Llandrindod Wells
Elan Valley
Herefordshire
Builth Wells
Lampeter
Cardigan
Llanwrtyd Wells
Hay-on-Wye
Hereford
Newcastle Emlyn
Cilgerran
Teifi
Mynydd Eppynt
Fishguard
Cenarth
Llandovery
Black Mountains
Monnow
Pembrokeshire Coast National Park
Mynydd Prescelly
Carmarthenshire
Usk
Brecon
Kilpeck
Ross-on-Wye
Tywi
Llandeilo
Libanus
Pen-y-Fan 885
St David's
Pembrokeshire
Carmarthen
Brecon Beacons National Park
Crickhowell
Abergavenny
Haverfordwest
St Clears
Taff
St Brides Bay
National Botanic Garden of Wales
Ammanford
Ebbw Vale
Monmouth
Raglan
Milford Haven
Laugharne
Neath
Merthyr Tydfil
Monmouthshire
Pendine
Pontypool
Dale
Pembroke
Tenby
Llanelli
Neath & Port Talbot
Rhondda
Cwmbran
Chepstow
Carmarthen Bay
Swansea
Caerphilly
Caerwent
Bosherston
Caldey Island
Gower
Rhondda Cynon Taff
Pontypridd
Caerleon
Newport
St Govan's Head
Llangennith
Port Talbot
Bridgend
Rhossili
Parkmill
The Mumbles
Port Eynon
Severn
Bristol
Porthcawl
St Fagans
Cardiff
Vale of Glamorgan
North Somerset
Barry
Bristol Channel
Weston-super-Mare
Cheddar
Somerset

PLACES

A detailed guide to Wales, with principal sites clearly cross-referenced by number to the maps

Like Richard Burton, its celebrated son, Wales can assume many different guises yet remain recognisably itself. There is the Welsh-speaking Wales in the north and the west, a community whose distinctive culture has been shielded by its ancient language from a world hell-bent on homogeneity. There is the close community of the Valleys, shaking the coal dust from its boots and redefining its future. There are the sparsely populated rural heartlands of central Wales where farming and forestry still underpin the local economy. And there is the "English" Wales in the east and southwest, where the two ancient enemies have reached an understanding of sorts.

The visual contrasts within this small community are as striking as the differences in character. The Wye Valley, the first stop for many visitors who cross the Severn Bridge, offers gentle scenery, sleepy villages, ruined abbeys and castles. The Brecon Beacons National Park combines mountain and moorland to convey a feeling of space rare in an overcrowded island. In the Valleys, the dramatic geological rifts that form the heart of South Wales, the coal mines have been eclipsed but the terraced communities remain.

Cardiff, like many capital cities, does not claim to be a microcosm of the country. It is noticeably anglicised, and has cosmopolitan convictions – though it assumed the role of Wales's capital as recently as 1955. Swansea, Wales's second (and indeed *only* other) city, is a personable and personal place – "an ugly, lovely town," as the poet Dylan Thomas called it. Glamorgan's Heritage Coast remains one of Britain's best-kept secrets: the seaside pleasures of past times have remained uncorrupted by the juggernaut of tourism.

The coastline continues to the southwest into the Pembrokeshire Coast National Park, an area where seafaring traditions combine with Celtic myth and tales of Merlin. Mid-Wales, unsullied by motorways, has retained its unspoiled rural charm. It's the most peaceful part of Wales, a region of green hills, lakes and small market towns. To the north lies Snowdonia National Park, a dramatic mountain landscape and a magnet for climbers and outdoors enthusiasts. Those looking for fun will head instead for the string of north coast resorts, doggedly maintaining the candy-floss tradition of the British seaside. North Wales does have its quieter shores, along the Llŷn Peninsula ("Snowdonia's Arm") and around the Isle of Anglesey, connected to the mainland by road and rail bridges. For such a small country, there's a surprising variety of landscapes and seascapes. ❑

PRECEDING PAGES: Gwynant Valley; coracle fishermen; New Quay, Cardiganshire.

SOUTHEAST WALES

The mountain ranges retain their beauty, but the Valleys have changed as the old heavy industries have faded

The scenery on the Welsh side of the Severn Estuary is very different from that on the English side, as drivers approaching from the east can observe. Through Wiltshire and Avon, the countryside is rolling but relatively flat; houses are built in the soft yellowing Cotswold stone; rich pasture land borders the road. Across the water it is very different. The Wye, one of Britain's great salmon rivers, at whose mouth Chepstow lies, is steep-sided, with traditional oak, beech, birch, ash and chestnut covering the slopes. It's not surprising to discover that the river valley between Chepstow and Monmouth is one of Wales's officially designated "Areas of Outstanding Natural Beauty".

Beyond Chepstow, in the distance, are the borderland Black Mountains, a line of lofty hills filling the eastern flank of the Brecon Beacons National Park. The park is a succession of mountain ranges rolling across the landscape from the Welsh border almost to the doorstep of Swansea. At its heart is the flat-topped summit of Pen-y-Fan, at 2,907ft (886 metres) the highest mountain in South Wales. The peak is clearly visible from Merthyr Tydfil, the former "iron capital of the world", the contrast between the two throwing into stark relief the sudden changes that occur in this part of Wales.

The terraced towns of the old industrial Valleys rudely infiltrate the thinly populated foothills of the Beacons. Between the National Park and the sea lies the commercial heart of Wales, a place which has seen great changes over the past 20 years or so as the traditional heavy industries have declined, to be replaced by high-tech and service sector companies. Cardiff, Wales's capital, is at the forefront of these changes, the wholesale regeneration of Cardiff Bay serving as a symbol of the confident, forward-looking Wales of the 21st century.

The Vale of Glamorgan, which separates Cardiff from Swansea, presents yet another face of South Wales – prosperous farmlands fringed by the cliffs of the unspoilt Glamorgan Heritage Coast and a few traditional seaside resorts. Swansea, like Cardiff, has brought new life to its old docklands. This breezy "city by the sea" enjoys a fortunate location along a sandy bay which leads to the beaches and headlands of the Gower Peninsula, Britain's first "Area of Outstanding Natural Beauty". ❑

LEFT: walking on the Brecon Beacons at Pen-y-Fan, South Wales's highest peak.

Map on page 102

THE WYE VALLEY

Chepstow, Tintern Abbey and Monmouth are the main attractions in this beautiful area. You can walk along the ancient Offa's Dyke Path and visit the "book town" of Hay-on-Wye

When you approach Wales from England along the tedious M4 motorway, two dramatic structures decisively demarcate the border between the two countries. The one, opened in 1996, is the new **Severn Bridge** or **Second Severn Crossing** ❶. This toll bridge, built at a cost of £330 million by an Anglo-French consortium, is the longest in Britain, stretching for 3¼ miles (5km) and is now the main route into South Wales. The other, 4 miles (7km) upstream, is the original **Severn Bridge**, opened in 1966 and a pioneer in its time as the world's first box-girder suspension bridge. This bridge, once so congested, now gives easy access to a beautiful part of Wales. Take the M48 spur off the M4 for the original bridge, which takes you across the water to the wooded, meandering **River Wye**, one of Britain's great salmon rivers.

Chepstow

At the mouth of the Wye lies the town of **Chepstow** ❷. As an introduction to the Wye Valley, Chepstow offers few hints of the magnificent pleasures to come. This small town was once one of the most handsome and prosperous places in South Wales. The years, however, have not been kind: industrial decline and a series of curious town planning decisions – the worst has involved driving a bypass through the most attractive quarter – have robbed the place of much of its charm and character. On the other hand, the diverted traffic has made the town centre a more amenable thoroughfare; it's now much easier to appreciate the preserved medieval street patterns and the Town Gate, dating from the 13th century, which still stands at the top of the High Street.

The Norman Castle, the town's greatest treasure, remains impressively intact, dominating the river with tremendous presence. According to some, it is a hugely significant historical landmark: the first stone-built castle in Britain. Although playing a key role in the Norman control of the turbulent Welsh, it really came into its own in the English Civil War, achieving particular significance during the ebb and flow of the battle between the Roundheads and the Royalists.

The castle is particularly associated with Henry Marten, a leading Parliamentarian who signed King Charles I's death warrant and suffered for this "treacherous" act when King Charles II was restored to the throne. He was kept prisoner in the castle for 20 years; the tower where he was held is still known as Marten's Tower. (In fairness to the Restorationists, Marten's imprisonment seems

FT: the ver Wye. **GHT:** nepstow astle.

not to have been especially arduous: he lived with his family in some comfort and was given permission to come and go from the castle.)

Near the river, in the old streets at the bottom of the town, one can imagine how Chepstow must have been 200 years ago: busy with ships and boats travelling further up the Wye and out to the Bristol Channel, its dozens of ale houses crammed with sailors and prostitutes. Like most ports, it was often mad, bad and dangerous to know. A plaque marks the quayside from which the leaders of the abortive Chartist march on Newport in 1839 were transported to Tasmania.

Two miles (3 km) from the centre of Chepstow, heading north towards Monmouth on the A466, you pass **Chepstow Racecourse**, a popular venue for enthusiasts of steeplechasing. On Sundays the car park here and part of the course is given over to a busy market.

Shortly after St Arvans, a mile (1.6 km) further on, the Wye Valley opens up to reveal its full grandeur. It is worth making a small detour up to the **Wyndcliff** which offers a breathtaking view of the valley, the horseshoe bend of the river and beyond to the Severn Bridge. This view was one of the high spots of the "Wye Tour" enjoyed by pioneer tourists of the late 18th and early 19th centuries who travelled in search of such powerfully romantic settings.

Tintern Abbey

For most visitors, however, then and now, the true high spot is probably **Tintern Abbey ❸**, 5 miles (8 km) north of Chepstow. It would be difficult to imagine a more handsome setting for an abbey, located as it is beside the river, framed by steeply wooded slopes. The abbey inspired William Wordsworth to write one of his finest poems, *Lines composed a few miles above Tintern Abbey*. The poem, which Wordsworth actually wrote in Bristol, isn't really about Tintern Abbey at all but rather a statement of his pantheistic belief that God is to be found in nature:

LEFT: Tintern Abbey

Map on page 102

And I have felt
A presence that disturbs me with the joy
Of elevated thoughts; a sense sublime
Of something far more deeply interfused,
Whose dwelling is the light of setting suns,
And the round ocean and the living air,
And the blue sky, and in the mind of man.

The area around Tintern is superb walking country. There are footpaths in all directions, many well-marked trails on signposted circuits. A few miles above Tintern, and perhaps the very spot where Wordsworth had his first inspiring glimpse of the ruined abbey, is **Devil's Pulpit**. There's a waymarked footpath from the village, crossing the River Wye over the footbridge: the early part of the climb is steep.

A more interesting route to Devil's Pulpit – and a more level one – is along the **Offa's Dyke Path**, which begins near Tidenham, Chepstow; for a couple of miles you can follow the line of the 170-mile (272-km) dyke built in the 8th century by the Mercian King Offa, which is still almost intact in certain sections. It was erected to mark the western boundary of his kingdom and to provide a defence against Welsh raiders. Perhaps it looked more of a barrier 1,000 years ago; today, a small dog could leap over it *(see page 104)*.

At Devil's Pulpit, a rocky knob which does look rather pulpit-like, legend has it that the devil stood and raged against the monks in their handsome abbey below, pelting them with rocks. Not much sign of the devil now, but there are still piles of small rocks lying around (discarded brimstones perhaps?). From the Pulpit, the view of the abbey, the Wye and the wooded valley is one of the best views in the world: enough to move anyone to verse.

Don't leave Tintern without visiting the abbey, a splendid Cistercian building surprisingly well preserved. The Cistercians are a strict order who eschew most comforts, including warmth. But they treated themselves with the site of the abbey and its handsome construction. Even without heat, you can almost have envied them.

ELOW: ıe Wye Valley.

Offa's Dyke

Crossing the border from England is an anticlimactic event – the most you're likely to see is a sign welcoming you to Wales. Things were different in the dim and distant past. Tenth-century travellers, for example, knew precisely where they stood, for Saxon law stated that "Neither shall a Welshman cross into English land nor an Englishman cross into Welsh land without the appointed man from that other land who should meet him at the bank and bring him back again without any offence being committed."

The "bank" was a reference to the earthen dyke which served as the first official boundary between England and Wales. Speculation surrounds the purpose behind the construction of this great earthwork known as Offa's Dyke, or *Clawdd Offa* in Welsh. It was built at the command of King Offa (AD 757–796), ruler of the Midland Kingdom of Mercia.

That much can be stated with certainty. But was it a military defence put up to keep out the unruly Welsh? Or did it serve as an administrative boundary – a demarcation line, if you like – to clear up, once and for all, any territorial ambiguities between the Welsh and the Anglo-Saxons? Was it intended as a lookout to give the Mercians a sense of security and control in dangerous hill country? Or was it simply meant to discourage cattle thieves?

Compared to Hadrian's Wall, built to keep the Scots at bay, Offa's Dyke can hardly be regarded as a serious line of defence. Unlike the heavily fortified Wall, it was not intended to be permanently manned. Neither was it a continuous structure. The dyke ran from Prestatyn on the North Wales coast to Sedbury near Chepstow on the Severn Estuary, a distance of 142 miles (227 km). But there were many breaks along the way: in thickly wooded river valleys, for instance, where construction would have been very difficult – and pointless, the forests acting as a barrier in themselves.

The building of the dyke must, nevertheless, have represented a monumental effort. A deep ditch was dug on the Welsh side. Above this, an earthwork barrier rose up to 20ft (6 metres) high. The overall structure, ditch and earthwork, was in places over 70ft (22 metres) wide.

This 1,200-year-old barrier has vanished along much of its route. Where it does survive – usually in high, lonely, obscure places – it conveys a profound sense of the past. The untravelled uplands around Knighton are such an area. Here, the earthwork still stands more or less to its full height, miraculously well preserved as it snakes across remote, grassy hill country like a miniature railway cutting.

Knighton's Welsh name of *Tref-y-Clawdd* means "the town on the dyke". It is a real meeting of the ways. Not only does it stand on both the ancient dyke and today's official border between England and Wales, it is also on the long-distance Offa's Dyke Path, which follows the line of the earthwork wherever possible. Moreover, Knighton is the home of the Offa's Dyke Centre, so is the perfect place at which to begin an exploration of the dyke. The long-distance footpath runs for 170 miles (272 km), sometimes through demanding, tough moorland but also along gentle lowlands of outstanding beauty. Walkers will regularly come across evidence of the earthwork, sometimes faint, at other times conclusive. ❑

LEFT: Offa's Dyke Path near Chepstow

Map on page 102

Old railway

Below the Offa's Dyke Path, running parallel to the river, is the route of the old Chepstow to Monmouth railway. The Wye Valley line was closed in 1964, and the tracks ripped up with indecent haste. It must have been a magnificent ride; memories of the line are preserved at **The Old Station** in Tintern, which offers an interesting exhibition on the Wye Valley Railway, leaflets for waymarked walks and picnic and café facilities. The old signal box houses a variety of changing displays.

One regular traveller on the Wye Valley line was journalist and writer Flora Klickmann. Born in 1867, she was editor of the *Girls' Own Paper* and *Woman's Magazine* for 22 years. She also wrote and edited more than 50 books, including the *Flower Patch* series which lovingly chronicled life in her small cottage near Brockweir, 1 mile (1.6km) north of Tintern. Flora Klickmann, who cared deeply about the ecology of the area, died in 1957 and is buried in the graveyard of the delightful Moravian church in Brockweir. Today a waymarked trail commemorates her name.

In autumn, the hues and tints of the Wye Valley rival the New England fall. The wooded stretch of valley from Brockweir to Llandogo is particularly fine.

Llandogo ❹, 2 miles (3 km) north of Brockweir, was once a busy river port. After the village, the road crosses over Bigsweir Bridge, and continues towards Monmouth on the English side of the river. During the highest spring tides, usually in April, both banks are crowded at night with men fishing for baby eels (or elvers, as they are known). These tiny, almost transparent creatures make their long arduous journey across the Atlantic Ocean from the Sargasso Sea only to be scooped out of the river in special nets. The elvers are boiled and then pressed into an elver "cheese" which can be fried with bacon.

Redbrook ❺, 5 miles (8 km) north of Llandogo, has a dour, industrial air about it. Indeed, like other places in the Wye Valley, it used to have a busy iron industry, linked to the streams that rushed down the valley sides. When, later on, large supplies of coal were discovered further east in South Wales, the iron industry soon moved away.

In the 2-mile (3-km) drive from Redbrook to Monmouth, the valley flattens out as the road re-enters Wales. The scenery is less dramatic but no less beautiful.

Monmouth ❻ can claim several places in history. Geoffrey of Monmouth, who might have been a monk of the Benedictine Priory in the town, produced a history of England, the *History of the Kings of Britain*, which contained more fantasy than fact but which, like Shakespeare's more popular history plays, became accepted by many as the unvarnished truth.

A more recent celebrity was Charles Rolls, the co-founder of Rolls-Royce, who until his death in 1910 in a flying accident lived in The Hendre, a handsome manor house near the town. (Near the former Rolls home are the Rockfield recording studios, frequented by more contemporary celebrities.)

Monmouth's most famous son, however, is without doubt Henry V (Good King Hal), who won the Battle of Agincourt – Monmouth's main square is called **Agincourt**

HT: nmouth's ified bridge.

Square. He was born in 1387 in Monmouth Castle, which was largely destroyed in the Civil War: a few walls are all that remain. The town museum has plenty of information on Henry, Rolls and Geoffrey – but its star exhibits concern quite a different character, Admiral Lord Nelson.

Nelson came to Monmouth only twice, but such was his status – equivalent to that of some sort of TV superstar today – that these visits had a profound effect on local sensibilities. A naval temple was erected on the **Kymin Hill**, which has a stunning view over Monmouth, to commemorate Britain's success at the Battle of the Nile and other naval victories. Lady Llangattock, Rolls's mother, built up a collection of Nelson memorabilia, bequeathed to the town after her death in 1923. These items, which include Nelson's sword and models of his ships, forms the basis of the town museum's Nelson Collection.

The town's most outstanding sight is the 13th-century **Monnow Bridge**, Britain's only surviving fortified bridge and still in regular use (its narrow portal constitutes a continuing menace to cars and buses).

Map on pag 102

Hay-on-Wye

After Monmouth, the River Wye leaves Wales. It recrosses the border almost 30 miles (48 km) northwest of Monmouth at **Hay-on-Wye** ❼, the famous "Town of Books". This once-sleepy border town has become the "Biggest Secondhand Bookshop in the World" *(see facing page)*, but retains a rural character. The dry business of book browsing can be remedied at one of the town's excellent old pubs.

From Hay, the road shadowing the Wye moves on northwards towards Builth Wells, following a particularly beautiful stretch of the river. Near Llyswen it passes **Llangoed Hall**, handsomely remodelled by Portmeirion architect Sir Clough Williams-Ellis *(see page 243)*. After falling into neglect, the house was acquired by Sir Bernard Ashley, widower of the late Laura Ashley (founder of the chain of shops bearing her name), and is now a luxury hotel. ❑

BELOW: Monmouth's twin heroes Henry V and the aero engine mak Charles Rol

How a Town Turned into a Bookshop

For bibliophiles, the small market town of Hay-on-Wye, straddling the border between England and Wales, is either paradise or a vision of hell. In nearly 30 bookshops, ranging from the cosy to the gargantuan, glossy art books rub spines with the battered works of long-forgotten novelists, battered Barbara Cartlands consort with frayed Ian Flemings, and antiquarian treasures share shelf space with volumes of *Pennsylvania Constitutional Development*.

It all began in 1961 when Richard Booth, who had local family connections, set up a books and antiques store in the town with the aid of a legacy. The antiques didn't do so well, but the old books moved. Booth was on his way. Every time a commercial property came on the market, he snapped it up. Soon the old Plaza cinema was packed with books; so was the former fire station, the workhouse, a chapel, even the castle.

His philosophy was simple. Hay was facing economic extinction as shoppers were lured to supermarkets in nearby towns, and its only salvation was to specialise. "Books are essentially an international and not a purely metropolitan market," he argued. "Hay is a suburb of nowhere, but there's a bigger market here than in London because people who live within 100 miles can easily take a trip here – and that includes Bristol, Manchester and Birmingham. Books are a part of tourism and I want to give bookselling a carnival image."

Booth installed himself in ramshackle Hay Castle, originally Norman but now late Tudor, which he bought for £6,500, and filled it with books. Outside stood wooden stocks "erected in 1690", complete with bookrest and a sign proclaiming that, even in the 17th century, Hay was a Book Town and that malefactors locked in the stocks were permitted to read. Tourists queued to photograph this "antiquity", which in reality had been cobbled together by a local carpenter for £55 plus value-added tax.

Soon bus tours began including Hay on their itineraries. Booth, ever quotable, became a celebrity. One day he would attack the "bureaucrassities" of the Wales Tourist Board; the next he would rage against the parish-pump politics of the "Hay Clown Council". It was time, he insisted, to ban the destructive motor car and reinstate the horse economy, thereby creating jobs for blacksmiths, grooms and stable boys. Declaring the town an independent state, he printed Hay passports (for carefree travel, 50p post-free) and national currency (denominations of £1,000, £5, £1).

Not everyone shared in the joke. Many of the 1,200 townspeople resented the razzmatazz and didn't take to the "trendy types" who were moving in. Hay divided into the supporters of "King Richard" and his detractors.

Inevitably, Booth's book-keeping abilities couldn't keep pace with his bookselling skills. As his empire withered, professional antiquarian booksellers moved in, happy enough to endorse Booth's stirring slogan: "Every publisher in the world is working for Hay-on-Wye." Antiques and crafts shops joined them and, in 1989, the first Hay-on-Wye Festival of Literature was held. Now the annual event is hugely popular, attracting internationally famous writers. ❑

HT: Richard
th, who
ted it all.

Map on page 112

BRECON BEACONS NATIONAL PARK

Even though 4 million sheep graze here, there's a fine feeling of empty space. Towns worth visiting include Brecon, Crickhowell, Abergavenny and Llandovery

People in South Wales used to regard the **Brecon Beacons National Park** almost as a private fief. Just as the world at large thought of Cardiff as a grimy and industrial coal city, so it vaguely imagined that the South Wales coalfield reached to the fringes of Snowdonia. A glorious landscape hid its secret behind the myth of black industry until the M4 motorway reached out, demolished the myth and abolished the fief.

But despite being the nearest serious hill country to London and the Southeast, Parc Cenedlaethol Bannau Brycheiniog, in the old tongue, still retains its remoteness and a certain sense of mystery. Its most valuable asset in an overcrowded island is the feeling of space presented by mile after mile of empty mountain and moorland, dappled by cloud shadows, ever-changing but planting an enduring mental snapshot.

The highest peak

The park is almost defined by its hills: the five ridges of the **Black Mountains** on the eastern border; the more isolated **Black Mountain** in the west, with its legend-haunted twin lakes, **Llyn y Fan Fach** and **Llyn y Fan Fawr**; and, dominating the centre, the Beacons themselves, crowned by South Wales's highest peak, **Pen-y-Fan** ❶ (2,907ft/ 886 metres).

These are soft-focus grassy heights with few rocky outcrops or glowering cliff faces, superb hillscapes of wide horizons, turning the colour of a lion's mane even in an averagely decent summer. But mountains – and wild ones – they certainly are: hard on the legs, sharp on the senses, demanding on the body. They would scarcely be the chief training ground for the soldiers of the SAS if they were otherwise. The Army, the Beacons and the Mynydd Eppynt ranges above Sennybridge have been partners for generations. In some places, we're told, they beat swords into ploughshares. Here, farmers' wives have been known to make stools and foot-rests out of spent artillery shells, stitching together covers to disguise their original purpose.

Half the park's 519 sq. miles (1,344 sq. km) is enclosed farmland with a patchwork of small fields whose soil turns red under the plough because of the predominant old red sandstone of much of the geology. The pinky-red stone is used in many of the older buildings on the eastern side of the park: travelling west, the

ECEDING ...ES: Black ...untains near ...ckhowell. **...T:** Cradoc ...f Course, ...con. **...HT:** statue ...Wellington ...Brecon's ...in square.

harder outlines of the villages are sometimes softened with painted plaster and the farms are lime-washed white or pink.

Hedges have survived to a far greater extent than in many other parts of Britain because this is cattle and sheep country and they are needed as shelters and windbreaks. The hills are the breeding grounds for Welsh ponies whose concave profiles and delicate muzzles are said to be a legacy of Arab blood brought in by Roman packhorses. The park's 4 million sheep easily outnumber the entire human population of Wales.

A recent law has enabled some upland commons to be fenced along the roadsides to save the sheep from cars but there are still too many "mutton miles" for comfort as they break through to get at the sweeter grass of the verges. There are at least two major roads crossing the park, the A40 London to Fishguard trunk road running east–west along the northern edge and the A470, north–south; sometimes the conflict between road engineering and National Park aims is blatantly obvious, and not just in the numbers of dead sheep. Who wants the standards of urban streets applied to country lanes – unnecessarily straightened, widened and given concrete kerbs? Or the excessively engineered stretches of highway leading to **Storey Arms** ❷, the landmark at the high point on the A470 through the Brecon Beacons?

The human hand has been in evidence in other directions. There are 18 reservoirs supplying Cardiff, Newport and the industrial Valleys – one of the earliest was built to supply clean water to Merthyr after a raging mid-19th-century cholera outbreak – and thousands of acres of conifer plantations. The environmental impact is limited, though; even together, they account for less than 10 percent of the park's extent.

Historically, the Welsh have never been great ramblers and even now many of the groups on the hills are visitors. Too often, these may be seen making the trek up the much eroded path from Storey Arms to the top of Pen-y-Fan, when there are at

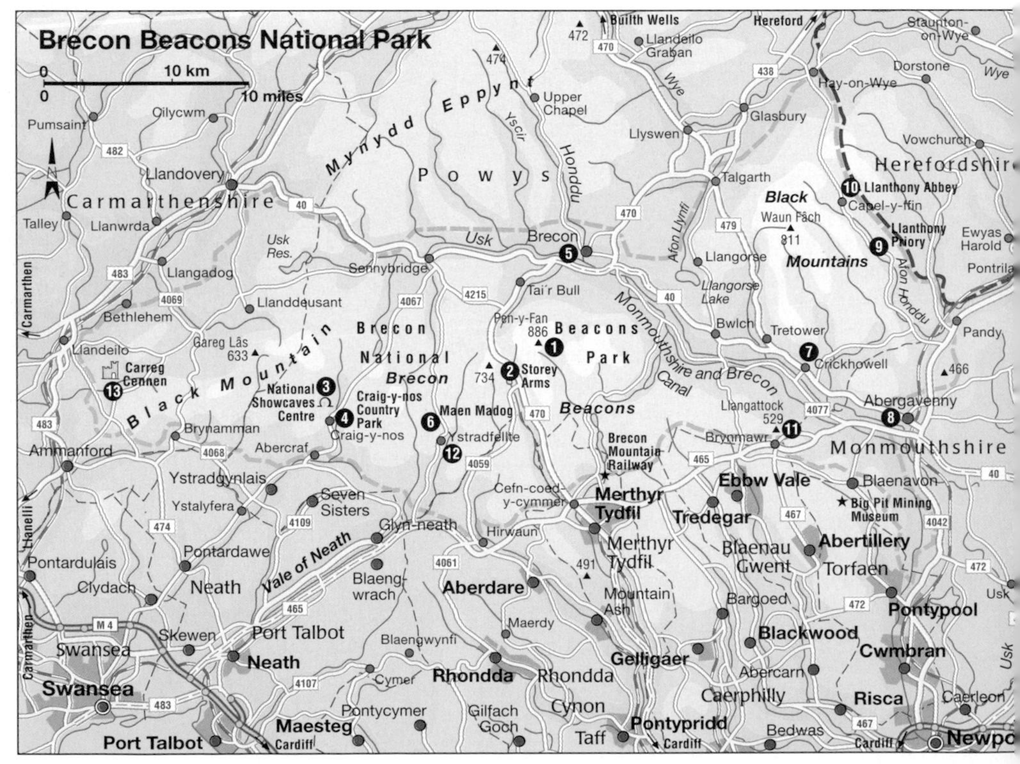

Map on page 112

least 45 to 50 known hill and ridge routes, mainly circular, to choose from in the Beacons and Black Mountains. Such walks do not include the uncharted ones here and further west on the remote Black Mountain for exploration by those who scorn nannying and who see that one of the greatest threats in any national park is the erosion not of footpaths but of the scope for finding your own way.

Protecting the environment is a difficult balancing act. By a happy geological accident, the park's most popular attraction – the **National Showcaves Centre** ❸ at Dan-yr-Ogof, near Abercraf, said to be the largest showcave system in Western Europe – is on the southwestern edge and heavy internal traffic is avoided. This family attraction offers more than the underground spectacle of narrow passageways, vast chambers and limestone formations; the large site also has a Dinosaur Park with life-size replicas of many prehistoric animals, an Iron-Age farm, shire horse centre and indoor adventure playground.

The nearby **Craig-y-nos Country Park** ❹, consists of 40 acres (16 hectares) of woods, a lake and gardens in the grounds of Craig-y-Nos Castle, once the home of Madame Adelina Patti, the Victorian opera singer. It is a classic example of the honey-pot – an attraction catering for family outings and casual day-out visitors which serves to ease pressures elsewhere.

Just off the A465 Heads of the Valley road, travelling along the park's southern boundary near Merthyr Tydfil, the narrow-gauge **Brecon Mountain Railway** runs a scenic 7-mile (11-km) round trip into the Beacons. Attached to the main station, with its high-quality shop and café, is a fascinating workshop where small locomotives from as far afield as South Africa are being restored for work on the line.

Brecon

Brecon ❺, population 7,200, a small town of great charm, is the park's "capital", internationally noted for its jazz festival held every August. The **Oriel Jazz**

ELOW: plastic nosaurs the an-Yr-Ogof howcaves.

Gallery on The Watton reflects the atmosphere of the festival and gives a lively introduction to the world of jazz.

Both the Romans and the Normans left their mark on Brecon (in Welsh, *Aberhonddu*) from its site at the meeting place of the rivers Usk and Honddu. Six Roman roads converged at Bannium, the fortress the Romans built near Brecon after the conquest of Wales, and much of the extensive Roman road network can be easily traced today.

One of the most remarkable features of the Beacons landscape are the memorial stones such as the 9-ft high (2.7 metres) **Maen Madog** ❻, the stone of Madog, alongside Sarn Helen (Helen's Causeway), the Roman road from Brecon to Neath. This is one of 12 such stones found in the area, and its Latin inscription tells us it is a memorial to Dervacus, son of Justus. A half-Welsh, half-Irish chieftain called Brychan was victor in the tribal battles that followed the Roman departure; Brecon is named after him.

It has always been a farmers' town – **Ship Street**, one of its main thoroughfares, refers to sheep rather than matters maritime – though with strong military and ecclesiastical overtones. Despite a reputation Brecon people have elsewhere in South Wales for a certain reserve, there is a pleasant intimacy about the place. So far, it has escaped developers' rash, the modern Bethel Square shopping development for once enhancing its surroundings.

Norman relics

William the Conqueror's half-brother, Bernard Newmarch, built **Brecon Castle**; its surviving tower and battlemented section of wall are nearly all in the garden of the Castle Hotel. That same Bernard Newmarch also had a hand in the building of nearby **Brecon Cathedral**, though the only relics of the Norman period are the north and south walls of the nave and the 12th-century font.

The largely 14th-century church is, in the words of E. A. Freeman, "noblest of a

LEFT: cycling in the Beacor

MAKING SENSE OF THE BEACONS

The Brecon Beacons Mountain Centre opened ir 1966 to a public not altogether convinced of the need for it. Today it attracts 160,000 visitors a year, sc time has given at least one answer to the doubters, though not perhaps the one they had in mind.

The centre, run by the Brecon Beacons Nationa Park, is 5 miles (8 km) southwest of Brecon on a stretch of wild moorland called Mynydd Illtud, about 1,100ft (330 metres) above sea level. Critics said its very existence was a contradiction, that it was bounc to damage the landscape the park was pledged to protect, bringing all the paraphernalia of cars, coach parties and crowds to a remote common once chiefly the haunt of lapwings, sheep and mountain ponies.

The centre, established with help from the Unitec Kingdom Carnegie Trust, achieves a balance betweer conservation, recreation and education with considerable success. The building itself, with its stone-facec and rough-cast walls and stone slated roof, merges discreetly into its surroundings and its car park is landscaped with plantations of native trees. Althougr there's a charge for parking, the centre itself – with its maps, photographs and information displays – is free.

Map
n page
112

class of which a good many structures occur in Wales, massive cruciform churches with central towers… invariably presenting a picturesque external outline". The cathedral was finally restored and completed by Sir Gilbert Scott no less than 650 years after work began. A **Heritage Centre** is sited in the restored 16th-century tithe barn in the cathedral close.

Across the Usk is **Christ College**, a public school founded by Henry VIII, and a riverside walk along the Promenade that allows superb views of the Beacons. From here, you can see **Newton Farm**, a Tudor house on the site of the birthplace of Davy Gam, the one-eyed Welsh squire (as his nickname, Gam, suggests) who saved the life of Henry V at Agincourt but lost his own, and is said to have been the inspiration for Shakespeare's Fluellen.

Brecon was also the birthplace of Sarah Siddons, the actress, in 1755, and of Dr Hugh Price, founder of Jesus College, Oxford's Welsh college.

When the Gurkhas were given the freedom of Brecon in 1988 they won an honour that had also been granted to the South Wales Borderers (24th Regiment) in 1948, commemorated by the numerals XXIV in the town's coat-of-arms. The Borderers have 23 Victoria Crosses on their roll, nine of them awarded in the battle of Isandhlwana and the defence of Rorke's Drift in 1879 that inspired the award-winning film *Zulu*. The splendid museum in **Brecon Barracks** illustrates the history of the regiment from its birth in 1689 to its amalgamation into the Royal Regiment of Wales in 1969.

The **Brecknock Museum and Art Gallery** in the colonnaded Shire Hall, built in 1842, encapsulates the history and life of bygone Breconshire. It houses the original Victorian assize court and a large collection of elaborately carved Welsh lovespoons (traditionally made for a loved one as long ago as the Middle Ages). The gallery has an excellent programme of exhibitions.

Captains' Walk, where the ground drops steeply to the river, is so called

.OW: Brecon z Festival.

HT: con Castle.

because it was used for exercise by French officers who were prisoners on parole during the Napoleonic Wars. Not far away on the Bulwark, the town's centre, stands a statue of their conqueror, the Duke of Wellington, put up four years after his death in 1852.

Imposing **Theatr Brecheiniog**, a short walk from the town centre, overlooks the picturesque canal basin at the terminus of the **Monmouthshire and Brecon Canal**.

Llangorse Lake, 6 miles (10 km) east of Brecon, is the largest natural lake in South Wales and has long been bedevilled by the demands of recreation and conservation. The lake is privately owned and, while sailing and fishing are both long-established, water ski-ing and power boating also have a slice of the action. You may need to belong to a local club or pay to use the facilities. The decline in wildlife has long been a source of concern, though the run-off of fertilisers from surrounding fields into the water may be as much to blame as the lake's long-term use as a playground. This has gone on so long that some of the birds have adapted their behaviour: sensibly, they fly off in the morning to spend the day elsewhere, returning in the evening when all is peaceful.

Crickhowell (*Crug Hywel*, Hywel's Fort) ❼ is the only other town in the park, 14 miles (23 km) along the incomparable **Usk Valley** from Brecon. Though scarcely more than a village, it has some excellent shops and good pubs and is popular with new settlers in search of the rural dream.

Abergavenny

So is **Abergavenny** ❽, 6 miles (10 km) along the A40, not actually in the park, but like Merthyr Tydfil, 17 miles (27 km) to the west, a gateway. A smart shopping centre complements the twice-weekly market (Tuesdays and Fridays) when farmers' wives still bring home-made butter, free-range eggs and fresh cut flowers as their perks to sell in the market. Abergavenny used to be noted for its Welsh white flannel and exported large amounts

BELOW: cottage in Abergavenny

Map n page 112

to India. Rudolf Hess spent the war here, imprisoned at Maindiff Court, once the home of Crawshay (Cosher) Bailey, the Victorian ironmaster.

The town is in a hollow, surrounded by hills, the **Sugar Loaf** (1,955ft/ 596 metres) **Skirrid Fach** and **Skirrid Fawr**, and the **Blorenge**, or Blue Ridge. On the Ridge's summit is a memorial to Foxhunter, a legendary showjumper of the 1950s, whose rider, Sir Harry Llewellyn, lived in the Usk Valley.

Black Mountains

Abergavenny is a splendid jumping-off point for the 80 sq. miles (207 sq. km) of the **Black Mountains** with their opportunities for pony trekking, caving and good old-fashioned exploring. Ruins of a high romantic order are to be seen in the Vale of Ewyas at **Llanthony Priory** ❾, an Augustinian monastery founded in the 12th century. Llanthony Priory – the name is an abbreviation of *Llandewi nant Honddu*, the church of St David on the Honddu brook – now houses a hotel and restaurant in what used to be the Prior's Lodge and south-west tower. The row of 14th-century pointed arches seen by moonlight is a sight not soon forgotten. Walter Savage Landor, a poet and author, once lived in the Priory house but died in 1864 without realising his plans to restore the ruins.

Four miles (6 km) up the valley is the confusingly named **Llanthony Abbey** ❿ at Capel-y-ffin where Father Ignatius, an Anglican monk who claimed to have seen a vision of the Virgin Mary in a nearby field, founded a monastery. It ceased to exist soon after his death in 1908 but was later the setting for a craft community led by the Catholic sculptor and graphic designer Eric Gill. Westward over the hills is **Partrishow** (or **Patricio**) **Church** whose early Tudor rood screen, beautifully carved from Irish oak, is one of the border country's chief glories.

Outlined on a map, the park resembles a miniature United States, with the Florida finger going down towards Pontypool, an

LOW: Sugar af Mountain.

enclave taking in a length of the 32-mile (51-km) **Monmouthshire and Brecon Canal.** This waterway is now navigable for the whole distance in a setting of the utmost rural charm, with the possibility of fishing and pleasant towpath walks.

Cave country

Sooner or later, though, you come back to geology, as you always must in South Wales. On these southern fringes of the park you are in the limestone belt with its wooded ravines, its graceful lime-loving ash trees, pale escarpments and above all its caves. **Llangattock Mountain ⓫** is riddled with them – the biggest **Agen Alwedd**, is 18 miles (29 km) long – but they are open (only with permission) to members of approved caving clubs.

Travelling west along the Heads of the Valleys road, with the old industrial Valleys stretching away to the south, their scars now rapidly vanishing, you reach, north of Glynneath, the minuscule settlement of **Ystradfellte ⓬**. A few houses surround a well-kept stone church sheltered by a set of magnificent yews, halfway down the valley of the **Mellte**, a little river with a great deal going for it.

Scoring deep into the limestone, the Mellte plunges from its source on the moor at **Fforest Fawr** into an impressive series of white cascades, from **Sgwd Clun Gwyn** (White Meadow Fall) to **Sgwd y Pannwr** (Fuller's Fall) with many another *swgd*, as the wonderfully expressive Welsh word has it, on neighbouring rivers. The most remarkable is **Sgwd yr Eira** (Fall of Snow) on the Hepste, an eastern tributary of the Mellte, where you can walk on a ledge and see the falls from behind.

Linked with the falls is another extensive cave system. The Mellte disappears into **Porth yr Ogof**, a long cave with a mouth like a hungry giant, from which the river re-emerges a quarter of a mile on. Ten miles (16 km) further west is the more visitor-friendly **National Showcaves Centre** at **Dan-yr-Ogof** *(see page 113)* in the upper Tawe Valley.

Searchers after solitude may well find the western reaches of the park more to their liking with quiet villages like **Bethlehem**, where people come to have Christmas letters stamped, and **Llandovery**, a delightful little market town (not actually *in* the park) whose public school is a friendly rival to Brecon's Christ College.

Carreg Cennen Castle

One of the greatest delights is to come across one of Wales's supreme visual experiences – the first sight of **Carreg Cennen Castle ⓭**, 3 miles (5 km) southeast of Llandeilo. This is the ruined medieval fortress someone once described as "a castle like a rock upon a rock". Steep crags on three sides fall precipitously to the valley of the Cennen below, while on the other, two towers guard the approach. On the south side, a passageway, bored for 150ft (45 metres) through solid rock, reaches a well that is supposed to have been the castle's water supply when under siege.

The present building may date from the 12th century but we are given more to conjure with in a British Museum manu-

LEFT: Maen
in Fforest Fa

Map n page 112

script that pinpoints the site as the stronghold of Urien, Lord of Is-Cenen, a Knight of the Round Table.

This is Welsh Wales and this is the language Urien would have spoken even though the Saxons might have been at the gate. It used to be said that the best Welsh was spoken in these southwestern areas and the best English, too, with the precise delivery and careful enunciation of those to whom it was a learned language.

The social map has changed markedly and perhaps irrevocably since the early 1970s when West Wales became the new frontier for city refugees (many from England) in search of alternative lifestyles. A second wave of incomers began in the latter half of the 1980s and the hill farms whose names identified the families who occupied them for generations – for instance, Tculu Beilidu, meaning the family from Beilidu farm – have become increasingly rare.

There are no very large hotels in the Brecon Beacons National Park, but many small hotels and guesthouses in and around Brecon, Crickhowell, Abergavenny, Llandovery and Llandeilo. The amount of farmhouse accommodation is on the increase; there are five youth hostels and, although there are not many official camping sites, farmers sometimes allow tents on their land.

The great outdoors

The National Trust owns much of the open mountains and does not permit *ad lib* camping. Perhaps it's to individuals – the back-packer, the naturalist, the historian, the rider – that the park yields its chief treasures. Within its boundaries there are all those variations of the British landscape that sharpen one's appreciation of its sheer variety – wilderness to woodland, farmland to riverside, with all their plant and animal life, domestic and wild. What makes it even better is that it is part of the feast of Wales that stretches wild, beautiful and open to the free spirit for 100 more miles (160 km) to the north. ❑

LOW: nmer ising in Brecons.

Map on page 102

NEWPORT AND CAERLEON

Newport, once a thriving industrial town, has seen its wealth gradually slip away. Caerleon, once a garrison for up to 6,000 Roman soldiers, today conveys a powerful sense of history

It must be admitted, right at the start, that **Newport** ❽ *(Casnewydd-ar-Wysg)* is not high on most people's priority list of places to visit in Wales. Although, like Cardiff and Swansea, it was a product of rapid industrial expansion in the 19th century, it is a poor relation to them when it comes to attracting tourists. Visitors usually turn a blind eye as they speed by on the M4, hardly captivated by the drab, urban skyline they see from the motorway as it skirts the town's northern fringe.

It's the same for those arriving by train. The railway runs through Newport's unprepossessing back yards before crossing the muddy, tidal banks of the Usk, the river that bisects the town.

But images and instant impressions can be deceptive. Although Newport, Wales's third-largest conurbation, doesn't have Cardiff's cosmopolitan confidence or Swansea's bright-and-breezy beside-the-sea charm, pockets of considerable interest are contained within that bland coat.

This first becomes apparent as the train crosses the Usk, and a ruined castle comes into view on the riverbank. This medieval shell was built in the 14th and 15th centuries to replace an earlier hilltop motte-and-bailey fortification. Today it is an isolated misfit surrounded by road systems, shopping precincts, tower blocks and the large, modern Newport Centre leisure complex. Its scant remains display decorative touches – the windows, for example – which point to a castle that once had a residential as well as an important military role.

In the beginning

Newport's history began long before medieval times. **St Woolos's Cathedral**, on the top of Stow Hill (also the location of Newport's original castle), occupies the site of a 5th- or early 6th-century religious settlement founded by Gwynllyw, lord of Gwynllwg (or Wentlooge, which became corrupted to *Woolos* – Wales is an etymological labyrinth). The cathedral has fine Norman nave arcades, though its most striking feature is a tall tower which was built around 1500.

Newport really came of age in the 19th century, because of its growth as an iron and coal exporting port serving the nearby industrial Valleys. The Victorian boom years are reflected in the architecture. A particularly fetching piece of Victoriana is the **covered market**, with its iron and glass barrel-vaulted roof, which has been restored to its original splendour.

The town's most infamous brush with history occurred on 4 November 1839, when thousands of ironworkers and

[LE]FT: a friendly [we]lcome.
[RI]GHT: [Th]ere are good [be]aches close [to] Newport.

coalminers marched to Newport in support of the Chartist cause for democratic reform of Parliament and the voting system. In the ensuing conflict outside the **Westgate Hotel**, troops fired on the crowd killing more than 20 Chartists and wounding a further 50. The leaders of the protest were transported to Tasmania and the mayor, who ordered the shooting, received a knighthood from Queen Victoria.

This episode has not been forgotten. The hotel still bears the marks of the bullets fired, and there are heroic murals depicting this and other events in the Civic Centre's entrance hall. The town's excellent **Museum and Art Gallery** in John Frost Square also contains material on the Chartist Rising, together with a noted collection of English watercolours.

The most conspicuous reminder of Newport's industrial past is the ingenious **Transporter Bridge**, its spindly framework dominating the view towards the docks. Built in 1906 to act as a "suspended ferry", this famous landmark carries vehicles and passengers on a gondola which glides across the mouth of the Usk.

LEFT: Tredegar House.

An earlier example of engineering on an ambitious scale can be seen at **Rogerstone** on the northwestern outskirts of the town, where a huge staircase of canal locks – 14 in all – are stepped into the hillside. The site, which boasts an interpretive centre and waymarked walks, has been imaginatively developed for visitors.

Tredegar House

Newport is justifiably proud of **Tredegar House** (open noon–6pm Tues–Sun in July and Aug, Wed–Sun in Apr, Jun & Sept, Sat–Sun in Oct), a splendid 17th-century mansion standing in a 90-acre (36-hectare) country park on the western approaches of the town close to junction 28 of the M4. As a result of local initiative, it was rescued from extinction by the authorities in the 1970s and has since been refurbished to a high standard. This red-brick mansion, regarded as the finest house of its kind in Wales, sums up the visible and the hidden sides of privileged life as visitors wander from gilded state rooms into functional servants' quarters.

Tredegar House can be seen as the flagship of a "new" post-industrial Newport: an unfairly maligned town situated on the doorstep of attractive, green countryside, a town with excellent communications at the western end of the M4 corridor, and a town which offers a quality of life absent in England's prosperous but beleaguered southeast. The official optimism seems generally to be justified. Ambitious redevelopment schemes are in the air, new high-technology companies have moved in, and major "white-collar" businesses have relocated here.

Caerleon

The promotional literature issued by the town authorities inevitably mentions Newport's proximity to Roman **Caerleon** ❾. This is another site that, in the past, has been overlooked – which is strange because Caerleon, alias *Isca*, was, along with the much more famous centres of Chester and York, one of only three Roman fortress towns in Britain, built to

Map on page 102

accommodate the elite legionary troops. But Caerleon's celebrity is on the up and up. This is partly due to the opening of an impressive excavated bath-house complex, the Roman equivalent of a modern sports and leisure centre.

Roman magnificence

Caerleon's lavish Fortress Baths, now equipped with audio-visual facilities, were built in AD 75. They were part of a huge 50-acre (20-hectare) camp that contained barracks, a headquarters, hospital, palace and amphitheatre, all laid out on an orderly gridiron ground plan. It's still easy to appreciate the Romans' enthusiasm for the place. Caerleon is a neat and tidy little town in a favoured location. Standing among green fields above the looping River Usk, it must have been an ideal place to set up camp well away from the heathen wastes of an upland Wales populated by uncooperative natives.

The various excavated sites here paint an illuminating picture of life in one of the largest Roman military strongholds in northern Europe. The crack troops were well looked after. Apart from the hot and cold baths, the games and the wine enjoyed under cover at the bath-house, there was entertainment – which included bloody gladiatorial combat and animal baiting – at the 5,000-seat amphitheatre.

The amphitheatre's arena and grassy, circular banks are well preserved, as are the foundations of the troops' accommodation blocks, the only remains of Roman legionary barracks on view in Europe.

Many of the finds unearthed at Caerleon, abandoned by the Romans in the 4th century, are on show in the town's **Legionary Museum**, which has one of the country's best collections of Roman artefacts. The exhibits, displayed in a bright, well-designed context, include life-size figures (a legionary, a centurion and a standard-bearer), arms and armour, mosaics, tombstones and a collection of gemstones found at the bath-house. Children can try on a Roman soldier's armour plating. ❑

[BE]LOW: [Ca]erleon, one [of] the Romans' [m]ost important [fo]rtresses.

Maps:
ity 128
rea 146

CARDIFF

Cardiff, dominated by its castle, hasn't been Wales's capital for very long. But the presence of the new Welsh Assembly and the transformation of the old docklands area have given it a new focus

In recent years **Cardiff ❶** (*Caerdydd* in Welsh) has been shaking off the reputation that it is not much of a Welsh city. These days all the road signs, as well as certain place names, are regularly presented in both Welsh and English, while several of the town's pubs and restaurants have been renaming themselves in the traditional language. Many of the suburbs have only Welsh names, such as *Maes y Coed, Heol y Deri* and *Llanedeyrn*, leaving you in no doubt that this isn't England.

Though some still complain that Cardiff remains a very anglicised city, this is a criticism that is becoming less and less valid. You'll certainly hear less spoken Welsh in Cardiff than in some towns in North and West Wales, but the visible evidence of the Welsh language is there in abundance. Many businesses are largely bilingual and there is even a nightclub which bars entry to non-Welsh speakers on Saturday nights.

Devolved power

The pervading presence of the Welsh language is probably a lot stronger now than it has ever been, and the atmosphere here is of a city finding a new personal identity. This may partly be explained by Cardiff's relative youth: compared to many British cities, it is a youngster, having nothing like the length of capital status enjoyed by the three other capitals that govern the United Kingdom. It was not designated as such until the 1950s.

Another factor in helping Cardiff to come of age as a real capital city has been the opening of the National Assembly for Wales, the centre of devolved power in the country, in Cardiff Bay. While the Assembly's powers are fairly limited, it has shifted the focus away from London on certain key Welsh issues such as agriculture, greatly adding to Cardiff's sense of importance.

Small beginnings

At the start of the 19th century Cardiff was little more than a township and bore no relationship in importance to Merthyr Tydfil, 25 miles (40 km) to the north. But when the quantities of iron and coal being produced around Merthyr grew big enough to need an export outlet, Cardiff began to grow.

The important influence was the Bute family, who owned much of the land around the docks and saw the opportunities for creating a city based on entrepôt trade. They built the docks, bringing in labour from far and wide to undertake the construction work. In the nature of things, many of the immigrants married and settled in the area, so that by the second half

RECEDING AGES: Cardiff ty Hall.
FT: resident St Fagans useum of elsh Life
ELOW: Mary's reet, Cardiff.

of the 19th century Cardiff had a far more cosmopolitan population than the great northern citadels that had already outstripped it in size and importance.

The strongest influence came from the Irish; many of those who did not emigrate to America or find their way to Liverpool after the potato famine of the 1840s came to build Cardiff's docks and the canal and railways that linked the city to its hinterland. Cardiff had, and continues to have, a strong Roman Catholic population, strong enough to warrant a Catholic cathedral alongside the Anglican one.

The Bute family

The Butes themselves are a leading Catholic family, which might be thought unusual in a country whose upper classes tended to be Anglican and whose working population were heavily Nonconformist. A Scottish family, they came to Cardiff in the 17th century, the third marquess becoming a Catholic in the 19th century.

Signs of the Butes can be seen all over Cardiff to this day, especially in docklands which they virtually created and which are now the subject of a huge waterfront redevelopment. There is the famous Bute Street, Bute Docks, a Bute Park and Butetown, probably better known as Tiger Bay. There is also a Mount Stuart Square, commemorating another of their titles.

They are not the only family whose ancestry is commemorated in the streets of Cardiff. Clare Road remembers a much longer established member of the nobility. The de Clares came over with William the Conqueror in 1066 and Gilbert de Clare, later Earl of Glamorgan, who died in 1292, did much to strengthen the defences of Cardiff by building the castle's Black Tower and rebuilding the Great Hall of the Keep. Memories of another Norman overlord can be seen in Despenser Street.

Much of Cardiff's (and later the Butes') wealth came from the Glamorganshire Canal that brought iron and coal down the Taff Valley from Merthyr Tydfil. The canal was built before the railway era changed the face of Britain; but, as iron gave way to steel and the new steelworks were built on

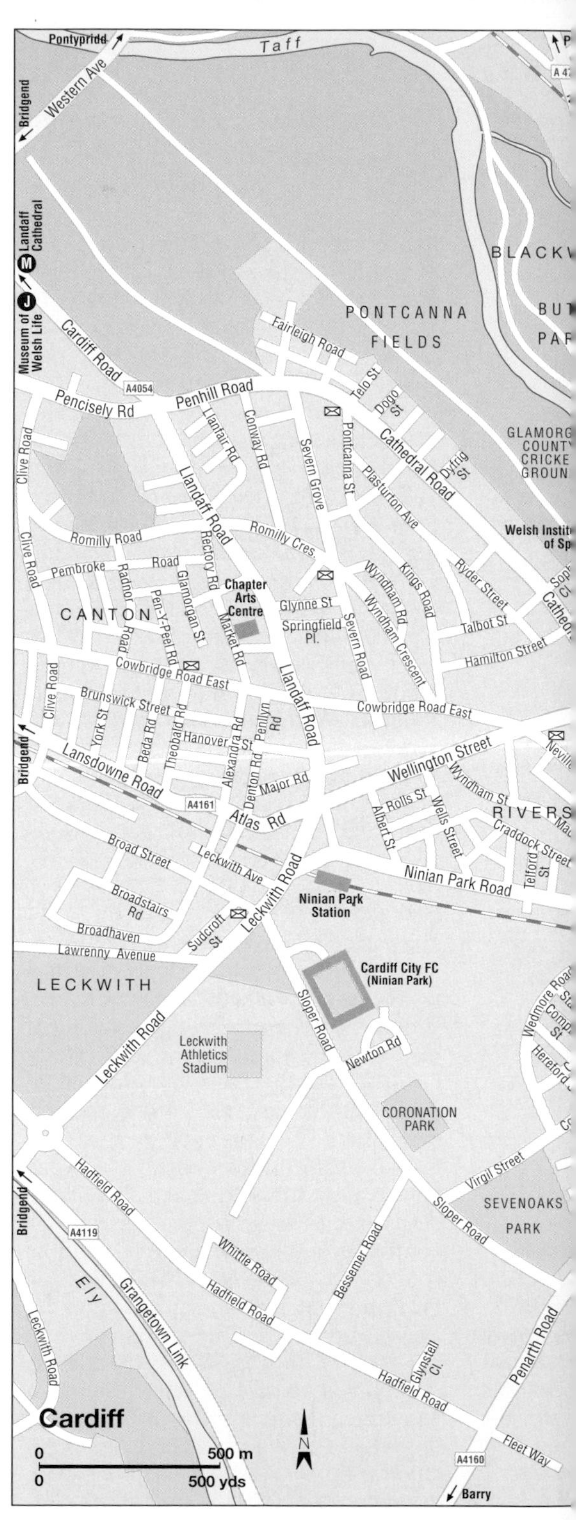

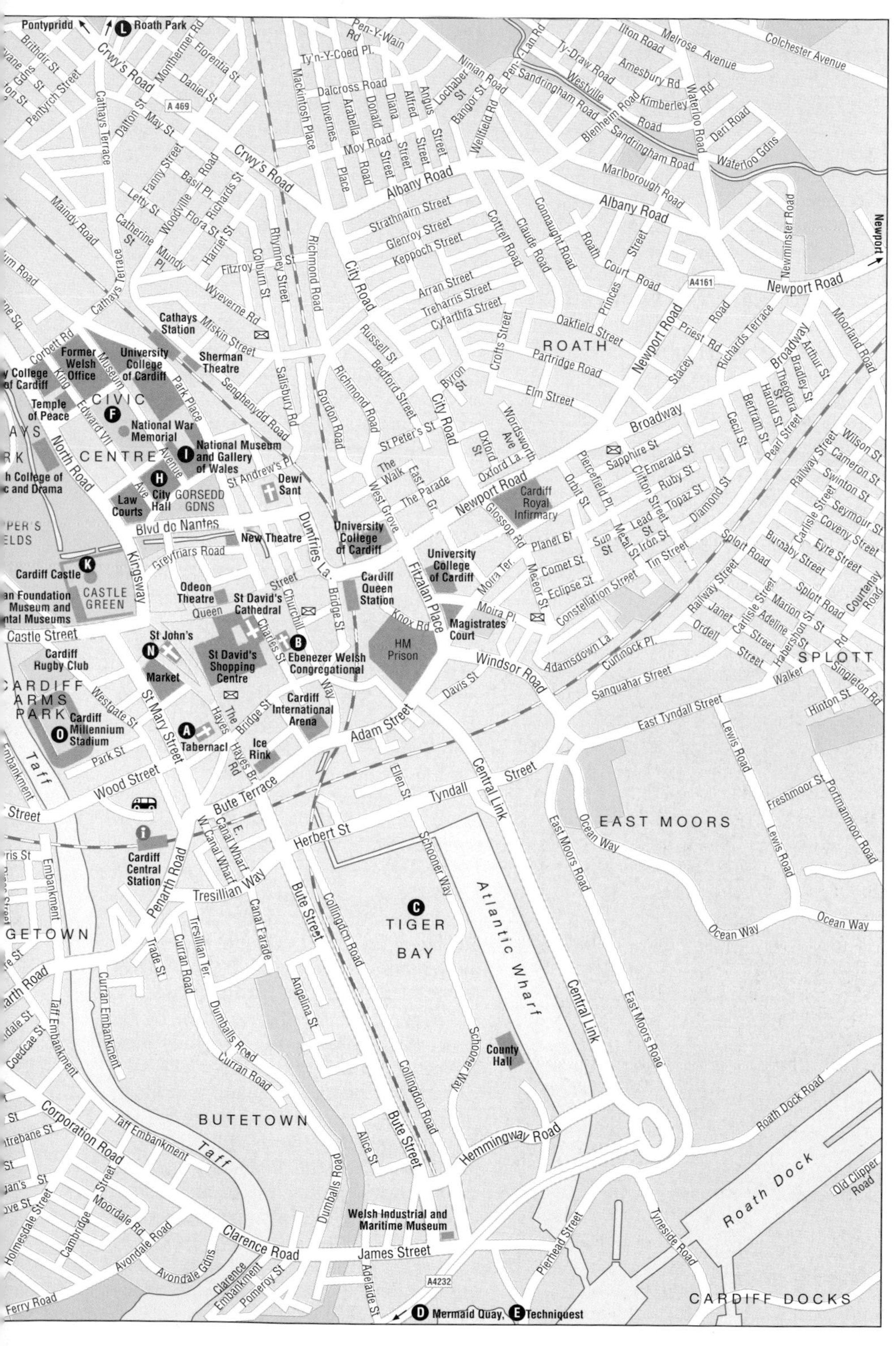

CIVIC CENTRE
ROATH
SPLOTT
EAST MOORS
TIGER BAY
BUTETOWN
CARDIFF DOCKS
Cardiff Castle
Cardiff Central Station
Cardiff Queen Station
Cathays Station
National Museum and Gallery of Wales
St David's Cathedral
St David's Shopping Centre
Cardiff Millennium Stadium
Cardiff International Arena
HM Prison
Cardiff Royal Infirmary
County Hall
Welsh Industrial and Maritime Museum
Mermaid Quay,
Techniquest
Roath Park
Pontypridd
Newport
Roath Dock
Atlantic Wharf

or near the coast, the canal's trade was increasingly restricted to coal. Eventually all that, too, was carried by the Taff Vale Railway (later to become part of the Great Western Railway) and gradually, section by section, the canal was closed.

The last section was shut down in 1942 – even then, the canal was not being used in any economic form. A small section, perhaps no more than half a mile long, existed by the sea-lock for another nine years, but eventually a dredger hit the gate, broke the lock and all the water ran out.

There were other influences on Cardiff's growth. Many men came from the border counties to work in the growing city. Gloucestershire, Somerset and Herefordshire supplied a lot while still others were attracted into the economic honeypot from Mid and West Wales. Until the 1930s the influence of the Welsh incomers could be seen in particular in the Welsh chapels.

Today, few remain. There are now only four which hold their services in Welsh, of which the leading one is **Tabernacl** Ⓐ, in The Hayes, bang in the centre of the city. Services here are at 10.45am and 6pm on Sundays. Another one nearby is **Ebenezer Welsh Congregational Church** Ⓑ in Charles Street, just behind Marks and Spencer's store and across the road from the Roman Catholic cathedral. There is one Church of Wales church, **Dewi Sant**, in St Andrew's Place. These would once have been the tip of the iceberg.

LEFT: modern buildings have transformed Cardiff Bay.

Immigrant areas

Then there were the overseas immigrants. Cardiff always had a small but vibrant coloured community, which is one reason why it has to this day enjoyed excellent inter-racial community relations. Originally, the coloured community came from the Lascars, often donkeymen on ships, the men who shovelled coal into the boilers. These men would be paid off, or jump ship, in Cardiff and stay in the city. The Lascars were in time supplemented by other races who found a home in the docklands area of **Tiger Bay** Ⓒ.

That coloured community was never large and mostly remained on the wrong side of the tracks, the Great Western Railway line that connected London's Paddington station with Fishguard in West Wales.

Good community relations probably arose because the coloured population remained within its ghetto. Whatever the reason, the vast majority in Cardiff always had a tolerant approach to the immigrants. Tiger Bay in its heyday was no place for the meek and mild, though. Even in a much more law-abiding era it was said that the policemen always patrolled in pairs.

The area is bounded on one side by the railway line which runs the length of **Bute Street**, almost to pier head, from which the Campbell's paddle steamers would, in summer, ply across the channel to Weston and Clevedon in Somerset and Ilfracombe in Devon. The other boundary was the canal so that Tiger Bay was in effect a long rectangle stretching from the commercial and shopping heart of the city down to the waterside. It was tough and torrid, housing Cardiff's red-light area, some seedy cafés, and some even more seedy pubs.

Map
n pages
128–9

Whatever its charms by night it was, by day, a place of rectitude where Cardiff's upright businessmen came to conduct their legitimate affairs, the sort of business that would have been highly regarded in Ebenezer or Tabernacl.

Service city

Despite the "smokestack" image under which it laboured for years, Cardiff was not then, indeed has never been, an industrial city. It could not hold a candle to those great northern monuments to Victorian wealth, Leeds, Manchester, Birmingham, Bradford and Sheffield. It was a service city. It existed to ship the coal and iron around the world. As in Liverpool – a place sometimes called the capital of North Wales since there were more Joneses there than along the Welsh coast – it oiled the wheels of trade.

At its centre was the **Exchange** in **Mount Stuart Square**, in the very heart of Tiger Bay, the place where coal was traded as stocks and shares were traded on the stock market in London. The price of coal in Bremen or Buenos Aires would be set by what happened on the floor of the Exchange in Cardiff. A large, gaunt Victorian building, it is now being slowly brought back to life. The metamorphosis of the Exchange is reflected in a gigantic redevelopment of the whole of docklands which is turning Cardiff into an exciting city for the 21st century.

The life began to ebb out of Cardiff's docklands after World War I and, although it received a shot in the arm during World War II, a long economic decline began again in the 1950s. By the early 1960s Cardiff's docklands were a shadow of their old self, and Tiger Bay was ripped apart as modern council flats and houses replaced the mean streets. The once torrid area became a place where in the 1960s the fashionable could come on a Saturday night to the Windsor pub, the first place in the city to serve decent French food.

Now a major multi-billion pound development scheme is taking place, culling

LOW: a
:torian dock
ilding in
rdiff harbour.

ideas from the best around the world. Baltimore, Toronto, Vancouver, Boston and New Orleans have all been visited to see how a waterside community can be rebuilt. So, too, has London's docklands. What has been created in London has become part-model for what is happening in Cardiff.

As part of the ongoing renovation, new housing has sprung up around the old East Bute Dock, now renamed **Atlantic Wharf**. This was the first of many new residential developments along the Bay that, despite the unfinished nature of the infrastructure, are commanding high prices. Confidence in the area is high. The county council, showing its faith, built a new county hall slap-bang in the centre of the docks development. A marina has been opened under **Penarth Head** which has all the chutzpah of London's Wapping. **Mermaid Quay** Ⓓ, a new waterfront complex of fashionable shops, bars and restaurants, is drawing people out from the city centre, while improved road and rail links are making the Bay really feel like part of Cardiff. Close by, there's the **Techniquest** Ⓔ science discovery centre, a popular attraction which tempts many visitors from the city centre.

From here, it's a pleasant walk along the refurbished waterfront to the clapboard **Norwegian Church**, originally built for visiting seamen but now an arts centre and café,

Dockland developments

At the heart of the whole development is the Cardiff Bay barrage. A **Visitor Centre**, housed in a space-age, tube-shaped silver structure that looks like a UFO, explains the scheme. It is based on a half-mile (0.8-km) barrier across the mouth of the Bay that has created an inland lake of some 500 acres (200 hectares) of clean water and an 8-mile (13-km) waterfront around which a vast variety of new development is taking place. Scheduled as the flagship building, but subject to much debate and delay, is the Wales Millennium

LEFT: Cardiff café quarter. **BELOW:** the Norwegian Church.

Map on pages 128–9

Centre, an £86 million, multi-purpose arts venue. The Bay will also be the home of the spectacular new **Welsh Assembly building**. Cardiff's inner harbour alone is larger than the whole dockside in Baltimore, and the rejuvenation of the American waterside is an international example of how such works can breathe new life back into a city.

As the building of Cardiff's docks was essentially the brainchild of one member of the nobility, the Marquess of Bute, so the present redevelopment is the brainchild of another, Lord Crickhowell. He wasn't Lord Crickhowell when the plan was launched: the Right Honourable Nicholas Edwards, PC, MP, to give him his original title, was Her Majesty's Secretary of State for Wales. A tall, spare, ascetic-looking man, he had become MP for Pembrokeshire in the early 1970s and entered government in 1979 when Margaret Thatcher formed her first Conservative administration.

Nick Edwards, as everyone called him, was an Anglo-Welshman, not a local at all. His father had been a leading figure in the London art world and he had been brought up more in the British capital than the Welsh one.

His early years as Secretary of State were dominated by the economic recession of 1979–81, which saw large parts of the two basic Welsh industries, coal and steel, decimated. It wasn't until 1984 that he had the opportunity of looking to the future rather than fighting to put out bush fires in the present.

The Edwards vision was that if Wales was to prosper then it needed a capital that could lead the country. It was little use sustaining individual parts of the country if the capital was falling apart. And the part that was so obviously disintegrating was the docklands. So he drew up a plan to rejuvenate the whole area. But his plan was not just to do something about the one major run-down area; it was to link this redevelopment back into the city through a mall or boulevard that would run the length of Bute Street down to pier head and the inner harbour. Tiger Bay, rebranded and revitalised for the new millennium, would revert to its former greatness. That greatness was built on coal. It is frequently said that Cardiff was the greatest coal-exporting port in the world. The truth of that assertion is open to question: it all depends on the definition of Cardiff docks.

In 1914, when the industry was going full blast, 10,278,963 tons of coal were shipped through Cardiff. However, Barry, located 10 miles (16 km) along the coast to the west, actually handled 10,875,510 tons and so could claim to be the greater.

Competition for coal

In between Cardiff and Barry, though, lies a third port: **Penarth**. It is normally considered to be part of Cardiff, though the people of Penarth have always regarded it as separate from, and slightly superior to, the big city. Penarth handled almost 4 million tons in 1914 and if this is added to the Cardiff figure it would make it the greater exporter. But it is a subject of some debate – and not a little controversy

[RI]GHT: low tide, [Ca]rdiff harbour.

– in Cardiff, which always likes to be thought of as the greatest.

Cardiffians also like to point out, with no little pride, what they consider to be the greatest **Civic Centre** ❻ in the Commonwealth. And, they say, they have royal backing for their assertion.

It is a wonderful neo-classical building, perfect in scale and scope, constructed in Portland stone around 1904. Most of the buildings put up since have been designed with an empathy for the whole. The buildings themselves enclose a large rectangle, within which wide, tree-lined avenues bisect **Cathays Park** ❼. The Prince of Wales, in one of his trenchant attacks on modern architecture and its failure around the country, specifically omitted Cardiff from his criticism. He pointed to the way in which the architecture blended as a whole and the way in which everything was in scale.

In the inter-war years Cardiff won architectural commendations for its overall design. More important, it was copied as well as envied. Town planners and architects from the new Commonwealth that emerged after 1945 came to Cardiff and took away ideas, much as an earlier generation had incorporated bits of the city into places as disparate as New Delhi and Canberra.

A cluster of institutions

The Civic Centre's southern flank comprises the Law Courts, the City Hall, dominated by its 194-ft (59-metre) campanile-type clock tower, and the National Museum of Wales. The eastern side has the University College of Cardiff, a constituent part of the federal University of Wales. The western flank comprises a number of buildings, including various university buildings. Its **Temple of Peace**, perhaps unique in Europe, opened in 1938 – just in time to see peace swept away by the approaching World War II.

The northern edge is topped off by the administrative buildings of the former **Welsh Office**. At the centre of this great

LEFT: City Hall cloc
BELOW: an ol pub in downtown Cardiff.

Map on pages 128–9

rectangle is Wales's national war memorial.

The **City Hall** **H** contains a particularly fine collection of paintings. Among the portraits of the civic dignitaries who have graced its parlours and presided over momentous events is a particularly good one of Edward VII at the opening of the Queen Alexandra dock in 1909. John Glover's *The Bay of Naples*, first shown in the Louvre in Paris, hangs near it, as well as two paintings – *The Shadow* by E. Blair Leighton and *Winter* by Joseph Farquhanson – which have hung in their present position since at least 1925.

Statues honour the great names of Welsh life as well as those of the city, for Cardiff has always considered itself the first city of the principality and so has never adopted the parochial approach to events that bedevils so much of Wales. David Lloyd George is here, for instance. He was not a native of the city, having been born in Manchester, but Cardiff treats Britain's former Prime Minister as an adopted son.

BELOW: City Hall luminaries include Queen Boudicca.

History's heroes

Inside the City Hall there are also statues of Owain Glyndŵr, who led an uprising against the English in 1400; Llewelyn ap Gruffydd, the last prince of Wales before modern times, killed in 1282 for defying the English whom he had earlier befriended; William Williams, known throughout Wales as William Williams Pantycelyn and throughout the world as one of the great hymn writers, a man at the very cornerstone of the Methodist Revival in the country; Harri Tudur, better known as Henry VII, born in Pembroke Castle, who overthrew the Lancastrian line to the throne and brought in the Tudors; Giraldus Cambrensis, the outstanding Welsh scholar of his age, another Pembrokeshire man, who made a historic journey around the country in medieval times; and Boudicca, the Celtic tribal queen who stands as a symbol of resistance to the Roman legions who invaded – and conquered – Britain in the 1st century.

And, of course, there is Dewi Sant, St

David, patron saint of Wales, founder of the cathedral that bears his name in the tiny city of St David's in the far west of Pembrokeshire.

The great politician, Aneurin ("Nye") Bevan, from the industrial Valleys, is also honoured by a statue. His stands at the end of Queen Street, overlooking the castle which, to him, represented the privilege he so much wanted to overthrow.

Cardiff's own sons and daughters comprise a varied and elegant crowd, with the emphasis very much on their musicality or artistic ability generally. Shirley Bassey was born in the city and sang her way to fame in the clubs of Tiger Bay. The composer Ivor Novello came from a posher part of town and the house in **Cathedral Road** where he was brought up by his mother, who led the famous Royal Welsh Ladies Choir, now has the obligatory plaque on it.

Howard Spring, whose novels include *Fame is the Spur*, was born here in 1899 at the very end of the great Victorian era, one of nine children; his ability as a wordsmith was honed on newspaper life in the city. Dannie Abse, poet and broadcaster, is of a more recent generation, as is the late playwright and children's author Roald Dahl. Another well-known novelist, Eric Linklater, was brought up in Cardiff during his formative years as a boy, though he never lost his Scottishness and looked back on Cardiff without much remembrance or affections.

National Museum and Gallery

The **National Museum and Gallery of Wales** ❶ (closed Mon), next door to the City Hall, is a "tidy" place, a Welsh use of the word denoting considerable approval. It boasts a wide variety of attractions, covering science, history, archaeology and art. It is also closely linked with the world-renowned Museum of Welsh Life at St Fagans, only 4 miles (6.5km) from the city centre (an hourly bus leaves from the Central station).

Fifteen art galleries dominate the east-

BELOW: the National Museum and Gallery of Wales.

Map
ı pages
128–9

ern side of the building, while the west is devoted to science and natural history. The latter comes to high-tech life in an "Evolution of Wales" exhibition, and there are strong botanical and archaeological collections.

At the heart of the museum's collection of paintings is the Davies Bequest, left to the museum by two Welsh sisters, Gwendoline and Margaret Davies, daughters of a notable coalmine-owner. The collection is of French rather than Welsh painters, though, since the sisters were among the first, in the early years of the 20th century, to appreciate the Impressionists. The collection, the largest outside France, has been called "exceptional"; it is certainly one of the best-kept secrets in the museums world." Cézanne, Daumier, Manet, Millet, Monet, Morisot, Renoir, Pissarro and Van Gogh are all represented. Other galleries range from the Pre-Raphaelites to abstractionism. The striking sculpture collection includes several Rodins, including a copy of *The Kiss*.

This being a Welsh museum, native artists are well represented, among them Frank Brangwyn, Cedric Morris, Ceri Richards and Kyffin Williams, as well as Augustus John and his sister Gwen who tended to remain very much in his shadow during his lifetime.

Working-class heritage

The **Museum of Welsh Life** at **St Fagans** **J**, where the city meets the Vale of Glamorgan 4 miles (7km) west of the city centre, is devoted to heritage and has a vast collection of buildings showing just how people lived in the past.

Of particular interest is a row of six ironworkers' cottages painstakingly relocated from Rhydycar in Merthyr Tydfil. Each cottage has been restored in the style of a different era, right down to the gardens and outbuildings. Ranging from 1805 to 1985, they give an excellent insight into working-class life in Wales over the past two centuries.

The museum, which opened in 1948, grew up in the grounds of St Fagans Castle, a handsome Elizabethan manor house. It is a pioneering folk museum, not just a host of artefacts: it lives. The Denwen bakehouse, which came from Aberystwyth, produces traditional bread and *bara brith* (a rich fruit bread) every day. Animals roam the grounds. A water wheel turns the grinding stones of Melin Bompren flour mill, which came from Cross Inn in West Wales, and a blacksmith works in the Llawryglyn smithy which originally stood at Llanidloes in Mid-Wales. There is also a tollhouse, which was originally put up at Penparcau, Aberystwyth, in 1771.

A more conventional modern museum block displays treasures such as a wide variety of cooking and dairying implements, musical instruments, including the Welsh *crwth* and *pibgorn*, and, of course, a large selection of Welsh lovespoons.

Cardiff Castle

The centrepiece of Cardiff, though, is not its museums but its castle, largely Norman in origin but with Roman traces still visible. **Cardiff Castle** **K** dominates its city in a way few others do because it is

HT:
Museum
Welsh Life.

part of the fabric of everyday life. Two of the main streets wind around it and the city fathers have ensured that it is not surrounded by high-rise modern buildings. So it's possible to see the battlements and walls from several directions and from a considerable distance.

The castle was originally a Roman fort, the Romans having arrived in AD 76. The fort, one of a chain across South Wales, was built on a strategic site alongside the river, the Taff, and intended to hold back the fiercely independent Silures.

The Normans rebuilt and enlarged the fort, something the Romans themselves had done at least once, and a keep, which still dominates the grounds, was added. William the Conqueror is said to have chosen the site in 1081 while on his way to visit the shrine of St David in Pembrokeshire. During the Civil War and the subsequent Commonwealth government, Cardiff was at first Royalist before succumbing to Cromwell's Parliamentarians in 1645. After that, the castle was allowed to decay badly, until the third Marquess of Bute appointed the imaginative William Burges in 1865 to undertake a major restoration; it was completed by 1872.

Rich tiles

Burges is not a household name among Victorian architects but his contribution to Cardiff Castle deserves a wider audience. He would be described today as a specialist in tiles, having been involved in the revival of interest in medieval tiles, and so his work in Cardiff is rich in this field. He created lavishly decorative interiors which today form the backdrop for many civic and other public functions.

The banqueting hall is particularly attractive, decorated with murals depicting the castle's history. There is also a Moorish room, a pleasant anachronism in a Welsh city, and a clock tower. Another interesting feature, often overlooked, is the tiled (and covered) roof-garden which again carries Moorish overtones.

The castle also contains the regimental

BELOW: Carc
Castle, prou
as a peacoc

Map
n pages
128–9

museum of the Welch Regiment, now incorporated into the Royal Regiment of Wales, and 1st The Queen's Dragoon Guards, the Welsh cavalry regiment.

The grounds are now a public park, one of the many that grace Cardiff. For the statistically minded, there are 2,700 acres (1,100 hectares) of them, about a third the size of London's docklands. The grounds of the castle, sometimes called **Bute Park**, stretch for 2 miles (3km), almost to Llandaff Cathedral, and contain an arboretum as well as superb flowerbeds.

Roath Park **L** is a small-scale version of London's Kew Gardens, with the addition of a lake that once incorporated a swimming pool but is now restricted to boaters, who may take out a skiff. No motor boats or noisy activities are allowed. Note the memorial to Captain Scott, built like a lighthouse, at one end of the lake.

The top of the **Wenallt**, a stiff climb, affords a panoramic view of the city and offers nature trails; also, in severe winters, a place for tobogganing. Nearby **Parc Cefn-onn** is a jewel of rhododendrons and azaleas in spring.

Llandaff Cathedral

Another jewel is **Llandaff Cathedral** **M**, set (in some ways similar to St David's Cathedral) in a hollow in an attractive "villagey" suburb a mile or so northwest of the city centre. A religious community was established by St Teilo in the 6th century but a 10th-century Celtic cross, in the south aisle, is the only pre-Norman reminder.

Oliver Cromwell did his damnedest here, as in the castle, turning part into a beer house; but the cathedral survived his depredations. Since then, though, God and man have played nasty tricks with it. A storm in 1703 blew down the pinnacles of the north west tower and caused them to fall through the roof; 20 years later the southwest tower collapsed. Then in 1941 German bombs severely damaged the whole edifice. Since it was rebuilt, the cathedral has incorporated the chapel of the Welch Regiment,

ELOW: acob Epstein's ontroversial culpture in andaff athedral.
GHT: Cardiff astle's Winter moking Room.

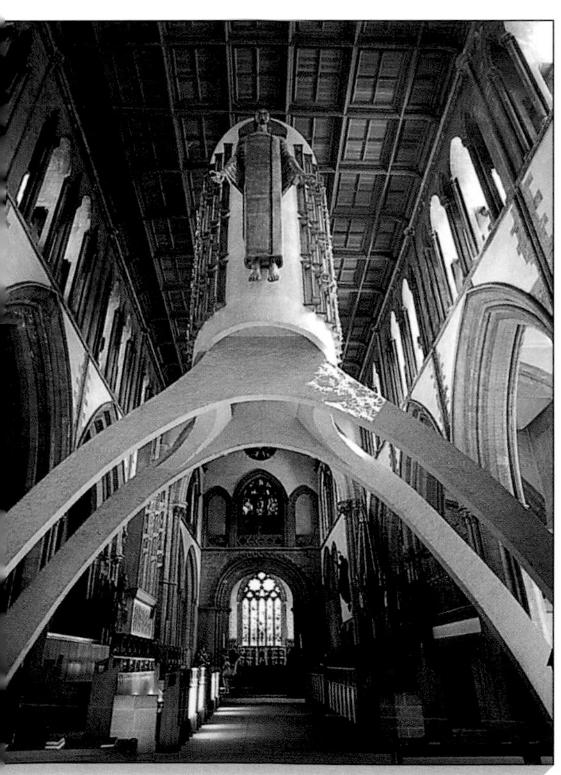

the regiment most closely associated with the city, and Sir Jacob Epstein's *Christ in Majesty*, a contemporary sculpture which dominates the centre aisle and provokes strongly opposing views. Elsewhere, on windows and panels, the Pre-Raphaelites are well represented.

Back in the city centre, **St John's Church** Ⓝ, opposite the market, is the parish church; the present building dates from 1453, though a place of worship has been on the site considerably longer. Its main interest is an indirect connection: the tower was put up by Lady Ann Nevill, wife of Richard, Duke of Gloucester, who became Richard III.

Opposite is the great indoor **market**, one of the features of Cardiff life, a place not just of vegetables and pans but also a point for buying traditional Welsh foods such as laverbread, made from seaweed, and a host of Welsh cheeses. Nearby, too, are the arcades that are another prominent feature of the city. Long before atriums and covered shopping centres became popular, Cardiff's Victorian shoppers moved about under cover. Cardiff has more arcades than any other city in Britain and they are an important reflection on Victorian and Edwardian shopping patterns and architecture.

Map on page 128–9

Millennium Stadium

For the sports-minded, there is the finest rugby ground in the world in the spectacular new 72,500 capacity **Millennium Stadium** Ⓞ, which dominates the Cardiff skyline and which offers guided tours to visitors. Soccer also has a stadium at **Ninian Park**, home of the Cardiff City club. Other sporting and leisure facilities include an **ice rink**.

Although Cardiff has been attacked by impassioned Welsh nationalists for being insufficiently Welsh, there is an understated sense of pride about the place and the language is certainly gaining ground. When the spirits are rouse on a rugby international day, there's no mistaking which capital you're in. ❑

BELOW: the Millennium Stadium.

Cool Cymru

Until recently, Richard Burton, Tom Jones, Shirley Bassey and Anthony Hopkins were the only international stars most people would have associated with Wales. However, the past few years have seen a steady increase in the number of younger Welsh musicians, actors and film-makers taking their places in the limelight and, as a result, it's a lot more cool to be Welsh.

Leading Welsh music's renaissance were the Manic Street Preachers, formed as a socialist art/punk/glam act in the South Wales town of Blackwood. They have had number ones in both the singles and album charts, attract an amazingly devoted following of fans, and have cemented their fame with a reputation as a compelling live band. Their crowning glory was the Manic Millennium show, at which they saw in the new century playing to a capacity crowd at Cardiff's Millennium Stadium.

Following in their footsteps have come bands such as the Stereophonics and Catatonia. Other acts such as the Super Furry Animals and Gorky's Zygotic Mynci often sing in Welsh and their eclectically experimental sounds have ensured them committed cult followings, if not chart-topping status.

Television and cinema are also chilling out to the cool of Cymru. Justin Kerrigan, writer and director of the hip, Cardiff-based clubbing movie *Human Traffic*, is just one of the young Welsh film-makers who, along with a fresh crop of acting talent, are emerging onto the international scene. A good example is Ioan Gruffud, the young Welsh actor who made a brief appearance in *Titanic*, followed by the title role in the epic TV mini-series *Hornblower*, and who has since starred in the Oscar-nominated film *Solomon and Gaenor*.

Rhys Ifans is another cinematic success story. After working in small-scale British films such as the Swansea-set *Twin Town*, he proceeded to steal the show from co-stars Hugh Grant and Julia Roberts in *Notting Hill*. Ifans has since proved his versatility by convincingly portraying a wide variety of characters.

Perhaps the most striking tale of rags to riches is that of Catherine Zeta Jones. The Swansea-born actress first came to the public's attention in the popular and long-running UK television series, *The Darling Buds of May*. When the show's run finished, she found limited success in British films such as *Blue Juice* before relocating to Los Angeles in an effort to further her career. She eventually landed a lead role opposite Antonio Banderas and Anthony Hopkins in the blockbuster *The Mask of Zorro*, quickly followed by a starring turn with Sean Connery in another big-budget smash, *Entrapment*. It wasn't just stardom that Zeta Jones found in the USA; she is now married to movie star Michael Douglas, making her not only an A-list performer in her own right but also a member of the illustrious Hollywood glitterati.

These major players are only the tip of the iceberg. Throughout Wales, unknown artists are attempting to make it big in their chosen field, perhaps spurred on by the very visible successes that have been documented here. Recognition seems somehow more attainable and the Welsh appear to be shaking off their traditional stereotypes. Only time, of course, will tell if it's all for real. ❑

HT: herine a Jones *The Mask Zorro.*

Map on page 146

GLAMORGAN'S HERITAGE COAST

The tired attractions of the traditional seaside resort have a decreasing charm for today's visitors, but the real appeal is the rugged beauty of the coastline

It is claimed that south Glamorgan could once be found somewhere around present-day Bermuda. It is also said its inhabitants at the time, dinosaurs, basked in tropical sunshine. Perhaps it was when they moved to their new location that they became extinct, for surely no evolutionary invention has been so crucial to survival as the wellington boot has been to this wet area.

For 14 miles (22 km), from the fairground, smutty postcards, caravan parks and hotdog stands of **Porthcawl** ❷ in the west to the sedate tea houses of **Llantwit Major** in the east, this coast displays an ever-changing, rugged beauty untouched by the juggernaut of tourism.

The mountainous **dunes** that stretch from the outskirts of Porthcawl and threaten to engulf all around them are the second highest in Europe and the source of much of the history and legend of the region; lost villages, phantom funerals, spirit hounds and red goblins vie with relics of the Beaker People, Romans and Vikings. Today the dunes are frequented by athletes and ornithologists alike and are a more popular rendezvous with courting couples than the Bridgend cinemas. A walk across the dunes' switchback from **Newton Point** (the Heritage Coast's westernmost boundary) to **Candleston** offers a profusion of unusual flora and fauna.

Commerce controlled

It would be fair to say that Welsh buildings are not exactly the talking point of the architectural world. There are exceptions, of course, and a notable one is **Merthyr Mawr** ❸, nestled behind the towering dunes just a mile inland from Candleston. The owners of the Merthyr Mawr estate have pursued policies that have discouraged pubs, tea houses and shops. Instead, there is a straggle of thatched cottages, a manor house, grey stone church, a red village telephone box concealed in a wall and a post office hidden inside someone's living room.

The 11th-century **Ogmore Castle** overhangs the River Ogmore like a discarded hunk of nibbled gorgonzola. Linking it to Merthyr Mawr are the stepping stones that were built, so legend has it, on the instructions of the mistress of the castle who feared her commoner lover's ardour might be dampened by wading the river.

The road continues climbing for a mile to **Ogmore-by-Sea**, the only coastal village along the stretch. Just 10 minutes by

...ECEDING ...GES: ...sh Point ...hthouse. **...T:** dunes ...Candleston ...stle. **...HT:** the ...itage Coast ...st of Cardiff.

car from Bridgend or half an hour from Cardiff, Ogmore is a nondescript ribbon of 1950s bungalows but with a perfect location overlooking this great unsung coastline. The village boasts a few shops and pubs. The most notable building, and the best pub, is the mock gothic Craig, a large friendly family pub with grounds overlooking Tusker Rock.

The coastal road hugs the cliffs, snaking its way eastwards from Ogmore. The sea is often swollen here, as if angry at being channelled from the vastness of the Atlantic into the narrow funnel of the Bristol Channel. The tides are the second highest in the world, with a 50-ft (15-metre) lift and a notorious undertow.

Victorian folly

A descent to **Southerndown beach** ❹ leads to the Heritage Coast Centre with its useful guidebooks to walks, folklore and the history of the region. Here you can hire a bike or arrange guided "family" or "study" walks. All 56 surrounding acres (23 hectares) of natural parkland are open to the public. The grounds belonged to **Dunraven Castle**, the Victorian folly which used to stand on the headland above the bay. It was supposedly destroyed in 1962 by the owner himself after a disagreement with the council. Its walled gardens have now been restored.

Above **Dunraven Gardens** are the defensive banks, ditches and burial mounds of an Iron-Age promontory fort. The balcony (with heritage information board) offers a panoramic view along the coast and across the waters to Somerset. A descent to the wave-cut platform when the tide is out provides a splendid opportunity to view at close hand the teeming marine life: mussels and barnacles cling to rocks while shrimps and sea anemones shelter in the crevices and pools.

In the distance, you can see the lighthouse at **Nash Point** ❺ which is the starting point for a short but pleasant nature trail across streams and through woodland towards **Marcross** ❻. The nearby manor

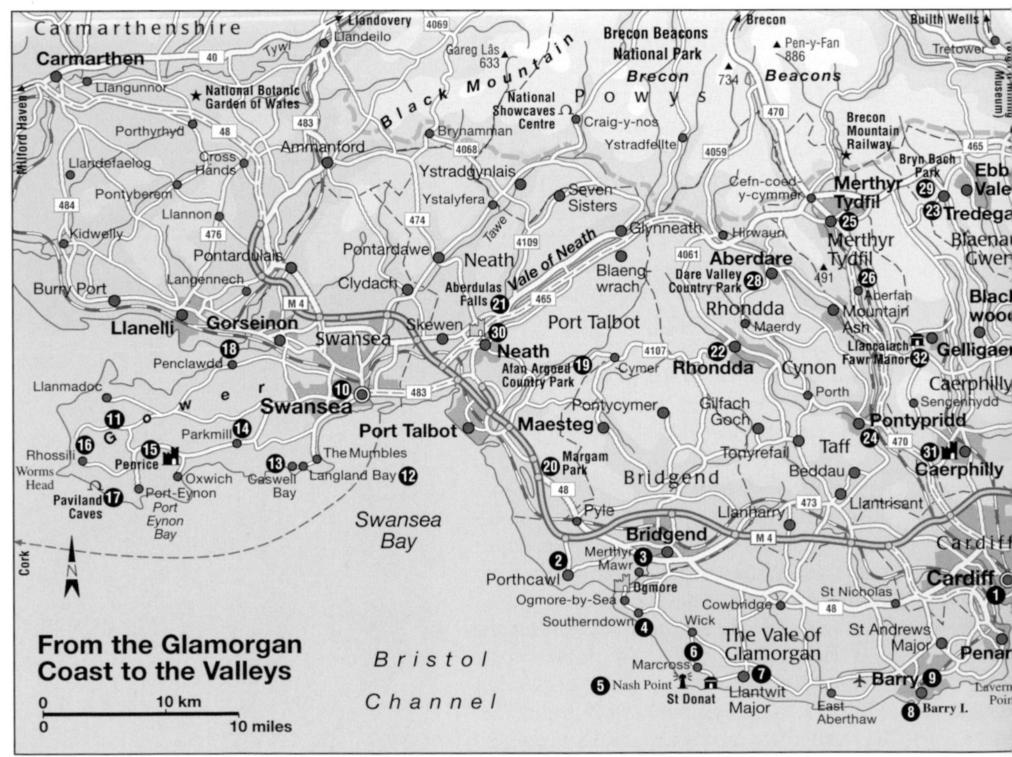

From the Glamorgan Coast to the Valleys

Map
n page
146

has seen better days, namely those when it auctioned off wrecking spoils. The Norman presence is clearly visible in the church here, as it is in those at Merthyr Mawr, Ewenny Priory and Newton. One of the most interesting features of this particular church is the "leper window" through which parishioners with contagious diseases participated in services.

Perhaps the most famous church is that founded by St Illtyd at **Llantwit Major** ❼ in the 5th century. Here the practice of *laus perennis* (unending prayer), also practised at Old Sarum and Glastonbury, was introduced. Next to the Celtic stone crosses of local kings, an incongruous palm tree adds its exotic touch.

Llantwit is one of most ancient villages in Wales and many of the narrow lanes, dotted with tea houses and bed-and-breakfast establishments, are under conservation orders. The Italianate town hall contains a tourist information office, and there's a fine parish church (actually two churches joined at the tower and containing some decorative Celtic crosses).

During term time, Llantwit's population swells with the influx of students from home or abroad who attend the world peace school of Atlantic College, located in a fairy-tale opening in the forest high above the landscaped gardens of **St Donat's** castle. In the 1930s the American publishing tycoon William Randolph Hearst created a small-scale Welsh San Simeon in this extensive, wonderfully preserved castle which had belonged for 700 years to the poets, knights, wreckers and adventurers of the Stradling family. Said to be the most haunted house in Wales, it also houses a lively arts centre and, in July, hosts the Wales International Storytelling Festival.

Old-fashioned resorts

To the east, the magnet for day-trippers is **Barry Island** ❽, a bucket-and-spade resort complete with funfair. The former Butlin's holiday camp has been turned into a less regimented collection of rides and end-of-the-pier shows. To the west, Pebble Beach is an unusual mile-long geological formation. Whitmore Bay and Jackson's Bay are popular beaches.

The town of **Barry** ❾, a major coal-exporting port in the 19th century intended to challenge the Bute family's shipping dominance in Cardiff, is now sedately residential.

Porthcawl, the other traditional seaside resort in this area, is at the western approach to the Heritage Coast. Its former cheerful image has given way to the usual dreary caravan parks and tacky souvenir shops, though efforts are being made to give it a more 21st-century appeal.

Fabulous walks

The great outdoors in this area has a lot more to offer than the towns. Because Glamorgan's 14-mile (22-km) Heritage Coast has largely been ignored, it has managed to retain all the most attractive, rugged features of an unspoilt British coastline. The weather options may often be Presbyterian grey or bucketing rain, but the region offers fabulous coastal walks and enough pubs on the way to stop you fretting about the climate. ❑

HT: nering weed, d in making erbread.

Maps:
[A]rea 146
[C]ity 152

SWANSEA AND ENVIRONS

Writers such as Dylan Thomas and Kingsley Amis have called Swansea ugly yet felt great affection for it. Contrastingly beautiful are the bays and parks within easy reach

"I was born in a large Welsh industrial town at the beginning of the Great War; an ugly, lovely town (or so it was, and is, to me) crawling, sprawling, slummed, unplanned, jerry-villa'd, and smug-suburbed by the side of a long and splendid curving shore." Dylan Thomas's unsentimental hymn to his home town still evokes the essence of the place, despite recent refurbishment.

In the middle of the 19th century, **Swansea** ⓾ was the metallurgical capital of the world, with 300 chimneys pumping their toxic gases into the Swansea Valley. Diseases included cholera, typhoid, and even an outbreak of yellow fever. There were 60 beggars' hotels and crime was endemic. What was left of Swansea after poverty, disease and crime had taken their toll, Hitler's Luftwaffe tried to finish off in the 1940s. Then postwar planners began ripping out its barely beating heart. With justification, it was said: "The only good thing to come out of Swansea is the road to Llanelli."

Urban forests

Swansea, *Abertawe* in Welsh (meaning "Mouth of the River Tawe"), is Wales's second city. As there *are* only two, it's hardly surprising that it has in the past suffered a chronic inferiority complex. Although seemingly soulless, Swansea is nevertheless a personable and personal city – it's the kind of place where someone honks a horn and everyone waves.

There are also unmistakable signs of a new-won confidence and vibrancy. Over the past 20 years 1,000 acres (400 hectares) of industrial wasteland in the Swansea Valley have been brought back to life to create one of Britain's largest urban forests, complete with pony trekking and river walks. The valley also houses an all-weather athletics track and Britain's first Enterprise Zone. Millions more have been spent on healing the industrial scars and providing yet more leisure facilities. As a sign of goodwill, the fish have returned to the **River Tawe**.

Indoor pursuits

A well-known Irish saying has been adapted to suit Swansea: "If you can see the hills of Somerset, it's going to rain; if you can't, it's already raining." Certainly, the city does seem to suffer an inordinate number of rainy days, but fortunately it does provide visitors with a number of options. The **Quadrant** Ⓐ, which opened in 1980, is a modern indoor shopping centre with all the usual retail outlets. Alongside is a vast glass aircraft hanger of an **indoor market** (the largest and one of the

[PR]ECEDING [PA]GES: Rhosili [He]ad, Gower. **[LEF]T:** Swansea [Ca]stle. **[RIG]HT:** marina [in] Swansea.

best in Wales) offering everything from ice cream to antiques and laverbread to carpets. **Plantasia** is an unusual city-centre attraction. It is a giant, pyramidal glasshouse, home to exotic plants, insects, fish, reptiles and a band of cotton top tamarin monkeys.

The development of the **Maritime Quarter** – a successful mix of residential and leisure facilities – got under way in 1982. On the quayside the excellent **Maritime and Industrial Museum** **B** (closed Mon) houses a 150-year-old working woollen mill alongside other exhibits of the city's industrial and maritime past, as well as a section on the World War II bombing of the city. There's also a replica tram from the world's first passenger tram line that trundled along the front from 1807 until 1960. The museum also boasts the largest collection of floating exhibits in Wales. Visitors are free to climb aboard a former Gower lightship and a steam tug. These are moored in the large **marina**, which can accommodate 600 sailing craft.

Remembering Dylan Thomas

Also skirting the Marina are the Dylan Thomas Theatre, cafés, pubs, restaurants and apartments, all festooned with carvings and sculptures that relate the city's maritime history. Two statues, one of Dylan Thomas himself and another of Captain Cat, a well-loved character from Dylan's *Under Milk Wood,* survey the scene.

Behind the museum is a **leisure centre**, as impressive inside as it is unimpressive out, offering indoor bowling green, spa pools, sauna, solarium and a pool with hydroslide and waves. **Ty Llên** **C**, also known as the **Dylan Thomas Centre**, in Somerset Place, is Britain's first purpose-built literature centre. It was opened by former US President Jimmy Carter, a great Dylan fan, in 1995, when it became the focal point of Swansea's Festival of Literature and Writing. It incorporates a theatre space, galleries, bookshops, a restaurant and craft shops.

For those seeking more information on Swansea's most famous son, the Informa-

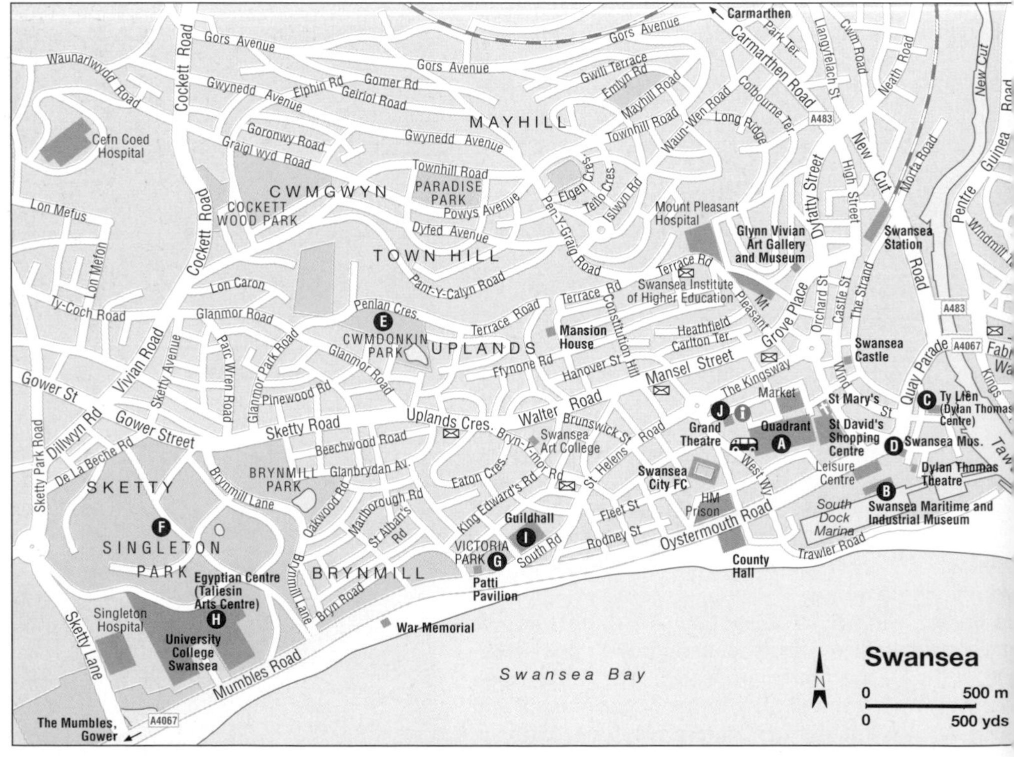

Map on page 152

tion Centre in Plymouth Street has leaflets on the **City Centre Trail** and the **Dylan Thomas Uplands Trail**.

Olden times

Not everything is modern. The city boasts **Swansea Museum** Ⓓ, the oldest in Wales (founded in 1838), with a marvellously eccentric pot-pourri of international and local exhibits including an ancient Egyptian mummy, a Welsh kitchen and a superb collection of Swansea and Nantgarw porcelain. Between the museum and the Marina is a small concentration of Victorian, Edwardian and Georgian streets (**Cambrian Place**, **Gloucester Place** and **Prospect Place**) under conservation orders. There's also a nibble of 14th-century **Swansea Castle** sandwiched between Castle Street and the High Street.

Dylan Thomas's "Return Journey" to the **Uplands** leads to "the still house over the mumbling bay" in **Cwmdonkin Drive** where the poet grew up. Like many of the residential streets that clatter down the Uplands, Cwmdonkin Drive is as steep as Everest's final ascent and would drive anyone to drink.

From the commemorative plaque on his home, you can ascend a little further before entering **Cwmdonkin Park** Ⓔ. This was Thomas's "eternal park", the setting of his early poem *The Hunchback in the Park*; it now has a memorial inscribed with lines from his famous poem *Fernhill.* The view over the bay is spectacular.

A short distance from the Uplands shops is **Brynmill Park** which connects with the larger **Singleton Park** Ⓕ, with its boating lake, botanic gardens and children's playground. This green space leads around **Swansea University** campus down to the front where locals do battle with bowls and tennis rackets in **Victoria Park** Ⓖ. Swansea is extraordinarily well endowed with grassland – no doubt courtesy of the 19th-century industrialists who realised the town must have lungs if they were to survive their own pollution.

If your appetite for ancient Egypt has

ELOW: ass castles commerce dge the umbling cade of vansea astle.

been whetted by the mummy in Swansea Museum, the **Egypt Centre**, at the **Taliesin Arts Centre** **H** on the university campus, is well worth a visit and admission is free. On display are more than 1,000 exhibits dating from pre-3500 BC to AD 500, including beautiful bead necklaces from the time of Tutankhamun and the painted coffin of a Theban lady musician.

The eastern **Promenade** leads past **St Helen's Cricket and Rugby Ground** to the **Guildhall** **I**, which contains the city's main concert hall as well as the garish **Brangwyn Panels** (the enormous canvases commemorate the British Empire and were originally earmarked for the House of Lords) and on to the Marina.

The Mumbles

To the west, the tree-lined seawall continues skirting the 4-mile (6-km) bay to the 900-ft (275-metre) Victorian pier at **The Mumbles**, a popular sailing centre and small resort. As the tide turns, the mudflats become populated by fishermen digging for lugworm. At **Oystermouth** (which is part of The Mumbles) a 13th-century castle overlooks the bay with a number of underground passageways leading to the courtyard of the nearby hotel.

In the graveyard, among the tombs to lost sailors, is a memorial to the legendary Thomas Bowdler who had the zealot's small-minded arrogance to delete everything from 10 volumes of Shakespeare "which cannot with propriety, be read aloud to the family".

The Mumbles is well stocked with pubs, those along the seafront being known as the "**Mumbles Mile**". Many of them, including The Antelope and The Pilot, were frequented by Dylan Thomas when, as a young man, he was a member of Swansea Little Theatre, a company which held its rehearsals in The Mumbles. The Mermaid, his favourite drinking hole, has now been demolished. When the nights are balmy, everyone seems to be drawn out of the city centre to this, the resort end of the bay.

BELOW: looki over Swanse towards Mumbles.

Maps:
Area 146
City 152

The entertainment zone

Back in Swansea, the **Grand Theatre ❿** is one of the finest provincial playhouses, with an impressive track record in operatic and dramatic performances, and is well worth a visit, if only in order to have a drink or a bite to eat in the eye-catching Rooftop Café bar.

There's also the **No Sign** wine bar at 56 Wind Street which some claim is the best bar in the world. There's sawdust on the floor, dust carefully preserved on the wine racks and antiques unselfconsciously littering the bars. Its chequered history has provided a marvellous riot of architectural styles that together create a charming harmony unmatched by any other public building in the city. If Dylan Thomas was drinking elsewhere, the man had no taste.

Wind Street itself has a growing reputation as the "café quarter" of Swansea and is a lively place full of pubs and bars.

October is a great time for festivals in Swansea. The **Cockles and Celts Festival** gets the ball rolling with a week's celebration of Celtic cuisine, music and dance. Next comes the **Swansea Festival of Music and the Arts** (incorporating the Fringe Theatre Festival), closely followed by the **Dylan Thomas Celebration** which attracts visitors from all over the world. For those wishing to extend their Celtic experience, the Swansea–Cork Ferries will transport you to Ireland at reasonable cost.

Back to nature

Designated as the first Area of Outstanding Natural Beauty in Britain in 1956 and strangely defined as part of the actual city of Swansea, the **Gower Peninsula ⓫** is a real magnet for the visitor. It has three National Nature Reserves and 21 Sites of Special Scientific Interest. It is both Swansea's dormitory and its playground.

From The Mumbles, the sheltered Mediterranean-like switchback shoreline plunges and soars out of pine-clad limestone bays, dotted with occasional palms. **Langland Bay ⓬** is the nearest to town and popular with surfers. It's a safe family

BELOW: Summer bathing at Mumbles Head.

beach with rock pools for the kids to explore. The large old changing huts that line the upper reaches of the beach can be hired as virtual beach homes but overnight stays are forbidden. There are all-weather tennis courts, and Langland Golf Club is on the hill.

Caswell Bay ⓭ has a fine deep bay but also a self-catering eyesore that arrived 20 or 30 years ago. From here a scenic cliff path leads to the tiny, old smugglers' lair of **Brandy Cove** which is inaccessible by car.

Caves and castles

At **Parkmill** ⓮ the coast road plunges under a leafy canopy through a valley suffused with wild garlic. **Parc-le-Breos Burial Chamber** and **Cathole Cave** are located here, together with the **Gower Heritage Centre**, a popular craft and countryside centre sited at a 12th-century water-powered cornmill.

The 13th-century **Penrice Castle** ⓯, owned by the old Gower Methuen-Campbell family, comprises a grand manor house and terraced water gardens (not open to the public) overlooking **Oxwich Bay**, which is popular with surfers.

Also overlooking Oxwich Bay (but open to visitors) is the impressive, ruined 16th-century mansion known as **Oxwich Castle** (open May–Sept daily).

Barely visible in a grove overhanging the wide sweeping bay, backed by heather and woodland, is the ancient **church of St Illtud**. The village itself is a quaint reminder of southwest England, just across the water. The **Great House** behind Horton's bay, now a restaurant, was once the home of the 17th-century pirate and wrecker, John Lucas, and is supposedly the oldest building in Gower.

Port Eynon Bay, like Oxwich, has a gently shelving sandy beach backed by dunes. **Culver Hole** and the **Salt House** are the principal attractions here. The finest beach is at **Rhossili** ⓰, the westernmost point on Gower facing the Atlantic and Ireland. A 4-mile (6-km)

BELOW: Rhossili Bay.

Map on page 146

arching cuticle of sand banked by dunes provides perfect surf. Sticking out of the water can be seen the blackened remnants of the *Helvetia* which ran aground here in 1887. The spectacular **Worms Head** promontory at one end of the beach is accessible on foot at low tide – make sure you check before setting off. Beyond is southwest Wales's Pembrokeshire coast.

There's a large seabird colony at Worms Head, a gaggle of homes, half a dozen bed-and-breakfast establishments, the Worms Head Hotel and a National Trust Information Centre. Here, too, you may catch Gower's hang-gliding lemmings throwing themselves off the cliff edge 632ft (193 metres) above the Atlantic. The village church has a memorial to Rhossili-born Petty Officer Edgar Evans who died in Captain Scott's tragic Antarctic expedition in 1912.

Old mysteries

The nearby **Paviland Caves** ⓱ are thought to be the oldest occupied site yet excavated in Europe, dating back 100,000 years. The skeleton of the Red Lady of Paviland (a man, actually), neolithic burial chambers like **Arthur's Stone** at **Reynoldston** and spooky names like Druids' Moor, Devil's Kitchen and Hangman's Cross evoke the Celtic mysteries.

Meanwhile the cockle women of **Penclawdd** ⓲ on the northern coast, who still traipse up to 7 miles (11 km) a day across the mudflats to collect the cockles and seaweed for laverbread, keep alive the region's more recent traditions. The northern-fringed saltmarsh stretches for 8 miles (13 km) round to Carmarthen Bay and has a desolate beauty which is in marked contrast to the golden sands of the south.

Just as the Landsker line divides Pembrokeshire's northern Welsh speakers from the Norman south, so the high central ridge, **Cefn Bryn**, divides Gower. Not too far from Arthur's Stone, which is on the high point of Cefn Bryn, is the country retreat of **Fairyhill**, a secluded restaurant and hotel, with lake, trout stream and 24 acres (10 hectares) of woodland frequented by a variety of wildlife such as buzzards and badgers.

Parks worth visiting

Within a radius of about a half-hour drive from Swansea are a number of other sights. **Afan Argoed Country Park** ⓳ has a Welsh Miners' Museum and a Countryside Centre in densely forested hills. There are forest walks, cycle hire facilities and tours.

An 18th-century Orangery in **Margam Park** ⓴ makes a visit worthwhile. The Tudor-Gothic Margam Castle, 12th-century Cistercian abbey remains, and sculptures pepper the estate. Children are well catered for: there's a maze, pony rides and Fairytale Land with Three Bears, ogres, pea-green boats, and houses of straw with tape-recorded tales.

Aberdulais Falls ㉑ in the Vale of Neath is a National Trust site combining natural beauty and historic industrial remains.

The National Showcaves Centre at Dan-yr-Ogof in the Upper Swansea Valley *(see page 113)* is the largest of its kind in Western Europe, with three separate caves plus lots of children's attractions.❑

IGHT: re-Norman ross at largam Park.

Map on page 146

THE VALLEYS

Once there were 66 coal mines in one valley alone. Now the pits have all but gone and efforts to reverse the environmental damage are changing the face of the land

From the top of the 2,000-ft (600-metre) **Mynydd Blaenrhondda** (the Blaenrhondda mountain), where the hang gliders use the escarpment to fly in some of Britain's best air currents, it's possible to look due north and not see a vestige of habitation. If you could walk in a straight line, the first signs of urbanisation would be met at Colwyn Bay, 110 miles (177 km) away on the North Wales coast.

Yet right behind is the **Rhondda** ㉒, most famous of the Valleys that comprise the heart of South Wales. Cardiff may be the capital of Wales; Newport, Bridgend and Swansea may dominate the plain; but the valleys are the inner sanctum of Wales.

Famous sons

Here, in the village of **Pontrhydyfen**, above Port Talbot, the actor Richard Burton was born and brought up. Anthony Hopkins was born a stone's throw away, in **Port Talbot** itself. Also in the Valleys, in **Tredegar** ㉓, Aneurin ("Nye") Bevan, creator of Britain's National Health Service and firebrand of British politics in the 1940s and 1950s, was born. Just down the road from Tredegar is the birthplace of Neil Kinnock, the former Labour Party leader. In **Merthyr Tydfil**, Jack Jones, novelist author of *Off to Philadelphia in the Morning* and other works, was born.

Here, the great choirs and brass bands of Wales practise and play. Here, the coal and steel that once fuelled the industrial greatness of modern Britain was mined and smelted. Here is history.

The Blaenrhondda mountain is a perfect place to see just what a valley is. From the top, on the A4061 road, the visitor looks down on a perfect geological rift. Steep sides rise to perhaps 1,500ft (460 metres) from a narrow floor that in places is not half a mile (800 metres) across.

The tops are plateaus, excellent for walking; the sides, deeply wooded higher up, have terraces of small houses lower down clinging to them like limpets. From the top, the view could be of South Africa's *veldt*, gently-waving long grass in the breeze turning to gold as autumn approaches. In the solitude the only sound you can hear is the whisper of the wind.

Below, the river cuts a roughly straight path down to the coast. It originates just a few miles north, in the Brecon Beacons, the southern edge of the great plateau of Mid-Wales. Major land reclamation programmes in the Valleys have resulted in the removal or grassing over of the old tips, which now resemble enormous prehistoric burial grounds. The rivers, which at one time ran black, have been cleaned up and the salmon are returning.

RECEDING AGES: ymmetry in ie Rhondda. **EFT:** detail, lerlin pub, ontypridd. **IGHT:** ringing home ie bottles in erthyr Tydfil.

Boundary lines

The Valleys themselves stretch from Pontypool in the east, close to the border with England, to west of Llanelli. What is known as "the Valleys" is in fact the geological South Wales coalfield. The natural barrier in the north for much of the way is the A465 Heads of the Valleys road. Where the road turns south, at Glynneath, the geographic Valleys area continues west to Ystradgynlais and Ammanford.

The southern line meanders irregularly west from Pontypool, curving through Risca, Caerphilly, Llantrisant (home of the Royal Mint), Maesteg and Neath.

By the time the rivers have reached the plain at the southern approaches to the Valleys they are running crazily like snakes on a snakes-and-ladders board through the soft alluvial soil of South Wales. The main ones run out in the big cities: the Taff into Cardiff, the Usk into Newport and the Tawe into Swansea.

But there are others. There are perhaps 20 valleys in South Wales running roughly north–south; it is difficult to be categorical because the rivers divide and sub-divide. One valley may be home to two or three "rivers"; the **Rhondda Fawr** (the Big Rhondda) and the **Rhondda Fach** (the Little Rhondda) join and become the Rhondda at Porth, then flow into the Taff at Pontypridd.

Pontypridd

Pontypridd ㉔, 12 miles (19 km) north of Cardiff and known locally as "Ponty", has many fine old buildings of local stone and a bridge which, when built in 1750, had the longest span in the world (140ft/ 45 metres); the three holes on either side lessen the weight and help stop it falling down as its predecessor did.

The town (pop. 33,500) is the birthplace of singers Tom Jones and the late Sir Geraint Evans. By the bridge, the **Pontypridd Historical and Cultural Centre** has an evocative collection of photographs and exhibits depicting life as it was in this area's coal-mining heyday.

BELOW: Pontypridd.

Map on page 146

John Hughes's **Grogg Shop**, on Broadway, has sculptures caricaturing rugby players and other Welsh celebrities. On Market Street, an old-fashioned **market** does a lively trade. The Victorian **fountain** in the town centre was erected in 1985 for a local MP, Sir Alfred Thomas, later Lord Pontypridd.

Merthyr Tydfil

The "capital" of the Valleys is **Merthyr Tydfil** ㉕, named after St Tydfil the Martyr, daughter of the Welsh chieftain Brychan killed at the hands of marauders in the year 480. At Morlais Castle, just north of the town, there are the remnants of a medieval stronghold started in about 1287 by Gilbert de Clare, one of the great Lords Marcher. But Merthyr's overriding historical claim to fame dates from the Industrial Revolution in the second half of the 18th century. It is here that iron ore and coal were first combined on a commercial scale to produce iron and then steel.

The cannon balls that sank Napoleon's fleets at the Nile in 1799 and Trafalgar in 1805 were made in Merthyr. So, too, were the railway lines that in the long era of peace after Waterloo were laid around much of the world – in France, Germany and the US as well as throughout the growing Empire.

It was here, in Homfray's Penydarren iron works, that Cornishman Richard Trevithick in 1804 built and ran the world's first railway locomotive whose "train" carried coal and iron and 70 men for 9 miles (14 km) down the valley to Abercynon, 21 years before the opening of Stephenson's pioneering Stockton-to-Darlington *Rocket* service.

The rails for the Stockton–Darlington line were actually made at John Josiah Guest's Dowlais works. Tramside Road in the town carries the name, and probably the route, of the Merthyr service. The tunnel along the route has been restored and may be inspected from the outside. The town contains a monument to the great railway achievement.

ELOW: finely rought emorial in erthyr Tydfil.

Fighting sons

Joseph Parry, perhaps the greatest of the 19th-century hymn writers, lived and died in the frontier-like town; and Dic Penderyn, in an 1831 uprising, raised the flag covered in blood that was to become the Red Flag of revolution around the world. Later, much later, Howard Winstone became boxing's featherweight champion of the world in 1968.

Today there are few signs – beyond the artefacts in the Museum in **Cyfarthfa Castle** – of the great iron works like those at Dowlais and Cyfarthfa that were so important in their day. Remains of some of the ovens in the Cyfarthfa works can just be seen alongside the Taff, and the **Ynysfach Engine House** has been restored; but the best view of what it must have been like when they opened the ovens and burnt the night sky red can be seen in a giant painting in the museum.

Parry has been more fortunate. His house has been restored and may be visited. The museum also houses artefacts of the coal industry, which has completely disappeared from the town. George Borrow, on his journey through Wales in 1854, was stunned by the glare of the iron furnaces, the dross shooting into the air like fireworks, the scorched and blackened appearance of the surrounding hills, the "low, mean" grey stone houses and "other remarkable edifices of a glowing, hot, Satanic nature."

Merthyr is far removed from this image now. The castle, surrounded by 160 acres (65 hectares) of parkland, was built as a private house for the Crawshay family who founded the Cyfarthfa works in 1825. From this castellated mansion, ironmaster William Crawshay II could keep a watchful eye on his investment. Now, refurbished in authentic Regency style, it houses a superb museum and gallery with a prestigious collection of fine and decorative art. Below stairs are exhibitions of Merthyr's social and industrial past.

Merthyr is well placed to take advantage of the green, open spaces of the Brecon Beacons, the northern edge of the

BELOW: Cyfarthfa Castle.

Map on page 146

borough lying within the National Park boundary. Three miles (5 km) north of Merthyr, the vintage steam locomotives of the **Brecon Mountain Railway** chug along a picturesque route into the Park. From the station in Pant, the 7-mile (11-km) round trip passes through Pontsticill and along the full length of the Taf Fechan reservoir to Dol-y-Gaer.

King Coal

Coal, the "Black Diamond", was the seminal influence on the Valleys. Iron and other ores, especially copper, were smelted and large numbers worked in the industry. But South Wales is associated with coal like Bavaria with beer.

At its peak, in 1921, some 271,000 men worked in the industry. The record production, however, was in 1913, just before World War I, when 56.8 million tons were produced. In the 1920s there were 66 pits in the Rhondda Valley alone. All have closed. Although the industry seems to be in terminal decline, a few privately owned pits are keeping mining proudly alive in the Valleys. One group of 240 miners at Tower colliery at Hirwaun, for example, used their savings to buy Wales's last deep pit for £1.9 million. Soon they were exporting to Europe and even began to undercut competitors in China, Cambodia and Vietnam – the source of so many of the pits' financial problems when they were under state ownership. The gamble paid off: in their first year, the miners showed a £2 million profit.

Aberfan ㉖, in the Taff Valley, is a place etched in the memory. It was here, on the morning of 21 October 1966, just after school had opened on a desperately wet day, that the tip moved and slid down on the little village school, killing 116 children and 28 adults. The sad rows of headstones in the cemetery can be seen for miles across the valley.

The best place to get a feel of what it must have been like to work underground is the **Big Pit Mining Museum** in **Blaenafon** ㉗. The mine closed in 1980 but is

ELOW: the ig Pit Mining useum, aenafon.

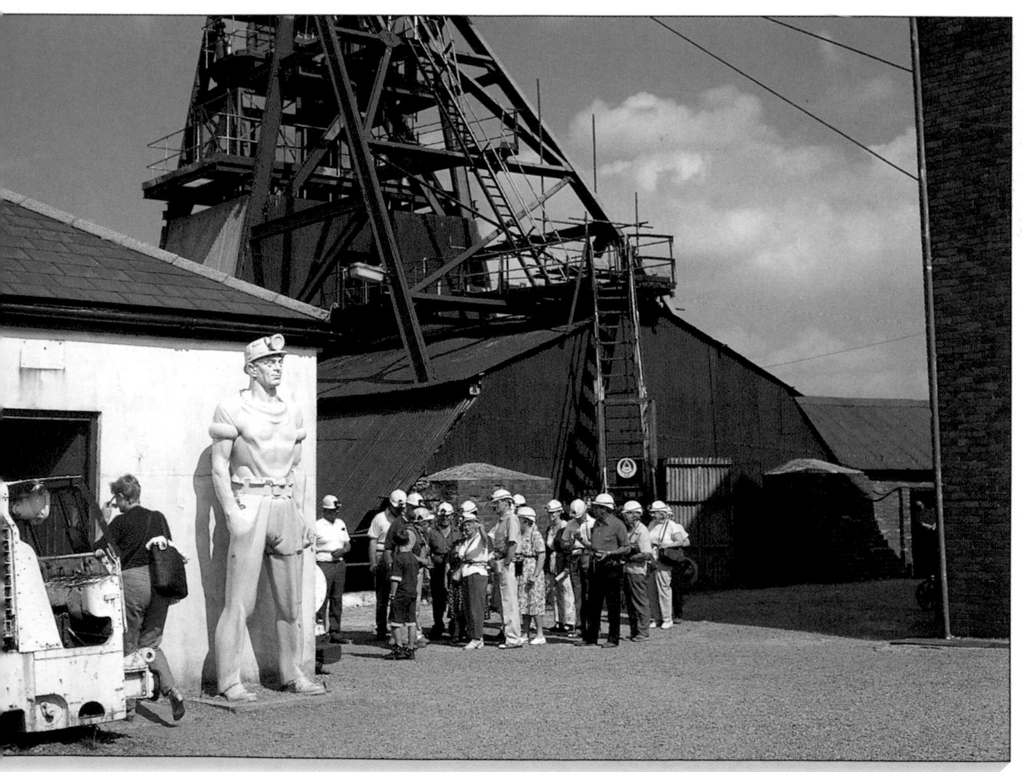

now a World Heritage Site. Visitors don a miner's safety helmet and ride down 294ft (90 metres) in the cage the miners used to take. For an hour they can experience the darkness and the stillness and get some idea of what it must have been like to work in the dank, humid conditions. Warm clothing and practical shoes are recommended.

There's a range of colliery buildings, including the winding engine house, blacksmith's shop, pithead baths and pitman's cabin, with a gift shop and cafeteria in what was the miners' canteen.

The drop in the cage was something few colliers welcomed, however often they did it. One, writing in 1925, recalled: "We sank rapidly down out of the daylight. The cage travels swiftly. About halfway down the engineman applies the brake. This checks the momentum and the queer sensation is experienced of coming back up again. Every miner experiences this. He knows, in fact, that the cage is still descending, but every physical sensation indicates that it is returning to the surface." Once down, the collier might still have a 3-mile (5-km) walk to the coalface. It's not possible to recreate all this in Big Pit, but it still gives a good impression of the claustrophobia and inhumanity of working underground.

Explosions were frequent; roof falls, preceded by the sickening sound of the wooden pit prop giving way and then snapping, commonplace. The very worst explosions took a monumental toll on life. On 18 October 1918, just before Armistice Day in the fields of Flanders, a massive explosion in the pit at **Sengenhydd**, then the nearest one to Cardiff, took the lives of 436 men. A quarter of a century earlier, on 23 June 1894, at the Albion colliery, **Cilfynydd**, 290 men and boys died.

From pits to parks

The greatest valley for coal was the Rhondda. Although the pits have all gone, the **Heritage Park** on the site of the former Lewis Merthyr pit at Porth ("The Underground Experience" that's also "fun", the brochures insist) is a historical evocation of the industry that once dominated everything.

Nowadays, through the creation of country parks, many of the Valleys are being restored to their pre-industrial green. In 1972, on the western fringes of Aberdare, the **Dare Valley Country Park** ㉘ was created from a despoiled industrial landscape. Where there were once 19 pits and drift mines there are now 480 acres (194 hectares) of grassland, woods, lakes and streams with an abundance of wildlife. The park, with its waymarked trails, informative visitor centre and wide range of facilities, is typical of many.

At **Bryn Bach Park** ㉙, just off the A465 Heads of the Valleys road near Tredegar, another transformation has occurred. In place of defunct pits and open-cast mines are more than 600 acres (240 hectares) of woodland and pasture with a man-made lake and visitor centre.

The greening of the Valleys is much in evidence at **Cwmcarn Forest Drive** (just off the A467 Risca–Brynmawr road). The scenic 7-mile (11-km) drive through the Ebbw Forest provides panoramic views

LEFT: Aberfan, scer of a slag-hea disaster.

Map on page 146

across the Severn Estuary to the north Devon coast. It is a popular spot for picnics, walking and cycling.

What's missing

The one shortage in the Valleys is castles. Wales has the greatest concentration of castles of any part of Britain but, because of the topography of the steep-sided valleys, there are few within the area.

Morlais, in Merthyr Tydfil, was the most important because it commanded the high ground in the area. **Neath Castle** ㉚ was founded by Richard de Granville in 1129. The remains of the gateway and its flanking towers can be traced to the 13th century, although it is of interest more for the number of times it changed hands than for its remains.

Guarding the southern approaches to the Valleys is mighty **Caerphilly Castle** ㉛, one of Europe's greatest surviving examples of medieval military architecture. Its presence in an ordinary – and slightly shabby – town is wholly unexpected, but it was strategically placed to control the exits from the Welsh strongholds in the Valleys. The huge 13th-century fortress, with its sophisticated system of water defences, concentric fortifications and leaning tower (which out-leans the one in Pisa) is Britain's biggest castle apart from Windsor. The 14th-century **Great Hall** has been restored. An exhibition covers Welsh castles in general – building methods and day-to-day life.

A few centuries younger than Caerphilly Castle and much less intimidating is **Llancaiach Fawr Manor** ㉜, near **Nelson**. Here, greeted by the servants of "Colonel" Edward Pritchard (all speaking in the style of the 17th century), the visitor is transported back to the year 1645. The time is the Civil War and the tours give a flavour of life in a household of the gentry at this time. The experience is varied, being based on a yearly calendar of events: if you visit on 5 August you will meet King Charles I. After Charles's visit in 1645 "Colonel" Pritchard sneakily switched sides and joined the Parliamentarians. ❑

ELOW: aerphilly astle.

S^T CATHERINES HOTEL

SOUTHWEST WALES

This is where to find the longest, emptiest beaches as well as elegantly understated resorts

The further west you travel, the more rural Wales becomes. Unlike its southeastern neighbour, this part of Wales is not a complicated mosaic of contrasting influences. Beyond Swansea there are no large urban conurbations. Comfortably sized country and market towns predominate; the landscape is a reliable green throughout, a patchwork of farmland, wooded river valley, moor and forest. And the coast offers the simple pleasures of the seaside that have all but vanished elsewhere beneath a tide of candyfloss and tacky funfair.

Heading west, you first travel through Carmarthenshire. The county town of Carmarthen sets the tone: modestly affluent and very much a part of the local farming community, with a large livestock market that almost spills over into the shopping centre. It's not a place known for its conspicuous use of mobile phones or internet cafés.

The countryside around and about is gentle. Rolling, rounded hills, not mountains, define the horizon. The River Tywi, which flows through a wide, fertile vale between Llandeilo and Carmarthen, is the main landscape feature. The river meets the sea along Carmarthen Bay, a shoreline fringed with the longest, emptiest and sandiest beaches in Wales. To the east of the estuary are the vast 7-mile (11-km) Cefn Sidan sands, while to the west there's the 6-mile (10-km) beach – once used for land-speed record attempts – leading to Pendine.

Pendine is at the gateway to one of Europe's finest stretches of coastal natural beauty. The Pembrokeshire Coast National Park is Britain's only coastal-based park. It stretches from Amroth all the way around Wales's rugged southwestern peninsula to the Teifi Estuary at Cardigan, a distance of around 180 miles (290km). Apart from the aberration of the oil refineries along the Milford Haven waterway, it's undiluted coastal spectacle all the way – pristine sandy bays, towering cliffs and sea stacks, rocky coves and headlands, the entire coast teeming with wildlife.

The resorts hark back to the good old days of the home-grown seaside holiday. There's nothing remotely tacky about Tenby. Fairground razzmatazz is kept at arm's length, the resort preferring to rely on its picture-book Georgian harbour and good beaches. Neighbouring Saundersfoot is popular with holiday sailors, while further along the coast the resorts are even smaller and less developed.

Although synonymous with coastline, Pembrokeshire does have an interior worth exploring – especially the Preseli Hills in the north, a bare, haunting upland scattered with prehistoric remains. ❑

PRECEDING PAGES: the harbour at Tenby.
LEFT: fisherman with a coracle, a boat made from animal hides stretched over a wicker frame.

Map on page 174

CARMARTHENSHIRE

This area includes an exquisite botanic garden, a gold mine and a nature reserve for birds, as well as the towns of Carmarthen, Llandeilo, Llandovery, Llanelli and Dylan Thomas's Laugharne

The county town of **Carmarthen** ❶ is a bustling market town on the banks of the Tywi with a truly Welsh atmosphere. The twice-weekly covered livestock market is the largest in the country and its indoor market one of Wales's finest.

Back in AD 75, the town was a Roman military settlement known as Moridunum and the partly exposed remains of a large amphitheatre can still be seen in Priory Street. There is less evidence for the romantic legend that the town was the birthplace of the famous wizard Merlin. His father is reputed to have ruled the area during the Dark Ages following the Roman evacuation. An ancient tree known as Merlin's Oak used to stand in Priory Street. In 1978 the council bravely decided to remove it to make way for road improvements despite the dire prophecy:

"When Merlin's oak shall tumble down,
Then shall fall Carmarthen town."

The town, we can report, remains upright and bits of the tree are on display in a glass case in St Peter's Civic Hall.

The most attractive part of the town is around Nott Square. This area has pleasant shopping streets, the scant remains of Edward I's **castle** and the elegant **Guildhall** dating from 1770.

Down on the banks of the Tywi is the **Carmarthen Heritage Centre** which records the history of the town. There are displays on Carmarthen's oldest industry – coracle fishing for salmon and sewin (sea-trout) – which pre-dates the Roman invasion. A fisherman carrying a coracle on his back is incorporated in the town's coat of arms.

Opposite St Peter's Church is **Oriel Myrddin Gallery**, housed in what was a Victorian purpose-built art school. This excellent gallery holds changing exhibitions of contemporary arts and crafts.

On the eastern outskirts of town at **Abergwili**, in the former Palace of the Bishop of St David's, is the **Carmarthenshire County Museum**. The exhibits from the region's past include displays of Roman gold, Welsh furniture and artefacts from local castles. Just east of Abergwili, a hill topped by an Iron-Age fort dominates the valley. This is **Merlin's Hill**, named after the ubiquitous local wizard.

The Vale of Tywi

The River Tywi charts a lazy course between Carmarthen and Llandovery, flowing through tranquil green countryside. The wide, fertile valley, edged by low, rounded hills, has a soothing, timeless quality about it. The A40 runs down the north side of the vale while the more

FT: rmarthen rket.
HT: cattle ction at rmarthen.

scenic B4300 follows the opposite bank. The two roads are linked at regular intervals by bridges which allow the visitor to explore in a meandering fashion.

National Botanic Garden

For those interested in horticulture the valley is a real delight. On the south side of the river near Llanarthne is the stunning **National Botanic Garden of Wales** ❷, opened in 2000. This £44-million millennium project is dedicated to conservation and sustainability and aims to show how the future of mankind depends on the potential and diversity of the world's plant life. The garden blends old and new. It is on a 568-acre (229-hectare) estate called Middleton Hall, developed by William Paxton in the 1700s. The regency buildings, walled gardens, lakes, waterfalls and cascades are being lovingly restored. At the heart of the garden is the futuristic Great Glasshouse. Designed by Sir Norman Foster, this elliptical glass dome is the largest single span glasshouse in the world. Containing the flora of five Mediterranean regions of the world planted in and around a deep sloping ravine, it is full of scent and colour. Overlooking the garden and one of the best viewpoints in the Tywi Valley is **Paxton's Tower**, a folly erected by the owner of Middleton Hall in memory of Lord Nelson.

Further east, near Llangathen on the opposite side of the river, is a very different, more intimate garden. **Aberglasney** ❸, known as "a garden lost in time", is tucked away in a sheltered hollow. The 16th/17th-century house and garden, which are being restored after half a century of neglect, have some unique features. There's the unusual parapet walk in the cloister garden with its pretty outlook over the walled gardens, woodland and pool garden. The yew tunnel is thought to be one of the oldest living garden features in Europe.

Across the river is **Gelli Aur Country Park** (it translates as Golden Grove), a swathe of wooded parkland surrounding

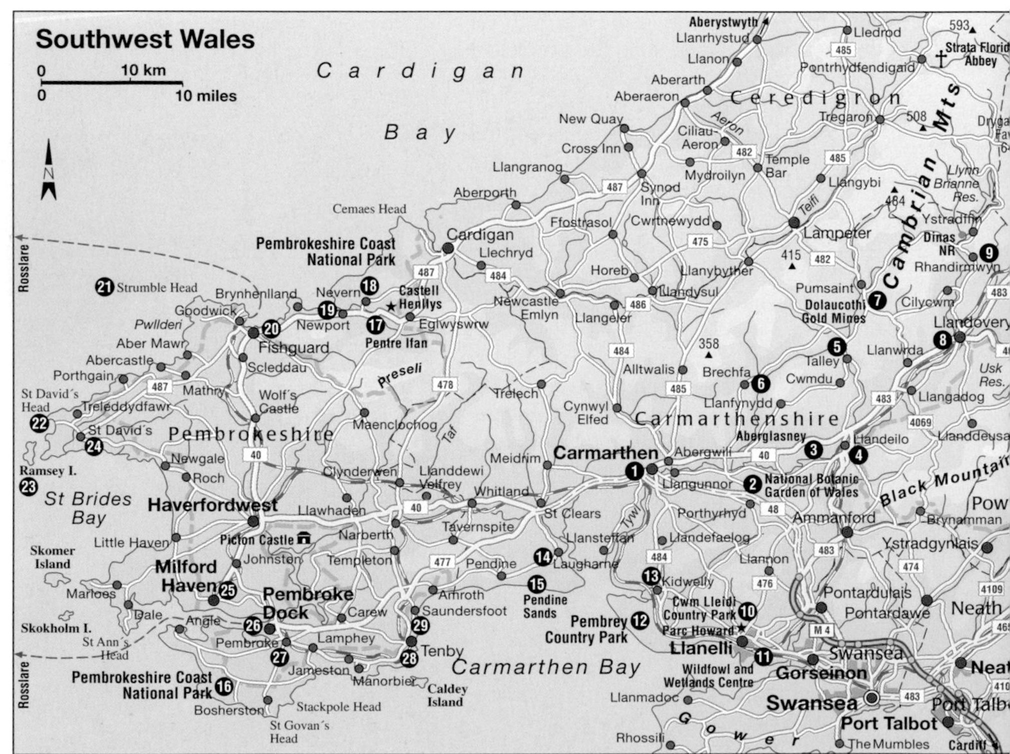

Map n page 174

a magnificent 19th-century mansion, with terraced gardens, arboretum, deer park and waymarked walks.

Llandeilo

The attractive market town of **Llandeilo** ❹ sits snugly on a bluff above the Tywi. Its streets cluster around St Teilo's Church, which, although rebuilt by G. C. Scott in 1848, has its origins in the 6th century. The elegant arched bridge which crosses the river is reputedly the longest single-span stone bridge in Wales. On the edge of the town is the historic National Trust site of **Dinefwr Park**, containing landscaped grounds and a small mansion known as Newton House.

Dinefwr Castle, at the edge of the park, occupies a strategic position on a wooded cliff overlooking the river – a site that has been fortified since the Iron Age. Legend states that the original castle was built in AD 877 by Rhodri Mawr, King of Wales. By AD 920 Dinefwr was the main court of Hywel Dda (Hywel the Good) who ruled over much of South Wales and created the first uniform legal system in the country. The castle we see today dates from the early 12th century when Lord Rhys ruled over the land. He was a patriotic, cultured Welshman who founded the first eisteddfod in Cardigan in 1176.

In the 17th century the descendants of Lord Rhys built the more up-to-date residence of **Newton House** just north of the castle. Much altered over the centuries, the house has now been completely restored. In the 18th century the whole estate with its, castle, house, gardens, woodlands and deer park were integrated into one huge rolling landscape. The famous long-horned Dinefwr White Park Cattle, referred to in the laws of Hywel Dda, still graze the land.

The area around Llandeilo is rich in castles. West of the town there's ruined **Dryslwyn Castle** atop a hill smack in the middle of the Vale of Tywi. This castle was held in the 13th century by a Welsh family, sworn enemies of Dinefwr. To the

LOW: National tanic Garden Wales.

south, spectacularly sited **Carreg Cennen Castle**, perched on a rocky outcrop near the isolated hamlet of Trapp, is a "must-see" *(see page 118 of the Brecon Beacons chapter for details).*

From Llandeilo the B4302 heads north to **Talley** ❺, an ancient religious site in a peaceful lakeside setting. Here are the evocative ruins of 12th-century **Talley Abbey**, founded by Lord Rhys for the Premonstratensians who were dedicated to "Devotion, Learning, Service". Close by, **St Michael's Church**, which dates from 1773, still retains its original box pews. In the lanes south of the village, at the pretty hamlet of **Cwmdu**, the National Trust has renovated a long range of disused buildings to create a working village shop, post office and inn – all fitted out in early 1900s style.

West of Talley is the huge swathe of **Brechfa Forest**, one of the largest conifer plantations in Wales. At its southern fringes the remote little village of **Brechfa** ❻, on the River Cothi, is a good centre for salmon and sewin (sea-trout) fishing or for exploring waymarked forest trails.

Amid wooded hillsides higher in the Cothi Valley, the sleepy village of **Pumsaint** (on the A482 between Lampeter and Llandovery) seems an unlikely place to have been of any interest to the Romans. Gold was the draw. Pumsaint is the only place in Britain where the Romans are definitely known to have mined gold.

The precious metal was extracted here between AD 75 and 140, producing Welsh gold for the imperial mint at Lyon. After the Romans left, the mines were abandoned. There was a brief revival of activity in the late 19th century, but mining proved uneconomic and the mines finally closed in 1938.

At the National Trust's **Dolaucothi Gold Mines** ❼ visitors can see the extensive remains by following the self-guided Miner's Way and by taking a fascinating underground tour of the 1930s workings. The National Trust Centre, in a converted coach house, houses a **Kite**

BELOW: Car Cennen Cas

Map
n page
174

Country Information Point and displays on the history and wildlife of the Dolaucothi estate.

Near the entrance to the mines is a large stone with five indentations which gives Pumsaint (meaning Five Saints) its name. It is said that five saints used the stone as a pillow during a storm, leaving behind the impressions of their heads.

Llandovery

George Borrow, in his 19th-century book *Wild Wales*, described the market town of **Llandovery** ❽ as "the pleasantest little town in which I have halted in the course of my wanderings". Not a lot has changed. Llandovery, with its cobbled market square, clock tower and Georgian facades, is still a pleasant little town with an interesting history. The Romans had a fort here on a site now occupied by the 12th-century church of Llanfair-ar-y-bryn (St Mary's on the hill). Roman masonry was incorporated into the church walls.

Little remains of the medieval castle which passed repeatedly between Welsh and English hands. It was captured in 1403 by Owain Glyndŵr as a reprisal for the hanging, drawing and quartering of one of his aides by Henry IV in the Market Square.

Llandovery lay at the junction of many drovers' routes. Every year 30,000 cattle were driven from Wales to London's Smithfield and Barnet Fair and by 1822 the town had 47 inns to cater for the trade. David Jones, a local farmer's son, set up a thriving bank for the drovers in 1799. Called the Bank of the Black Ox, it was located in what is now the King's Head and was incorporated into Lloyds Bank in 1909.

The town was also an important staging post on the "Great Road" to London. Both the droving and coaching trade were decimated by the arrival of the railway in 1868. Today's travellers can still use the scenic **Heart of Wales** line which crosses the spectacular Cynghordy Viaduct and links the town with Swansea and Shrewsbury.

Llandovery Heritage Centre, located above the Tourist Information Centre in a tastefully restored Georgian building, celebrates the history and legends of the area. It has excellent displays on the 12th-century herbal healers, the Physicians of Myddfai, and on Twm Sion Cati, the Welsh Robin Hood. Under the clock tower is the **Dinefwr Crafts Centre**, an attractive collection of craft studios under one roof.

The road north of Llandovery passes through the idyllic countryside of the upper Tywi Valley as it climbs up to the vast reservoir of Llyn Brianne. The peaceful village of **Rhandirmwyn** ❾ (land of minerals) was not always so. In the 19th century it was the site of one of Europe's largest lead mines.

Beyond Rhandirmwyn is the Royal Society for the Protection of Birds' **Dinas Nature Reserve**. A beautiful waymarked path winds alongside the tumbling river around a wooded conical hill. It was here in the 16th century that Twm Sion Cati hid from the Sheriff of Carmarthen. His supposed hiding place is a very damp cave near the top of the hill that is so difficult to find it is no wonder he evaded capture. At the roadside by the reserve is the little

HT:
enacting a
nous battle
r cattle
vers' gold
Llandovery.

12th-century church of **Ystrad-ffin** which was a stopping off point for Cistercian monks walking the mountain track to their abbey at Strata Florida.

This part of the world was totally remote and only accessible by foot or on horseback until as recently as the 1970s when the construction of **Llyn Brianne** took place and a tarmac road was built. Large sections of the monk's trail now lie beneath the waters of this huge reservoir, which serves the city of Swansea.

Although it has submerged a beautiful landscape it is nonetheless an impressive sight. A high, rock-filled dam holds back the waters of the Tywi and Camddwr, which spread like tentacles into the folds of the hills. The road around the eastern shore of the dam (which links up with the vertiginous Abergwesyn Pass across the remote "roof of Wales") is spectacular.

Llanelli

For a complete change of scene and a breath of sea air follow the A476 down from the green spaces of Llandeilo to the friendly rugby-playing town of **Llanelli**. The town grew up around its tinplate works and the "Sospan Fach" (Little Saucepan) of its famous rugby anthem remains a symbol of the industry which sustained the town's growth. Its rugby team, the famous "Scarlets", play at Stradey Park, west of the town, where even the rugby posts are decorated with saucepans.

The town has a modern pedestrianised shopping centre, a lively indoor market, an ornate Victorian Town Hall and some pleasant parklands. On a hill above the town centre is **Parc Howard**, the former home of Llanelli's first Mayor, Sir Stafford Howard. The Mansion House situated amid lawns and rose gardens houses a museum with an extensive collection of rare Llanelli pottery. Just north of the town **Cwm Lleidi Country Park** ❿, dubbed locally as "Swiss Valley", has lakes, fishing and woodland walks.

Llanelli sits facing the Gower Peninsula across the Loughor Estuary and since 1996 a huge £27.5-million project has been underway to transform the town's 14-mile (22-km) coastline into the **Millennium Coastal Park**. Pockets of industrial coastal dereliction are being swept away and the park – with its footpaths, cycleways and leisure facilities – stretches westwards from Loughor Bridge to Pembrey.

At its eastern end the park overlooks an area of fenland, sand and saltmarsh. Here at Penclacwydd is the excellent **Wildfowl and Wetlands Centre** ⓫. Its acres of ponds, lakes and reedbeds attract thousands of the world's most spectacular ducks, swans and geese, which can be viewed from walkways and secluded hides.

From the estuary, the park sweeps around the town of Llanelli, through the former docklands, travelling westwards hugging the coastline and providing panoramic views of tidal waters, sandbanks and the Gower Peninsula. It continues through woodland and open countryside to the popular little harbour at **Burry Port**. This town was put on the aviation map in 1928, when Amelia Earhart, after a 21-hour flight, landed her plane *Friendship* here in the mistaken belief that

LEFT: Kidwelly Cas

Map on page 174

she had arrived in Ireland. An exhibition at the harbour marks the occasion.

Pembrey Country Park

The final stretch of the Millennium Park links up with the established attraction of **Pembrey Country Park** ⓬. This area was once the site of a Royal Ordnance Factory which produced munitions for Allied forces in World War II and employed 3,000 people. A major land reclamation project took place after its closure and by 1984 the area had been transformed into a 500-acre (200-hectare) spread of woods and parkland with a wide range of amenities – these include nature trails, cycle paths, dry ski slope, toboggan run and miniature railway, to mention just a few.

The focal point of the park is the beautiful long stretch of sand at dune-edged **Cefn Sidan** beach. On the edge of the park a disused airfield has been developed into the **Welsh Motor Sports Centre**, Wales's premier venue for a comprehensive range of two- and four-wheeled competitive events. The circuit is also used by international Formula One teams for test and development work.

Standing guard over **Carmarthen Bay** on the three-pronged estuary of the Gwendraeth, Tywi and Taf rivers are the imposing castles of Kidwelly, Llansteffan and Laugharne.

Kidwelly ⓭ has packed its businesses, housing and ancient church on the southern bank of the **Gwendraeth Fach** river. This keeps the northern side clear, across the 14th-century bridge, for its showpiece medieval cobbled alleyways and remarkably complete 12th-century castle. It looks just as a medieval castle should and is much in demand by film-makers trying to recreate the period. In the 19th century, Kidwelly was a major tinplate manufacturing centre and in the old works on the outskirts of town the **Kidwelly Industrial Museum** preserves the machinery which produced the tinplate. The large site also has a coal museum with exhibits from now-defunct local collieries.

Llansteffan is a picturesque, uncommercialised coastal village which lies below its imposing Norman castle. The estuary was not always so peaceful – it was once busy with sail-powered coal boats travelling back and forth to Kidwelly. The 12th-century castle, built on the site of an Iron-Age promontory fort, has a strategically commanding position which provides panoramic views across Carmarthen Bay right down to the western tip of the Gower Peninsula.

Laugharne

Dylan Thomas's "heron-priested shore" at **Laugharne** ⓮ (pronounced *Larne*), overlooking the Taf Estuary, is a real joy. Georgian houses clatter down the hillside to the shore where the ivy-clad 13th-century castle guards the estuary's mud flats (the subject of a stormy Turner painting). This tranquil town provided Dylan Thomas with inspiration for the wonderful creation of Llareggub (spell it backwards) in *Under Milk Wood,* his famous "play for voices".

The Boathouse, where he lived for the last four years of his life, is open seven days a week throughout the year and con-

HT: Dylan ...mas's ...athouse ...Laugharne.

tains original furnishings, memorabilia, audio-visual presentations, themed bookshop and tearoom. The sea views from both the Boathouse and the nearby shed where he worked are certainly inspiring.

Brown's Hotel, one of Dylan Thomas's favourite watering-holes, doesn't capitalise cheaply on its most famous bar prop. There are a few faded photographs of the poet on the wall alongside rugby heroes, but it's an unsentimental place with atmosphere and lively conversation.

Both Thomas and his wife Caitlin are buried unostentatiously in St Martin's churchyard. Within the church itself there's a plaque, a replica of the one located in Poet's Corner at Westminster Abbey.

The less celebrated but equally accomplished poet Edward Thomas also resided in Laugharne and Richard Hughes, author of *A High Wind in Jamaica* wrote his novel *In Hazard* here. Clearly there must be something in the air that makes the imagination dance. In times gone by it was believed that fairies travelled to Laugharne from their offshore enchanted islands to shop in the market, returning home via secret subterranean passageways.

Map on pag 174

Landspeed record

The A4066 from Laugharne leads down to the vast sweep of **Pendine Sands** ⓯, a wide, flat, 6-mile (9-km) beach that extends eastwards from the resort off into the distance. It was here in the 1920s that the dangerous battle over the land speed record took place. In 1927 Sir Malcolm Campbell in *Bluebird* set a new world record of 174.88mph (279.8 kph). His rival, J. G. Parry Thomas, died challenging this record.

The wreckage of his car *Babs* was dug out of the dunes in 1971 and completely restored by motoring enthusiast and engineer Owen Wyn Owen. *Babs* now spends every summer on display in the **Museum of Speed** at Pendine where the "Sands of Speed" story is told. The museum also pays tribute to Amy Johnson who took off from here on her non-stop transatlantic flight attempt of 1933. ❑

BELOW: the room where Dyla Thomas wr

Dylan Thomas

Dylan Thomas, whose exhortation to his dying father to "Rage, rage against the dying of the light" is one of modern poetry's most defiant lines, didn't follow that advice himself. On 5 November 1953 he slipped into a final coma in a New York hotel room, after a heavy drinking bout. He was 39.

Thomas spent the first 20 years of his life in Swansea, the son of an English teacher with a love of words. He left school at 16 and had only one full-time period of employment (the 15 months he served as a junior on the *South Wales Daily Post*). He decided to be a poet almost before he was out of short trousers, dubbing himself "The Rimbaud of Cwmdonkin Drive".

His evocation of the passions and mysteries of childhood in his first three volumes of poetry were rooted in notebooks he kept between the ages of 16 and 20. Happy childhood memories of holidays spent around Carmarthen Bay, recaptured in *Fern Hill* and the short story *The Peaches*, led him back to Laugharne in the spring of 1938, though he was not to settle here until 1949. The Boathouse (bought for him by the first wife of the historian A.J.P. Taylor) appears to have been hewn out of the rock face and shares the same spectacular views across the bay as his workplace, "the Shed", just up the hill. The Boathouse is now a museum dedicated to his memory.

At the Boathouse, Thomas lived with his wife Caitlin and their three children. In the Prologue to his *Collected Poems* he describes "the scummed starfish sands... the breakneck of rocks, tangled with froth, flute, fin and quill" and "shells that speak seven seas." Although he spent much time getting drunk in the pubs and clubs of London, he could write only in Wales. It was here that he found fresh inspiration and his instinctive and elemental themes reached their final fruition.

His final work, *Under Milk Wood*, was also written at Laugharne. It was in his own words, an attempt "to write a sort of Welsh *Ulysses* where all the action takes place in 24 hours" and it revealed his sure eye for suburban pretensions. The real setting for the radio play may have been Laugharne but the fictional setting, Llareggub, when read backwards, displays Thomas's healthy irreverence for both the BBC (they changed the spelling) and propriety in general. However, it was the 1954 BBC recording with fellow Welshman Richard Burton that won the work instant acclaim.

Some accuse Thomas, in Nietzsche's words, of "muddying the water to appear deep"; others hail him as the greatest 20th-century British poet on the strength of a total oeuvre of little more than 100 poems. His paean to South Wales and his lyricism continued the long Welsh tradition for oratory and music. His own sonorous readings have been the single most telling factor in the growth of live and recorded poetry readings. His short life served as a blueprint for the modern rebel without a cause who feels it "better to burn out than to rust".

Dylan Thomas's body was flown back from New York and buried in Laugharne. In 1982 a memorial to him was placed in Poets' Corner in London's Westminster Abbey. Caitlin died in 1994, having lived for many years in Sicily. ❑

HT: poetic uvenirs.

Map on page 174

PEMBROKESHIRE

The main attraction is one of Britain's finest coastlines, now a national park. Urban areas include Fishguard, Haverfordwest, Pembroke, the tiny city of St Davids, and the popular resort of Tenby

According to *The Mabinogion*, the book of Welsh folklore, southwest Wales was *Gwlad hud a lledrith*, "The Land of Mystery and Magic". The siren-like quality of the Pembrokeshire coastline – especially the peaceful but savage rock-bound shoreline between St David's and Fishguard – still seems to cast a powerful spell. Tales of lost kingdoms gain credence when ancient submerged forests at Amroth, Manorbier and Newgale reveal themselves as the tide peels back. Romans, Vikings and Normans who came to tame the region have only added to its deep mystery, leaving behind them their castles, forts, people and placenames.

Historic coastline

Alongside the romance is the beauty of one of Britain's finest coastlines. The **Pembrokeshire Coast National Park** ⓰ is the only designated park in Britain that is predominantly coastal. In southwest Wales, bordered on three sides by the ocean, seafaring was a way of life long before tourists took to paddle boats. The Irish Sea was the major highway westwards both for copper and culture, with saints and pilgrims making their way to and from Ireland on the frailest of craft.

The farmers who have tilled the land for thousands of years were equally dependent on the sea, always eager to supplement their income with a little fishing, smuggling, wrecking – or even piracy. Nowadays economic necessity has led them to turn outhouses into self-catering units and to nailing "Bed & Breakfast" signs to their farmhouse doors.

"Little England"

The castles at Kidwelly, Llansteffan and Laugharne mentioned in the Carmarthenshire chapter are just three of the Norman strongholds dating from the 12th century that run in a line across the county through Llawhaden and Haverfordwest to Roch on the west coast. The **Landsker line**, as it is known, protected the Norman south from the native Celts in the north.

The division is clearly linguistic and cultural as well as military. Although people may no longer be ostracised for marrying across the divide, the villages to the north are more scattered, the small bell-coted churches showing their Celtic origins, and the Welsh language still in common use; to the south the villages gather tightly round the larger churches and the English language reigns (earning the region the sobriquet of "Little England Beyond Wales").

To the north of the Landsker are the **Preseli Hills**, the only large tract of hilly

T: the ...ge church ...osherston, ...nbrokeshire. **HT:** ... coast ...orthgain.

upland in Pembrokeshire; pretty rather than dramatic, having neither the austerity of the Beacons nor the grandeur of Snowdonia. Yet these gently sweeping hills are steeped in the mystery that gives meat to the bones of *The Mabinogion*'s folklore. Stone circles, burial chambers and standing stones are scattered over these hills and from here, around 2000–1500 BC, huge "blue stones" were somehow transported to Stonehenge, 200 miles (320 km) away, where they form the inner circle. Theories abound as to how these stones, weighing up to 4 tons, were moved. The most plausible suggests a combination of tree-trunk rollers and rafts.

The Long Barrow burial chamber at **Pentre Ifan** ⓱ is said to be the finest neolithic *cromlech* in Britain, dating back 4,500 years. Like some monstrous, double-trunked toadstool, the *cromlech* dwarfs everything round it. The vast capstone (16½ ft/5 metres long) rests on its tripodal perch 7½ft (2.3 metres) above the ground. This feat of engineering genius and sheer strength, together with its seemingly sculpted beauty, is awesome. The site offers uninterrupted views to Newport Bay.

Two miles (3 km) southeast of Nevern, at **Castell Henllys**, an Iron-Age hillfort is being reconstructed on its original foundations. In the thatched and wattled roundhouses, visitors can learn about the lives of the Celts who inhabited this site more than 2,000 years ago.

Nevern

North of the Preselis, across the A487 main road from Fishguard to Cardigan, lies the elysian churchyard at **Nevern** ⓲. Skirting the horseman's mounting block in the lane outside St Brynach's, you enter a short shaded avenue of yew trees. One tree has become fabled as "the bleeding yew" because it produces a thick red sap. Beside the church is the 5th-century **Vitalianus Stone** which is thought to commemorate a Celtic soldier of the Roman legion. The inscriptions are in both Latin and Ogham (as are the inscriptions on the

BELOW: artists at wo in Nevern churchyard.

Map n page 174

Maglocunus Stone inside the church).

Nearby is the 13-ft (4-metre) 10th-century Celtic **Great Cross**, perhaps the finest in Wales. The Pilgrims' Path to St David's skirts the church and leads across a clapper bridge over a stream. A short way up the hill, pilgrims have cut a cross into the rock face and below it there is a recess with another small one incised.

A little further on, pilgrims' footprints have worn 9 inches (23cm) into the rock. Crosses appear in the heels of the steps where successive pilgrims made the sign. Overlooking the valley is a 12th-century motte-and-bailey castle.

Newport ⓳, just a few miles to the west along the A487, is a holiday spot popular for its beaches, sailing and sea-fishing. The pubs, cottages offering B&B, book and gift shops are overlooked by a medieval castle and, on the mountain above, the Carningli Iron-Age fort. The Boat Club is based on Parrog Beach. The fascinating Eco Centre in Lower St Mary Street has the smallest solar power station in the UK, a solar bicycle and displays and information on sustainable living.

Cwm Gwaun, separating the Preselis from Fishguard, is a deeply wooded valley gouged out by meltwater surging under the Irish Sea glacier 15,000 years ago. It is a lush place, full of ancient woods and wildlife and has a remote and timeless quality. The locals keep to the pre-1752 Julian calendar (introduced by Julius Caesar in 46 BC) and celebrate their New Year in the middle of January.

Fishguard

Fishguard ⓴ is the main shopping town of north Pembrokeshire, with a busy Thursday market in the Town Hall selling local butters, bacon and laverbread (made from seaweed). It is a Stena ferry port with regular crossings to Rosslare in Ireland. Outside the Royal Oak in the town's main square is a stone commemorating the signing of the peace treaty at the end of the last invasion of Britain in 1797. Inside is a copy of the treaty itself. A few

LOW:
the beach.

doors down is the 19th-century parish church of St Mary's (built on a medieval church) where there is a gravestone to the great heroine Jemima Nicholas, who, if legend keeps on growing, will soon be hailed as having put down this shambolic invasion single-handedly. The true story is slightly less glorious.

Understandably, the invading French troops, consisting almost totally of convicts, felt no inclination whatsoever to fight the Welsh and instead spent the few hours of freedom they had getting drunk. Jemima, meanwhile, rallied an army of women dressed in the local costume of tall pillar-box black hats and red flannel coats and marched round the headland. The drunken French, convinced the mighty militia were upon them, surrendered without a peep. Jemima managed to round up 14 recidivists single-handedly with a pitchfork.

Two hundred years later the women of Fishguard once more joined together. This time, to celebrate the bicentennial of the doomed invasion, they created a 100-ft long (30-metre) tapestry, similar in format to the Bayeux Tapestry. The piece, which took over 40,000 hours of intricate stitching in 178 different colours of wool, is on display in St Mary's Church Hall.

Lower Town, the older, more picturesque part, was a flourishing port in the past. It's photogenic, with a row of gabled cottages clustered around the old quayside where the River Gwaun meets the sea. It has been the setting for a number of films, the most celebrated of which was *Under Milk Wood* starring Richard Burton and Elizabeth Taylor. Fishguard's main harbour, across the bay from the Lower Town, opened in 1906, but World War I and the lack of an industrial hinterland killed off the dream of making Fishguard a great transatlantic port to rival Liverpool.

Coastal splendour

The **Pembrokeshire Coast National Park** was created in 1952. It extends from St Dogmael's near Cardigan in the north to Amroth in the south, 180 miles (290 km)

LEFT: Fishguard, which once had ambitio to be a trans atlantic port. **BELOW:** a pu in Fishguard

Map on page 174

of truly spectacular coastal scenery. The only inland tracts in the park take in the Preselis and Cwm Gwaun.

Although each of the coastal stretches has charm, the finest section starts at Fishguard, continues round the lighthouse at **Strumble Head** ㉑ (one of Britain's finest sites for studying migrating birds and the nearest point to Ireland) and runs south around St David's Head and Ramsey Head to **Caerfai Bay**.

The coast road runs only a short distance inland with easy access to the hamlets and bays. The views over this rugged, untamed stretch from the youth hostel above **Pwllderi** and the lay-by a little before it are quite breathtaking. Waves break over a thick gorse-covered humpbacked promontory that juts out into the ocean hundreds of feet below.

Aber Mawr (the Great Bay) once dreamed of becoming a great transatlantic port. But hubris struck, the dream died, and Aber Mawr remains quite unspoilt with no facilities whatsoever.

Abercastle, once a coal, grain and limestone trading port, still has a lime kiln on view, and up on the hill at Longhouse is **Carreg Samson**, another dramatic *cromlech*. **Porthgain** has a long narrow harbour overlooked by the hoppers of an abandoned stone-crushing plant. The "Scots Houses" (cottages where Scottish workers lived) have been converted into homes and the Alun Davies Art Gallery.

On the opposite side of the bay is the 18th-century **Sloop Inn**, a marvellously infectious good-time pub with a fine collection of photographs charting maritime and mining history. After the "Blue Lagoon" at **Abereiddy** (a flooded quarry) you get back to the wildness again at **St David's Head** ㉒, the location of another *cromlech* and the fortified cliff site of Warrior's Dyke.

A less than gruelling detour will take you to the top of **Carn Llidi**, from which, on a clear day, you can see the peaks of Snowdonia and right across the Irish Sea to the Wicklow Mountains. **Whitesands**

LOW: umble Head hthouse, a -saving acon.

is the coast's most popular bucket-and-spade beach and is a surfer's paradise.

From the lifeboat station near **St Justinian's** medieval chapel, you can catch boats to **Ramsey Island** 23 to see the huge seal population. The ruins of the chapel stand on the hill. It was here that St David's sidekick walked across a fabled bridge to Ramsey, cutting it behind him with an axe as he went and thus creating the infamous wrecking rocks, "The Bitches", through which the waters bubble like some witch's cauldron. His followers, tiring of his model asceticism, chopped off his head. The saint, undaunted, picked it up and walked back to the mainland.

The coastal path continues round **Ramsey Sound** where more seals and pups can be spotted. Offshore are the islands of **Skomer** (a National Nature Reserve), **Skokholm** (Britain's first bird observatory) and **Grassholm** (one of Britain's few gannetries). Boat trips to all three islands depart from **Martin's Haven** further south along St Bride's Bay.

St David's

If it weren't for its cathedral, the most important ecclesiastical centre in South Wales, **St David's** 24 would be just a pretty village instead of Britain's smallest city. A cluster of shops and restaurants surround the main square; there are a couple of hotels, a few pubs, a few chapels (backs turned resolutely to the cathedral), and that's about it.

Apart from the **cathedral**, that is. St David founded a monastery here in the wooded Alun Valley in the 6th century. The saint is reputed to have been born during a fierce storm in the fields above St Non's Bay around AD 520. The site is marked by the ruins of an ancient chapel close to a holy well. A more recent tiny chapel on the headland is also dedicated to his mother, St Non. A vegetarian and teetotaller, David was clearly too good to be true as far as the wife of the local Irish chieftain, Boia, was concerned. Deciding to test the ascetic with a few pagan pleasures, she sent naked young girls to frolic

BELOW: St David's, a grand tribute to an austere saint.

Map on page 174

in the nearby river and throw a few lewd suggestions across to the monks. Legend has it all succumbed but David.

It is believed that Patrick, patron saint of Ireland, was born close to where the cathedral stands. The monastic site became a major centre of pilgrimage for kings and common people alike. Two pilgrimages here were worth one to Rome and three were worth one to Jerusalem.

The striking grandeur of the purple-grey stone cathedral is an ironic commemoration to the austere monasticism favoured by the saint himself. Inside the clarity and limpidity of light adds even greater majesty to the sublime interior. The floor rises sharply (some say deliberately to get the congregation nearer heaven) and the arcade piers splay outwards to the heavens to meet an intricately carved grey Irish oak 15th-century ceiling, surely the cathedral's greatest glory.

Inside Bishop Vaughan's chapel rest the remains of St David and St Justinian; these were discovered during 19th-century restoration, bricked for safe keeping behind a wall. At the far end of the cathedral is the mausoleum of a local notary who used to spend her afternoons knitting, dog at her feet (it's still curled up there now in marble), keeping an eye on the artisans carving her vault. Occasionally she would raise herself and try it out for size at various stages in construction.

Next to the cathedral are the equally impressive ruins of Bishop Gower's **palace** built in 1340. In the 16th century Bishop Barlow had the lead from the roof slowly stripped away as dowries for his five daughters – who, strangely enough, all married bishops. The grounds are often used for Shakespearean or historical productions over the summer months.

Haverfordwest is 16 miles (26 km) and 17 hills away from St David's. The main A487 offers fine views across to **St Bride's Bay** where smuggling, piracy and wrecking were all popular pastimes. **Lower Solva** is the only memorable stop-off point – unless you take the narrow coastal road south, calling in at **Little Haven** and the superb sandy beach at **Marloes**, undoubtedly one of the finest in Wales. The lack of immediate car access adds greatly to its peaceful charm The sheltered waters of **Dale** are a water sports mecca (and on the headland there's the Fort Field Centre specialising in marine biology).

Five miles (8 km) east of Haverfordwest is **Picton Castle**, a country house inhabited by members of the same family since the 13th century. It is surrounded by beautiful woodland gardens.

Haverfordwest

Haverfordwest itself is a historic town of steep streets built around one of Gilbert de Clare's castles. The main western railway terminus (and once a busy port before the railways arrived), it serves as the commercial, shopping and administrative centre of Pembrokeshire. Its new shopping precinct, the Riverside Market, is an attractive waterfront development located between the old and new bridges.

The town has a ruined 12th-century castle (partly destroyed by Oliver Cromwell) which crowns a steep hill and com-

RIGHT: Solva.

mands panoramic views. Haverfordwest Town Museum is located next door at Castle House. Few traces of the Norman walled garrison remain apart from the churches (St Mary's being the finest example on offer). The ruins of the old priory are on the river beside the Bristol Trader Inn. The town is an interesting place in which to spend a few hours, exploring the riverside setting and streets lined with elegant Georgian homes.

Milford Haven ㉕, Europe's deepest waterway, fully tests Baudelaire's dictum that beauty can be true beauty only if it contains an element of ugliness. The industrial skyline can provide fabulous petro-chemical sunsets but most of the time the snaking pipes are ugly scars on an otherwise unblemished coast. Admiral Lord Nelson considered the Haven to be one of the world's finest natural harbours.

The town of Milford Haven has an interesting history. Charles Francis Greville began building this 'new model town' on a grid pattern in the late 18th century. He persuaded two great Nantucket whaling families to relocate here and for several decades these Quaker settlers helped in the town's development. The Friend's Meeting House, built in 1811, is a reminder of this unusual twinning.

From the 1950s the fishing industry declined and the oil industry took over. As a major oil port, Milford Haven is still home to the mega-tankers. However, with the demise of fishing and the closure of the Esso refinery the area suffers high unemployment. Tourism is the new hope and the docks have been brought to life again with a leisure marina, historic ships, museum, family attractions and restaurants.

Across the toll bridge is **Pembroke Dock ㉖**, a town which boomed in the 19th century when the Admiralty Dockyard was established here. Its broad streets, with some imposing Victorian houses, were constructed on a rigid "gridiron" plan. The town claims many seafaring firsts. Built here were the first Royal Yacht *(Victoria and Albert)* the first steam man-of-war (HMS *Tartar)* and the first iron-clad warship *(Warrior)*. Today Pembroke Dock is an Irish Ferries terminal for Rosslare.

Pembroke

Pembroke ㉗, more elegant and less austere than its neighbour, caters far more for the tourist market. Its long, bustling main street of Victorian and Georgian houses leads up to the imposing castle. **Pembroke Castle's** present limestone fortress, with its 16-ft (5-metre) thick walls, was built by the Normans between 1190 and 1245 on an older site and, like Tenby Castle, has the dubious distinction of having been attacked by both sides during the Civil War.

Bounded on three sides by a tidal inlet of the Milford Haven Waterway, it is deservedly the most famous castle in southwest Wales and was the birthplace of Harry Tudor (Henry VII), founder of the mighty Tudor dynasty. Opposite the castle is the quirky **Museum of the Home** with its fascinating collection of 3,000 household bygones. A few miles from Pembroke you can visit the medieval world of walled gardens, orchards and fishponds at **Bishop's Palace, Lamphey**.

LEFT: St Govan's Cha[illegible] Pembroke.

Map
n page
174

East of the Cleddau toll bridge, away from the industrialisation and supertankers of Milford Haven, is the **Daugleddau**, a tidal estuary formed by the meeting of the Western and Eastern Cleddau rivers. Known as the "inner sanctuary" of the national park, it is an area of tranquil beauty – a birdwatcher's and sailor's paradise – totally unspoilt by tourist development. This self-contained, secret corner of Pembrokeshire is quite unlike any other part of the park. Walkers can follow the Landsker Borderland trail along the river banks; cruises operate out of Neyland and Hobb's Point through the oak-forested creeks. Life was not always so peaceful: in the 19th century there were coal mines, limestone quarries and boat-building yards here and the estuary was busy with coal barges and working vessels.

Overlooking a tidal creek in the lower Daugleddau just 5 miles (8 km) from Pembroke Castle is **Carew Castle** and corn mill. Over the centuries this stronghold has been transformed from Norman fortress to Elizabethan mansion. The impressive remains also house one of the three finest early Celtic crosses in Wales (the others are at Nevern and Maen Achwyfan in northeast Wales).

Spectacular cliffs

At the opposite end of the Milford Haven Waterway is **Angle Bay** and the peerless wild waters of **Freshwater West**. Continuing along the Pembrokeshire coast eastwards, the next stretch contains some of the most spectacular cliff scenery in Wales, especially around **Stack Rocks, St Govan's Head and Stackpole Head**. Nestling amongst this towering cliff scenery, battered by crashing waves, are the calm waters of **Bosherston Lakes**, man-made lakes which are covered in waterlilies in June. This stretch of coast also contains two beautiful sandy beaches at **Broad Haven** (not to be confused with the small resort of the same name on St Bride's Bay) and **Barafundle**.

A short hop from here is **Manorbier's**

LOW:
nbroke
stle, the
a's most
nous
tress.

Norman Castle – a particularly well preserved specimen – where Giraldus Cambrensis (Gerald of Wales) was born in 1145. Said to be Britain's first travel writer, he toured through Wales in 1188 with the Archbishop of Canterbury and kept detailed notes of his travels as he tried to drum up support for a third holy crusade. Eloquent and perceptive, he saved his finest passage for his birthplace: "Heaven's breath smells so wooingly... In all the broad lands of Wales, Manorbier is the most pleasant place by far."

Tenby

Tenby ㉘ is the major resort along Pembrokeshire's golden south coast and has been for the past 200 years. Though it's prosperous now, you could have bought the whole town and hinterland in 1348 for the princely sum of £38 8s 2d (£38.41 in today's decimal currency). Its name is most readily associated with Pembrokeshire's own species of daffodil, renowned for its early flowering and its vibrancy of colour. The Tenby daffodil came close to extinction in just three mad years in the 1880s when half a million bulbs were dug up for export to London's flower stalls.

The idyllic **Harbour Beach**, like a child's bath full of brightly coloured bobbing craft, is overlooked by the hilltop castle ruins and elegant pastel-shaded Georgian town houses. There are three more beaches, one of which, **South Beach** – banked with dunes and woodland and 1½ miles (2.4 km) long – is quite superb. The esplanade high on the limestone cliff is graced with a succession of four-storeyed hotels and offers views along the beach to Giltar Point as well as to the islands of **Caldey**, **St Catherine's** and **St Margaret's**.

From the harbour you can take a boat trip to Caldy. The island is owned by an order of monks who make perfume to supplement their income *(see below)*.

Tenby is justified in calling itself a historic resort because, apart from its seaside holiday facilities, the town's 13th-century medieval walls are mostly still intact,

LEFT: bakin bread on Caldey Islar

THE MONKS OF CALDEY

Virtually closed to the world, yet barely 3 miles (5 kn from one of Wales's most popular resorts, a commun ty of monks pursues the timeless rigours of religious li in a Cistercian monastery on Caldey Island. Their da begins at 3.15am, when they rise for the first of seve services which punctuate a day ending at 7.30pn Novices are allowed to communicate during daytim hours, but the routine forbids "unnecessary" conversatic and periods of silence lasting 12 hours form part of th probationers' training.

A largely self-supporting community, the dozen or s monks – the numbers vary – work the land and gath raw materials for a unique industry they established 1953: the manufacture of perfume from the gorse ar lavender which carpet the tiny island. Caldey perfume the worldly means by which an unworldly communi keeps afloat, and is on sale in Tenby.

Like many of the islands off the west coast of Britai Caldey has long been inhabited by monks. The first them is said to have been a hermit called Pyro who live a solitary life in a simple cell 1,300 years ago. The islar can be visited during the summer when small boats car tourists across from Tenby.

Map n page 174

although only one of its five gates remains. The walls encircle narrow labyrinthine lanes which make it easy to visualise medieval times. **Frog Street** is the most famous of these with its indoor market, adjoining cobbled mews, small pottery shops, tea rooms and crafts.

The mullioned windows of the gabled 15th-century **Tudor Merchant's House** project into the narrowest of alleys at Quay Hill. Housed next to the remains of medieval **Tenby Castle** on the breezy headland is **Tenby Museum and Art Gallery**. The museum has local exhibits dating back 12,000 years and the art gallery's permanent collection includes works by Augustus John and his less famous, but some say more talented, sister Gwen John. Born in Tenby in 1878, Augustus John declared, perhaps a little parochially, of his home town, "You may travel the world over, but you will find nothing more beautiful: it is so restful, so colourful and so unspoilt."

St Mary's is one of Wales's largest parish churches. On the secular side, the **De Valence Pavilion** in Upper Frog Street provides a variety of entertainments from theatre to wrestling.

Sandy beaches

A few miles to the north is **Saundersfoot** ㉙, a small family resort. Although there is a rather unkempt tourist strip, it does not spoil the beauty of the town's setting. The resort's large, sandy beach and harbour – a popular sailing and water sports centre – lie beneath a wooded headland. In the 19th century, in its pre-tourist days, Saundersfoot was a port exporting coal from the mines of south Pembrokeshire. A little further around Carmarthen Bay is **Wiseman's Bridge** where, on the small, steep beach in 1944, Sir Winston Churchill watched a rehearsal of the D-Day landings.

The national park ends (or begins, depending on your perspective) at **Amroth**, a pleasant village with a popular beach. In the hills above is the National Trust's **Colby Woodland Garden**. ❑

LOW: Tenby.

MID-WALES

This is "Wild Wales", where you can leave the tourist beat and enjoy the simple pleasures of rural life

The central heartlands are a region of small market towns and large, empty spaces. This is the undiscovered – and in tourism terms – understated part of Wales. While Snowdonia in the north and Pembrokeshire in the southwest capture the lion's share of the leisure market, Mid-Wales carries on, much as it has always done, at its own, unhurried pace. There are no major resorts here, no motorways, no big concentration of hotels and attractions.

What you get is countryside, pure and simple. Mid-Wales attracts walkers, bird-watchers and outdoors enthusiasts. It's a place for those who love solitudes and the fascinating rhythms of rural life. The big event of the week in many of Mid-Wales's country towns is market day, when farmers descend from the hills to buy and sell livestock and catch up on the local gossip.

Farmland and forestry – and, increasingly, the intrusive presence of wind farms – dominate the landscape. Although the countryside to the east tails off into the gentler, more amenable hills and vales of border country, this region is still in essence the "Wild Wales" which 19th-century author and traveller George Borrow wrote about in his classic travel book.

The region is dominated by the massive bulk of the Cambrian Mountains, the "backbone" of Wales. Their sweeping moors and plateaus have a compelling, elemental quality. It was here that endangered red kite made a comeback – to such an extent that much of central Wales now labels itself "Kite Country" in a bid to attract more visitors.

Man-made intrusions have been mostly benign. At the turn of the century the Elan Valley reservoirs were created to supply water to Birmingham. These were later followed by other new lakes – Clywedog, Brianne and the like – which for the most part have blended well into their mountain habitats.

The Cambrian Mountains are also the source of the headwaters of the River Teifi. The Teifi's course between Lampeter and the sea at Cardigan is one of the loveliest in Wales, a mix of thickly wooded riverbanks and tumbling falls. The historic town of Cardigan gives its name to Cardigan Bay, a stretch of beautiful coastline dotted with old fishing ports and trading centres, which mirrors its rural hinterland in its low-key approach to tourism. ❑

PRECEDING PAGES: a hill farm near Llandrindod Wells.
LEFT: Cenarth Falls, on the River Teifi.

Map on page 200

Cardiganshire and the Teifi Valley

Aberystwyth, a resort and university town, is the commercial centre of this region, whose roots lie in farming and fishing. The area is a popular haunt for bird-watchers

The **River Teifi** stands guard at the southern edge of this seductive territory. **Cardigan** ❶, a town with agricultural and seafaring connections, is the lowest crossing place. A crumbling castle overlooks a fine arched bridge. Huge timbers shore up the castle's outer walls which rise from a public street.

The sailing ships for which Cardigan was once famous are long gone – hounded to near-extinction more than 100 years ago by the railway; ironically, Cardigan lost its rail link after World War II, and today, despite a bypass, the motor car is supreme in the town's narrow streets. Market day – on Monday – is worth taking in. The covered Guild Hall, with its arches and clocktower, makes an imposing venue for displays of local produce – and for the itinerant traders' stalls piled with everything from jeans to digital watches.

Theatr Mwldan on Bath House Road is the venue for a varied programme of film, drama, art and music. It is also home to the Tourist Information Centre and has a good café.

Wildlife on view

By the bridge stands Geoffrey Powell's sculpture of a Teifi otter presented to the town by naturalist David Bellamy. There's a chance to see real life otters at the **Welsh Wildlife Centre** a few miles south of the town at Cilgerran. This 270-acre (109-hectare) nature reserve on the banks of the Teifi has 5 miles (8 km) of footpaths crossing woodland, marshland, reed beds and meadowland. You can survey the tree canopy from the Tree-Tops Hide, while the restaurant overlooks the second largest reed bed in Wales.

Cardigan Island, offshore, is inhabited only by a flock of wild Soay Sheep. The island is in the care of the Welsh Wildlife Trust and access is restricted. To get a good view of it and of the waters of beautiful Cardigan Bay visit **Cardigan Island Coastal Farm Park** situated on a scenic headland near Gwbert-on-Sea. Cardigan Bay is Britain's first Marine Heritage Coast and is home to the only resident population of bottlenose dolphins in English and Welsh waters along with Atlantic grey seals and porpoise. The farm park has tame domestic animals to pet and a cliff walk from which to spot the wilder variety. The path continues to delightful little **Mwnt** where an isolated, whitewashed medieval church stands on the cliffs above a sandy cove. Its unspoilt

[L]EFT: [bo]at farmer [in] Mid-Wales.
[R]IGHT: seeing [th]e sights at a [h]orse's pace.

future is secure thanks to its ownership by the National Trust.

Inland from Cardigan the A484 winds close to the banks of the Teifi. Upstream, **Cenarth** survives as a centre for coracle fishermen. The flimsy craft, looking for all the world like overgrown walnut shells split in two, are traditionally made of animal hides stretched over a wooden frame. A competent coracle maker is said to be able to construct one in less than 24 hours. Working in pairs with a net stretched between them, the coracles float down the river to catch salmon on their way upstream. Then the fishermen carry the craft on their backs to the starting point for another sweep. You can learn about this ancient craft at Cenarth's **National Coracle Centre,** set in the grounds of a 17th-century flour mill.

Farming centre

Newcastle Emlyn is a friendly market town serving a wide agricultural area. The ruined castle, built on a loop of the Teifi, is not outstandingly spectacular but has extensive river views. Markets bustle with talk of fatstock prices and forecasts of wool clip. Southeast of the town, in a cavernous woollen mill at Dre-fach Felindre, the National Museum of Wales's **Museum of the Welsh Woollen Industry** ❷ evokes the glory days of the industry in the Teifi Valley. There is an interpretive centre and working woollen mill on site.

The era of steam can be experienced at nearby Henllan on the **Teifi Valley Railway**. Trains chug for 2 miles (3km) on a narrow-gauge line through unspoilt woodland along the banks of the Teifi.

Twenty miles (32 km) further east, on the A475, **Lampeter** ❸ (pop. 2,000) unassumingly plays host to several hundred students at one of Britain's smallest seats of learning – St David's College, a constituent of the University of Wales. It was founded in 1822 for Welsh students who couldn't afford to go to Oxford or Cambridge and its fine old quadrangle is modelled on the layout of the Oxford colleges.

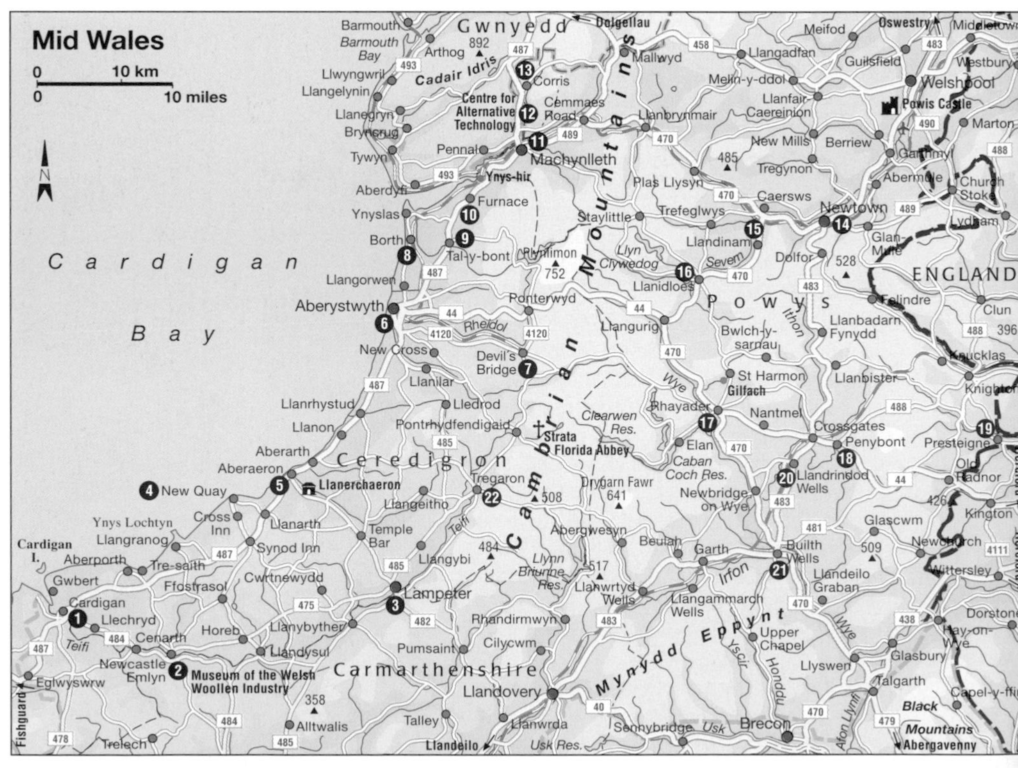

Map
page
200

Along the bay

From Cardigan the A487 leads north, sometimes swooping down to a seaside settlement, but mostly staying a couple of miles inland. An airstrip and a cluster of buildings laid out with military precision stand on a headland near the little resort of **Aberporth**. Mysterious aerials and similar impedimenta are sited on the cliff-top which is home to a rocket research establishment. Fortunately it is not visible to holidaymakers staying in the village.

Tre-saith has a small beach and is backed by a waterfall where the River Saith tumbles into the sea. At low tide you can walk around to the National Trust beach of **Traeth Penbryn**. Just along the coast, it's hard to believe that peaceful **Llangranog**, with its sandy beach, was once a centre for shipbuilding. From here there is a breathtaking cliff walk to spectacular **Ynys Lochtyn**, a National Trust-owned promontory which juts out into Cardigan Bay.

New Quay ❹, like Cardigan, once boasted important shipping connections. The last ship was built there in 1898, and now yachting holds sway. The huge curved quay is delightful – just the place for sitting in the sunshine and dreaming. A privately-run hospital for sea birds and marine creatures is one of New Quay's more recent claims to fame. Commercial fishing concentrates on skate, plaice and sole. Lobsters and scallops are also a major catch, most of them being hauled away by lorry to customers in England and the Continent.

A list of harbour dues, a venerable piece of Victoriana, tells of a time when a ton of ivory could be landed at a cost of 2s. 6d. (12½p in today's money). A cliff walk around New Quay Head leads to Bird's Rock with its teeming colonies of razorbills and guillemots.

For opportunities to view the plentiful marine life of Cardigan Bay, including the famous bottlenose dolphins, there are boat trips from the harbour.

The A487 winds north through **Llanarth**, an inland village in a steep valley.

ow:
Teifi Valley
r Cenarth.

Horse lovers home in on Llanarth Stud every October for the annual sale which attracts buyers from all over the world.

Aberaeron ❺, like some of its neighbours, was once a busy port and shipbuilding centre. The last boat was built in 1884 and the town is now a sailing and holiday centre. The town's well-ordered design is a result of it having been built almost from scratch in the early 19th century by the Reverend Alban Thomas Jones-Gwynne, who combined religion with property development. The result is a delight – a stone-walled harbour, elegant streets and squares with brightly painted Georgian houses. One of the grandest houses overlooking the harbour was the home of Sir Geraint Evans, the famous opera singer.

The harbour more than compensates for the beach which is pebbly and uninspiring. The fish on sale here is freshly caught and excellent value. Attractions on the quayside include the **Aberaeron Sea Aquarium** and the **Hive on the Quay**, which has a honey-bee exhibition and a restaurant with delicious honey ice cream on the menu. The Tourist Information Centre, located by the harbour in a pre-Georgian converted warehouse, has well-presented displays on the Cardigan Bay coastline. At the southern end of town **Clos Pengarreg** is a craft workshop complex in attractively converted stone farm buildings.

The **Vale of Aeron** runs back to Lampeter, a drive through some of the most relaxing countryside in Wales. Three miles (5km) from Aberaeron is **Llanerchaeron**, a rare survivor of a once typical 18th-century Welsh country estate now owned by the National Trust. The compact, elegant house designed by John Nash is under restoration but visitors can wander round the pleasure grounds, the unaltered Home Farm complex and the huge walled gardens. The Trust plan to bring the estate back to working life without compromising its historical significance.

Near the head of the vale, **Llangeitho**, a bastion of Welsh culture, is now a quiet

LEFT: tower [of] the Universit[y] of Wales.
BELOW: Aberystwyth['s] inviting bay.

Map
n page
200

village, but in the 18th century thousands gathered here every Sunday to listen to the sermons preached by Daniel Rowland, one of Wales's most charismatic evangelists.

Mid-Wales's "capital"

No town can better the claims of **Aberystwyth ❻** to be considered the capital of Mid-Wales. Others, inland, towards the English border, may dispute. But Aber, as it is affectionately called, wins the vote.

To describe the town as the terminus of the scenic Cambrian main line from Shrewsbury and the sea-end of the narrow-gauge Vale of Rheidol Railway, as train buffs tend to do, is to ignore its many charms. Aber is a university town, a commercial centre, a popular holiday resort and a convenient base from which to explore the haunting hinterland of sheep walks and lonely lakes. It is also the headquarters of the Welsh Language Society (Cymdeithas yr Iaith Cymraeg) founded here in 1963.

Aberystwyth University was opened in 1872 after a country-wide funding campaign. Both rich and poor contributed, with at least a 100,000 people giving less than half a crown (12½p). The original university buildings are on the seafront, while the 20th-century additions, including a magnificent arts centre, are located on Penglais Hill a mile away. There are numerous outstations of learning, notably college farms and pastures where agriculture is studied by undergraduates from many parts of the world. A College of Librarianship and the **National Library of Wales** are located on the sloping campus with views over the town and bay. The library holds a treasure trove of Welsh manuscripts including the *Black Book of Carmarthen,* the oldest existing manuscript in the Welsh language, and the earliest complete text of the great medieval folktales, *The Mabinogion.* The Reading Room houses some 5 million books, genealogical services, and huge collections of maps, photographs and personal letters. As one of Britain's few copyright

LOW:
erystwyth,
nagnet for
-trippers.

libraries it has copies of nearly every book, newspaper, map and piece of music published in the UK.

Aberystwyth's wide Victorian promenade curves between two hills. In the south Pendinas is topped by an Iron-Age hillfort and Constitution Hill stands 430ft (131 metres) high to the north. At the top of Constitution Hill is an updated version of a Victorian **Camera Obscura** which gives a unique 1,000-sq. mile (2,500-sq. km) panoramic view of sea, coast and mountains. Those with insufficient energy to walk up the hill can travel to the summit on the **Aberystwyth Cliff Railway**, "a conveyance for gentlefolk since 1896" and Britain's longest electric cliff railway.

Down in the town is **Ceredigion Museum** (Amgueddfa Ceredigion), housed in a wonderfully evocative, refurbished Edwardian theatre and music hall, better known as the Coliseum. Gracie Fields sang here and Lloyd George addressed a political meeting here in the fiercely contested election of 1921. The museum has exhibits reflecting the building's previous role and the economic and social history of the area.

Many of the gravestones in **St Michael's churchyard** recall the town's seafaring past. One memorial is to a deputy harbourmaster who fought at the Battle of Trafalgar. The **Welsh Christian Heritage Centre** is located in the church and tells the story of the Christian faith in Wales.

Vale of Rheidol Railway

The **Vale of Rheidol Railway** is steam-operated and is by far the best way of seeing the lovely valley which spears into the wooded hills above Aberystwyth. The line opened in 1902, to service the lead mines, timber and passenger traffic of the vale, linking the coast to Devil's Bridge, 12 miles (19 km) inland. It was built on a narrower gauge track than was usual, partly to save money and partly because of the difficulties of the terrain. It was the last steam railway owned by British Rail until it was privatised in 1989.

The countryside at **Devil's Bridge** 7

BELOW: wat stop on the Vale of Rhei Railway.

Map page 200

so inspired the poet Wordsworth that he composed verses praising its beauty. George Borrow, writer of the classic 19th-century travel book *Wild Wales,* thought it "one of the most remarkable locations in the world". The name is said to be derived from legend, not unknown elsewhere in Europe. An old woman's cow had strayed across the gorge; a monk appeared, and said he would build a bridge if she promised to give him the first living creature to cross it. She gave her word, the bridge was built, and the monk beckoned her to cross. But she spotted his cloven hoof, called her dog, and threw a crust across. The dog followed, and she told the devil he could keep it.

To confuse the tourist there are actually three bridges here, one above the other, spanning the 300-ft (90-metre) deep chasm of the River Mynach. There's the iron road bridge of 1901, the 1753 stone bridge and the original Pont-y-gwr-Drwg (The Bridge of the Evil Man) which is linked with the legend. From the viewing platform below the three bridges you can see the "Devil's Punchbowl" where the river has gouged out strange shapes in the rocks before spilling over spectacular falls. One hundred steps, known as "Jacob's Ladder", drop down into the gorge where you get the best view of the waterfalls.

Another legend – some say an absolute truth – concerns the people of **Cardiganshire** (known as Cardis) and their reputed financial caution. They are said to have deep pockets and short arms; in other words, they're held to be mean. Joked about by their compatriots, Cardis are sometimes unnervingly hospitable and only occasionally reluctant to come forward when it's their turn to buy the drinks. But legends die hard.

Nature reserves

Five miles (8 km) north of Aberystwyth is the strung-out holiday village of **Borth** ❽, consisting of one long rather windswept street facing the sea, with 3 miles (5 km) of unbroken sand. Behind the resort is the impressive raised expanse of marshy peat bogland known as Cors Fochno (Borth Bog). Now a protected area, it is home to many rare plants and a refuge for birds and wildlife. Built on the rocky outcrops rising from the bog are the Church of St Matthew and the hamlet of Llancynfelin.

A little further north is **Ynyslas** which lies at the southern lip of the Dyfi Estuary. This low-lying area of sandy foreshore and delicate sand dunes is a naturalist's paradise. It is an excellent place for bird-watching and many species of orchids grow in the damp hollows among the dunes. Information on this 3,867-acre (1,564-hectare) Dyfi National Nature Reserve can be found at Ynyslas Visitor Centre. In the days when the Dyfi Estuary was shallower, drovers, en route to English markets, would herd their animals across the river to Ynyslas at low tide. For protection on the long trek, cattle were fitted with iron shoes and geese had their feet covered with tar and feathers.

Tal-y-bont ❾ (incidentally, there are many Tal-y-bonts in Wales: the name means "end of the bridge"), a straggling

...HT: ...king near ...-y-Bont.

village back on the A487, has rival chapels and rival pubs. One chapel is Gothic in design, the other Classical. The pubs' differences are starker – one's the Black Lion, the other the White Lion – and they stand cheek-by-jowl overlooking the village green. Tal-y bont is also home to Y Lolfa, a thriving Welsh language press.

A side road from Tal-y-bont climbs into the mountains at **Cwm Ceulan**, where the gaunt ruins of lead mines, long since worked out, testify to Mid-Wales's forgotten industrial muscle. If you venture for a closer look, beware of the old shafts.

A gigantic water wheel stands by the bridge at **Furnace** ⑩, an elongated village. In the 17th century it – or rather its predecessor – powered machinery which was used to refine silver; later, in the mid-18th century, a blast furnace produced iron from ore shipped from northwest England. The present wheel dates from a later period when the building was used as a sawmill. Visitors can enter the large stone building and gaze down into the heart of the furnace.

The River Einion, which powered the furnace, flows through a picturesque wooded vale which is known as **Artist's Valley** because of its popularity with Victorian landscape painters. A narrow, dead-end road climbs alongside the river into the wooded foothills of the Plynlimon mountains.

On the opposite side of the road to the furnace is the entrance to **Ynys Hir**, a Royal Society for the Protection of Birds reserve. This 900-acre (360-hectare) site has a wide variety of habitats. Along the estuary shore, red kites, peregrines and hen harriers hunt over the saltmarshes. The road north follows the edge of marshes fringing the River Dyfi. On the landward side, wooded hills rise steeply. The climb through trees to the open mountain brings a rich reward: the view over the river to the outriders of Snowdonia beyond is superb. At sunset, when the golden ball sinks into the sea, it is particularly entrancing. ❑

Map on page 200

BELOW: Furnace Falls, near Machynlleth

Bird-watching

In summer, there are few lovelier places from which to watch birds than the hills of Wales. The rocky hillsides are vibrant yellow with gorse, the melancholy calls of curlew drift across sheep-nibbled valleys and the hanging oakwoods, stunted, gnarled and dripping with lichen, burst with birdsong.

As well as the resident woodland birds – woodpeckers, nuthatches, tits and treecreepers – these woods hold thousands of summer visitors from Africa. There are pied flycatchers, the males dapper individuals with contrasting black and white plumage, wood warblers filling the woods with their shivering, vibrating song, redstarts – the most colourful of all – as well as tree pipits, garden warblers, siskins and crossbills.

Above the woods, on the open hillside, quite different birds are found. Wheatears skim low across the rocky ground and sing their rattling song from lichen-studded rocks. Among heather and gorse, where knuckles of rock bulge from the rough ground, ring ouzels, stonechats and whinchats nest. Higher still, rocky crags provide nesting ledges for ravens, buzzards and peregrines.

On vast windswept stretches of open moorland, curlew, redshank, golden plover, dunlin, snipe, lapwing, red grouse and black grouse nest on the ground among rough grass and heather. And on the lakes and reservoirs, goosanders dive deep for fish while common sandpipers forage at the water's edge. In the skies above, buzzards circle.

This is also the heart of red kite country. The red kite, until recently found nowhere else in the British Isles, can often be seen wheeling above the hillsides of central Wales, coaxing the gusty air currents with its long, crooked wings and rufous, forked tail. By the end of the 18th century their numbers in Wales were down to just a few pairs but now there are over 200 pairs. At some of the six Kite Country Centres in Mid-Wales visitors can witness the unique spectacle of kite feeding. At Gigrin Farm near Rhayader there are four large hides sited just 100ft (30 metres) from where the kites swoop down to feed. The number of kites using the station varies between a dozen and 90.

Countless places in Wales offer good opportunities for bird-watchers. Some are reserves where entry is by permit only; others have completely open access. Among the more famous areas are the Gwenffrwd and nearby Dinas, Ynys Hir and Lake Vyrnwy (reserves owned by the Royal Society for the Protection of Birds), Cors Caron, near Tregaron (National Nature Reserve), the Elan Valley area, the Brecon Beacons and Snowdonia.

The hills of Wales are also home to two birds in decline. The merlin, a beautiful and dashing falcon, is fast disappearing as large expanses of heather-clad upland are "improved" for agriculture or converted into conifer plantations. The dipper – a dumpy, action-packed little bird of fast-flowing mountain streams – is also fighting a losing battle as the acid level of the water rises, killing the insect larvae upon which it depends for food.

Around the Welsh coast, especially in winter, are some of Europe's finest seabird breeding colonies. Among the most important are the islands of Grassholm, Skomer, Skokholm and Ramsey. ❑

HT: a
e redstart.

Map on page 200

LAKES AND MOUNTAINS

Many young people moved to this rural area of Mid-Wales in search of alternative lifestyles. Llanidloes is an attractive market centre and Llandrindod Wells is a dignified spa town

Machynlleth ⓫ is as Welsh as its formidable name suggests. It's a name which causes panic among monoglot English broadcasters who are sometimes called on to pronounce it. *Mac-un-cleth* would be a approximation; locally, "Mach" suffices.

The town boasts wide airy streets and a prominent clock tower which provides a focal point where young people congregate on warm summer evenings. The elaborate tower was erected in 1873 by the Marquess of Londonderry to celebrate the coming of age of his heir, Lord Castlereagh. Their country residence, the imposing 17th-century **Plas Machynlleth**, stands in nearby parkland. It is now home to **Celtica**, an attraction which recreates the sights and sounds of Wales's Celtic past using the latest audio-visual technology.

The work of Wales's top artists is on display at **Y Tabernacl, The Museum of Modern Art**, in both permanent and temporary exhibitions in six beautiful exhibition spaces. Y Tabernacl is a former Wesleyan chapel converted into a centre for performing arts. The auditorium, with its pitch-pine pews, seats 400 people and is the venue for the **Machynlleth Festival**, a mix of classical music, jazz and art held annually in late August.

The town has a special significance for Welsh nationalists. Owain Glyndŵr, the rumbustious Welsh native prince who played cat and mouse with English armies, established a short-lived parliament there in 1404 when he led an uprising against English rule. This event is commemorated in the **Owain Glyndŵr Centre, Parliament House**, alongside the Tourist Information Centre. The Glyndŵr Centre contains exhibits reflecting Wales in the Middle Ages and the life of this enigmatic revolutionary who disappeared without trace in 1412.

Many walks, ranging from leisurely strolls to tough treks, start at the town's edge. Serious walkers can access two long-distance trails here. The spectacular 123-mile (196-km) **Glyndŵr Way**, is a circular highland route which stretches from Knighton to Welshpool via Machynlleth, while the **Dovey Valley** walk extends for 108 miles (172km) following the river valley deep into the mountains from Aberdyfi to Llanuwchllyn (near Bala) and back to the sea at Borth.

The Dovey is also popular with anglers who line its banks in search of salmon and sewin (Welsh sea-trout). Floods can close the bridge over the Dovey just north of Machynlleth. Heed the warning notices which police, through long experience,

...FT: ...e Elan Valley ...servoirs at ...aig-goch.
...GHT: ...eping time ...Machynlleth.

Alternative Living

Some may consider the trend as the modern alternative to Welsh mysticism. For an increasing number of people, it is the path to a healthier future for a polluted planet. Whatever the motivation, both organic farming and alternative technology have gained a strong foothold in the rough hill country of south, west and central Wales.

Organic Farm Foods (OFF), for example, is a successful company which operates an extensive packaging and distribution network from an industrial estate in Lampeter. A market town since 1284, Lampeter has become the UK's largest centre for the preparation, packaging and distribution of organic fruits, vegetables and dairy products.

Some of the exotic fruits and vegetables, raised without the boost of chemical fertilisers or the protection of potentially harmful pesticides, are imported by OFF. All the produce is certified as organically grown to official national and international standards. Much of the seasonal produce is home-grown by committed organic growers on farms and smallholdings within a 100-mile (160-km) radius of Lampeter. Other produce is raised outside West Wales in England and Scotland as well as abroad through partnerships with organic farmers in France, Israel, Egypt, South Africa, Namibia, Australia, the United States, Canada and Eastern Europe. OFF's distribution network covers the whole of the UK and France.

OFF is keen on recycling, too. All its produce arrives in reusable containers and is distributed in returnable crates. Effluents are filtered prior to discharge, waste packaging materials are separated and recycled and waste produce is composted or fed to animals raised on organic farms.

West Wales has a long tradition of co-operative and organic farming. In the old university town of Aberystwyth, 23 miles (37 km) northwest of Lampeter, the University of Wales offers a full-year course in organic farming and has close links with OFF.

Organic dairy farming is also thriving in the area. At Aberystwyth, Rachel's Dairy (founded in 1984) is one of Britain's leading organic dairies whose tasty cheese and yoghurts can be bought in supermarkets and other outlets throughout the UK. Back near Lampeter at Goetre Isaf Farm, Ty'n Grug Organic Farmhouse Cheese has won the coveted Soil Association award for the best organic cheese.

North of Aberystwyth, just off the A487 about 3 miles (5 km) past Machynlleth, lies an unusual microcosm of what some see as tomorrow's world: the Centre for Alternative Technology. Built on the foundations of an abandoned slate quarry, the centre, which celebrated its 25th birthday in 2000, both entertains and instructs with its real-life application of techniques which save resources and eliminate waste and pollution. It has its own reservoir, water supply and sewage system. It runs not on mains electricity but on renewable energy sources: windmills, water turbines, solar energy and biofuels. Cottages, some of which are occupied by centre staff, are built of recycled materials and are heated by solar power and wood stoves. Even human sewage, provided by visitors who use the centre's public lavatories, is recycled into organic fertiliser for use in the all-organic vegetable garden.❑

LEFT: energy conservation the Centre f Alternative Technology.

Map n page 200

erect in good time; many a stalled motorist has needed a tow from an obliging tractor driver.

Up in the hills just off the A487 a few miles north of Machynlleth is the unique **Centre for Alternative Technology** ⓬ – accessed, appropriately enough for this "green" attraction, by an environmentally friendly water-powered cliff railway *(see also panel on facing page).*

Here you can learn all about "green living" and see solar, wind and water power in action. There are organic gardens, farm animals, picnic areas, a cafeteria and book shop. At the visitors' car park, one boards a water-powered railway for the short but steep ascent to the Centre. On 7 acres (2.8 hectares) of the 40-acre (16-hectare) cliffside site, there are working examples of wind, water and solar power in operation as well as energy conservation, environmentally sound buildings and alternative sewage systems.

Transport of people and materials is confined to non-pollutant bicycles, water turbine-charged electric vehicles and a hand-operated steel track site railway. It's a fascinating place for children and adults alike and after a hard day saving the planet, visitors can indulge in a vegetarian meal at the restaurant.

The centre, which works closely with the University of Wales, also offers short residential courses on alternative energy, low-cost building and organic gardening. It is open throughout the year from 10am to 5pm (tel: 01654 702400; fax: 01654 702782; e-mail: cat@gn.apc.org).

Slate centre

Continue a little further along the A487 and you come to the old slate mining village of **Corris** ⓭. In the second half of the 19th century Corris was a bustling place, its narrow streets busy with narrow-gauge trains transporting slate from the quarries down to Machynlleth. The line, which also carried passengers, closed in 1948 and was dismantled soon after. Since 1970 volunteers of the Corris Railway Society have

.OW: feeding e at a farm .lanwrthwl.

been working to restore a section of the line and at the **Corris Railway and Museum** you can see old rolling stock and a fascinating collection of artefacts and photographs from the railway's heyday.

Also at Corris is a **Craft Centre** which houses a variety of craft workshops and a Tourist Information Centre. Next door a former slate cavern has been transformed into **King Arthur's Labyrinth**, a popular family attraction where visitors take a subterranean boat ride back in time to the Celtic world of King Arthur.

From Machynlleth the road inland, the A489, joins the A470, the main north–south highway, at **Cemmaes Road.** Much of the criticism levelled at the A470 is explained by geography. Twisting and turning round mountains, swooping under (and over) the railway which connects Shrewsbury to Machynlleth and beyond, it is a route to test a driver's skill. But for those who prefer interesting driving in beautiful scenery to boringly direct motorways, the route is a joy.

Newtown

Southeast of Cemmaes Road along the A470/A489 is **Newtown** ⓮, the commercial and industrial centre of Mid-Wales. The town is the regional headquarters of the Welsh Development Agency, a government body set up to extend and support economic activity throughout Wales. New factories, housing estates and the excellent **Theatr Hafren** have brought the town into the front rank of the post-war designated new towns.

Once a centre of the flannel industry, when it was dubbed "the Leeds of Wales", Newtown is remembered as the home of the world's first mail-order business, founded in 1859 by Pryce Pryce-Jones in an inspired attempt to improve business. **The Textile Museum** in Commercial Street, housed in a row of 19th-century weavers' cottages, records the history of the industry from 1790 to the beginning of the 20th century.

In the High Street, the local branch of **W. H. Smith** has been restored to how it

BELOW: a Welsh blank

Map n page 200

was on its opening in 1927. On the first floor a museum chronicles the firm's progress from its beginnings in 1792.

The town's most famous son, Robert Owen, was born here in 1771. This philanthropic capitalist who started the co-operative movement is buried in the churchyard of the ruined 13th-century church of St Mary's, close to the River Severn which flows through the town. **The Robert Owen Museum** on Broad Street reconstructs his home and tells his story.

Soon after the A470 swings south past Caersws, a riot of flowers in carefully manicured front gardens announces **Llandinam ⓯**, a frequent winner of Wales's best-kept village competition. It was the home of one David Davies, a self-made millionaire who started on the road to riches in the middle of the 19th century by buying a tree for £5, sawing it up and selling the pieces for £80. He went on to develop mines in South Wales, and even built Barry docks, through which he exported coal all over the world. His statue, sculpted by Sir Alfred Gilbert, the creator of *Eros* in London's Piccadilly Circus, stands by the old railway station.

Set in extensive parklands near **Tregynon**, north of Newtown on the way to Llanfair Caereinion, stands a magnificent black-and-white mansion called **Gregynog Hall**. It was the home of of Margaret and Gwendoline Davies, avid patrons of the arts and granddaughters of David Davies of Llandinam. Gregynog is now run by the University of Wales, but following the traditions that the sisters began, the fine art press, educational courses and the prestigious **Gregynog Festival of Music** (held in June) are still integral to its life. The Davies sisters' world-class art collection can be seen at the National Museum of Wales in Cardiff.

Llanidloes

Llanidloes ⓰, a market town located almost at Wales's geographic centre, is not to be missed. A timbered market hall in the middle of the town dates from the early

LOW: how stay awake ile counting eep.

17th century and looks as though it has been built specially to frighten road users. Lorries have difficulty negotiating the historic chicane. A stone in the cobbled market place marks the spot where John Wesley preached in 1748, 1749 and 1764.

The Town Hall **Museum** tells the story of Llanidloes' silver and lead mining past and has an extensive natural history collection. A major refurbishment of the museum has included the incorporation of a **Kite Country Information Point**, providing information on this beautiful bird of prey which is making such a successful comeback in Mid-Wales after having been on the verge of extinction.

Unspoiled and unsophisticated, Llanidloes is a friendly place, with a good selection of shops and a splendid wholefood café. A pleasant riverside walk along the banks of the Severn is recommended for those with a taste for strolling. For the more energetic, the surrounding hills are invitingly open.

The **Clywedog Valley** is within easy reach, offering angling and sailing on the waters trapped behind a massive man-made dam, one of the tallest in Britain. Another new **Kite Country Information Point** is located here. It includes a viewing platform with panoramic views of the reservoir. This 6-mile (9.5-km) long lake is a popular spot for its waterside trails, sailing and trout fishing.

Near the dam a waymarked trail leads through the extensive remains of the 19th-century **Bryn Tail Lead Mine**. Past the lake, a spectacular mountain road winds waywardly back to Machynlleth, passing one of Wales's remotest pubs, the Star Inn, which lurks behind a copse.

Rhayader

The next town of any significance on the way south is **Rhayader** ⓱. It guards the entrance to the **Elan Valley** where in the late 19th century the canny burghers of Birmingham built reservoirs to supply water to the thirsty city. In Elan village stands the **Elan Valley Visitor Centre**, which gives a good introduction to the lakelands and the important wildlife habitats which surround the waters. Pony trekkers and bird watchers, as well as tourists, can be spotted among the wooded slopes and deep ravines. A **Kite Country Centre** is part of this impressive visitor centre and information, shows and hands-on exhibitions about this striking "Bird of the Century" can be found in the centre's Kite Country Theatre. It is believed that in 1977 the bird was so close to extinction that the entire population of Welsh kites subsequently came from just one female.

Rhayader is remembered by generations of war veterans as the base from which they sallied forth to fight imaginary foes in the inhospitable mountains. It is also recalled for the high quality of its fish and chips at the end of soggy days spent slogging through bog and bracken in preparation for real combat.

At the eastern approach to Rhayader is **Welsh Royal Crystal** where visitors can see demonstrations by master cutters creating designs on blown glass, and purchase items in the factory shop. Just south of the town is **Gigrin Farm**, another Kite

LEFT: publica at Rhayader.

Map
n page
200

Country Centre where there are regular feedings each afternoon.

To the north, **St Harmon** – more a straggle of farms than a defined settlement – is one of the coldest places in Britain; at least it always feels that way on a winter morning when the snow clouds come scudding in and the sheep huddle behind the windswept hedges.

Nearby **Gilfach** is a 418-acre (169-hectare) nature reserve on a wild hill farm, home to many threatened plants and animals. At its heart is a beautifully restored medieval Welsh longhouse. The reserve, yet another Kite Country Centre, has video links direct to nest boxes.

The source of the **River Severn** is a bog up in the **Cambrian Mountains**, accessible from several sides if you trudge across the boggy approaches. **Plynlimon**, the highest peak, stands in the centre of a lofty plateau. The summit is topped with a sizeable cairn which is added to all the time by walkers following the tradition of tossing a stone, however small, onto the pile. This is remote territory, little visited outside summer, but home to hardy sheep farmers who claim it to be one of the most peaceful places on earth.

New lifestyles

The road east from Rhayader, the A44, heads towards the English border 30 miles (48 km) away. The countryside becomes progressively softer. Black-and-white timber-framed houses begin to appear. Place names become decidedly un-Welsh. Off the main road there are tiny valleys which seem to want to hide themselves away. But discovered they have been – by young people seeking an alternative lifestyle. Some try to support themselves by subsistence farming; others engage in rural crafts, selling their carvings, weavings and embroideries at markets on both sides of the border.

Penybont ⓲, a handsome village, was once renowned for its market. Now it is notable for its trotting races, an activity seemingly as much appreciated by the horses as by the knowledgeable crowds.

LOW:
n Valley
itor Centre.

Knighton, a thriving market town, is right on the border; its train station is, in fact, in England. Handsome St Edward's Church, with its squat tower, sits at the bottom of the hill, from which streets climb steeply to the inevitable 19th-century clock tower in the market place, and upwards again through the Tudor "Narrows" to the mound of the Norman castle. Knighton is the only original settlement on **Offa's Dyke** and its Welsh name, Tref-y-Clawdd (Town of the Dyke) reflects this. King Offa of Mercia built the barrier between his kingdom and Welsh land in the 8th century *(see page 104)*. Today all nationalities are free to walk the 168-mile (268-km) **Offa's Dyke Path** which runs the length of the Wales/England border. The **Offa's Dyke Centre** on West Street has information on the Dyke and its history.

Ten miles (16 km) south, **Presteigne** ⓳ also stands sentry on Offa's Dyke. The town is famous in Wales for its annual festival, the **Presteigne Festival of Music and the Arts**, held in August. Its leading hotel, the Radnorshire Arms, built in 1616, is a fine example of black-and-white architecture. Once an important coaching town between London and Aberystwyth, it was also an administrative and legal centre and, until 1970, conducted Radnorshire's quarter sessions and assizes. Shire Hall, where the courts were held has become an award-winning museum called **The Judge's Lodging**, which recreates the 1870s when Reverend Richard Lister Venables was Chairman of the Magistrates. An audio-tour conducts you round the house, through courtroom, kitchen, parlour and pantry and lets you into the lives of the Victorian inhabitants.

Much of the borderland is heavily forested with conifers, concealing many unexpected streams, ponds and tiny valleys which older folk remember as positive features of the landscape.

Llandrindod Wells

One of Mid-Wales's gems, the spa town of **Llandrindod Wells** ⓴, has an air of

BELOW: studying form at the sheep dog trials.

Map on page 200

Victorian splendour. Tall houses, once owned by the wealthy and now mostly converted into flats, look down on broad streets. Above the town an artificial lake beckons strollers, anglers and standers-and-starers. The fish may be too domesticated for real sport – they stay inshore, waiting to be fed by visitors. A short step away, the local golf course offers a hilly challenge to would-be Faldos and Lyles.

The pump room, at the **Rock Park Spa Centre** down in a wooden glen across town, has been lovingly restored, reviving the atmosphere of 100 years ago when thousands came to Llandrindod Wells to "take the waters". Health-giving water was until recently dispensed here; then someone discovered that it contravened the zealous rules laid down by the European Commission in Brussels.

In previous, less bureaucratic times, a glass (or a cup) could be taken while watching chess matches being fought out with Grand Master concentration on a giant board in the courtyard. Splendid public gardens abound and the bowling green, where international tournaments are held, is smoother than smooth.

Llandrindod's annual **Victorian Festival**, held in late August, returns the town to the leisurely days of hansom cabs, top-hatted railway staff, frock coats and mutton-chop whiskers. Events include street theatre, walks, talks, drama and music. Local tailors and dressmakers are skilled at kitting out festival-goers in authentic costume.

The flat-roofed **Automobile Palace**, a listed building dating from 1913, holds the **National Cycle Exhibition**, a fascinating collection of over 120 cycles, with displays and exhibits on the history of cycling.

Builth Wells

Ten miles (16 km) south of Llandrindod is another Wells: **Builth Wells** ㉑. The Royal Welsh Agricultural Society's showground, on which one of Britain's premier farming jamborees, the **Royal Welsh Show**, is staged in July, stands on one bank of the River Wye – the town on the other.

ELOW: andrindod ells, a fine a town.

Prize bulls, home-made jam, equestrian displays, scores of firms selling everything from tractors to toffee – all are ingredients of this immensely popular annual show, jollied along with outdoor brass band and jazz concerts. Builth itself boasts a fine tree-lined walk along the River Wye and an enterprising arts centre, which stages films, plays and concerts.

Just west of Builth at Cilmery on the A483, a huge stone by the roadside marks the spot where Llewelyn the Last, the last native Prince of Wales, was slain by English soldiers in the 13th century.

Two other Wells come next: **Llangammarch**, where Victorians congregated to drink water containing barium (recommended for scrofulous cases according to hucksters of that era), and **Llanwrtyd**, a bigger place where the favoured flavour was sulphur. These days, enterprising Llanwrtyd is gaining a growing reputation as a centre for outdoor activities and offers an imaginative programme of events including a "Man versus Horse Marathon", mountain biking, pony trekking, Four-Day walks and the decidedly weird World Bog-Snorkelling Championship.

Ty Barcud (Welsh for "Red Kite House") in the town centre is a Kite Country information point. Outside stands a striking steel sculpture of a kite entitled *Spirit in the Sky*. On the outskirts of town, the **Cambrian Woollen Mill** offers tours and a factory shop.

There are unresolved arguments about Llanwrtyd's status – the weight of opinion believes it to be a small town ("the smallest in Britain" according to its publicity-conscious local entrepreneurs) rather than a large village. Whichever, it is a pleasant place – and the jumping-off point for a spectacular journey over rugged mountains to Tregaron 15 miles (24 km) away.

The road, known as the **Abergwesyn Pass**, discourages anyone in a hurry; the views are breathtaking, but drivers should concentrate on the way ahead. The pass – now with a proper surface, of course – follows a famous track across the remote

BELOW: arour Tregaron.

Map on page 200

"roof of Wales" once used by drovers taking their livestock to markets along the Wales/England border. Some gradients are said to be one in four, but often seem steeper. The area is almost uninhabited. Sheep speckle the vast hillsides, an occasional shepherd can be seen, birds on the lookout for a meal circle warily. It is a slightly scary journey when the weather turns wet, as it can do unexpectedly.

Tregaron

Tregaron ㉒, at the other end of the pass, has the air of a frontier town. A workmanlike place, it considers sheep more important than tourists, although there is an excellent craft shop which has an extensive range of Celtic jewellery, some in Welsh gold. There's also a Kite Country Centre in the old schoolhouse. Tregaron was the birthplace of two disparate characters – Twm Sion Cati, the Welsh equivalent of Robin Hood, and Henry Richard, the "Apostle of Peace", founder of the Peace Union which predated the League of Nations. Richard's statue stands in the town square.

Cors Caron (Tregaron Bog), a National Nature Reserve, lies on the outskirts of town. This rather eerie raised peat bog is home to a wide range of plants and birds and can be entered along a disused railway line beside the B4343. Further along the same road at **Pontrhydfendigaid** are the evocative ruins of **Strata Florida Abbey.** This Cistercian abbey lies beside meadows carpeted with seasonal flowers – its Welsh name, Ystrad Fflur, means "the way of the flowers". Founded in the 12th century, it was a renowned medieval centre not only of religious but also cultural, political and educational influence within Wales. It is thought to be the burial place of many of the native Welsh rulers and of the 14th-century poet Dafydd ap Gwilym. Mid-Wales's 20th-century centre of things cultural and commercial, **Aberystwyth**, is 16 miles (25 km) distant across the mountains *(see page 203 of the "Cardiganshire and the Teifi Valley" chapter).* ❑

LOW: Welsh ld on sale Tregaron.

NORTH WALES

Snowdonia's mountain peaks and valleys provide the drama. The varied coastal resorts provide the amusement

The first tourists to discover North Wales were the early Victorians, following in the footsteps of William Wordsworth in search of the "sublime experiences" that the majestic peaks of Snowdon could grant in abundance. These were shortly followed by a new wave of visitors who, for the first time, could escape by railway from the industrial towns and cities of the North West to the generous sands and therapeutic seas along the Welsh coast.

North Wales continues to appeal to visitors on these two broad fronts. There are those who come here for the mountains, and those who prefer the coast. A huge chunk of this region is taken up by the Snowdonia National Park, which contains Britain's highest mountains south of the Scottish Highlands. Snowdonia's crags, boulder-strewn slopes and wooded valleys manage to keep all kinds of outdoors enthusiasts happy, from the rock climbers drawn to the challenge of the fearsome slabs which line the Llanberis Pass to the weekend walker looking for a gentle stroll in the countryside.

Along the coast it's the same story – the North Wales seaboard manages to cater for all tastes. To prove that the traditional British seaside holiday is not dead and buried – though on certain evidence it's certainly past its sell-by date – there are places like Rhyl and Prestatyn, where you can still buy candy floss and spend a listless wet afternoon in amusement arcades (Llandudno, an altogether more spick-and-span, upright place, should not be placed in this category). If big resorts aren't your cup of tea, then North Wales can provide miles of peaceful shoreline and abundant wildlife – along the Isle of Anglesey and Llŷn Peninsula in particular, two officially designated Areas of Outstanding Natural Beauty dotted with nothing more raucous than coastal villages and sailing ports.

In landscape terms, Snowdonia is the unchallenged star. But east of the Conwy Valley (which forms the boundary of the national park) there's a gentler countryside of heather moorlands and forests. Travel further east again and you come to the Vale of Clwyd, a rich and fertile strip of farmland which lies in the shelter of the Clwydian Range, another Area of Outstanding Natural Beauty. ❑

PRECEDING PAGES: a train heads for Snowdon's summit.
LEFT: Blaenau Ffestiniog.

Map on page 226

SNOWDONIA

Walkers flock to this mountainous national park. Other attractions include narrow-gauge railways, old slate caverns, resorts such as Barmouth, and the imposing Harlech Castle

Half a million people walk on **Snowdon** every year – which means that one mountain has done more to attract visitors to Wales's greatest national park than any advertising agency could ever have managed. There's more to the **Snowdonia National Park ❶**, however, than the mountainscape centred on Snowdon. At nearly 850 sq. miles (2,200 sq. km), it runs from near Conwy on the north coast all the way down to within a few hundred metres of Machynlleth in the south. On its western edge it is bordered by the A487 Porthmadog–Caernarfon road. Bala sits on its eastern boundary.

Although the highest point in Snowdonia is a modest 3,560ft (1,085 metres) above sea level, you can still get the feeling of being very alone in the surrounding wild country. The area around **Llanberis** especially gives the impression of being in the midst of a major mountain range – even though the landscape suddenly becomes tame just a few miles down the road. Hilaire Belloc wrote: "There is no corner of Europe that I know which so moves me with the awe and majesty of great things as does this mass of the northern Welsh mountains."

As well as being out of doors, you're likely to be out of breath: walking, orienteering, pony trekking, mountain biking, fishing, canoeing, sailing and water skiing are all pursued with equal vigour. There are more than 1,500 recognised rock climbing routes in the Snowdonia National Park. And each winter, more and more mountaineers visit Snowdonia to climb on snow and ice. Names like the **Carneddau Range**, the **Glyder Range** and the **Hebog Range** get climbers' adrenalin flowing.

Southern approach

There are hints of the landscape to come a few miles north of Machynlleth. As you approach the small community of **Corris**, steep pine-clad slopes mimic a sort of mock-Alpine landscape. No longer does the land undulate gently. Things have changed. Corris has a museum devoted to its old slate railway, and forest trails begin here *(for more details see the fuller description of Corris on pages 211–2).*

A few minutes beyond Corris, as you negotiate a bend in the road, the sudden bulk of **Cadair Idris** looms into view. At 2,927ft (892 metres), it's an imposing sight; you'd be excused for missing the small roadside sign which officially confirms your presence in the Snowdonia National Park. Cadair Idris takes its name from a 7th-century warrior killed in a battle against the Saxons. This means that the National Park begins and ends with mountains named

LEFT: Llyn Gwynant. **RIGHT:** Walkers on the Pyg Track up Snowdon.

after national heroes: the northern counterparts of Cadair Idris are **Carnedd Dafydd** and **Carnedd Llywelyn**, each more than 3,400ft (1,040 metres) high.

Although Cadair Idris doesn't make the 3,000-ft (900-metre) mark, its accessibility means that it comes a close second to Snowdon in popularity. There are several routes up to the summit of **Pen-y-Gader** from Dolgellau and Tal-y-Llyn lake. The two highest glacial lakes – **Llyn y Gadair** to the north and **Llyn Cau** to the south – are favourite destinations.

A very prominent geological feature in this vicinity is the **Bala Fault**. This 12-mile (19-km) crack in the earth's crust originates on the eastern side of Cadair Idris and is responsible for the lakes at Tal-y-Llyn and Bala.

The Talyllyn Railway

For railway enthusiasts, this quiet south-western corner of Snowdonia has one claim to fame. The **Talyllyn Railway** has the distinction of being the first of the Welsh narrow-gauge railways to be saved. Like most of the "Great Little Trains" *(see page 85)*, the Talyllyn line has its origins in the slate quarries of the 19th century. Slate mining opened up in 1847 near Abergynolwyn and packhorses were used to transport the slate to Aberdyfi on the coast. In the 1860s, the narrow-gauge railway was built to make a connection with the mainline railway at Tywyn.

When the line was reopened by enthusiasts in 1951, it carried fewer than 16,000 passengers; today, in summer, it carries many times that number. Its story and that of other narrow-gauge railways is told at a museum at **Wharf Station** in the small resort of **Tywyn**.

Nearby, in the small village of **Llanfihangel-y-Pennant** ❷, can be traced the origins of an international religious organisation. In 1800, so the story goes, a girl called Mary Jones, having saved for six years, set out for Bala 25 miles (40 km) across the mountains to purchase a Welsh Bible from the minister, Thomas Charles.

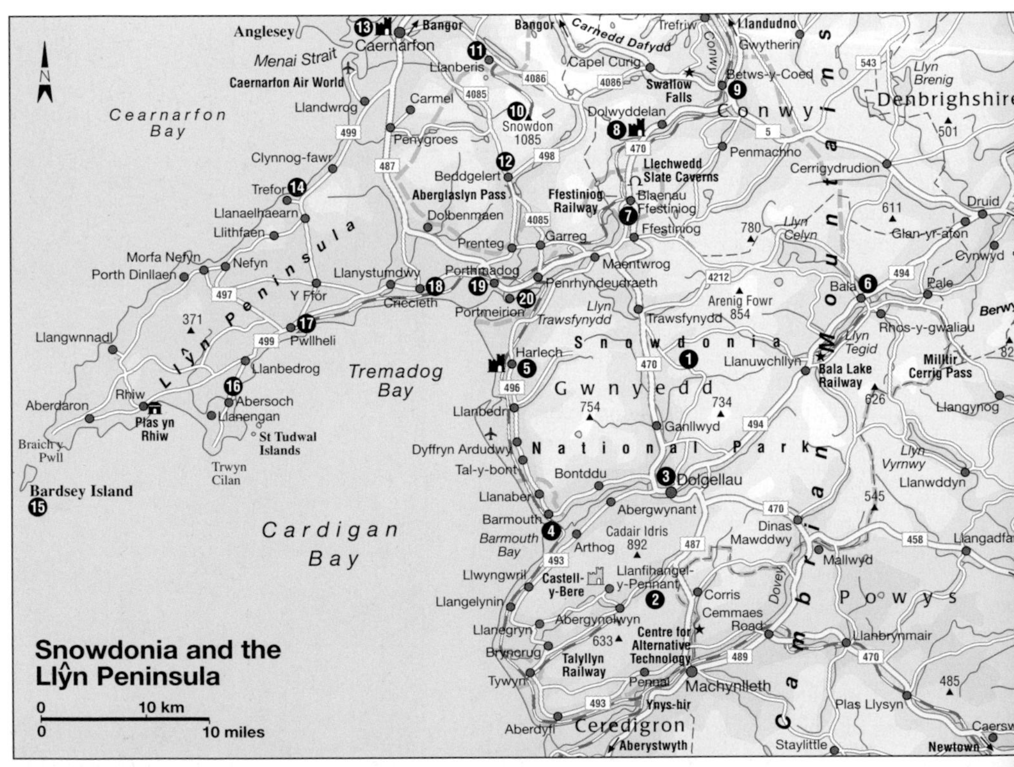

Snowdonia and the Llŷn Peninsula

Map on page 226

On her arrival, she found that the last Bible had been sold. Moved by the young girl's disappointment, the minister gave her his own. The incident prompted Thomas Charles to found the internationally known British and Foreign Bible Society, a group dedicated to the worldwide distribution of local-language Bibles. Since then, the Bible's fortunes have been assiduously promoted in the society's London offices. Mary Jones's Cottage has fared less well: it's a ruined building marked by a plain memorial.

Little remains of **Castell-y-Bere**, a short distance away. It is one of the few castles in Wales which owes its origins to a Welsh rather than an English sovereign. While this site may lack architectural presence, its mountain-locked location is a stirring one. The presence of a cormorant nesting ground at nearby **Craig-yr-Aderyn** (Bird Rock) suggests that the sea was at one time much nearer; it is possible that Castell-y-Bere was not far from a navigable marine channel.

Dolgellau

At the other side of Cadair Idris, it's worth diverting off the bypass to visit the old market town of **Dolgellau** ❸ (pronounced *Doll-geth-lie*). Standing in the river meadows of a valley, it lies encircled by the mountains of Snowdonia – Cadair in particular, which looms menacingly above the rooftops. The town, with its quaint narrow streets and 17th-century seven-arched bridge, gets its neat and tidy look from the uniform use of the local boulderstone and granite which went into the building of the sturdy three- and four-storey Victorian houses. A riverside woollen industry once thrived here and in the 19th century there was a Welsh gold rush when the precious metal was discovered in local rocks.

Intrepid visitors can head for the hills north of **Bontddu** on the northern shore of the beautiful Mawddach Estuary to seek out the remains of the gold mines which supplied the precious metal for many royal wedding rings.

Today Dolgellau makes its living from

:LOW: e Talyllyn ailway, the dest of its nd in the orld.
GHT: going r gold at the ogau mine ar Dolgellau.

farming and tourism. In the heart of the town there's an interesting **Museum of the Quakers**, which recounts the past persecution and emigration of local Quakers.

Eight miles (13 km) north of Dolgellau, on the A470 near Ganllwyd, is the **Coed y Brenin Visitor Centre**, where audio-visual displays explain the magnificent **Coed y Brenin** woodlands ("The King's Forest"), with their wooded gorges, crags, waterfalls, abandoned gold workings and scattering of farmsteads. The centre also has details of forest trails and mountain biking.

To escape from the busy roads, you can travel up the Welsh coast by rail by catching the highly scenic **Cambrian Coaster** train, which runs from Aberystwyth all the way to Pwllheli on the Llŷn Peninsula (you can hop on and off at a number of stations and halts along the coast).

The old railway bridge carrying the line across the **Mawddach Estuary**, just out of Fairbourne station, only adds to the view that William Wordsworth called a "sublime sight" when he came here in 1824. If you want to spend more time walking beside this lovely estuary ask for directions to the **Panorama Walk**, which runs for more than 3 miles (5 km) along the shore.

Railway enthusiasts can take a trip on the **Fairbourne Steam Railway**, the smallest of the narrow-gauge railways of Wales. Its northern terminus is at **Porth Penrhyn** at the entrance to the Mawddach Estuary.

Barmouth ❹ lies just outside the official boundary of Snowdonia National Park, but that doesn't stop people coming here in summer. Having grown up as a resort in the 19th century, this seaside town (its Welsh name is Abermaw) owes its popularity to its wide, sandy beaches and pretty harbour, though the commercial side to the resort is now looking a little tired. The National Trust was born here in 1895 when it acquired its first piece of land, the Dinas Oleu headland above the resort.

Harlech

Just 10 miles (16 km) further up the coast, **Harlech** ❺ is an altogether different

BELOW: the Cambrian Coast Railway at Barmouth.

Map on page 226

coastal community. In the 13th century it was dominated by Edward I's sturdy castle, built between 1283 and 1289. Seven centuries later it's the same story. This is still only a small community and **Harlech Castle** still dominates everything around it. The only thing that has changed is the proximity of the sea. At one time, Harlech stood at the water's edge; today a golf course occupies land from which the sea has retreated.

Harlech Castle played a key role in the events of the uprising led by Owain Glyndŵr in the early 15th century. Harlech's capture, together with that of Aberystwyth Castle (both after long sieges) in the spring of 1404, gave Owain authority over central Wales. Harlech became the residence of his court and, with Machynlleth and Dolgellau, one of three places to which he summoned his parliament. Five years later, Harlech was retaken by the English after a long siege and heavy bombardment.

Sixty years later Harlech played its part in the Wars of the Roses when it was held for the Lancastrians by Dafydd ap Ienkin ap Enion. Asked to surrender, he replied: "I have held a castle in France until every old woman in Wales heard of it, and I will hold a castle in Wales until every old woman in France hears of it!" It was this siege which is supposed to have given rise to the song *Men of Harlech*.

Around Bala

A natural port of call for many travelling into North Wales is **Bala** ❻ and a particularly dramatic approach road is the B4391. As the road leaves **Llangynog** village, it climbs until it runs precipitously along the steep-sided glacial valley of the Eirth.

Milltir Cerrig Pass marks the end of this ascent and leads out onto wide, open moorland. From here, the B4391 marks the easternmost boundary of Snowdonia National Park and, fittingly, there is usually a fine view most of the way down into Bala of the northern highlands of Snowdonia in the distance.

ELOW: arlech Castle.

Standing at the eastern end of **Bala Lake** (Llyn Tegid), Bala attracts some energetic visitors. This 4-mile (6-km) long stretch of water is the largest natural lake in Wales and an established inland sailing centre, hosting major events in the yachting calendar. Bala is also a popular windsurfing and canoeing centre.

North of Bala there's another lake, this time man-made. Llyn Celyn was created in the 1960s to supply drinking water to Liverpool by the flooding of the Tryweryn Valley and the drowning of the village of Capel Celyn. The dam at the southern end of Llyn Celyn has not dampened the ardour of canoeists; in fact, quite the contrary. World Slalom and Wild Water Racing Championships have been successfully staged downstream of the dam on the River Tryweryn and it is now established as a leading European canoe slalom course. You can watch and/or participate by going to Canolfan Tryweryn – the **National White Water Centre** – just 2 miles (3 km) out of Bala.

Water sports comprise the most modern chapter in Bala's history. Before the Industrial Revolution, the town was an important centre for the woollen industry, being the market outlet for garments knitted in the area. It is said that George III wore Bala stockings when he suffered from rheumatism. The introduction of machine-made garments led to the decline of Welsh wool just as quickly here as in other parts of Wales.

Religion has also figured strongly in Bala. Thomas Charles, the minister who gave his own copy of the Welsh Bible to Mary Jones of Llanfihangel-y-Pennant *(see page 226)*, is commemorated by a statue in Tegid Street (just off the main street).

Another local clergyman who made a name for himself was Michael Jones. In 1865, he took 150 people to Patagonia to set up a Nonconformist colony on the Chabut River (now part of Argentina). The settlement survives, its inhabitants speaking Welsh and Spanish.

Narrow-gauge railways

If you prefer a more sedate prospect of Bala Lake than the one canoe and sailing enthusiasts enjoy, you can take the 25-minute train journey along Bala Lake's southern shore. The **Bala Lake Railway** is a "remnant" of the Great Western Railway standard-gauge line which opened in 1868 and ran from Ruabon (near Wrexham) to Barmouth, skirting the lake. Closed in 1965, the line was partially resurrected in 1971 in the form of a 23-inch narrow-gauge railway which by 1976 ran 4½ miles (7 km) from Bala to Llanuwchllyn.

It's tempting to wonder how Victorian slate entrepreneurs would react to today's environmental lobbyists. Not too far from Llyn Celyn, **Blaenau Ffestiniog** ❼ is the kind of monumental blot on the landscape that is matched in Wales only by the slag heaps of the old mining communities in the south. The scenic route traced by the B4391 across open moorland provides little warning of the astonishing grey wasteland that lurks just a few miles away.

The effect is the same if you take the **Ffestiniog Railway** up from Porthmadog; picture-postcard views of the Vale of

LEFT: statue of Methodism pioneer Thomas Charles in Ba

Map on page 226

Ffestiniog quickly fade from mind when you arrive at the terminus. More than a century of slate mining has covered the surrounding slopes with thousands of tons of grey waste.

Blaenau Ffestiniog is not technically part of the Snowdonia National Park. It sits there in the middle of things rather like a Black Hole, the park boundary skirting cautiously around the town and its immediate vicinity. And yet the town, under certain climatic conditions, can have a strange beauty, the man-made mountains of jagged slate offsetting the natural cragginess of the surrounding Moelwyn and Manod mountain ranges.

Slate was to North Wales what coal was to the south. At its peak in 1898, the North Wales slate industry employed 16,766 men, of whom a quarter worked in the mines and quarries in and around these hills. Ffestiniog Parish had a population in 1801 of just 732 – a figure which had risen to 11,433 in 1901. At the turn of the 20th century the town of Blaenau Ffestiniog had 22 taverns and 37 places of worship. Other towns too – **Porthmadog** is one example – owe their origins entirely to slate.

Today Blaenau is still dependent upon slate. Many tourists come to the town to visit the popular **Llechwedd Slate Caverns**. You can choose one of two (or both) tours through the 19th-century mines. The Miners' Underground Tramway enters the side of the mountain through an 1846 tunnel leading to a succession of enormous chambers. The Deep Mine tour takes you underground on Britain's steepest passenger railway, after which you follow on foot a self-guided audio tour telling the story of a typical slate miner. On the surface is a reconstructed Victorian mining village complete with shops, pub and smithy.

Just 3 miles (5 km) further along the road towards Betws-y-Coed, **Dolwyddelan Castle** ❽ is said to be the birthplace of Llywelyn the Great. It is more likely that he was born elsewhere in the area and that it was Llywelyn himself who built Dolwyddelan's first keep in the early 1200s.

ELOW: ;aenau ;estiniog, town ;uilt on slate.

Northern Snowdonia

Draw a line from Betws-y-Coed to Beddgelert and you mark a rough-and-ready boundary for what many people call Snowdonia proper. In this northeastern corner of Snowdonia National Park there are 14 peaks over 3,000 ft (900 metres).

Betws-y-Coed ❾ ("Chapel in the Wood" and pronounced *Betoos-ah-Coyd*) is rather a tame first stop if you approach North Wales from the east. Sitting sensibly along the banks of the **River Llugwy**, it is deliberately quaint – sombre grey Welsh buildings enlivened by white ornate garden railings and pretty porches. You can hear the sound of the river in the picturesque high street – but only in the early morning or late evening when the traffic is light.

Betws-y-Coed is Snowdonia at its most touristic. There are the usual craft shops selling pottery, brass, woollens and other souvenirs, but, more usefully, there are also outdoors equipment stores. Several easy walks – all waymarked –start here, particularly up to **Llyn Elsi** by the Jubilee Path, to forest-fringed **Llyn y Parc**, and along the River Llugwy to the **Miners' Bridge**.

Close to the railway station – on the **Conwy Valley Line** from Llandudno Junction to Blaenau Ffestiniog – is the unspoilt 14th-century **Old Church of St Michael and All Angels**. If closed, obtain a key from the **Royal Oak Stables**, which house the National Park and Royal Society for the Protection of Birds information centres – a good source for walkers' maps.

Along the A5 is a popular beauty spot, **Swallow Falls**, where the Afon Llugwy drops 30ft (9 metres) into a deep pool.

Serious walkers will head for **Capel Curig**, a small village a few miles further along the A5. North Snowdonia is a centre for rock climbing and trekking and the National Centre for Mountain Activities provides training for these and a range of outdoor pursuits, including skiing, orienteering and canoeing.

Snowdon ❿ (Yr Wyddfa in Welsh, meaning "monument" or "tomb", a reference to the burial place of a legendary

BELOW: the River Conwy a Betws-y-Coec

Map on page 226

ogre) is not only the highest, but also the most distinctive of Welsh mountains. Along with one or two other peaks in the Glyder Range, it even has a plant species – the Mountain Spiderwort – found nowhere else in the British Isles.

Although in height Snowdon beats Carnedd Llewelyn, to the northeast, by just 75 ft (23 metres), the unobscured outlook alone places it at the top of the league. One reason Snowdon is so popular is that you don't have to be a very serious climber to reach its 3,560-ft (1,085-metre) summit.

In 1998, the future of a huge slice of the mountain was secured when it was bought by the National Trust. Welsh-born actor Sir Anthony Hopkins weighed in with a £1 million donation.

Snowdon was popularised as a walking destination in the 19th century. In 1892, Britain's former prime minister William Gladstone – at the age of 83 – opened one of the main ascents and walked as far as what is known as **Gladstone's Rock** where, in front of a crowd, he saw fit to make a speech on freedom for small states. A century of tramping later, Snowdon is suffering severe erosion and a programme of footpath restoration work is in progress.

Walking routes

There's a choice of six main walking routes: **Llanberis Track**, **Miners' Track**, **Pyg Track**, **Snowdon Ranger Path**, **Watkin Path** and **Rhyd Ddu Path**. The Snowdonia National Park advises all walkers to wear appropriate footwear and clothing and to check the weather forecast before setting out.

If you prefer to ascend Snowdon less energetically, you can try **Snowdon Mountain Railway** (mid-Mar to end-Oct daily, first train 9am), Britain's only public rack-and-pinion railway. On the day it opened, 6 April 1896, an accident occurred, closing it for a year while the rack system was modified. It has operated safely since then – the round trip from Llanberis to the Summit and back lasts two hours, including 30 minutes on the top to enjoy the view.

Llanberis ⓫ sits at the very foot of Snowdon (though just outside the park). On a cold, wet day the **Llanberis Pass** can look distinctly forbidding; on a warm summer's day it is a magnet for the many tourists meandering through Snowdonia's glaciated landscape.

There are good reasons to come here all the same. The **Welsh Slate Museum** occupies the workshops of the **Dinorwig Quarry**, which stopped work in 1969. A short distance along the Caernarvon road, the **Llanberis Lake Railway** runs along the north shore of Llyn Padarn. **Padarn Country Park** tempts visitors with lakeside picnic sites, woodland walks and craft shops. The mountainside at Llanberis has been hollowed out to create the awesome **Dinorwig Pumped Storage Power Station**. You can take a bus trip into these workings from the **Electric Mountain Centre** on the south shore of Llyn Padarn.

Between Llyn Peris and Llyn Padarn, **Dolbadarn Castle** is a 13th-century fortress with a grim history.

Before the wide estuary of the Glaslyn was reclaimed by the construction of the

[RI]GHT: [Sn]owdon [Mo]untain [Ra]ilway.

embankment at Porthmadog, boats came as far inland as the bridge at **Pont Aberglaslyn**. Overland routes from here to Caernarfon and Bangor allowed ships to ply their trade without having to navigate around the dangerous seas of the Llŷn Peninsula. A short distance north of Pont Aberglaslyn, through the dramatic **Aberglaslyn Pass**, is the picturesque mountain village of **Beddgelert** ⓬, another popular walking centre.

A Celtic monastery, ranking second only to the one on Bardsey Island, was established here in the 6th century. In the late 12th or early 13th century this was superseded by an Augustinian priory, of which Beddgelert's parish church is the sole surviving building. Beddgelert means "Grave of Gelert". The village does a good trade in postcards which tell the story of the legendary wolfhound, mistakenly killed by Prince Llywelyn after it had saved his baby son from a wolf. Unfortunately this heart-rending tale appears to have been a 19th-century invention to attract tourists. But we all love a good story and today's visitors still make the pilgrimage a little way along the right bank of the River Glaslyn to the spot which is allegedly Gelert's final resting place.

In more modern times, Alfred Bestall, creator of the comic-strip character Rupert Bear, was born here; he died in 1986.

To the west, **Beddgelert Forest Park** has a large, well-appointed campsite and a number of waymarked trails.

Map on page 226

Threat to the environment

Snowdonia, like Venice, has become too popular for its own good. When the Queen Mother heard Sir Clough Williams-Ellis outlining in 1943 his vision of a national park in Snowdonia, she is reported to have said: "It's fine… preparing this splendid countryside for the people, but are you doing anything about preparing the people to make proper use of it?" The damage caused by the half million people who trample the slopes of Snowdon each year suggests that more needs to be done. ❑

BELOW: the Precipice Walk, which starts near Llanfachreth

The Story of Slate

To learn about Wales's once-great slate industry is to learn about Wales itself – not just its economy but its religion, its culture, politics and education. In the heart of mountainous Snowdonia, which was the centre of the slate industry, the scars left by the quarries, mostly now silent, are the most significant man-made feature of the landscape.

At Llanberis, Bethesda, Blaenau Ffestiniog and the Nantlle Valley in the far north, and around Corris and Abergynolwyn to the south, 16,000 men once toiled, practising skills of a higher order in harsh and hazardous conditions. A practised quarryman (*chwarelwyr*) could tell how well a piece of rock would split even before it was blasted, and how many slates of what size he and his gang – often a family group – could extract from it. It was a skill on which the gang's livelihood depended.

The skill of slate splitting is still demonstrated at the Llechwedd Slate Caverns near Blaenau Ffestiniog. It is now a tourist attraction; visitors are taken underground by rail to view the giant caverns where men clung to the rock walls like flies and worked by candlelight to prise out roofing tiles for the world.

Some of the little ports in the north – such as Porthmadog and Port Dinorwic – owed their origins to the industry which, in its heyday in the late 1800s, transported thousands of tons of slate on narrow-gauge railway lines for shipment to destinations all over the world.

The workmen's cabins on the quarry floor served not only as shelter but also as chapels and classrooms, where brighter youngsters could be started on a route that might eventually lead them to university. And in those same cabins there must have been sown the seeds of revolt which led to an heroic dispute between the infant Quarrymen's Union and autocratic quarry-owners over minimum pay; this led, in 1900, to a lockout which lasted for three bitter years.

There was frequent violence, but the dispute ended in a crushing defeat for the workers. The hardships of those times have been told and retold in prose and poetry, not least by Kate Roberts, whose writing has been compared to that of Katherine Mansfield and Chekhov, and some of whose work has been translated into English. But the lockout was the beginning of the end for Welsh slate. By the time it finished, not only was there a depression in British building but new types of roofing material had arrived on the scene, as well as tiles from the United States. The departure of whole quarrying families to South Wales to seek work in the coal mines is poignantly described by Alexander Cordell in *This Sweet and Bitter Earth*.

Though the culture of the quarrymen and their villages survives and slate is used in many craft workshops, most of the major quarries closed down after World War II. The exception is Dinorwig, at Llanberis, no longer a quarry but the biggest pumped-storage electrical generation plant in Europe. Behind the grand quarry face, engineers constructed a cathedral-like cavern housing turbines powered by water cascading from an artificial hilltop lake to another on the old quarry floor. Here, as at Llechwedd, visitors can learn something of the hard way of life of the quarryman, for Dinorwig's workshops form the centrepiece of the Welsh Slate Museum.❑

GHT:
ate workers.

Map n page 226

THE LLŶN PENINSULA

This is the Land's End of Wales, encompassing Caernarfon's splendid castle, resorts such as Abersoch, Pwllheli and Porthmadog, and the fantasy village of Portmeirion

Long before tourist boards perfected hyperbole, the Llŷn Peninsula was exercising its own subtle charisma on visitors. In the 1930s, one writer, reading up on Llŷn the night before setting out from Caernarfon, was informed that this "Cornish-like arm which thrusts itself westward below Anglesey, is one of the last provinces of Arcady." Aberdaron was "a remote wilderness 17 miles from a railway station" whose inhabitants "live in happy ignorance of this modern world."

Centuries earlier, Gerald of Wales, while on his celebrated tour of 1188, also succumbed to the peninsula's sense of mystery. He wrote of Bardsey Island: "Either because of its pure air, which comes across the sea from Ireland, or through some miracle occasioned by the merits of the holy men who live there, the island has this peculiarity, that no one dies there except in extreme old age, for disease is almost unheard of. In fact, no one dies there at all, unless he is very old indeed."

Just 16 miles (25 km) long and 3–10 miles (5–16 km) broad, the Llŷn Peninsula still trades on its sense of being "different" from the rest of Wales. Shaped uncannily like Cornwall, it boasts of being the Land's End of Wales.

Caernarfon and its castle

The coastline alone, designated in 1956 an Area of Outstanding Natural Beauty, attracts a good proportion of Llŷn's visitors. Inland too, however, there are small communities which do indeed have a sense of peace and remoteness that give the region its own character. And, depending on where you mark the geographic starting point of Llŷn, the peninsula boasts the star attractions of Caernarfon and Portmeirion.

Few who visit Wales for any length of time miss out **Caernarfon** ⓭. The Romans certainly didn't. The name Caer-yn-Arfon is ancient; there has been a castle on this spot for many centuries.

The castle and town walls built by Edward I between 1285 and 1322 were successors to a strategic Roman fortification built in the vicinity more than 1,000 years earlier. Taking its name from the River Seiont, Roman Segontium was garrisoned by the 20th Augustan Legion. Its excavated ruins are open to the public, together with a museum run by the National Museums and Galleries of Wales.

The fortification that still stands today, **Caernarfon Castle**, was part of one of the most ambitious military construction projects of the Middle Ages – spawned by two 13th-century conflicts with Llywelyn ap Gruffydd, prince of the ancient king-

T: ernarfon bour.
LOW: ernarfon stle.

dom of Gwynedd. Caernarfon, a designated World Heritage Site, is part of a network of fortifications that includes Conwy, Rhuddlan, Beaumaris and Harlech. They were built by Edward 1 as an "iron ring" around Snowdonia, symbols of English dominion over the Welsh. How it all came about is explained in an excellent permanent exhibition within the castle walls. There's also the Royal Welch Fusiliers Museum, which, thanks to a substantial Heritage Lottery grant, is the most up-to-date regimental museum in the country. In the northeast tower another display explains the long and complex history of the many Princes of Wales, the most famous of whom is the present Prince Charles. His Investiture was held in Caernarfon Castle in 1969.

In the 19th century, when Caernarfon's military importance had long declined, it became a thriving port exporting slate to all parts of the world. Urbanisation accompanied this and the town's population more than doubled in the first half of the 1800s.

The castle and town were originally built as a single structure, though when the town walls ceased to serve their original purpose as a defence, the ditches were filled in to make roads and new archways were added in the 18th and 19th centuries to ease the flow of traffic. The town also began to spread along the banks of the Seiont and by the end of the 19th century it was three times as large outside its walls as within.

Despite this, Caernarfon has kept its simple grid pattern of medieval streets and it is this feeling of compactness and enclosure that gives the old part of the town its character. Caernarfon's connections with the British royal family give it an additional resonance.

The Roman garrison at Segontium stood guard over what in medieval times came to be called Watling Street, a line of communication of great strategic importance. Evidence of an outlying fort, guarding the approaches to Watling Street, can be seen at Dinas Dinlle, southwest of Caernarfon. But it's an uninspiring sight.

BELOW: open air motoring and eating in Caernarfon.

Map on page 226

A more exciting spectacle is provided by **Caernarfon Air World** which adjoins the sandy Dinas Dinlle beach. It offers a hands-on Air Museum and breathtaking flights over the mountains, castles and coastline of North Wales.

If you prefer a more sedate form of transport, take a ride on the **Welsh Highland Railway** (Rheilffordd Eryri). The ultimate aim of the railway is to restore, after 60 years of disuse, the 25-mile (40-km) track from Caernarfon to Porthmadog, creating the longest restored narrow-gauge steam railway in Britain. The track is now open for 7 miles (11 km) from Caernarfon to Waunfawr.

But if you don't have a head for heights or a love of trains you should, like pilgrims on their way to Bardsey, stop off at St Beuno's Church at **Clynnog-fawr**. This unspoiled 16th-century Tudor relic is dedicated to Wales's second most important saint after St David. St Beuno is said to have founded a church here in the 6th century.

The three-peaked mountain overlooking Trefor and Llanaelhaearn is **Yr Eifl** (the Forks), though this name has been anglicised into The Rivals. The easternmost summit (accessible from the B4417) is the site of Tre'r Ceiri, a hillfort-village thought to date from the 2nd century.

Old wounds

While Llŷn is rightly praised for its scenery, the lure of slate in the 19th century has left its scars on the landscape around **Trefor** ⓮. The quarry here closed years ago and Trefor is a quiet, run-down backwater. The steep quarry tracks zigzagging up the mountainside behind this village are still visible from a distance.

There are good beaches along this coast. The sand runs uninterrupted for more than a mile near **Morfa Nefyn**, culminating in the quiet – and exceedingly picturesque – village of **Porth Dinllaen**, now owned in its entirety by the National Trust.

As the B4413 leads down to **Aberdaron** and a wide panorama of Cardigan Bay

LOW: misty rth Dinllaen.

opens up, it's tempting to think of medieval pilgrims journeying to the Abbey of St Mary on Bardsey Island. For them, Aberdaron was the last staging post on their journey. They stayed in the small cottage of Y Gegin Fawr (The Big Kitchen), today a café. This building, however, isn't the only remnant from that time. The small church nearby, St Hywyn's, dates from the 12th century. Aberdaron's hump-backed bridge is thought to be the original medieval structure.

Bardsey Island

Today **Bardsey Island** ⓯ is a lonely nature reserve. Its Welsh name, Ynys Enlli, translates as Island of Currents or Island of Tides, but its strong religious association has given it another name: the Island of 20,000 Saints. From the 5th century onwards, it was an important ecclesiastical centre and a major place of pilgrimage. It is said that two pilgrimages (some think three) to Bardsey could be reckoned as the equivalent of one to Rome.

The first monastery was founded here in AD 429 by St Cadfan from Brittany. In the early part of the 7th century it was a refuge for monks fleeing the destruction of the monastery at Bangor-is-y-Coed.

The sense of the ancient fades away in **Abersoch** ⓰, a small and smart resort with a leisurely and distinctly nautical atmosphere. Boats are very much in evidence, whether bobbing around colourfully in the harbour or parked in private front gardens with For Sale signs displayed. Add a sprinkling of sporty cars topped by surfboards, and on a good summer's day there's an air of ease and affluence that seems a thousand miles away in a small village like Trefor.

If this makes Abersoch a little too crowded in the summer, there are other diversions nearby. Less than 2 miles (3 km) away, the 15th-century church of **Llanengan** is thought to be the oldest in the Llŷn Peninsula. Midway between Aberdaron and Abersoch is **Plas yn Rhiw**, a 17th-century Welsh manor house overlooking Porth Neigwl (Hell's Mouth).

BELOW: Aberdaron, once a staging post for pilgrims.

Map on page 226

You can take a boat to the **St Tudwal Islands**, east of Abersoch. Sir Clough Williams-Ellis purchased them in 1934 to save them from development.

A few miles along the coast is another of Llŷn's resorts: **Pwllheli** ⓱. There is little of Aberdaron's neatness and tidiness here. Pwllheli may have a noble past, having received its first charter in 1355 from the Black Prince, but today it is the unashamed commercial centre of Llŷn's tourist trade. The old town of Pwllheli is overshadowed by the seaside suburbs of South Beach and West End offering pony rides, adventure playgrounds, crazy golf, bowling and a craft centre.

Lloyd George's Wales

It would be interesting to know what Lloyd George, one of Britain's most gifted Prime Ministers, would have made of Pwllheli's seaside-resort incarnation. He was brought up just a few miles from here along the coast at **Llanystumdwy** in a cottage called Highgate – he was born not in Wales but in Manchester – and was educated at the church school at the west end of the village. He died here, too, in 1945, and there is now a **Lloyd George Museum** devoted to his life.

Criccieth ⓲ is a pretty resort, just 2 miles (3 km) along the road, which has retained its air of Victorian gentility. A writer visiting here in 1932 noted: "The ruined castle and Mr Lloyd George are the only 'sights' in Criccieth. Those who visit in the summer are not happy until they have seen Mr Lloyd George and even, perhaps, thrust their cameras through the gate."

That total of two sights in Criccieth is today reduced to just one. Lloyd George bought a house in 1939 back in Llanystumdwy. But the aforementioned **Criccieth Castle**, built around 1230, then sacked and burnt in 1404 by Owain Glyndŵr, still stands on its prominent headland overlooking the sweep of Tremadog Bay.

Porthmadog

On the south side of Llŷn, the staging point for the peninsula is **Porthmadog** ⓳. In the early years of the 19th century this small town didn't exist. It owes its origins to William Alexander Madocks, who in 1798 acquired land near here in order to reclaim it from the estuary. Following bigger projects, the community of Tremadog was born and by 1811 the great embankment of The Cob across the estuary had been completed.

Meanwhile Madocks had been exploiting the infant slate industry in Snowdonia and there was soon a need for a port for shipping slate. Porthmadog was opened in 1824 and rapidly became a bustling port and an active shipbuilding centre, producing between 1891 and 1913 a total of 33 elegant top-sailed schooners known as Western Ocean Yachts. They sailed the world, carrying out slate and returning with every conceivable cargo.

Porthmadog is still a bustling place, popular with shoppers, sailing enthusiasts and railway buffs. The **Ffestiniog Railway**, instead of transporting slate, now carries tourists along a scenic route from the harbour to Blaenau Ffestiniog. The **Welsh Highland Railway** only travels a

[RI]GHT: [Ab]ersoch [be]ach, packed [in] summer.

little way into the countryside to Pen-y-Mount. It will eventually link up with the railway of the same name which is being reinstated all the way from Caernarfon.

On the quayside, in the last surviving slate shed, is the **Maritime Museum**. Here you can see see how the fledgling seaport looked in the 19th century. The images of so many tall ships moored in a harbour populated by today's modern but unremarkable small craft is enough to recreate just that sense of romance, of time gone by, and conjure up the charisma that has attracted people to Llŷn since Gerald of Wales first related his modest knowledge of a modest peninsula in 1188.

Portmeirion's fantasy

If you ever thought that warnings over architectural insensitivity and bad taste were a symptom of the 1980s, spend a day in **Portmeirion** ⑳. Sir Clough Williams-Ellis, its gifted creator, was hammering home the same message in the 1920s.

He built this quirky Italianate village – which was to achieve fame when Patrick McGoohan's cult TV series, *The Prisoner*, was filmed there – as a "living protest in wood and stone against the havoc being wreaked by so-called development." He renamed his cherished site Portmeirion ("port" because of its natural harbour and "Merion" after the old county of Merioneth). Suspecting that most people did not readily appreciate architecture and landscape, he adopted a "light opera approach".

Portmeirion grew gradually and not to a preconceived plan. Built round a central courtyard flanked by the Campanile and Dome, this colourful community of buildings was originally inspired by the Italian town of Portofino.

But Portmeirion amounts to more than the often-used label of "Italianate" implies. Knitted into its architectural fabric is a complicated thread that includes Georgian houses, a Jacobean country hall, ornate Victorian facades and even gilded Burmese dancers on Ionic columns.

Building work, which often resembled the putting together of a jigsaw puzzle, began in 1925, the Campanile being one of the first buildings to pop its head up above the surrounding countryside as a portent of things to come. A second phase of building began in 1954, following the end of postwar restrictions.

To sample the Portmeirion experience visitors can buy day tickets or really indulge themselves by staying in secluded Hotel Portmeirion or in one of the charming cottages dotted around the village.

Few visitors are prepared for the elegant and compact dreamscape they find as they walk through Portmeirion's gates. As they explore the stairways and passageways, investigate the grottoes and courtyards, listen to the soothing sound of fountains, and come across unexpected architectural jokes and follies, expressions of amazement are everywhere to be seen and are just as entertaining as the buildings themselves.

But it's surely what Sir Clough Williams-Ellis eccentrically intended: that even after his death, the thousands of visitors who pass through Portmeirion every year still hear his rallying cry to the cause of sympathetic architecture. ❑

Map on pag 226

LEFT: Portmeirion unpredictab

The Man Who Built Portmeirion

To most visitors, the fantasy village of Portmeirion is just another attraction – slightly eccentric but beautiful. It was, of course, conceived as a visual entertainment; but at its heart lies a serious purpose.

In 1925, a successful architect, Sir Clough Williams-Ellis, bought the site – a beautiful headland near Porthmadog – with the intention of building a complete miniature seaside town. Sir Clough said that he had first had the dream of building "such a place to my own fancy" when he was five years old. "Throughout the years of my war service abroad [*in World War I*] I had to dream of something other than the horror, destruction and savagery – and what more different than to build with whatever serenity, kindness and loveliness one could contrive on some beautiful unknown site, yet to be miraculously discovered?"

Portmeirion was to be a demonstration that "one could develop even a very beautiful site without defiling it and indeed, given sufficient loving care, that one might even enhance what nature had provided as your background". His aim was to show that "architectural good manners can also mean good business".

Taking his inspiration from Portofino in Italy, and from buildings he had seen while travelling in Austria, Sir Clough gradually built up Portmeirion using odds and ends of houses rescued from demolition ("the home for fallen buildings," he called it). In its construction, he developed what he described as his "light opera approach to architecture" to produce what he hoped would be "beauty without solemnity".

An example of this rescue process is the village's town hall. After seeing by chance that a Flintshire mansion, Emral Hall, was to be demolished, he hastened to the house sale where he bought the Hall's ballroom ceiling for £13: there were no other bidders for "so awkward and speculative a lot". With considerable effort – and vast expense – the 17th-century ceiling was brought back to Portmeirion in 100 different pieces to form the centrepiece of the Hercules Hall.

Sir Clough was chairman of the first of Britain's New Towns, Stevenage, and his ideas on sympathetic town planning were a radical force. Without the economic depression of the 1930s and then World War II, one wonders what Sir Clough might have achieved on a national scale.

Portmeirion remains, however, as a fitting tribute. When Sir Clough died in 1978, some feared the dream of Portmeirion might die with him. The buildings were mostly of lightweight construction, not designed to last. However, under the direction first of Sir Clough's daughter Susan Williams-Ellis, then of his grandson Robin Llywelyn, the Portmeirion Foundation has worked to ensure the village's preservation. In 1988, the Portmeirion hotel, burnt down in 1981, reopened, elegantly restored. Guests can also stay in the village's individually designed cottages.

Noel Coward wrote his play *Blithe Spirit* while on holiday in Portmeirion. But the village is best known as a backdrop to the cult TV series *The Prisoner,* filmed there during the 1960s. Naturally, Sir Clough found this surreal programme entirely to his taste. ❑

HT: Clough iams-Ellis.

Map on page 248

THE ISLE OF ANGLESEY

Britain's largest offshore island contains Neolithic sites, remnants of the ancient Druids, a flourishing wildlife, and the village of Llanfairpwllgwyngyllgogerychwyrndrobwllllantysiliogogogoch

Some visitors to Wales don't bother with Anglesey. It's flat and featureless, they've heard. There's not much there, they've been told. And how can it compare to Snowdonia?

The Druids would certainly have welcomed such apathy. Nearly 2,000 years ago the Romans made every effort to cross the narrow stretch of water of the Menai Strait. Suetonius Paulinus, in the reign of Nero, arrived in AD 61. He sent his infantry across in boats and had his cavalry ford the shallows. On the far shore the Druids and the Britons were lined up ready for battle, but it was an easy victory for Rome.

Yet the lure of Anglesey didn't last long and Suetonius Paulinus cut short his stay on receiving news that Boudicca was marching on London. Some years later Agricola arrived. Not content to mess around in boats, he had trained a special corps in swimming and it is said they could fight in mid-stream. The Druids were beaten once more and this time nearly exterminated into the bargain.

Prehistoric sites

Ancient remains are, however, not difficult to find. Anglesey was populated in prehistoric times and the legacy of ancient settlements and burial chambers is plain to see. One of the best-known ancient sites is **Bryn Celli Ddu**, a burial chamber in the southeast of the island which is thought to date from as far back as 2,000 BC.

Facing the Menai Strait, the village of **Brynsiencyn** ❶ was once a Druid settlement. Close by is **Bodowyr**, another prominent burial chamber. There's a long list of similar sites scattered around the island.

Since the 19th century, Anglesey has received far more welcome visitors than the Romans. It was Thomas Telford who first bridged the Menai Strait when his Menai Suspension Bridge was completed in 1826. Robert Stephenson increased the flow of traffic with his railway bridge in 1850. The original Britannia Bridge was originally built by Stephenson too, being completed in 1850, but was damaged by fire in 1970 and replaced by a new structure. The original Stephenson road bridge has long since failed to keep up with modern traffic; although still open, most vehicles now cross the strait on the modern Britannia Bridge. Despite decades of being connected to the mainland of Wales, many visitors to Anglesey are just passing through – the Holyhead ferry service to Ireland ensures that. Anglesey has never escaped the charge that it doesn't have much going for it.

Anglesey's flatness and undulating low hills give this island an extremely un-

ECEDING GES: e Menai spension idge.
FT: Moelfre, Anglesey's rtheast ast.
GHT: the arquess of glesey.

Welsh look. Yet it has deep-seated cultural associations which root it in the Welsh nation. As well as being the home of the Druids, it was known as the "Mother of Wales" (*Mam Cymru*) because – in the words of medieval chronicler Gerald of Wales – "when crops have failed in all other regions, this island, from the richness of its soil and its abundant produce, has been able to supply all Wales."

Nonetheless, **Beaumaris** ❷ is regarded by the real Welshman as essentially an English town. **Beaumaris Castle** was the last of Edward I's Welsh fortifications but today it is often the first place visited by tourists. *Beau Marais* (Beautiful Marsh) was named after a nearby marsh that was drained by the castle's moats.

The town grew up around Edward's imposing castle. Although declared defensible in 1298, the castle fortifications never reached their full height due to a lack of money and supplies. It is nonetheless a magnificent sight, which academics regard as an almost perfect example of medieval military architecture. These days Beaumaris is a yachting resort and the short main thoroughfare of Castle Street is a tidy line of pastel-coloured Regency and Victorian houses which give the street an upmarket look.

The town boasts much older buildings. Tudor Rose, one of the oldest houses in Britain, is said to have been built around 1400. It was restored by Hendrik Lek, an artist who died in 1985. His son, Karel Lek, has inherited both the house and the talent of his father and exhibits oil paintings, watercolours, drawings and engravings.

Nearby there are more historic buildings. The **Olde Bull's Head Hotel**, dating from 1472 and rebuilt in 1617, was the headquarters of Cromwell's soldiers when they attacked the castle. The **Court House**, built in 1614 and unchanged since the 19th century, is the oldest active court in Britain; and the **town jail** is a 19th-century building which provides the visitor with a taste of the harshness of the Victorian judicial system.

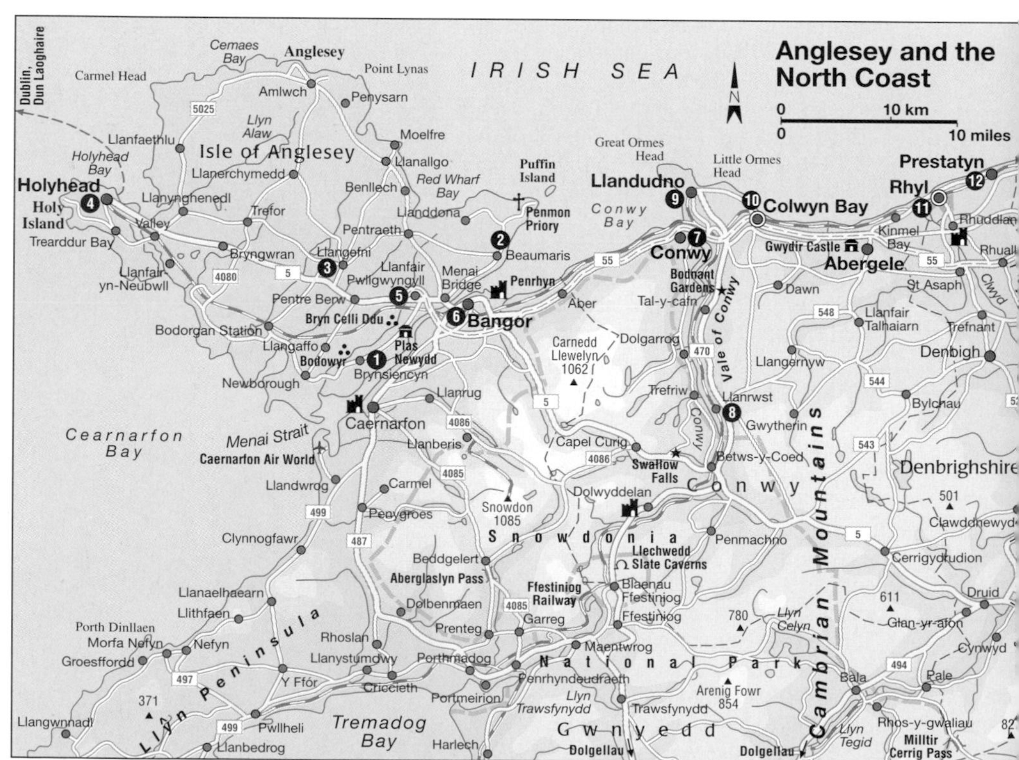

Map on page 248

The Beaumaris **Museum of Childhood Memories** (Easter–1 Nov), which lies on the other side of the road from Tudor Rose, has assembled a collection of antique toys and games that includes oddities such as Polyphons, Zoetropes and Praxino-scopes. This studious museum might have little to tell you about Anglesey but it adds to the charm and interest of Beaumaris.

Rich veins

Once you've wandered around Beaumaris, keep wandering. Your reward will be to stumble across quiet coves like **Red Wharf Bay** or **Benllech** on Anglesey's east coast, which are especially fine at low tide.

Llangefni ❸, near the middle of the island, is home to **Oriel Ynys Môn**, a museum and art gallery which offers an imaginative portrayal of Anglesey's history, folklore and wildlife and displays the meticulous work of the noted bird painter Charles Tunnicliffe, who spent the last 30 years of his life on the island. The art gallery holds up to nine exhibitions annually.

Amlwch, near the island's northern coast, exercised its own attraction in the 18th century, but not through any scenic virtues. While the Romans had worked copper mines near here, it wasn't until 1768 that some especially rich veins of copper ore were tapped. Amlwch became the most populated part of the island and a port was built here in 1793. The source of the ore, Parys Mountain, was eventually exhausted and its scarred remains overlook this small community.

Further along the northern coast at **Cemaes Bay**, secrecy was an ingredient for success for smugglers who used its secluded beaches. The secrets today take the form of **Wylfa nuclear power station** which, in a desire to keep its public relations sweet, dispels secrecy by inviting visitors on educational tours of the plant. Nearby, rival energy is provided by a large wind farm. Cemaes Bay itself, Wales's most northerly village, is a picturesque little port with an attractive sandy beach.

For visitors to Wales, **Holyhead** ❹ is

LOW: the useum of ildhood emories.

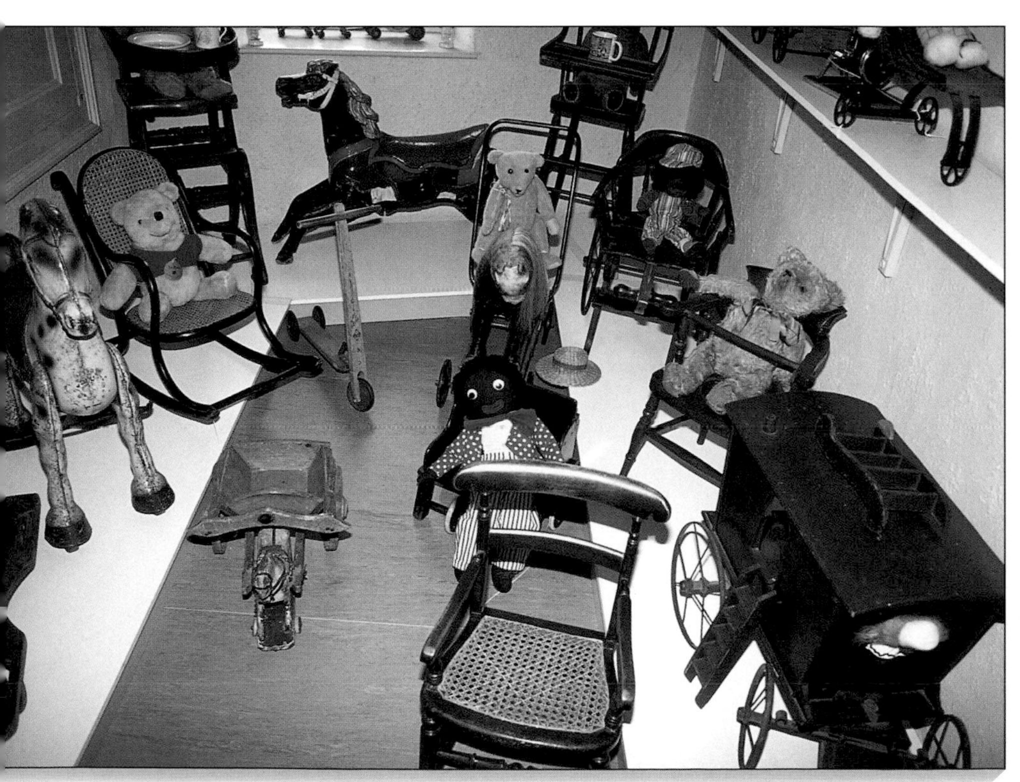

the end of the road; for those bound for Ireland, it is just the beginning. There are records of passenger boats between Anglesey and Ireland as far back as 1573. In 1801, Holyhead became the official crossing point and the opening of the road bridge (1826) and the railway bridge (1850) across the Menai Strait ensured the London to Ireland route's future.

Ireland became much more accessible in 1965 when the first car ferry service was introduced. After decades of so much passing through, Holyhead these days still fails to capture a tourist market. It's a fairly ordinary town with the usual ferry-port infrastructure. The only interesting remnant of the past is the **parish church of St Cybi**. The churchyard takes the form of rectangular walls which are part of a Roman fort built in the 3rd or 4th century. In the 6th century St Cybi set up his oratory within the protection offered by these Roman walls. Today's church dates from between the 15th and 17th centuries.

In summer, visitors who aren't just passing through make their way up **Holyhead Mountain**, which at more than 700ft (210 metres) can provide fine views of Snowdonia, Ireland and even the Isle of Man. These slopes were a natural choice for ancient inhabitants and hill-fort ramparts are visible. The signposts to the Irishmen's Huts refer to the remains of a large Celtic settlement that thrived between the 2nd and 4th centuries. At **South Stack**, 2 miles (3 km) west of Holyhead, the **Ellin's Tower Seabird Centre** allows you to observe nearly 3,000 nesting birds in early summer.

Tongue-twister

The village with the world's second longest name (a New Zealand hamlet is even more prolix) is famous only for having 58 letters. In 1988, Gwynnedd County Council, conscious of how long the name took to type, grasped the nettle and shortened **Llanfairpwllgwyngyllgogerychwyrndrobwllllantysiliogogogoch** ❺ on its documents and maps to a more man-

BELOW: sailing in the Menai Strait

Map on page 248

ageable Llanfair Pwllgwyngyll (others settle for Llanfair PG). "It would be impractical to use the full name on road signs," argued the council chairman. "Each sign would need its own bypass." The full name does have a meaning, translating as "St Mary's Church by the white aspen over the whirlpool and St Tysilio's Church by the red cave."

Sign-writers at least have earned a good living from the name. It is writ large – more than once – on James Pringle's woollen store which dominates the unassuming railway station (on the line between Bangor and Holyhead). The station itself sports a nameboard 15 ft (4.5 metres) long, supported by five steel posts.

Plas Newydd, as well as having a more manageable name, has much more to offer. Run by the National Trust, this 18th-century mansion has opulent interiors, fine furniture and paintings, and stately gardens. Plas Newydd's Rex Whistler Exhibition has the artist's largest wall painting, a 58-ft (18-metre) *trompe l'oeil* seascape. The **Cavalry Museum** devotes one room to the First Marquess of Anglesey, an officer whose stoicism has gone down in history. Losing his leg while on horseback at the Battle of Waterloo, so the story goes, the marquess (at that time he was the Second Lord Uxbridge) announced solemnly to Wellington: "By God, sir, I've lost my leg!" Back came the stiff-upper-lip reply: "By God, sir, so you have!"

Nearby, just along the coast at Brynsiencyn, the **Anglesey Sea Zoo** is a deservedly popular attraction. In imaginative simulations of local sea conditions, a huge variety of sea-life can be seen at close quarters. As part of a conservation project, lobsters and seahorses are bred here. The visitor can stroke a ray, walk through a shipwreck bristling with conger eels and see how pearls are created.

From the Sea Zoo, follow the coast road for a short while. There are stunning views across the Menai Strait to Caernarfon, its castle set against a backcloth of Snowdonia's peaks. ❑

LOW: e name esn't fit on train ticket.

7651 GRASSHOPPER

Map on page 248

THE NORTH COAST RESORTS

Bangor, Conwy, Llandudno, Colwyn Bay, Rhyl and Prestatyn range from the brash to the dignified. But can such traditional resorts adapt to the demands of the 21st century?

The 30-mile strip from Bangor to Prestatyn is no riviera – the best Welsh beaches are in the west. In summer, though, it still manages to draw significant numbers of people from Liverpool, Manchester and the Midlands. The traditional two-weeks beside the sea may well be in decline, but this, to some extent, has been counteracted by improved road links with the upgrade of the A55 along the North Wales coast. Former bottlenecks have been relieved, making this part of Wales more accessible for the increasing market in short breaks, which is taking over from the old style of holiday.

This small stretch of coast has been working hard to attract visitors since Victorian times, and the emphasis has always been on family holidays. The British seaside town comes brashly into its own on the North Wales coast, with Colwyn Bay, Rhyl and Prestatyn each trying to forge its own inimitable version of what a day by the sea should offer, and Llandudno coming up with a more dignified formula. The fare that they dish up is surprisingly varied, with Llandudno putting its money on Victorian seaside elegance, while Rhyl goes for the Coney Island approach – complete with rollercoaster.

Bangor

If you are setting off from **Bangor ❻**, however, you should be prepared for something much more sober. This cathedral city, a place of learning and an ancient religious centre, has a serious atmosphere that won't greatly appeal to those solely in search of seaside amusement. The name Bangor has its origins in a word meaning great circle or wattle enclosure – a reference perhaps to the wattle fence which surrounded the monastic community founded here in the 6th century by St Deiniol. The **cathedral**, originally constructed in the early 12th century, received its most damaging assault at the hands of Owain Glyndŵr in 1402 and lay in ruins until 1496 when repair work began. Today's building dates from a restoration by Gilbert Scott, begun in 1866.

Bangor is best known for its university; but it's not the kind of ancient institution found in England, Scotland or Ireland. Even though the idea of a Welsh university was one of Owain Glyndŵr's dreams in the Middle Ages – letters in which he wrote about this are preserved in archives in Paris – it wasn't until five centuries later that it finally became a reality.

Bangor College was established in 1883, although at that time, along with colleges at Aberystwyth and Cardiff, it was not allowed to confer degrees. In 1893 all three colleges were incorporated as the

RECEDING **AGES:** North ›ast beaches ›t crowded. **FT:** Borthy ›st harbour. **GHT:** the pier Llandudno.

University of Wales, and were later joined by colleges in Swansea and Lampeter.

Bangor was by that time well established on the north Welsh map. In the early 19th century the Penrhyn slate quarries inland at Bethseda were producing riches for Liverpool entrepreneur Richard Pennant, and the port of **Penrhyn**, to the east of Bangor, developed quickly. The construction from 1815 of Telford's road (today the A5) marked Bangor's coming of age. One good place to investigate all this is the **Bangor Museum and Art Gallery**. Exhibits help build up a picture from prehistoric times, through the Roman era and on into the Middle Ages and Victorian times. The downstairs art gallery has a varied programme of temporary exhibitions.

Although Bangor is on the coast, its waterside location is not apparent from the town centre. It's worth seeking out **Bangor Pier**, built in 1896 and since restored to its Victorian splendour, for views out across the Menai Strait.

Some of the profits from the Penrhyn slate quarries went into creating **Penrhyn Castle**, just outside Bangor, into a vast, quite overpowering mansion said to represent "the masterpiece of the Norman Revival in Britain."

The man behind this lavish residence was George Pennant (a cousin of Richard Pennant), who in 1820 commissioned an architect called Thomas Hopper. Penrhyn Castle was described in 1844, shortly after the project had been completed, as "stately, massive and stupendous." Those words barely do justice to the intricate interior woodwork and masonry – or the furniture and decor. As a monument to pride and excessive wealth there's nothing quite like it in the rest of Wales. It is now in the care of the National Trust.

Conwy

Conwy ❼ owes much to successful engineering. In 1824 Thomas Telford displayed architectural good manners when he started work on the elegant suspension

LEFT: Conwy Castl

CASTLES

There are two distinct kinds of castle in North Wales "native" structures and those built by Edward I following his successful campaigns against the Welsh in the late 13th century. Those in the former category, such as Powis and Criccieth, were built by Llywellyn the Great (d.1240), who as Prince of Gwynedd devoted his life to securing the territorial integrity of Wales. His grandson, Llywellyn the Last sought to establish his own authority as Prince of Wales but his refusal to pay homage to Edward I resulted in the invasion that put an end to any hopes of independence.

The last of the Welsh castles to fall was Castell-y-Bere on the western flanks of Cadair Idris, in 1283. Long since abandoned to the elements, the ruins lack the grandeur of other castles in Wales, but remain today one of the most poignant reminders of Welsh resistance, made all the more so by the magnificent mountain scenery in which they lie.

Edward's own castles at Conwy, Beaumaris, Caernarfon and Harlech, supported by fortified town walls, are fine examples of medieval military architecture. Their theatrical siting to guard strategic points against Welsh resistance would have intimidated any enemy. Even so, all except Caernarfon were taken, if only briefly, by the Welsh rebel Owain Glyndŵr's uprising at the start of the 15th century

Map on page 248

bridge across the Conwy Estuary. The now pedestrianised bridge has been restored and its toll house furnished as it was a century ago. Its towers match those of **Conwy Castle**, itself a fine piece of medieval engineering, so that the two structures not only blend together but even enhance each other.

The much celebrated Conwy Castle, begun in 1283, is another link in the network of fortifications erected by Edward I. Conwy's town walls, nearly a mile long and with 22 towers and three original gateways, are among the most complete anywhere in Europe. The town itself, however, was for a long time less important than the strategic defences: records from the late 16th century show that there were just 60 houses here.

The coming of the railway helped the town expand and gave rise to the need for a second bridge across the Conwy Estuary – this one built by Robert Stephenson in the mid-19th century.

Conwy has retained much evidence of its past. Of all the architectural riches within Conwy's narrow streets, **Plas Mawr** is the undisputed gem. Built between 1576 and 1585 for Robert Wynne, a prominent Welsh merchant, it is the finest surviving Elizabethan town house in Britain and has been painstakingly restored to its original glory. Close by, an imaginatively converted chapel houses the excellent **Royal Cambrian Academy Art Gallery**.

Remains of the Cistercian abbey of Aberconwy, built between 1172 and 1187, have been incorporated into **St Mary's Church** nearby. A gravestone on the floor of St Mary's states that Nicholas Hookes died in 1639, the 41st child of William Hookes and himself the father of 27 children.

Aberconwy House is a stone-and-timber medieval merchant's house dating from the 14th century. The rooms are furnished to portray the lifestyles of its various inhabitants over the past 600 years.

Tucked away on the quayside is the self-styled **Smallest House in Britain**,

[BE]LOW: [Pl]as Mawr. **[RI]GHT:** the [Sm]allest House [in] Britain.

measuring 6ft (1.83m) wide and 10ft 2in (3 metres) high. It was last occupied in 1900 by a 6ft 3in (1.9-metre) fisherman.

You'll see more than one advertisement in Conwy or Llandudno for bus tours of the fertile **Vale of Conwy**. Edward I moved the Cistercian monks of Conwy into the Vale of Conwy at Maenan, north of Llanrwst, in 1283, where they remained until Henry VIII's Dissolution of the Monasteries in 1536.

Between Dolgarrog and Trefriw, on the B5106, stands **Trefriw Wells Spa**, believed to have been discovered by soldiers of the 20th Roman legion. The Victorians added a Pump Room and Bath House. A tour includes sampling water from the chalybeate spring. At Trefriw, a turbine-powered **Woollen Mill** has demonstrations of traditional weaving of tweed and tapestry.

The Conwy River's source is just a few miles northeast of Blaenau Ffestiniog and its swift run down to the sea has carved out a formidable tourist route: the B5106 runs for 14 miles (22 km) along its west side and the A470 returns you to the coast via its eastern flank. Excursion coaches busily lap each other between Conwy and Llanrwst all summer long.

LEFT: hotel at Llandudno

Change of scenery

The Vale of Conwy more or less marks the eastern border of Snowdonia National Park, as if to point out that the really rugged territory is not to be found here. The vale is in fact rather neat and tidy.

At **Bodnant Garden**, just before the village of Tal-y-cafn, the landscape has actually been carefully manicured. Laid out in the late 19th century by Lancashire industrialist Henry Pochin and then added to by later members of his family, this is a celebrated piece of landscape gardening that makes imaginative use of conifers, rhododendrons, yews, roses, waterlilies and many rare varieties. This 100-acre (40-hectare) garden, one of the best in Britain, is now owned by the National Trust.

At the top of the Vale of Conwy, **Llanrwst** ❽ has actually declined rather than grown in the past 100 years. In the middle of the 19th century it was home to twice the population of today, an industrious town that made its living from wool, malting and tanning. An early resident was William Salesbury, who translated the New Testament into Welsh in the 16th century. Llanrwst's most renowned feature is its graceful old bridge, said to have been built by Inigo Jones in 1636.

The Wynne family, one of the most important in the vale, has left its mark in the form of **Gwydir Castle**, over on the west side of the river. Over the years this Tudor mansion has suffered fires and neglect, but is now being lovingly restored by a descendant of the Wynne family. The Wynnes also built two impressive chapels that still stand. In Llanrwst, **Gwydir Chapel** (1633) may have been designed by Inigo Jones. Near Gywdir Castle, **Gwydir Uchaf Chapel** (1673) retains an elaborate 17th-century painted ceiling.

Llandudno

Dignified **Llandudno** ❾ is Wales's largest resort. For more than 100 years it has been the jewel in the North Wales

Map
n page
248

crown. On a sunny day, the Victorian houses lining the North Shore bay are a picture of gleaming white symmetry. For once, the tourist office brochure has got it right. Llandudno can indeed "lay strong claims to be the most beautifully situated resort in the whole of the British Isles."

Lying on a wide, gently curving bay between the headlands of **Great Orme** and **Little Orme**, in the mid-19th century Llandudno was little more than a collection of fishermen's cottages. It was the Mostyn family that stood behind and helped finance the town's growth. Mostyn Street, Mostyn Avenue and Mostyn Broadway are the most visible legacy of the town's benefactors. The family also gave its name to the **Oriel Mostyn Art Gallery**, North Wales's major public art gallery.

A century of growth has allowed Llandudno to dominate the headland, with Great Orme separating the wide beaches of the North Shore and the quieter West Shore. Llandudno's earliest known visitor, St Tudno, from whom the town takes its name, made Great Orme his home in the 6th century. Today, the 12th/13th-century church of **St Tudno** stands overlooking the sea, on the site of St Tudno's original cell.

The Great Orme is well endowed with attractions. The summit can be reached by road, by the vintage **Great Orme Tramway**, which has been in operation since 1902, and by the more recently installed **Cabin Lift** from the **Happy Valley** formal gardens. At the top are the **Great Orme Country Park Visitor Centre** and the **Bronze-Age Copper Mines** (underground tours Feb–end Oct, daily 10am–5pm). Lower down the Orme **Ski Llandudno** has a dry ski-slope and toboggan run.

The **North Shore** offers just about everything the seaside has ever dreamed up. Its pier, all 2,296ft (700 metres) of it, was said by Sir John Betjeman to be one of the finest examples of a Victorian pier in Britain. The fact that the pier is now home, in the summer months, to an amusement arcade, candy floss, advertisements for boat rides and coach rides

LOW: ndudno wed from eat Orme.

and still more entertainments for young and old has not detracted from it. Down on the beach there are donkey rides and a Punch and Judy show.

On the quieter **West Shore** is a memorial, portraying Lewis Carroll's White Rabbit, unveiled by David Lloyd George in 1933. Alice Liddell, the inspiration for *Alice In Wonderland*, spent holidays in Llandudno as a child. At the **Alice In Wonderland Visitor Centre**, there is an exhibition in the Rabbit Hole of Alice's adventures.

The growth of **Colwyn Bay** ❿ as a resort was more recent than that of Llandudno and it can hardly hope to compete. In the 1940s it was just a village. Today the 4-mile (6-km) stretch between Llandrillo-yn-Rhos, Rhos-on-Sea and Old Colwyn has become a continuous built-up area liberally sprinkled with guesthouses. **Eiras Park** on the 3-mile (5-km) long promenade offers, among much else, bowls, tennis, a boating lake and **Dinosaur World**.

Overlooking the bay is the **Welsh Mountain Zoo**. Best known for its birds of prey displays, sea-lions and chimpanzees, it aims to show its animals as far as possible in their natural surroundings. The semi-circle of hills to the south and west of the town protect it from rain and wind. Local people claim that Colwyn Bay has its own "local climate".

Rhyl

Rhyl ⓫ is surely a lesson in how not to develop a seaside resort. As one drives in from the west, the first sights to catch the eye are the huge amusement park dominated by its rollercoaster and the 262-ft (80-metre) high **Skytower** which provides impressive views over the North Wales coast. From then on, however, Rhyl seems content to be average. Its long promenade is uninviting and gimmicky, and the resort relies on indoor attractions like the **Palace Fun Centre** and **Sealife Aquarium**.

The amusement park and extensive beaches are about the only thing that Llandudno, Colwyn Bay and Conwy can't compete with. Its only other selling point

BELOW: on t[h]e beach at Rh[y]

Map on page 248

is the **Sun Centre** at the eastern end of the promenade, a kind of indoor beach resort that combines under one roof a swimming pool, surfing pool, monorail, sunbeds, a 200-ft (60-metre) water slide and Tropical Bar.

A few miles inland the story is a little different. **Rhuddlan Castle** was one of the most important locations in the battle for Welsh independence; it was here in 1284 that Edward I announced the formation of the government of the conquered principality. Rhuddlan Castle was the second to be erected as part of Edward's strategic chain. The River Clwyd was diverted so that the castle could be supplied by sea and Rhuddlan was a port until a century ago.

Just 3 miles (5 km) south of Rhuddlan is **St Asaph Cathedral**, a building that makes the small community of St Asaph (Llanelwy) a city. The cathedral, dating to the 14th century, is Britain's smallest. A copy of the first Welsh-language Bible, translated in 1588 by the local bishop, William Morgan, is on display.

Prestatyn

Prestatyn ⓬ is a disappointing resort, and the building of a long concrete promenade hasn't done much for it. Its main attraction is the **Nova Centre**, an indoor water park and leisure complex. The town is the most northerly point of the Offa's Dyke path and the **Offa's Dyke Interpretative Centre** explains all about this 170-mile (272-km) route. Prestatyn was once the site of a castle held by the Prince of Powys. Following three major victories as they repelled invasion attempts by Henry II in the 12th century, Welsh leaders missed a unique chance to unite against the English.

As you follow the coast road east, the caravan parks around Rhyl and Prestatyn soon give way to the dockyard cranes and factories of the approaching industrial landscape. This was the way Henry II came in his first attempt to invade Wales. And it's the way many English visitors come now as they speed along the A55 Expressway from Lancashire, Cheshire and the Midlands. ❑

LOW: the ating lake Colwyn Bay.

Map on page 266

THE NORTHEAST

Wales meets England here, resulting in a mixture of undistinguished industrial estates and pleasant market towns such as Mold, Ruthin, Denbigh, Llangollen, Chirk and Welshpool

This corner of Wales is a strange hybrid. In the remote, thinly populated moors and mountains to the west of the region, you'll find the small, grey-stoned villages typical of traditional Wales. In parts of the east, where England meets Wales, the flat landscape is filled with busy roads, bleak industrial estates and anonymous, this-could-be-anywhere towns. So potent are the cross-border influences that some people on the Welsh side can sound as if they come from Liverpool.

Northeast Wales is a cultural amalgam. There's the mainstream traditional Wales of the rural hill communities; and, in complete contrast, there are the industrial and urban incursions into the flatlands around the Dee Estuary and Wrexham which have brought with them an anglicised culture.

Wrexham

Wrexham ❶, the biggest town in these parts, is a rather plain place. Its main source of interest is the **Church of St Giles**, with its 16th-century tower ("Wrexham Steeple", one of the so-called Seven Wonders of Wales). East-coast Americans make a pilgrimage to this spot, for the church contains the tomb of Elihu Yale, the benefactor of the eponymous American university, who died here in 1721. Look out for his long epitaph, part of which reads:

Born in America, in Europe bred,
In Africa travell'd, and in Asia wed,
Where long he liv'd and thriv'd;
at London dead.

Don't miss **Erddig**, on the outskirts of Wrexham. This 17th-century house, in the care of the National Trust, is not the usual opulent country mansion. Its individuality comes from the vivid insight it gives into "upstairs, downstairs" life in a country house of old. The well-preserved kitchen, laundry, bakehouse and smithy are as important as its decorative finery and period furniture.

Erddig's well-rounded character is partly a reflection of the benevolent attitude the Yorke family, who lived here from 1773 to 1973, had to their staff. The relationship, by all accounts, was an untypically happy and equitable one, the Yorkes even decorating their walls with specially commissioned portraits of their servants.

The landscape around Wrexham bears plentiful evidence of past and present industrial activity. More recently, this has been a coalmining area, though iron was the speciality in early industrial times. At **Bersham**, just west of Erddig, ironmaking took place from 1670, reaching its peak in the 1780s. At **Bersham Ironworks and**

PRECEDING PAGES: Valle Crucis Abbey. **LEFT:** Ruthin Castle, now a luxury hotel. **RIGHT:** Erddig.

Heritage Centre those interested in industrial archaeology can see the remnants of this pioneering enterprise which produced cannons for the American War of Independence and cylinders for James Watt's steam engines. Exhibitions tell the story of John "Iron-Mad" Wilkinson the Cumbrian ironmaster who took over the works in 1762. These industrial reminders are part of the 7-mile (11-km) **Clywedog Valley Trail**. This links a number of attractions, including the **Minera Lead Mines and Country Park** and visitor centres such as **King's Mill** which reflects Wrexham's agrarian past.

Mold ❷, a small town to the northwest of Wrexham, is noteworthy as the home of Theatre Clwyd, a large, modern arts complex. At **Flint**, on the Dee Estuary, you'll have to search for the town's important historical landmark. This was the home of the first castle built – in 1277 – by the all-conquering King Edward I as part of his campaign to subdue Wales. Edward's sturdy fortress – the harbinger of even greater castles which were constructed at Caernarfon, Conwy, Harlech and Beaumaris – is hidden away behind the very ordinary façades of the town centre.

Indecent exposure

Just up the coast at **Holywell ❸**, there's a cluster of places worth a mention. The little town has yet another of those Seven Wonders: the **holy well of St Winifride**, dating from the 7th century and possibly the most famous healing well in Britain. The much-travelled Dr Johnson was offended when he visited this "Lourdes of Wales" in 1774; he noted disapprovingly that "the bath is completely and indecently open: a woman bathed while we all looked on."

The **Greenfield Valley Heritage Park**, leading down to the coast, has been developed on a site where textiles, copper and brass were once produced. At the estuary end of the park is **Basingwerk Abbey**, a monastic ruin founded in 1131.

The **Clwydian Range**, which runs northwest to southeast above the Vale of

LEFT: Flint Castle.

Map on page 266

Clwyd, is the first natural upland barrier between England and Wales. These hummocky, rounded hills – an "Area of Outstanding Natural Beauty" – rise to 1,821ft (554 metres) at **Moel Famau**.

From the spectacular little mountain road that cuts through the hills between Ruthin and Mold (the main road, the A494, takes a southern loop through lower terrain), a number of paths lead to this windy summit, which is crowned by the ruins of the **Jubilee Tower**, built in Egyptian style in 1810 to commemorate the Jubilee of King George III. Go to the top to wonder not only at the views (you'll see Snowdonia and Liverpool on a clear day) but also at the profligate enthusiasm, so typical of Britain in the 19th century, which inspired the construction of a 115-ft (35-metre) tower on top of a weather-lashed Welsh hill.

Ruthin and Denbigh

Spread out beneath Moel Famau is the fertile Vale of Clwyd, a rich farming area. **Ruthin** is a pretty market town, "unique in North Wales for its number of timber-framed buildings" according to the Council for British Archaeology. Its architecture – a delightful black-and-white half-timbered jumble – is indeed irresistible. This is more than can be said, purists would argue, for the so-called "medieval banquets" held at the Ruthin Castle Hotel (an otherwise commendable establishment which incorporates into its fabric parts of the town's original medieval castle). On the approach to the historic centre of Ruthin, there is a good crafts centre.

Denbigh ❹, further up the vale, is another fine medieval town. It has grown up around its hilltop castle – ruined, but with a most impressive Great Gatehouse – and boasts a well-preserved, and almost complete, circuit of town walls.

When you leave the fertile, sheltered pastures of the Vale of Clwyd and head westwards, you are entering the *real* Wales, the harsh, marginal uplands of economic value only to the hill-sheep farmer and – more recently – the forester. The empty, exposed moorlands between the vales of Clwyd and Conwy are bleakly beautiful, resembling a Scottish moor when the purple heather is out.

In the 20th century, man radically altered the southern part of this lonely plateau. **Llyn Brenig** is a massive, man-made reservoir, completed in 1976 to accompany the smaller Llyn Alwen, built in the early 1900s. Casting aside, for a moment, the concerns often expressed by conservationists, the construction of the reservoir has at least given the public access to this previously untravelled upland. Overlooking the dam there's an excellent visitor centre which explains the local history and ecology, and also serves as the starting point for a number of lakeside footpaths.

Conservationists have particularly strong feelings about the spread of the ubiquitous, conformist conifer. The **Clocaenog Forest**, Wales's second-largest commercial plantation, covers much of the southern moor. Along with the water authorities, the Forestry Commission is nowadays acutely aware of its public

RIGHT: waitresses burst into song at Ruthin Castle's medieval banquets.

image and makes considerable efforts to welcome visitors to its woods.

The **River Dee**, which flows eastwards from Bala to Llangollen, is a convenient dividing line between the northern and southern halves of northeast Wales. Whereas the north is a mixture of moor, vale, hill and urban and industrial areas, the south presents a much more consistently rural picture. Centred around the bulky Berwyn Mountains, the south is an area of green, steep-sided valleys, remote mountains and undulating border country, dotted with unpronounceable villages such as **Llanfihangel-yng-Ngwynfa** and **Llansantffraid ym Mechain**.

Llangollen

Llangollen ❺, on the fast-flowing Dee, stands at one of the most dramatic entry points into Wales. As one drives westwards along the A5 (the route pioneered by that extraordinary Victorian engineer, Thomas Telford), the wide borderland vistas are suddenly replaced by a form of tunnel vision as the road funnels into the claustrophobic, cramped **Vale of Dee**. Llangollen, guarding the entrance to this narrow, severe valley, is a pretty town now famous the world over as the home of the International Eisteddfod.

Welsh *eisteddfodau* can disappoint non-Welsh speakers, though the major events now have translation facilities. Nonetheless, their main focus is Welsh-speaking Wales. Llangollen's event, held for a week each July, is different. Taking the traditions of the eisteddfod and applying them to a world stage, the event is a colourful, extrovert, outward-looking celebration of international fraternity. Started in 1947 to help rebuild a war-ravaged world, it has become one of Wales's largest festivals, an event attracting around 12,000 visitors as well as musicians and dancers from more than 50 countries (*see pages 69–72*).

Llangollen's **Plas Newydd** is a fine "magpie-style" black-and-white mansion (those cross-border influences, once again) which was the home from 1780 of the

BELOW: Llangollen.

Map on page 266

town's most unconventional inhabitants, the "Ladies of Llangollen". The lesbian ladies in question were two aristocrats of Anglo-Irish extraction, Lady Eleanor Butler and the Honourable Sarah Ponsonby, who with their maid Mary Carryll established an eccentric, gossipy household visited by the likes of Wordsworth, Byron, Shelley and the Duke of Wellington. The house is noted for its elaborate panelling. The ladies now lie in the graveyard of the town's 15th-century **Church of St Collen**, on Bridge Street.

On Castle Street can be found the **Postal Museum** and the **European Centre for Traditional and Regional Studies**, which specialises in folk studies and holds regular displays from other European Union countries. Llangollen does well for museums: there's also a museum here which takes the theme of a **Victorian school.**

An eerie drive

There's a stiff climb from the town to the stump of **Castell Dinas Bran**, a ruined fortress perched on a magnificent vantage point 1,000ft (300 metres) high. Alternatively, you can drive much of the way to the top, past an eerie line of cliffs (which would not look out of place in a spaghetti western). Another interesting drive through the narrow, steep lanes north of Llangollen takes you to **World's End**, a secluded, spectacular spot. For easier motoring, stick to the A542, which passes the ruins of the Cistercians' **Valle Crucis Abbey** and the 9th-century **Eliseg's Pillar** before climbing in a loop along the Horseshoe Pass.

The easiest, most relaxing travelling of all is by boat along the **Llangollen Canal** which runs east from the town, though you'll need a head for heights as it crosses the Dee Valley by Telford's superb 120-ft (37-metre) high **Pontcysyllte Aqueduct**, the longest in Britain.

Chirk ❻ is another gateway town – and has the gateway to prove it. The approach to **Chirk Castle** is protected by wrought-iron entrance gates, made in 1719–21 by the Davies brothers of Bersham, which

BELOW: The steam-powered Llangollen Railway.

display remarkable intricacy, finesse and painstaking detail. The castle, a National Trust property, is not what you might expect judging by its name. Although it began life as a rough-and-ready border fortress, over the centuries Chirk evolved into a stylish stately home embellished by neoclassical and neo-Gothic influences. Its fabric reflects its record, unique amongst North Wales castles, of continuous occupation from medieval times.

To get to **Glyn Ceiriog** from Llangollen, you can either drive via Chirk (the easy but long way around) or hold your breath and take an as-the-crow-flies route direct over the mountain on narrow, steep country lanes. Either way, this out-of-the-way village merits a visit, if only for the surprising evidence it displays of its past role in North Wales's great slate-mining industry.

The village stands at the entrance to the **Vale of Ceiriog**, a popular pony-trekking and walking area. This narrow valley ventures into the obscure **Berwyn Mountains**. Although not, in statistical terms, monumentally tall (they rise to around 2,500ft/750 metres), precious few inroads have been made into this often-ignored corner of Wales. There are few villages, few facilities for visitors; and few ways of getting to grips with the area other than on foot or horseback, for it does not lend itself to relaxed car touring, the topography having thwarted the efforts of the road-builders.

But its shortcomings are also its strengths. This tranquil backwater is peace and quiet personified. It's worth making the effort to get to **Pistyll Rhaeadr**, the tallest waterfall in Wales, which plunges 240ft (74 metres) into a rocky, wooded valley. The fall can be found right at the end of the road which sidles into the Berwyns northwestwards from **Llanrhaeadr-ym-Mochnant**, a village whose place in Welsh history is assured through its 16th-century associations with Bishop William Morgan, translator of the Bible into Welsh.

Llyn Vyrnwy is also mountain-locked, though a little more accessible. This reservoir, built at the end of the 19th century to

BELOW: Pontcysyllte, the longest aqueduct in Britain.

Map on page 266

supply Liverpool with water, can hardly be criticised on aesthetic grounds. Its location, surrounded by thickly wooded mountains, is superb, its inky-black waters adding a sense of extra drama to a powerful backdrop of peaks.

Perhaps the reservoir's dramatic personality also has something to do with the period in which it was built. The Victorians, never renowned for doing anything by halves, brought an architectural embellishment to Lake Vyrnwy's twin-spired water tower that owes much to the Gothic excess which also inspired Bram Stoker's *Dracula*. Call in at the **Vyrnwy Visitor Centre**, which is located in a converted chapel near the dam, if you want information on the rich wildlife in the woods around the lake.

Welshpool

Welshpool ❼ is a handsome, prosperous border and market town of tall buildings, a wide main street, and pleasing half-timbered and Georgian architecture. There's an interesting local museum and, for steam-train enthusiasts, the chance to ride on the narrow-gauge **Welshpool and Llanfair Light Railway**, which runs on a scenic route through the hills to **Llanfair Caereinion**, 8 miles (13 km) away.

The town's most significant site lies a mile to the south. The mellow red walls of **Powis Castle**, an opulent property given to the National Trust in 1952, rise above a magnificent series of terraces. The castle's links with a kinsman of the Earls of Powis, Clive of India, are reflected in its **Clive Museum**, which contains more than 300 objects associated with the celebrated soldier and administrator who helped consolidate British power in India in the 18th century.

Rivalling the exotic grandeur of the castle itself are the gardens, a series of four grand terraces of Italianate design. Created between 1688 and 1722, they are horticulturally and historically important because they are the only formal gardens of this date to survive in their original form. ❑

.LOW: wis Castle.
'ERLEAF: rnyard at la Lake.

INSIGHT GUIDES
TRAVEL TIPS

Global connection
h the AT&T Network

AT&T
direct
service

www.att.com/traveler

AT&T Direct® Service

The easy way to call home from anywhere.

AT&T Access Numbers

Argentina .0800-555-4288	**Czech Rep.▲.00-42-000-101**
Australia...1-800-881-011	**Denmark........8001-0010**
Austria●....0800-200-288	**Egypt●(Cairo) ...510-0200**
Bahamas..1-800-USA-ATT1	**France.....0800-99-00-11**
Belgium● ..0-800-100-10	**Germany..0800-2255-288**
Bermuda✚ 1-800-USA-ATT1	**Greece● 00-800-1311**
Brazil 000-8010	**Guam 1-800-2255-288**
Canada...1 800 CALL ATT	Guyana○ 165
Chile 800-225-288	**Hong Kong ..800-96-1111**
China, PRC▲ 10811	**India▲ 000-117**
Costa Rica .0-800-0-114-114	**Ireland 1-800-550-000**

AT&T Direct® Service

The easy way to call home from anywhere.

AT&T Access Numbers

Argentina .0800-555-4288	**Czech Rep.▲.00-42-000-101**
Australia...1-800-881-011	**Denmark........8001-0010**
Austria●....0800-200-288	**Egypt●(Cairo) ...510-0200**
Bahamas..1-800-USA-ATT1	**France.....0800-99-00-11**
Belgium● ..0-800-100-10	**Germany..0800-2255-288**
Bermuda✚ 1-800-USA-ATT1	**Greece● 00-800-1311**
Brazil 000-8010	**Guam 1-800-2255-288**
Canada...1 800 CALL ATT	Guyana○ 165
Chile 800-225-288	**Hong Kong ..800-96-1111**
China, PRC▲ 10811	**India▲ 000-117**
Costa Rica .0-800-0-114-114	**Ireland 1-800-550-000**

Israel 1-800-94-94-949	**Portugal▲..........800-800-128**
Italy●. 172-1011	**Saudi Arabia▲........1-800-10**
Jamaica● 1-800-USA-ATT1	Singapore.........800-0111-111
Japan●▲ 005-39-111	**South Africa......0800-99-0123**
Korea, Republic● ...0072-911	**Spain 900-99-00-11**
Mexico▽● ..01-800-288-2872	**Sweden.............020-799-111**
Netherlands●..0800-022-9111	**Switzerland● 0800-89-0011**
Neth. Ant.▲❂001-800-USA-ATT1	**Taiwan............0080-10288-0**
New Zealand● 000-911	Thailand❮.......001-999-111-11
Norway...............800-190-11	**Turkey●...........00-800-12277**
Panama 00-800-001-0109	U.A. Emirates●..........800-121
Philippines● 105-11	**U.K. 0800-89-0011**
Poland●▲...00-800-111-1111	**Venezuela 800-11-120**

FOR EASY CALLING WORLDWIDE

1. Just dial the AT&T Access Number for the country you are calling from. *2.* Dial the phone number you're calling. *3.* Dial your card number.*

For access numbers not listed ask any operator for **AT&T Direct®** Service.
In the U.S. call 1-800-222-0300 for **AT&T Direct** Service information.
Visit our Web site at: **www.att.com/traveler**
Bold-faced countries permit country-to-country calling outside the U.S.

- ● Public phones require coin or card deposit to place call.
- ✚ Public phones and select hotels.
- ▲ May not be available from every phone/payphone.
- ○ Collect calling only.
- ▽ Includes "Ladatel" public phones; if call does not complete, use 001-800-462-4240.
- ❂ From St. Maarten or phones at Bobby's Marina, use 1-800-USA-ATT1.
- ❮ When calling from public phones, use phones marked Lenso.
- * AT&T Calling Card, AT&T Corporate, AT&T Universal, MasterCard®, Diners Club®, American Express®, or Discover® cards accepted.

When placing an international call ***from*** the U.S., dial 1-800-CALL ATT.

WW ©6/00 AT&T

CONTENTS

Getting Acquainted

Planning the Trip

Practical Tips

Getting Around

Where to Stay

Eating Out

Attractions

Festivals

Outdoor Activities

Shopping

Sport

Language

Further Reading

Getting Acquainted

The Place

Area: 8,021 sq. miles (20,780 sq.km)
Capital: Cardiff
Highest mountain: Mount Snowdon (3,560 ft/1,085 metres)
Population: 2.89 million (326,000 in Cardiff)
Language: Welsh (19 percent) and English
Religion: nonconformist Protestant and Roman Catholic minority
Time zone: Greenwich Mean Time
Currency: pounds sterling
Weights and measures: imperial/metric
Electricity: 220 volts
International dialling code: 44

The land area of Wales is about the size of Massachusetts or half the size of Switzerland. It is approximately 170 miles long by 60 miles wide (270 by 100 km) and has 750 miles (1,200 km) of coastline. Wales is mainly an upland country with the greater part being over 600 ft (183 metres) above sea level. One quarter of it is above 1,000 ft (305 metres).

The population numbers slightly less than that of New Zealand. Over 75,000 of the total population of Wales live within half an hour of Cardiff – a population that grew as the Industrial Revolution exploded in the late 18th century.

Each part of Wales possesses physical features that have given it qualities of their own. The south has its beautiful sandy beaches, Mid-Wales has its gently rolling hills and the north craggy mountains and Yr Wyddf – Mount Snowdon, at 3,560 ft (1,085 metres) the highest point in England and Wales.

Time Zones

Wales, like the rest of Britain, lies in the Greenwich Mean Time Zone. In spring, the clock is moved forward one hour for British Summer Time and in the autumn moved back again to GMT. In the early summer months, it is light until 10pm, especially on the west coast of Wales. Zones west of Greenwich have earlier times (e.g. New York, five hours), whereas zones to the east have later times (e.g. Tokyo, nine hours).

Climate

Welsh weather is always unpredictable. Because of the mountainous nature of the country, it can be raining on one side of the mountain and dry and sunny all day on the other. Always be prepared and carry a lightweight raincoat or a collapsible umbrella.

May/June and September/October are usually the most pleasant and comfortable times to travel in Wales and although July and August were once considered to be the warmest months, they are now often quite wet. The month of April a few years ago was the warmest and driest since records have been kept and one recent December was the mildest in living memory. Heavy snow is something of a rarity and generally only remains on the higher ground for no more than a few days at a time.

Culture & Customs

Dewi Sant, or Saint David, a saint of the Celtic Church, was son of Sandde, Prince of Powys, and his wife Non. He became the Abbot of Ty Ddewi/Saint David's and died on 1 March AD 588. He was buried in what is today Ty Ddewi (Saint David's Cathedral) in Pembrokeshire. So respected was he that medieval pilgrims believed that two pilgrimages to Ty Ddewi were worth one pilgrimage to Rome. Fifty churches in South Wales alone bear his name.

St David's Day (1 March) is now the traditional day of the Welsh, celebrated by Welsh people all over the world, wearing either of the national emblems: a leek or daffodil. Usually the day's celebrations would include either a concert, an *eisteddfod* (festival) or a dinner with guest speaker.

THE NATIONAL FLAG

The national flag depicts a red dragon passant on a green and white field. No-one really knows how the red dragon became the emblem of Wales. However, it seems that the early Britons probably used it as a battle standard after the Roman occupation and that the design may derive from a Roman standard. One clue to this theory is that the English word "dragon" and the Welsh *draig* both come from the same Latin root, *draco*.

Draig was used in Welsh poetry to symbolise a warrior or a leader, while a British leader was sometimes called Pendragon, or chief dragon, as was King Arthur's father.

In the 7th century, Cadwaladr, Prince of Gwynedd, carried a battle standard bearing a Red Dragon. Legend gathered around the prince asserting that he would return to deliver his people.

The same idea appears in a legend recorded by an 8th-century historian about a fight between a Red Dragon (Wales) and a White Dragon (England) which foretold the eventual triumph of the Red Dragon. These deeply rooted convictions that a Welsh prince would reign again were preserved by the bards.

Centuries later they helped Henry Tudor to gain support as he marched through Wales, bearing the Red Dragon as his standard. After winning the English Crown at Bosworth Field, he placed the standard in St Paul's Cathedral. Henry also introduced the Red Dragon into the Royal Arms. This was later displaced by James VI of Scotland with the Scottish Unicorn.

In 1801 the Red Dragon again won heraldic recognition – this time as a Royal Badge representing Wales. An addition was made to it in 1953 by placing it on a shield, surrounded by a ribbon bearing the quotation *Y Ddraig Goch ddyry Cychwyn* (The Red Dragon lends impetus). The whole of this was surmounted by a crown.

For a time, this badge was used on the Welsh flag, but did not find universal favour in Wales and, in 1959, the Queen commanded that the original Red Dragon on a green and white field be flown as the official Welsh flag.

Welsh flags of varying sizes may be purchased from:

United Flag Traders, 20 Clarian Court, Clarian Close, Llansamlet, Swansea SA6 8RF. Tel: (01792) 700795.

Jaymie High Class Gifts and Fine Arts, 43 Queens Arcade, Cardiff CF10 2BY. Tel: (029) 2022 8718.

The Economy

Well over half of the land area of Wales is in agricultural use, although conditions vary considerably from the high moorland and mountainous regions of North Wales to such arable areas as part of southeast and southwest Wales. Farmers have not been too happy of late. The European Union has at various times introduced stringent milk production quotas and weakened the support system for beef. The crisis over BSE-infected animals hit many farmers hard.

As the cereal surplus problem is being faced, Welsh sheep farmers too are concerned about their future. Many farmers are therefore diversifying – some with considerable success as cheese producers and fish farmers but primarily as tourism entrepreneurs. Tourism is Wales's major growth industry, now employing directly or indirectly around 100,000.

The "How Green Was My Valley" image of Wales, of miners trudging their way home is no more. Wales is now in the forefront of a range of new technologies. More than one in five of Welsh manufacturing workers are employed by foreign-owned companies – North American, European and Japanese. Wales now boasts disc production, optics, electro-acoustics, office furniture, petrochemicals, instrument and automotive engineering, oil refining, electricity generating, financial services – and even Welsh wine industries.

In the early 1990s, the Welsh Development Agency, one of the first such agencies to take Japan seriously, was netting more than 20 percent of the UK's new inward investors. That share fell to 11 percent by the mid-1990s as other areas such as Scotland and the West Midlands fought back, and the weakness of the Japanese yen at the end of the decade caused some concern, but the general outlook remained good.

But the shedding of jobs in mining and other industrial sectors during the 1980s had been brutal, and so, despite the new vibrancy and the exciting regeneration of dock areas in Cardiff and Swansea, parts of Wales still experience a high level of unemployment.

Government

Wales returns 38 members to the (British) House of Commons in Westminster. The Conservative government's devastating defeat in the 1997 general election left them with no MPs at all in Wales, and the incoming Labour administration promised a referendum on Welsh devolution. The poll produced an extremely narrow margin for a limited transfer of local powers to a Welsh Assembly in Cardiff.

Made up of 60 elected members, the National Assembly for Wales has taken over from the Welsh Office in dealing with a variety of Welsh issues. Headed by the First Secretary, the Assembly is responsible for developing and implementing policies relating to agriculture, economic development, transport, health, tourism and the Welsh language. Previously, most of these areas were under the remit of the Secretary of State for Wales, a position that still exists but which now appears to be rather pointless. After a turbulent early period during which the Assembly has had to cope with a crisis in agriculture and a certain amount of internal wrangling, it now appears to be becoming more assured and effective, though many still regard it as an expensive talking-shop.

On 7 June 1979 there was a new representation when Wales elected its four members to sit in the European Parliament. The country, for this purpose, was divided into South Wales, Southeast Wales, Mid and West Wales and North Wales.

Local government in Wales, as elsewhere in Britain, has long been a playtoy of the politicians. In 1974, it was structured into two tiers, comprising eight large counties (Clwyd, Dyfed, Gwent, Gwynedd, Mid Glamorgan, Powys, South Glamorgan and West Glamorgan), within which there were 37 districts. The counties were responsible for strategic planning, transportation planning, education, the police and fire services and the personal social services. The districts provided more local services.

This organisation was never popular, and in 1996 the two-tier system was replaced by 22 unitary authorities. Old county names such as Flintshire and Monmouthshire were revived, and a new tier of county boroughs such as Cardiff and Caerphilly were created to represent the more densely populated south. You'll still see a mixture of old and new names – a reality reflected in this book – and it's always possible that the new Welsh Assembly will try to shift things around yet again.

Planning the Trip

What to Bring

Apart from your own special personal requirements, there is no need to bring any equipment other than a travel plug adaptor. Medications are available at chemists (drug stores) and photographic supplies are readily available everywhere. Any Tourist Information Centre should be able to advise you as to where to go to buy your particular needs.

Clothing

The visitor to Wales should bring comfortable, practical clothing and have a good pair of walking shoes. Casual clothes are perfectly acceptable, even for medieval banquets, but a few of the upmarket country hotels will expect men to wear a collar, tie and jacket for evening dinner.

A light raincoat (a "mac") is highly recommended as Welsh weather is so unpredictable. In recent years Wales has experienced a heatwave in April, snow in May and a drought in November! So be prepared and bring a small selection of clothes for all seasons.

Many visitors to Wales enjoy walking in the countryside and some also attempt to walk to the summit of Mount Snowdon and other peaks. The mountains are to be respected; as the weather can change in a matter of minutes on higher ground, adequate clothing, footwear, a map and a compass are essential. If one's visit coincides with a period of heavy rainfall an inexpensive pair of "wellies" (Wellington boots) obtainable for a few pounds from most shoe shops is a very good investment, even though you may decide to leave them at your favourite hotel or guest house rather than take them home with you.

Maps

Good road maps can be brought from petrol stations throughout the country. If you are taking a walking holiday, it is recommended that you visit a good book shop and buy your maps there.

Entry Regulations

The same regulations apply to Wales as to the rest of Britain. Overseas citizens must have a valid passport, but in the majority of cases do not need a visa. US and Canadian citizens generally receive a stamp on their passports, entitling them to stay for up to six months.

Customs Regulations

Items which may not be brought into Britain include plants, vegetables, fresh meats, controlled drugs, animals or pets, firearms and ammunition.

A red and green system is in operation for non-European Union visitors at most ports and airports in Britain. EU citizens can use a separate blue channel. Go through the Red Channel if you have goods to declare (or if you are unsure of importation restrictions), or the Green Channel (which is subject to spot checks by a Customs Officer) if you have nothing to declare (i.e. are not exceeding your permitted allowance of tobacco, perfume, spirits and wine).

Visitors arriving in cars from Ireland can obtain red or green windscreen stickers on the boat.

You must declare anything you intend to leave or sell in Britain.

Quarantine

The new "passport for pets" system allows visitors to bring cats and dogs into Britain from certain countries without placing them in quarantine. In order to comply, all animals must be vaccinated against rabies and fitted with a special microchip. Detailed information can be obtained from the Ministry of Agriculture, Fisheries & Food, Animal Health Dept., Hook Rise South, Tolworth, Surbiton, Surrey, KT6 7NF. Tel: (020) 7270 8080; website: www.maff.gov.uk

The penalties for landing an animal or bird without the "passport" or attempting to avoid quarantine are severe – at present the maximum penalty is an unlimited fine and/or one year's imprisonment. There are no exceptions to this rule, which is enforced to keep out rabies.

Health

Should you have any medical problems, consult your doctor before you travel and ask for a card with your medical profile. This, if kept with your other identification, could prove very useful in the case of an emergency.

Make sure that your health insurance coverage is adequate. Should you have to be hospitalised or be in need of what would be classified as non-emergency treatment, you will have to pay the full fees but would be able to recoup these from your insurance company on your return home.

The National Health Service in Britain charges no fees for the treatment of accidents, emergencies and infectious diseases. For more information on Medical Services, see section on *Emergencies*.

Money

The pound sterling is a decimal currency, divided into 100 pence. Coins come in the following denominations – £1 (100p), 50p, 20p, 10p, 5p, 2p, and 1p; and notes in four denominations, £50, £20, £10 and £5. No £1 notes remain in circulation.

You can bring any amount of money into the UK in any form, but for security the bulk should be in travellers cheques. Many people find it helpful to buy these in pounds sterling so that they can be exchanged easily in most places. Banks are the best places to convert foreign currency, not hotels or privately owned *bureaux de change*.

Major international credit cards are acceptable in an increasing number of British hotels, shops and restaurants but not necessarily away from major towns and cities or in small privately owned hotels and guest houses. The most popular cards are Access, American Express, MasterCard and Visa. It is advisable to purchase a small amount of currency before you arrive for immediate necessities and tips at the airport, rail station or ferry terminal. But as this currency would be in notes with the smallest denomination being £5, buy a bar of chocolate or a newspaper on arrival so that you have a selection of coins readily available.

Public Holidays

Public holidays in Wales are identical to those in England and usually amount to eight days a year. These are:

New Year's Day Bank Holiday, 1 January
Good Friday
Easter Monday
May Day Holiday (1st Monday after 1 May)
Spring Bank Holiday (a Monday in late May)
Late Summer Bank Holiday (last Monday in August)
Christmas Day, 25 December
Boxing Day, 26 December

Getting There

BY AIR

You can fly straight into Wales via Cardiff International Airport, 12 miles (19 km) from the city's centre (Tel: 01446 711111, website: www.cial.co.uk). It has direct all-year-round services to Orlando and summer only services to Toronto. There are also connecting scheduled services into Cardiff via Amsterdam and Dublin from a wide range of North American airports. In addition to Amsterdam and Dublin, scheduled flights also operate between Cardiff and Belfast, Aberdeen, Glasgow, Guernsey, Jersey, Brussels and Paris.

For those wishing to visit North Wales first, Manchester Airport is less than an hour's drive from the Welsh border, and is served by a variety of European and intercontinental carriers.

BY SEA

The only direct sea routes into Wales are from Ireland. Five services operate:
Dublin to Holyhead, **Rosslare to Pembroke Dock** (Irish Ferries, tel: [08705] 171717, website: www.irishferries.com); **Dun Laoghaire to Holyhead**, **Rosslare to Fishguard** (Stena Line, tel: [08705] 707070, website: www.stenaline.co.uk); and **Cork to Swansea** (Swansea/Cork Ferries, tel: [01792] 456116, website: www.swansea-cork.ie).

BY TRAIN

The 125 InterCity Service is a real distance-shrinker – less than two hours, capital to capital, from London (Paddington Station) to Cardiff – though it's not cheap. Speedy 125 trains also link Birmingham, Sheffield, York and Newcastle with Cardiff, and there's a fast, regular service from London (Euston Station) to Holyhead in North Wales, calling in at the north coast resorts. This coast is also served by direct services from Manchester, Liverpool and Hull. Tel:(08457) 484950; website: www.thetrainline.com

Great Little Trains

Narrow-gauge railways still operate in some parts of Wales. For more information contact: The Station, Llanfair Caereinion SY21 OSF, tel: (01938) 810441.

Members of Wales's Great Little Trains include:
Bala Lake Railway; Brecon Mountain Railway (Merthyr Tydfil); Ffestiniog Railway (Porthmadog); Llanberis Lake Railway; Rheilffordd Eryri/Welsh Highland Railway (Caernarfon); Talyllyn Railway (Tywyn); Vale of Rheidol Railway (Aberystwyth); Welsh Highland Railway (Porthmadog) and Welshpool and Llanfair Railway (Llanfair Caereinion).

BY COACH

Good road links also mean quick journey times – at surprisingly low prices. Convenient express services to Wales operate from almost all major towns and cities throughout England and Scotland. London services usually start at Victoria Station. For National Express services, tel: (08705) 808080; website: www.nationalexpress.co.uk

BY ROAD

Continual motorway connects Wales with London, Heathrow and Gatwick airports. And the motorway extends deep into southwest Wales; the scenic Pembrokeshire coast in the far west, for example, is an easy, straightforward drive of no more than a couple of hours from Cardiff.

Along the North Wales coast, there's the excellent A55 "Expressway". This road, which avoids all the old bottlenecks and links with Manchester Airport and Britain's motorway network, has resulted in dramatic improvements in communications between North Wales and the rest of the country. Similar improvements to roads into Mid-Wales from the M5/M6 via the M54 make for quick and easy access, especially from Birmingham Airport and central England.

Doing Business

Welsh Development Agency, Principality House, The Friary, Cardiff CF10 3FE. Tel: (0345) 775577; website: www.wda.co.uk

Confederation of British Industry, 3 Columbus Walk, Atlantic Wharf, Cardiff Bay CF10 4WW. Tel: (029) 2045 3710; website: www.cbi.org.uk
Dept. of Trade and Industry, Companies House, Crown Way, Maindy, Cardiff CF14 3UZ. Tel: (029) 2038 8588; website: www.companieshouse.gov.uk
Chamber of Commerce & Industry, Corys Building, 57 Bute Street, Cardiff CF10 5AS. Tel: (029) 2048 1648.

Travellers with Disabilities

For specific information contact:
Disability Wales, Llys Ifor, Crescent Road, Caerphilly CF83 1XL. Tel: (029) 2088 7325.

A publication produced by the Wales Tourist Board, listing attractions, etc. accessible to disabled guests and titled *Discovering Accessible Wales* is available from the Wales Tourist Board and information centres.

An all-Britain holiday information service for disabled visitors is available from:
Holiday Care, 2nd Floor, Imperial Buildings, Victoria Road, Horley, Surrey RH6 7PZ. Tel: (01293) 774535.

Tourist/Visitor Information

Wales Tourist Board, Brunel House, 2 Fitzalan Road, Cardiff CF24 0UY. Tel: (029) 2049 9909; website: www.visitwales.com
Wales Tourist Board (London), Britain Visitor's Centre, 1 Regent Street, London SW1Y 4XT. Tel: (020) 7808 3838; website: www.visitwales.com
Welsh Arts Council, 9 Museum Place, Cardiff CF10 3NX. Tel: (029) 2037 6500; website: www.ccc-acw.org.uk
Urdd Gobaith Cymru, Welsh League of Youth, Swyddfa'r Urdd, Llanbadarn Road, Aberystwyth, Ceredigion SY23 1EN. Tel: (01970) 623744; www.urdd.org.uk
National Eisteddfod Office, 40 Parc Ty Glas, Llanishen, Cardiff CF14 5WU. Tel: (029) 2076 3777; website: www.eisteddfod.org.uk
The National Trust, Office For Wales, Trinity Square, Llandudno LL30 2DE. Tel: (01492) 860123; website: www.nationaltrust.org.uk
Snowdonia National Park, National Park Office, Penrhyndeudraeth LL48 6LS. Tel: (01766) 770701.
Brecon Beacons National Park, 7 Glamorgan Street, Brecon, Powys LD3 7DP. Tel: (01874) 624437; website: www.breconbeacons.org.uk
Pembrokeshire Coast National Park, Winch Lane, Haverfordwest, Pembrokeshire SA61 1PY. Tel: 01437 764636; website: www.pembrokeshirecoast.org.uk
Wales Craft Council, Henfraes Lane, Welshpool, Powys SY21 7BE. Tel: (01938) 555313; website: www.walescraftcouncil.co.uk
National Museum and Gallery Cardiff, Cathays Park, Cardiff CF10 3NQ. Tel: (029) 2039 7951; website: www.nmgw.ac.uk
The Royal Welsh Agricultural Society, Llanelwedd, Builth Wells LD2 3SY. Tel: (01982) 553683; website: www.rwas.co.uk
European Centre for Traditional and Regional Cultures, Parade Street, Llangollen LL20 8RB. Tel: (01978) 861514.
Prince's Trust, Shire Hall, Mold, Flintshire. Tel: (01352) 700179.
CADW – Welsh Historic Monuments, Cathays Park, Cardiff CF10 3NQ. Tel: (029) 2050 0200; website: www.cadw.wales.gov.uk
Welsh National Opera, John Street, Cardiff CF10 5SP. Tel: (029) 2046 4666; website: www.wno.org.uk
Youth Hostels Association, Regional Office, 1 Cathedral Road, Cardiff CF11 9HA. Tel: (029) 2039 6766; website: yha.org.uk
Museum of Welsh Life, St Fagans, Cardiff. Tel: (029) 2057 3500; website: www:nmgw.ac.uk
National Library of Wales, Aberystwyth. Tel: (01970) 632800; website: www.llgc.org.uk
The Sports Council for Wales, Sophia Gardens, Cardiff CF11 9SW. Tel: (029) 2030 0500; website: www.sports-council-wales.co.uk

Practical Tips

Business Hours

Business hours are generally 9am–5.30pm Monday–Saturday. In cities such as Cardiff, Newport and Swansea many "corner shops" are open seven days a week until 10pm. In country areas, many small villages and towns still have an "early closing day". This is often on a Wednesday afternoon.

WEIGHTS & MEASURES

In Wales, weights and measures now generally follow the metric system, though it is possible that certain smaller shops and markets will still use imperial measurements. To calculate metric equivalents, use the following formulae:

To convert	Multiply by
Inches to centimetres	2.540
Feet to metres	0.3048
Yards to metres	0.9144
Miles to kilometres	1.60934
Sq. inches to sq. centimetres	6.4516
Sq. feet to sq. metres	0.0929030
Sq. yards to sq. metres	1.19599
Sq. miles to sq. kilometres	2.58999
Acres to hectares	0.404678
Gallons to liters	4.546
Ounces to grams	28.3495
Pounds to grams	453.592
Pounds to kilograms	0.4536
Tons to kilograms	1016.05

Tipping

This is very much left to the individual. The following is intended as a guide to customary practice:

Hotels: Many hotel bills include a service charge, usually 10–12.5 percent, but in some larger hotels 15 percent. Where a service charge is not included, it is customary to divide 10–15 percent of the bill among the staff who have given good service.
Restaurants: Some restaurant bills include service charges. Where a service charge is not included it is customary to leave a tip of 10–15 percent of the bill.
Taxis: 10–15 percent of the fare.
Hairdressers: £1 plus about 50p to the assistant who washes your hair.
Petrol (Gas) Stations: Tips are not expected.

PORTER SERVICES

Porters are a rare sight at railway stations these days. Most of the larger hotels, however, employ porters, whereas in smaller hotels the waiter or barman, or even the owner himself will help you with your baggage. About 50p per suitcase would be considered a reasonable tip.

Religious Services

Wales can boast a long and continuous history of Christian conviction, although church attendances have declined in recent years. Wales is largely non-conformist – with a great number of chapels, churches and a few spectacular cathedrals. The Archbishop of Wales is head of the disestablished church of the Anglican communion.

Most church services are held on a Sunday morning and evening. Details of these and other services are usually available at hotel reception desks and Tourist Information Centres.

Media

NEWSPAPERS

The *Western Mail*, printed in Cardiff, claims to be "The National Newspaper of Wales". It is the only daily paper with a good coverage of Welsh news as well as British and foreign news. Its "News of Wales" has tended to be biased towards South Wales but a North Wales edition was introduced in 1988. In North Wales, the *Daily Post*, printed in Liverpool, has Welsh news in its Welsh edition.

The three main cities – Cardiff *(South Wales Echo)*, Swansea *(Swansea Evening Post)* and Newport *(The Argus)* have evening papers which concentrate on local news, sport and entertainment. There's a lot of advertising in each of these papers. There are many local weekly papers throughout Wales and one weekly "national" newspaper, *Y Cymro* (The Welshman) which is printed in the Welsh language. *Buzz* is an excellent magazine, available free of charge, which contains comprehensive "what's on" listings for events, cinema, arts, music, etc in Cardiff and southeast Wales.

All major daily British papers are readily available at newsagents throughout Wales. The principality's first Sunday paper, *Wales on Sunday*, was created in 1989 to provide national news with a Welsh focus, and has proved popular.

TELEVISION

Cardiff has major television studios for both the BBC and commercial television (HTV). Both companies provide programmes of local interest which are slotted into the national schedules. Welsh language programmes are transmitted via the local counterpart of the national Channel 4: S4C *(Sianel 4 Cymru)*; this channel also includes some Channel 4 programmes in English at non-peak times.

BBC Wales (located at Broadcasting House, Llandaff) is the biggest and most productive broadcasting centre outside London. In television, BBC Wales originates nearly eight hours a week of English television programmes as an opt-out service for BBC 1 or BBC 2. Welsh news and events are featured in *Wales Today* each lunchtime and evening.

BBC Wales is one of the major contributors to the S4C Welsh language service, supplying most of the news and sporting programmes as well as a nightly "soap" about the inhabitants of Cwm Deri.

The commercial station in Wales, HTV, has invested about £20 million to create the most modern television production centre in Europe on a 60-acre (24-hectare) site on the outskirts of Cardiff. Welsh news and events are featured in an early evening programme. The company maintains close links with major national events in Wales and produces programmes of high quality, including current affairs, music and entertainment and agriculture.

Although BBC Wales has studios in Swansea and Bangor and HTV Wales have a presence in Mold, more broadcast television is produced in Cardiff than anywhere else in the UK other than London. Many of Wales's new independent companies are based in the regenerated dockland area of Cardiff whilst Caernarfon is undoubtedly the thriving media centre of North Wales.

Several dozen cable and satellite channels, such as CNN and Discovery Channel, are available.

RADIO

As well as its five national channels, the BBC runs Radio Wales (English language) and Radio Cymru (Welsh language). Both services provide on average 65 hours a week of programmes. A variety of commercial radio stations also have a presence – Marcher Sound in the northeast, Radio Maldwyn in Mid Wales, the bilingual Radio Ceredigion in West Wales, Red Dragon Radio, Touch AM and Bay FM in Cardiff and southeast Wales, and Swansea Sound covering southwest Wales. Programming ranges from community coverage to bland pop.

Postal Services

Post offices in cities and major towns throughout Wales are open from 9am–5.30pm Monday–Friday and from 9am–12.30pm Saturday. Most villages have post offices, but these are referred to as sub-post offices and are usually part of a grocery or general store. Opening hours are the same as main post offices but in some villages shops often close for a half-day (usually Wednesday) during the week.

The postage rate within the UK for letters is 26p (1st class) and 20p (2nd class). Airmail cards or letters to EU countries cost 30p, 31p for the rest of Europe or 43p to anywhere else in the world.

The Post Office will receive mail for you providing you instruct the sender to label the envelope "Poste Restante". It should be sent to a main post office nominated by you from where it may be collected.

Telephone

There is a minimum charge of 10p to use a public telephone. Telephone booths accept 10p, 20p, 50p and £1 coins. You can direct dial any number in Britain for the minimum charge of 10p, although the time you buy for your money is dictated by the distance involved. A local call will give you three minutes for 10p. If you think you may need to make a lot of calls from public kiosks, it would be worthing buying a phone card for convenience; this looks like a credit card, operates in many call boxes and is good for multiple calls to the amount of the card's value (typically £2 or £5).

To access the international network, dial 00 followed by your country code (e.g. 1 for the United States, 61 for Australia).

To contact the operator for assistance or if you experience difficulty in obtaining a dialled call, dial 100. Dial 153 for international directory enquiries. For directory enquiries within the UK dial 192. No money is required to call the operator or to call directory enquiries from a public telephone but a charge is made when calling directory enquiries from a private phone.

Americans with a credit phone card should use the following access numbers:
AT&T 0500 890 011
MCI 0800 890 222
Sprint 0800 890 877

Most hotels in Wales have **facsimile** facilities, available to guests at a small charge. You may also be able to send a facsimile from retail outlets in the High Street and from some village shops.

Internet Services

Travel and tourist information is available on the Wales Tourist Board web site. The Wales Tourist Board internet address: **www.visitwales.com**

Tourist Information Centres

** Indicates seasonal opening only*

MID WALES

Aberaeron
The Quay, Aberaeron, SA46 0BT. Tel: (01545) 570602.
Aberdyfi
Wharf Gardens, Aberdyfi, LL35 0ED. Tel: (01654) 767321.*
Aberystwyth
Terrace Road, Aberystwyth, SY23 7AG. Tel: (01970) 612125.
Bala
Penllyn, Pensarn Road, Bala, LL23 7SR. Tel: (01678) 521021.*
Barmouth
The Old Library, Station Rd., Barmouth, LL42 7SR. Tel:(01341) 280787.*
Borth
Cambrian Terrace, Borth SY24 5HU. Tel: (01970) 871174.*
Builth Wells
Groe Car Park, Builth Wells LD2 3BT . Tel: (01982) 553307.*
Cardigan
Theatr Mwldan, Bath House Road, Cardigan SA43 2JY. Tel: (01239) 613230.
Corris
Corris Craft Centre, Corris SY20 9SP. Tel: (01654) 761244.*
Dolgellau
Ty Meirion, Eldon Square, Dolgellau LL40 1PU. Tel: (01341) 422888.
Harlech
Gwyddfor House, High Street, Harlech LL46 2YA. Tel: (01766) 780658.*
Knighton
Offa's Dyke Centre, The Old School, West Street, Knighton LD7 1EW. Tel: (01547) 529424.
Lake Vyrnwy
Unit 2, Vyrnwy Craft Workshops SY10 0LY. Tel: (01691) 870346.*
Llandrindod Wells
Old Town Hall, Memorial Gardens, Llandrindod Wells LD1 5DL. Tel: (01597) 822600.
Llanidloes
54, Longbridge St., Llanidloes SY18 6EF. Tel: (01686) 412605.
Llanwrtyd Wells
Ty Barcud, The Square, Llanwrtyd Wells LD5 4RB. Tel: (01591) 610666.
Machynlleth
Canolfan Owain Glyndwr, Machynlleth SY20 8EE. Tel: (01654) 702401
Newcastle Emlyn
Market Hall, Newcastle Emlyn SA38 9AE. Tel: (01239) 711333.*
New Quay
Church Street, New Quay, Cardiganshire SA45 9NZ. Tel: (01545) 560865.*
Newtown
Back Lane, Newtown SY16 2PW. Tel: (01686) 625580.
Presteigne
The Judge's Lodgings, Broad St., Presteigne LD8 2AD. Tel: (01544) 260650.*
Rhayader
Leisure Centre, North St., Rhayader LD6 5BU. Tel: (01597) 810591.
Tywyn
High Street, Tywyn LL36 9AD. Tel: (01654) 710070.*
Welshpool
Vicarage Garden, Church Street, Welshpool SY21 7DD. Tel: (01938) 552043.

NORTH WALES

Bangor
Town Hall, Deiniol Road, Bangor LL57 2RE. Tel: (01248) 352786.*

Beddgelert
Canolfan Hebog, Beddgelert LL55 4YE. Tel: (01766) 890615.*

Betws-y-Coed
Snowdonia National Park/ Wales Tourist Board Information Centre, Royal Oak Stables, Betws-y-Coed LL24 0AH. Tel: (01690) 710426.

Blaenau Ffestiniog
Snowdonia National Park/Wales Tourist Board Information Centre, Unit 3, High Street, Blaenau Ffestiniog LL41 3HD. Tel: (01766) 830360.*

Caernarfon
Oriel Pendeitsh, Castle Street, Caernarfon LL55 1ES. Tel: (01286) 672232.

Colwyn Bay
Imperial Buildings, Station Sq., Colwyn Bay LL29 8LF. Tel: (01492) 530478.

Conwy
Conwy Castle Visitor Centre, Castle Street, Conwy, LL32 8LD. Tel: (01492) 592248.

Holyhead
Penrhos Beach Rd., Holyhead LL65 2QB. Tel: (01407) 762622.

Llanberis
41b High Street, Llanberis LL55 4EU. Tel: (01286) 870765.*

Llandudno
1–2 Chapel Street, Llandudno LL30 2YU. Tel: (01492) 876413.

Llanfair P.G.
Station Site, Llanfair P.G., LL61 5UJ. Tel: (01248) 713177.

LLangollen
Town Hall, Castle St., Llangollen LL20 5PD. Tel: (01978) 860828.

Mold
Library, Museum and Art Gallery, Earl Road, Mold CH7 1AP. Tel: (01352) 759331.

Porthmadog
High Street, Porthmadog LL49 9LD. Tel: (01766) 512981.

Prestatyn
Offa's Dyke Centre, Central Beach, Prestatyn LL19 7EY. Tel: (01745) 889092. *

Pwllheli
Min y Don, Station Square, Pwllheli LL53 5HG. Tel: (01758) 613000.

Rhos on Sea
The Promenade, Rhos on Sea LL28 4EP. Tel:(01492) 548778.

Rhyl
Rhyl Children's Village, West Parade, Rhyl LL18 1HZ. Tel: (01745) 355068.

Ruthin
Craft Centre, Park Road, Ruthin LL15 1BB. Tel: (01824) 703992.

Wrexham
Lambpit Street, Wrexham LL11 1WN. Tel: (01978) 292015.

SOUTH WALES

Abergavenny
Brecon Beacon National Park/ Wales Tourist Board Information Centre, Swan Meadow, Monmouth Road, Abergavenny NP7 5HH. Tel: (01873) 857588.

Barry Island
The Promenade, The Triangle, Barry Island CF62 5TQ. Tel: (01446) 747171.*

Blaenavon
Blaenavon Ironworks, Stack Square, Blaenavon NP4 8SJ.*

Brecon
Cattle Market Car Park, Brecon LD3 9DA. Tel: (01874) 622485.
Brecon Beacons National Park Visitor Centre, The Mountain Centre, Libanus, Brecon LD3 8ER. Tel: (01874) 623366.

Bridgend
McArthur Glen Design Outlet, The Derwen, Bridgend CF32 9SU. Tel: (01656) 654906.

Caerleon
5, High St., Caerleon NP6 1AE. Tel: (01633) 422656.

Caerphilly
Lower Twyn Square, Caerphilly CF83 1XX. Tel: (029) 2088 0011.

Cardiff
Cardiff Visitor Centre, 16, Wood St., Cardiff CF10 1ES. Tel: (029) 2022 7281.

Carmarthen
113, Lammas Street, Carmarthen SA31 3AQ. Tel: (01267) 231557.

Chepstow
Castle Car Park, Bridge Street, Chepstow NP6 5EY. Tel: (01291) 623772.

Crickhowell
Beaufort Chambers, Beaufort St., Crickhowell NP8 1AA. Tel: (01873) 812105.

Fishguard
Town Hall, The Square, Fishguard SA65 9HA. Tel: (01348) 873484

Kilgetty
Kingsmoor Common, Kilgetty SA68 0YA. Tel: (01834) 814161.*

Haverfordwest
Pembrokeshire Coast National Park/ Wales Tourist Board Information Centre, Old Bridge, Haverfordwest SA61 2EZ. Tel: (01437) 763110.

Llandeilo
Car Park, Crescent Road SA19 6HN. Tel: (01558) 824226.*

Llandovery
Heritage Centre, King's Road, Llandovery SA20 0AW. Tel: (01550) 720693.

Llanelli
Public Library, Vaughan St., Llanelli SA15 3AS. Tel: (01554) 772020.*

Llanidloes
54, Longbridge St., Llanidloes SY18 6EF. Tel: (01686) 412605.

Magor
First Services and Lodge, Jct 23a/M4 NP6 3YL. Tel: (01633) 881122.

Merthyr Tydfil
14a Glebeland Street, Merthyr Tydfil CF47 8AU. Tel: (01685) 379884.

Milford Haven
94, Charles St., Milford Haven SA73 2HL. Tel: (01646) 690866.*

Monmouth
Shire Hall, Agincourt Square, Monmouth NP5 3DY. Tel: (01600) 713899.

Mumbles
The Portacabin, Oystermouth Square, Mumbles SA3 4DQ. Tel: (01792) 361302.*

Newport
Newport Museum & Art Gallery, John Frost Square, Newport NP9 1HZ. Tel: (01633) 842962.

Newport (Pembs)
2, Bank Cottages, Long St., Newport SA42 0TN. Tel: 901239) 820912.*

Pembroke
Pembroke Visitor Centre, Commons Road, Pembroke, Pembrokeshire SA71 4EA. Tel: (01646) 622388.*

Pembroke Dock
The Guntower, Front St., Pembroke Dock SA72 6JZ. Tel: (01646) 622246.*
Penarth
Penarth Pier, The Esplanade, Penarth CF64 3AU. Tel: (029) 20708849.*
Pont Abraham
Pont Abraham Services, Junction 49/ M4, near Cross Hands SA4 1FP. Tel: (01792) 883838.
Pont Nedd Fechan
Pont Nedd Fechan, near Glyn Neath SA11 5NR. Tel: (01639) 721795.*
Pontypridd
Pontypridd Historical & Cultural Centre, The Old Bridge, Pontypridd CF37 4PE. Tel: (01443) 409512.
Porthcawl
The Old Police Station, John Street, Porthcawl, Bridgend CF36 3DT. Tel: (01656) 786639. *
St Davids
Pembrokeshire Coast National Park Centre, The Grove, St Davids SA62 6NW. Tel: (01437) 720392.
Saundersfoot
The Barbecue, Harbour Car Park, Saundersfoot SA69 9HE. Tel: (01834) 8133652.*
Swansea
Plymouth St., Swansea SA1 3QG. Tel: (01792) 468321.
Tenby
The Croft, Tenby SA70 8AP. Tel: (01834) 842402.

Tourist Information Centres in England

Cheshire

Chester
Town Hall, Northgate Street, Chester, Cheshire CH1 2HF. Tel: (01244) 313126.

Shropshire

Oswestry
Mile End , Oswestry, Salop SY11 4JA. Tel: (01691) 662488.
Manchester
Terminal 1, Manchester International Airport, International Airways Hall, Greater Manchester, M22 5NY. Tel: (0161) 436 3344.

Embassies & Consulates

Belgium: Belgian Consul, 10 Marine Parade, Penarth, Vale of Glamorgan CF46 3BG. Tel: (029) 2070 1457.
Italy: Italian Vice Consulate, 14 Museum Place, Cardiff. Tel: (029) 2034 1757.
Netherlands: Netherlands Consul, 3 Harbour Drive, Capital Waterside, Cardiff CF10 4WZ. Tel: (029) 2082 4405.
Norway: Norwegian Consul, 55 High Street, Cowbridge, Vale of Glamorgan. Tel: (01446) 774018.
Thailand: Royal Thai Consulate, 9 Mount Stuart Square, Cardiff CF10 5EE. Tel: (029) 2046 5777.
Turkey: Turkish Consul, Empire House, Docks, Cardiff. Tel: (029) 2048 7841.

Emergencies

Dial **999** on the nearest telephone (no coins required) and ask for the emergency service you want – **Fire**, **Police**, **Ambulance** or **Coastguard**.

MAIN POLICE STATIONS

Mid Wales

Aberystwyth: Tel: (01970) 612791.
Newton: Tel: (01686) 625704.

North Wales

Colwyn Bay: North Wales Police, Colwyn Bay. Tel: (01492) 517171.
Dolgellau: Tel: (01341) 422222.
Llandudno: Tel: (01492) 860260.
Wrexham: Tel: (01978) 290222.

South Wales

Bridgend: South Wales Constabulary, Bridgend. Tel: (01656) 655555.
Cardiff: Tel: (029) 2022 2111.

Southeast Wales

Cwmbran: Gwent Constabulary, Croesyceiliog, Cwmbran. Tel: (01633) 838111.
Chepstow: Tel: (01291) 623993.
Monmouth: Tel: (01600) 712321.

Southwest Wales

Carmarthen: Dyfed Powys Constabulary, Carmarthen. Tel: (01267) 236444.

MEDICAL SERVICES

Although it is advisable to have your own medical insurance, citizens of EU countries and some other countries are entitled to medical treatment under reciprocal arrangements. Emergency treatment is given free at hospital accident and emergency departments. Major hospitals are listed here.

Mid Wales

Aberystwyth: Bron Glais Hospital, Aberystwyth. Tel: (01970) 623131.
Shrewsbury: Royal Shrewsbury Hospital, Mytton Oak Road, Shrewsbury. Tel: (01743) 231122.

North Wales

Bangor: Ysbyty Gwynedd, Penrhos Road, Bangor. Tel: (01248) 370007.
Llandudno: Llandudno General Hospital, Llandudno. Tel: (01492) 860066.
St Asaph (for Rhyl & Prestatyn): Glan Clwyd Hospital, Bodelwyddan, St Asaph. Tel: (01745) 583910.
Wrexham: Ysbyty Maelor Wrecsam, Croesnewydd Road, Wrexham. Tel: (01978) 291100.

South Wales

Abergavenny: Nevill Hall Hospital, Abergavenny. Tel: (01873) 852091.
Bridgend: Bridgend General Hospital, Quarella Road, Bridgend. Tel: (01656) 6662166.
Cardiff: Cardiff Royal Infirmary, Cardiff. Tel: (029) 2049 2233. University Hospital of Wales, Cardiff. Tel: (029) 2074 7747.
Newport: Royal Gwent Hospital, Newport. Tel: (01633) 234234.
Swansea: Morriston Hospital, Heol Maes Eglwys, Cwnrhydyceirw, Swansea. Tel: (01792) 702222.

Southwest Wales

Carmarthen: West Wales General Hospital, Glan Gwili, Carmarthen. Tel: (01267) 235151.

Haverfordwest: Withybush General Hospital, Fishguard Road, Haverfordwest. Tel: (01437) 4545.

LOST PROPERTY

Lost credit cards must be reported immediately to:
Access/MasterCard, Southend on Sea. Tel: (01702) 354040.
American Express, Brighton. Tel: (01273) 696933.
Diners Club, Farnborough. Tel: 0800 460800.
Visa, Northampton. Tel: (01604) 230230.

Valuables: Most hotels have a safe where your valuables may be deposited. When travelling, it is always advisable to conceal cameras, etc. when left unattended in a car or coach. Always lock your car.

Gay & Lesbian Travellers

Two sources in Cardiff for gay and lesbian information and advice are **Friend** (Tues–Sat, 8–10pm, tel: 029-20340101) and **Lesbian Line** (Tues, 8–10pm, 029-2937 4051). They can advise of activities throughout Wales.

Alternative Lifestyles

New Age beliefs have always been strong in Wales, but have burgeoned since the 1960s when many dropouts sought alternative lifestyles on the Celtic fringe. As a result, the incidence of health food shops, organic gardening and vegetarian cafés is far higher than in England. The Centre for Alternative Technology (see page 000) is a notable example of the trend.

Getting Around

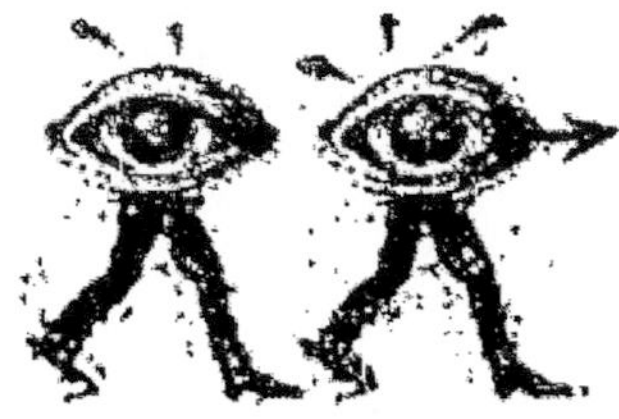

On Arrival

Wales is much more accessible than most people think. It takes only two hours to travel from London to Cardiff by high-speed Intercity train. These trains run during most of the day at hourly intervals and depart London from Paddington Station.

But, having arrived in Wales, how does one get around? There are only two answers: with difficulty or by car. To see the best of Wales and to explore its quieter areas, a car is essential. With four people sharing, it may well be worthwhile having the services of a knowledgeable chauffeur-guide but if you are happy to rent a car and do the driving yourself, don't pick up your car in London or another large city – travel by train or bus to Wales first and rent your car in a smaller city or town where the traffic is much lighter and quieter country roads are virtually on your doorstep. This will give you a confidence booster, especially if you aren't used to driving on the left-hand side of the road.

Car hire in Britain is not cheap, although many excellent deals are available if you can pick up and return your car to the same destination. Some of these smaller companies, however, have very few automatic cars available, so it's advisable to book this type in advance.

There is no air link between South and North Wales, nor is it possible to travel by train from south to north without going through England. The "Britrail Pass" holder needs to work hard to get value for money in Wales. The two main lines run east to west along the north coast (Chester–Holyhead) and the south coast (Newport–Fishguard). Both services link up with ferry services to and from Ireland.

In Mid-Wales it is possible to travel by rail, again from east to west (Shrewsbury to Aberystwyth), but the two railway journeys that are the most scenic and memorable are the Central Wales line through the heart of Wales (Swansea–Llandrindod Wells–Shrewsbury) and the Cambrian Coaster service (Aberystwth–Aberdyfi–Harlech–Criccieth–Pwllheli).

There is only one way of travelling between North and South Wales by public transportation in one day, and that is by coach. This daily year-round service, operated by First Cymru (tel: [08706] 082608), is known as Traws Cambria. It runs between Bangor (North Wales) and Cardiff via Aberystwyth, Swansea and a number of small towns on the west coast. Journey time is eight hours and sample fares are around £17 single for entire journey or around £30 period return (three months). There is a 25 percent discount on adult fares for men and women over 60.

Another ticket worth condidering is the 'Freedom of Wales' Flexi Pass, which offers unlimited travel on all mainline rail services in Wales plus most scheduled bus services. For narrow-gauge railway enthusiasts there's the bonus of free travel on a few of the "Great Little Trains" too. Eight- and 15-day tickets are available. The North and Mid Wales Flexi Rover and the Freedom of South Wales Flexi Rover Tickets give much the same unlimited travel benefits by train/bus as Flexi Pass, though on a regional basis. Seven-day tickets are available. For further Flexi Pass/Rover details tel: (08457) 484950 or (01766) 512340; website: www.travelwales-flexipass.co.uk

Travellers arriving in Wales through Cardiff Airport (12 miles/19km west of city centre) can take a taxi (cost to Central Railway

Station approx. £10–£12) or a bus. Service X91 operates hourly between the airport during the day while the 345 service runs in the evenings.

Maps

The best general map of Wales is published by the Wales Tourist Board. This map lists all major tourist sites and is packed with useful information and telephone numbers, town maps, a gazetteer and suggested road tours (cost approx. £2). Other useful maps are available at most offices of the British Tourist Authority worldwide.

Walkers heading for the Snowdonia region can choose from six Ordnance Survey Landranger maps at a scale of 1:50,000. They are: 115 for Snowdon, 114 for Anglesey, 123 for the Lleyn Peninsula, 124 for Porthmadog and Cadair Idris, 125 for Bala, and 135 for Aberdyfi and Machynlleth. Outdoor Leisure maps (1:25,000) cover Snowdon and Conwy Valley areas (Sheet 17), Harlech and Bala areas (Sheet 18) and Cadair Idris area (Sheet 23).

Car Hire

Avis

Website: www.avis.com
Cardiff: 14–22 Tudor Street, Cardiff CF11 8RF. Tel: (029) 2034 2111.
Swansea: N.C.P. Car Park, Orchard Street, Swansea. Tel: (01792) 460939.
Wrexham: Crescent Car Sales, The Beast Market, Wrexham. Tel: (01978) 351747.

Hertz

Website: www.hertz.com.
Cardiff: 9 Central Square, Cardiff CF1 1EP. Tel: (029) 2022 4548/9.
Fishguard: Fishguard Harbour Garage, Goodwick, Fishguard SA65 0BU. Tel: (01348) 874701.
Holyhead: Swift Service Station, London Road, Holyhead, Anglesey. Tel: (01407) 763818.
Swansea: Ael-Bryn Service Station, Carmarthen Road, Fforestfach, Swansea. Tel: (01792) 587393.

Europcar

Website: www.europcar.com
Cardiff: Cardiff Airport, Terminal Building, Cardiff Wales Airport, Rhoose. Tel: (01446) 711924.
1–11 Byron Street, Cardiff, . Tel: (029) 2049 8978.
Newport: 670 Chepstow Road, Royal Oak, Newport. Tel: (01633) 281810.
Swansea: 187.189 Lower Oxford Street, Swansea. Tel: (01792) 650526.

Kenning

Website: www.kenning.co.uk
Cardiff: Unit F, St. Catherine's Park, Pengam Road, Tremorfa, Cardiff Tel: (029) 2049 9333.
Carmarthen: W.L. Silcox & Sons Limited, Pensarn, Carmarthenshire. Tel: (01267) 221420.
Holyhead: 22 Welsh Road, Garden City, Holyhead, Anglesey. Tel: (01244) 836 300.
Pembroke: Waterloo Garage, Pembroke Dock, Pembroke. Tel: (01646) 684252.
Swansea: Sway Road, Morriston, Swansea. Tel: (01792) 781782.

NATIONAL CAR RENTALS

Website: www.nationalcar-europe.com.
Cardiff: 10 Dominions Way Industrial Estate, Newport Road, Cardiff. Tel: (029) 2049 6256.
Holyhead: Kingsland Road, Holyhead, Anglesey. Tel: (01407) 764614.
Swansea: 46-50 Lower Oxford Street, Swansea. Tel: (01792) 456646.

Travel Packages

Wales is often not included in package tours of Britain or only forms a minor part of an all-Britain coach tour. Nevertheless, Wales is an ideal destination for people seeking the unusual and the tour operators listed in this section, although mainly small organisations, do cater for a wide range of special interests.

FISHING TRIPS

Starida, Little Bryn, Bryn Lane, Beaumaris, Anglesey. Tel: (01248) 810251.
Sea Cruises
Coastal & Island Cruises, 3 Seaman's Rooms, Penniless Cove, Tenby SA70 7BY. Tel: (01834) 845400/843545.
Thousand Island Expeditions, Cross Square, St David's SA62 6SL. Tel: (01437) 721686; website: www.thousandislandexpeditions.co.uk

COACH TOURS

Alpine Coaches Garage, Builders Street West, Llandudno. Tel: (01492) 879133.
Stratos, Poole Road, Newtown SY16 1DL. Tel: (01686) 629021; website: www.stratostravel.co.uk
Walking Tours
Acorn Activities, PO Box 120, Hereford HR4 8YB. Tel: (01432) 830083; website: www.acornactivities.co.uk

SPECIAL INTEREST GROUP TOURS

EuroWales, Princes Square, Montgomery SY15 6PZ. Tel: (01686) 668030; fax: (01686) 668029; website: www.eurowales.co.uk

Tour Guides

The Wales Official Tourist Guide Association can be contacted at Alun Booth, 54 Allt-yr-yn Road, Newport NP20 5EB. Tel: (01633) 663364. Guides can be booked through Tourist Information Centres.

Members are the only qualified tourist guides in Wales registered by the Wales Tourist Board. Association Members will undertake any kind of guided tour, ranging from hourly tours by car and coach from a designated centre, to extended tours throughout Wales.

Language Key

D/G	Driver/Guide	**I**	Italian
D	Dutch	**S**	Spanish
W	Welsh		
Da	Danish	**Sw**	Swedish
F	French	**G**	German
GB	Round Britain Tours		

NORTH WALES

Derek Jones, Y Stabl, 30 Acton Gardens, Box Lane, Wrexham. Tel: (01978) 351212.

SOUTHWEST WALES

Susanna Van Eeghen, Ty Poeth, Llandysul SA44 4RS. Tel: (01559) 384483. **F D**

SOUTHEAST WALES

Cardiff

Audrey Griffiths, 3 Church Street, Taffs Well, Cardiff CF4 7PG. Tel: (029) 2081 1970. **GB**
William O'Keefe, 76 Conwy Road, Pontcanna, Cardiff CF11 9NN. Tel: (029) 2066 6879.
Philip Boots, 9 St Pauls Avenue, Barry CF62 8HT. Tel: (01446) 722277
David Thompson, 59 De Braose Close, Danescourt, Cardiff CF5 9LR. Tel: (029) 2025 0495.

Llantwit Major

Michael Gill, 7 Tewdrig Close, Llantwit Major. Tel: (01446) 793740. **W/F**

Newport

Alun Booth, 54 Allt-yr-yn Road, Newport NP20 5EB. Tel: (01633) 663364. **GB**
Phil Coates, 288 Pilton Vale, Newport NP20 6LS. Tel: (01633) 774796.

Swansea

Len Ley, 2, Alder Avenue, Ystradgynlais, near Swansea. Tel: (01639) 844102. **D/G I**

Usk

Rosemary Phillips, Willowdene, Llantrisant, Near Usk NP5 1LR. Tel: (01633) 450397.

ENGLAND

London

Katrine Prince, 33 Greencroft Gardens, London NW6 32N. Tel: (020) 7372 7578. **F G I**
Liza Spencer, 7 Baronsmede Court, Baronsmede, London W5 4LN. Tel: (020) 8567 9409. **F I**
Mike Wale, 7 Baronsmede Court, Baronsmede, London W5 4LN. Tel: (020) 8567 9409. **F**

Wiltshire

Joan Robertson, Glebe House, Chitterne, Warminster BA12 0LJ. Tel: (01985) 850382.

Surrey

Inge Garstang, Solbakken, Grafton Road, Worcester Park KT4 7JN. Tel: (020) 8337 7659. **Da**

Where to Stay

Booking Accommodation

When moving on, it is always advisable to make an advance reservation. If staying at a hotel which belongs to a chain or consortium such as "Welsh Rarebits" or "Great Little Places" the hotel will make the reservation on your behalf and at no cost to you. But if your requirements are not straightforward your best advice is to call at your nearest TIC (Tourist Information Centre) and ask about their "Book a Bed Ahead" scheme.

Hotels

Wales offers a wide range of accommodation from small cottages and farmhouses offering Bed and Breakfast to hotels of international standard. There are very few hotels with more than 100 bedrooms outside the capital, Cardiff. Prices vary from about £16 a night to over £100 at the luxury end of the hotel market.

Hotels and guest houses as well as self-catering properties and caravan parks are inspected and graded by the Wales Tourist Board. The Board publishes *Where to Stay in Wales* annually; it contains the most comprehensive list of accommodation available.

Information on where to stay in Wales is also available at all British Tourist Authority offices worldwide.

In London, one can obtain this information and make the necessary reservations at the Wales Centre in the heart of London's West End: Wales Tourist Board London, Britain Visitor's Centre, 1 Regent Street SW1Y 4XT. Tel: (020) 7808 3838. Once you arrive in Wales, call in at a Tourist Information Centre. Most operate a Bed Booking Service.

Welsh Rarebit Hotels and Historic Inns

This listing includes a complete cross-section of accommodation. All are highly individualistic, are privately owned and personally run, offer genuine Welsh hospitality – and good value for money.

PRICES

Prices are as guidelines only. Per person, per night for a double room (two people sharing) and including full Welsh breakfast.

£ = under £40
££ = £40–£50
£££ = £50–£60
££££ = over £60

MID-WALES

Aberdyfi

Penhelig Arms, Aberdyfi. Tel: (01654) 767215. Email: penheligarms@saqnet.co.uk. Friendly inn beside the harbour, with outstanding views of the estuary and noted for its good food. **£**

Aberystwyth

Conrah Country Hotel, Chancery, Aberystwyth. Tel: (01970) 617941. Email: hotel@conrah.freeserve.co.uk. An elegantly restored 19th-century mansion. **£££**

Dolgellau

Penmaenuchaf Hall, Penmaenpool. Tel: (01341) 422129. Email: relax@penhall.co.uk. Website: www.penhall.co.uk. An elegant country house hotel in its own grounds overlooking the Mawddach estuary. **£££**

Knighton

Milebrook House Hotel, Milebrook. Tel: (01547) 528632. Email: hotel@milebrook.kc3ltd.co.uk. A handsome mid-18th-century small hotel with formal gardens and watermeadows, set on the Welsh/English border. **££**

Llangammarch Wells

The Lake Hotel, Llangammarch Wells. Tel: (01591) 620202. Email: lakehotel@ndirect.co.uk. Website: www.ndirect.co.uk/~lakehotel. A superb country house set in 50 acres (20 hectares). **£££**

Machynlleth

Ynyshir Hall, Eglwysfach. Tel: (01654) 781209. Email: info@ynyshir-hall.co.uk. Website: www.ynyshir-hall.co.uk. A charming Georgian country house hotel set in landscaped grounds. **££££**

Presteigne

Radnorshire Arms, Presteigne. Tel: (01544) 267406. Black-and-white timbered historic inn with lots of charm. **££**

NORTH WALES

Beaumaris

Ye Olde Bull's Head, Tel: (01248) 810329. Email: info@bullsheadinn.co.uk. A 500-year-old coaching inn of great character. **££**

Near Betws-y-Coed

Tan-y-Foel, Capel Garmon. Tel: (01690) 710507. Email: tanyfoel@wiss.co.uk. Website: www.tyf@tyfhotel.co.uk. A 16th-century country house with fine restaurant. **££**

Caernarfon

Tŷn Rhos, Llandeiniolen. Tel: (01248) 670489. Email: enquiries@tynrhos.co.uk. Website: www.tynrhos.co.uk. A farmhouse and restaurant, with the highest standards of accommodation and food. **££**

Near Conwy

The Groes, nr. Conwy. Tel (01492) 650545. Friendly 15th-century inn with modern accommoadation. A popular spot. **££**

The Old Rectory, Llansantffraid Glan Conwy. Tel: (01492) 580611. Email: oldrect@aol.com. Website: www.wales.com/oldrectory/. Elegant Georgian-style country house with superb views of Conwy Estuary and Snowdonia. **£££**

Near Corwen

Tyddyn Llan Country House, Landrillo. Tel: (01490) 440264. Email: tyddynllanhotel@compuserve.com. A Georgian house converted with exquisite taste and situated in the beautiful and unspoilt Vale of Edeyrnion. **£££**

Harlech

Hotel Maes-y-Neuadd, Talsarnau. Tel: (01766) 780200. Email: maes@neuadd.com. Website: www.neuadd.com. Beautiful country house in a superb setting. **££££**

Holyhead

Trearddur Bay Hotel. Tel: (01407) 860301. Email: markdgul@aol.com. Website: www.trearddur-bay-hotel.com. A superior seaside hotel with heated indoor pool. **£££**

Lake Vyrnwy

Lake Vyrnwy Hotel. Tel: (01691) 870692. Email: res@lakevyrnwy.com. Website: www.lakevyrnwy.com. Supremely comfortable country house hotel in magnificent lakeside setting. **££££**

Llandudno

Bodysgallen Hall. Tel: (01492) 584466. Email: info@bodysgallen.com. Website: www.bodysgallen.com. One of Britain's most popular country house hotels. **££££**

St Tudno Hotel. Tel: (01492) 874411. Email: sttudnohotel@btinternet.com. Website: www.st-tudno.co.uk. A luxury seaside resort hotel, winner of many awards. **£££**

Near Llangollen

West Arms Hotel, Llanarmon Dyffryn Ceiriog. Tel: (016917) 600665. Email:

gowestarms@aol.com. A charming traditional hotel located in a tranquil village in the Berwyn Mountains. **££**

Northop

Soughton Hall, Northop. Tel : (01352) 840811. Outstanding Georgian country mansion providing elegant surroundings and excellent cuisine. **£££**

Portmeirion

Hotel Portmeirion. Tel: (01766) 770000. Email: hotel@portmeirion-village.com. Website: www.portmeirion-village.com. A uniquely situated luxury hotel. **££££**

Pwllheli

Plas Bodegroes, Pwllheli. Tel: (01758) 612363. Email: gunna@bodegroes.co.uk. Website: www.bodegroes.co.uk. A small Georgian house with acclaimed elegant restaurant. **£££**

SOUTH WALES

Brecon

Griffin Inn, Llyswen. Tel: (01874) 754241. Email: info@griffin-inn.freeserve.co.uk. Website: www.griffin-inn.co.uk. An atmospheric inn-with-rooms, which runs its own Field Sports courses. **£**

Llangoed Hall, Llyswen. Tel: (01874) 754525. Email: llangoed_hall_co_wales_uk@compu serve.com. Website: www.llangoedhall.com. An impressive country house hotel owned by Sir Bernard Ashley, noted for its and modern classical British cuisine. **££££** Email: llangoed_hall_co_wales_uk@ compuserve.com

Nant Ddu Lodge, Cwm Taf. Tel: (01685) 379111. Email: enquiries@nant-ddu-lodge.co.uk Website:www.nant-ddu-lodge.co.uk. Award-winning Georgian hotel in beautiful National Park setting. **££**

Bridgend

The Great House, Laleston. Tel: (01656) 657644. Email: greathse1@aol.com. An historic Grade II listed building beautifully restored with outstanding restaurant and small health spa. **£££**

Near Cardiff

Egerton Grey Country House, Porthkerry. Tel: (01446) 711666. Email: info@egertongrey.co.uk. Website: www.egertongrey.co.uk. A small luxury manor house of great character. **££**

Chepstow

The George Hotel. Tel: (01291) 625363. Former coaching inn in town centre, incorporating part of medieval town walls. Friendly relaxed atmosphere. **££**

Crickhowell

The Bear Hotel, Crickhowell. Tel: (01873) 810408. Email: bearhotel@aol.com. Website: www.bear-hotel.co.uk. An historic coaching inn of great character. **££**

Near Monmouth

The Crown at Whitebrook, Whitebrook. Tel: (01600) 860254. Email: crown@whitebrook.demon.co.uk. An auberge style inn with award-winning restaurant. **£**

Near Swansea

Fairyhill, Reynoldstone, Gower. Tel (01792) 390139. Email: postbox@fairyhill.net. Website: www.fairyhill.net. A characterful 18th-century house set in 24 acres on the beautiful Gower Peninsula. **£££–££££**

SOUTHWEST WALES

Fishguard

Wolfscastle Country Hotel, Wolfscastle. Tel: (01437) 741225. Email: andy741225@aol.com. Small and friendly. Superb restaurant. **£**

Llanwrda

Glanrannell Park Hotel, Crugybar. Tel: (01558) 685230. Email: glanparkhotel@btinternet.com. Website: www.btinternet.com/~glanparkhotel. Set in beautiful parklands, this friendly hotel is a haven for all country lovers. **£**

Tenby

Penally Abbey, Penally. Tel: (01834) 843033. A characterful hotel with many four-poster beds. Close to the sea and golf course. **£££**

St David's

Warpool Court Hotel. Tel: (01437) 720300. Email: warpool@enterprise.net. Website: www. stdavids.co.uk/warpoolcourt. Wonderful location overlooking the magical Pembrokeshire coastline. Imaginative cuisine and good leisure facilities. **££££**

Small Hotels, Inns, Farms & Guesthouses

The following listing is based on a scheme which offers the best, most charming, most charismatic, most comfortable small places to stay in Wales. There are farmhouses, country hotels, guesthouses and inns. All are personally run by the owners and have fewer than 10 bedrooms – en-suite unless otherwise stated.

PRICES

Prices are given as guidelines only – per person per night in a double room, and include full Welsh breakfast. Most Great Little Places can also offer dinner.

£ = under £25
££ = over £25

Anglesey

Llwydiarth Fawr, Llanerchymedd. Tel: (01248) 470321. Large Georgian farmhouse providing beautifully furnished accommodation and delicious country cooking. 3 rooms. **£**

Wern Farm, Menai Bridge. Tel:

(01248) 712421. 17th-century farmhouse full of country comforts. 3 rooms. **£**

PRICES

Prices are given as guidelines only – per person per night in a double room, and include full Welsh breakfast. Most Great Little Places can also offer dinner.

£ = under £25
££ = over £25

Bala

Fron Feuno Hall. Tel: (01678) 521115. Elegant 16th-century family home in its own grounds on a wooded hillside overlooking Lake Bala. 3 rooms. **££**

Barmouth

Llwyndu Farmhouse, Llanaber. Tel: (01341) 280144. Email: peter.thompson@btinternet.com. Website: www.llwyndufarmhouse.co.uk. Comfortable 17th-century farmhouse overlooking Cardigan Bay. 7 rooms. **££**

Beddgelert

Sygun Fawr Country House Hotel. Tel: (01766) 890258. 17th-century Welsh manor house with relaxing atmosphere and lovely mountain views. 9 rooms. **££**

Betws-y-coed

Pengwern Country House, Allt Dinas. Tel: (01690) 710840. Email: marilyn@pengwern49.freeserve.co.uk. Website: www.snowdoniaaccommodation.com. Country house comfort on an intimate scale in charming woodland setting. 3 rooms. **££**

Brechfa

Tŷ Mawr Country Hotel. Tel: (01267) 202332. Website: www.tymawrcountryhotel.co.uk. A jewel deep in the green forested hills near Carmarthen, noted for its excellent food. 5 rooms. **££**

Brecon

Cantre Selyf. Tel: (01874) 622904. Email: cantreselyf@imaginet.com. Website: www.imaginet.co.uk/cantreselyf. Beautifully furnished and renovated 17th-century townhouse. 3 rooms. **£**

Caernarfon

Hafoty, Rhostryfan. Tel: (01286) 830144. Website: www.accomodata.co.uk/310898.htm 18th-century farmhouse, with award-winning accommodation and breath-taking views. 4 rooms. **£**

Cardiff

The Town House, 70 Cathedral Road. Tel: (029) 2023 9399. Email: thetownhouse@msn.com. Small hotel of distinction a mere 10 minute walk from castle and shops. 9 rooms. **££**

Conwy

Sychnant Pass House. Tel: (01492) 596868. Hospitable and comfortable country house in own grounds on hillside above Conwy. 10 rooms. **££**

Near Corwen

Delfryn (The Old Rectory), Betws Gwerfil Goch. Tel: (01490) 460387. Email: delfryn@zetnet.co.uk. Relaxing country hideaway serving delicious homemade food. 3 rooms. **££**

Crickhowell

Tŷ Croeso Hotel, Dardy, Llangatock. Tel: (01873) 810573.. Email: tycroeso@ty-croeso-hotel.freeserve.co.uk. Website:www.wiz.to/tycroeso. Set in a historic building this small hotel offers imaginative Welsh cooking. 8 rooms. **££**

Dolgellau

Borthwnog Hall, Bontddu. Tel: (01341) 149271. Email: borthhall@enterprise.net. Website: http://homepages.enterprise.net/borthwnoghall. A Regency house in an outstanding location overlooking the Mawddach Estuary, and a favourite with ornithologists and art lovers. 3 rooms. **££**

Harlech

Castle Cottage. Tel: (01766) 780479. A small hotel standing almost in the shadow of Harlech's mediaeval castle and noted for its award-winning restaurant. 6 rooms **££**

Haverfordwest

Lower Haythog Farm, Spittal. Tel: (01437) 731279. Attractive old farmhouse on working dairy farm serving excellent food. 4 rooms. **£**

Hay-on-Wye

Three Cocks Hotel. Tel: (01497) 847215. A traditional hostelry of great historic character, renowned for its excellent restaurant. 7 rooms. **££**

Near Llangrannog

The Grange Country House, Pentregat. (01239) 654121. Email: paul.kimber@btinternet.com. Pink-washed Georgian house with high standards of comfort and cuisine. 3 rooms. **££**

Lampeter

Dremddu Fawr, Creuddyn Bridge. Tel: (01570) 470394. A genuine taste of Welsh farming life and a winner of the All Wales Top Cook award. 2 rooms. **£**

Llandrindod Wells

Guidfa House, Crossgates. Tel: (01597) 851241. Email: guidfa@globalnet.co.uk. Website: www.guidfa-house.co.uk. A Georgian guest house providing comfortable accommodation, excellent food and a warm atmosphere. 6 rooms . **£**

Llandudno

Bryn Derwen Hotel, Abbey Road. Tel: (01492) 876804. Email: brynderwen@msn.com. Website: www.bryn-derwen-hotel.co.uk. This seaside resort hotel offers stylish accommodation and imaginative, award-winning cuisine. 9 rooms. **££**

Llanfyllin

Cyfie Farm, Llanfihangel-yng-Ngwynfa. Tel: (01691) 648451. A picturesque 17th-century farmhouse serving delicious, home-cooked food. 4 rooms. **££**

Newbridge-on-Wye

Lluestnewydd, Llysdinam. Tel: (01597) 860435. Website: www. wiz.to.zzz. Immaculately restored former hill sheep farm with breathtaking views. 3 rooms. **£**

Pendoylan

Llanerch Vineyard, Hensol. Tel: (01443) 225877. Email: llanerch@cariadwines.demon.co.uk. Guests staying in the modernised farmhouse can tour Wales's largest vineyard. 3 rooms. **£**

Pwllheli

The Old Rectory, Boduan. Tel: (10758) 721519. Immaculately furnished and friendly country house ideally located for visitors to the lovely Llyn Peninsula. 4 rooms. **££**

Near st Clears

Coedllys Uchaf, Llangynin. Tel: (01994) 231455. Outstanding accommodation in peaceful wooded valley. 3 rooms. **£**

Saundersfoot

White Horses, Pen-y-Graig. Tel: (01834) 812182. Former sea captain's home on wooded headland above the sea. 3 rooms. **££**

Talyllyn

Minffordd Hotel. Tel: (01654) 761665. Email: info@minffordd.com. Website: www.minffordd.com. Former 17th-century coaching inn close to the lovely lake of Tal-y-llyn lake. Cuisine with a Welsh flavour. 7 rooms. **££**

Tenby

Heywood Lodge, Heywood Lane. Tel: (01834) 842684. Email: kt@lodge95.freeserve.co.uk. A handsome Victorian gentleman's residence, now offering all modern comforts, a friendly atmosphere, and excellent cuisine. 10 rooms. **££**

Welshpool

Buttington House. Tel: (01938) 553351. Beautiful gentleman's residence with well-proportioned rooms, set in attractive gardens. 3 rooms. **££**

Gungrog House, Rhallt. Tel: (01938) 553381. A spotless 16th-century farmhouse specialising in Welsh home cooking, with view across the Severn Valley. 2 rooms. **£**

Youth Hostels

Website: www.yha.org.uk

MID-WALES

Blaencaron

Youth Hostel, Blaencaron, Tregaron, Ceredigion SY25 6HL. Tel: (01974) 298199.

Borth

Youth Hostel, Morlais, Borth, Ceredigion SY24 5JS. Tel: (01970) 871498.

Dolgellau

Youth Hostel, Kings, Dolgellau LL40 1TB. Tel: (01341) 422392.

Dolgoch

Youth Hostel, Dolgoch, Tregaron, Ceredigion SY25 6NR. Tel: (01974) 298 680.

Corris

Youth Hostel, Old School, Old Road, Corris, Machynlleth SY20 9QT. Tel: (01654) 761686.

Tyncornel

Youth Hostel, Tyncornel, Llanddewi-Brefi, Tregaron, Ceredigion SY25 6PH. Tel: (01629) 581399.

NORTHWEST WALES

Bangor

Youth Hostel, Tan-y-Bryn, Bangor, Caernarfon LL57 1PZ. Tel: (01248) 353516.

Youth Hostel, Idwal Cottage, Nant Ffrancon, Bethesda, Bangor, Caernarfon LL57 3LZ. Tel: (01248) 600225.

Bryn Gwynant

Youth Hostel, Bryn Gwynant, Nant Gwynant, Caernarfon LL55 4NP. Tel: (01766) 86251.

Capel Curig

Youth Hostel, Plas Curig, Betws-y-Coed, Conwy LL24 0EL. Tel: (01690) 720225.

Llanbedr

Youth Hostel, Plas Newydd, Llanbedr, Barmouth LL45 2LE. Tel: (01341) 241287.

Llanberis

Youth Hostel, Llwyn Celyn, Llanberis, Caernarfon, LL55 4SR. Tel: (01286) 870280.

Lledr Valley

Youth Hostel, Lledr House, Pont-y-Pant, Dolwyddelan, Conwy LL25 0DQ. Tel: (01690) 750202.

Pen-y-Pass

Youth Hostel, Pen-y-Pass, Nant Gwynant, Caernarfon LL55 4NY. Tel: (01286) 870428.

Rowen

Youth Hostel, Rhiw Farm, Rowen, Conwy LL32 8YW. Tel: (01492) 650089.

Rhyd Ddu

Youth Hostel, Snowdon Ranger, Rhyd Ddu, Caernarfon, LL54 7YS. Tel: (01286) 650391.

NORTHEAST WALES

Cynwyd

Youth Hostel, The Old Mill, Cynwyd, Corwen, Denbighshire LL21 0LW. Tel: (01490) 412814.

Llangollen

Youth Hostel, Tyndwr Road, Llangollen, Denbighshire LL20 8AR. Tel: (01978) 860330.

Maeshafn

Youth Hostel, Maeshafn, Mold, Denbighshire CH7 5LR. Tel: (01286) 650391.

Chester

Youth Hostel, Hough Green House, 40, Hough Green, Chester CH4 8JD. Tel: (01244) 680056.
Southwest Wales

Broad Haven

Youth Hostel, Broad Haven, Haverfordwest, Pembrokeshire SA62 3JH. Tel: (01437) 781688.

Manorbier

Youth Hostel, Manorbier, nr. Tenby, Pembrokeshire SA70 7TT. Tel: (01834) 871803.

Marloes Sands

Youth Hostel, Runwayskiln, Marloes, Haverfordwest, Pembrokeshire SA62 3BH. Tel: (01646) 636667.

Poppit Sands

Youth Hostel, Sea View, Poppit, Cardigan, Cardiganshire SA43 3LP. Tel: (01239) 612936.

Pwll Deri

Youth Hostel, Castell Mawr, Trefasser, Goodwick, Pembrokeshire SA64 0LR. Tel: (01348) 891385.

St David's

Youth Hostel, Llaethdy, St David's, Haverfordwest, Pembrokeshire SA62 6PR. Tel: (01437) 720345.

Trefin

Youth Hostel, 11, Ffordd-Yr-Afon, Trefin, Haverfordwest, Pembrokeshire SA62 5AU. Tel: (01348) 831414.

SOUTHEAST WALES

Llanddeusant

Youth Hostel, The Old Red Lion, Llanddeusant, Llangadog, Carmarthenshire SA19 9UL. Tel: (01550) 740218.

Capel-y-Ffin

Youth Hostel, Capel-y-Ffin, Abergavenny NP7 7NP. Tel: (01873) 890650.

Cardiff

Youth Hostel, 2 Wedal Road, Roath Park, Cardiff CF2 5PG. Tel: (029) 2046 2303.

Llwyn-y-Celyn

Youth Hostel, Libanus, Brecon, LD3 8NN. Tel: (01874) 624261.

Port Eynon

Youth Hostel, The Old Lifeboat House, Port Eynon, Swansea, SA3 1NN. Tel: (01792) 390706.

Tŷn-y-Caeau

Youth Hostel, Tŷn-y-Caeau, Groesffordd, Brecon LD3 7SW. Tel: (01874) 665270.

Ystradfellte

Youth Hostel, Tai'r Heol, Ystradfellte, Aberdare CF44 9JF. Tel: (01639) 720301.

Self-catering

Self-catering cottages, farmhouses, flats, chalets and static caravans are numerous. Low season weekly tariffs from as little as £80 represent good value, although in the peak season (when advance booking is essential) weekly rentals rise to £300 or more depending on the unit's size and location. Short breaks are widely available at attractive prices. One of the specialist self-catering agencies is Wales Holidays, Bear House, Broad Street, Newtown, Powys SY16 2QZ, tel: (01686) 628200. There are many excellent campsites in Snowdonia, usually costing between £5 and £8 for an overnight pitch.

Where to Eat

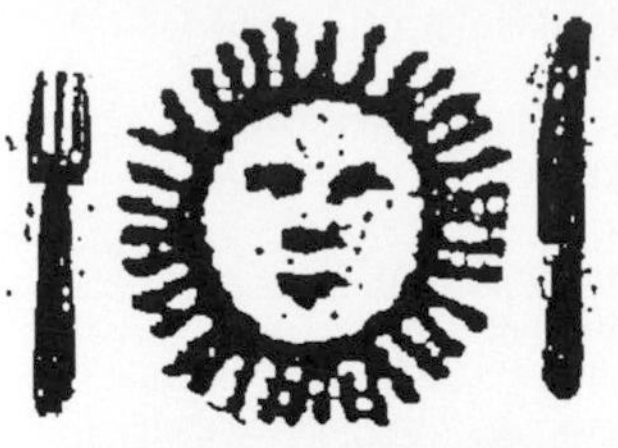

What to Eat

In many Welsh seaside resorts it is regrettably still chips with everything, and the increase in fast-food, hamburger and pizza restaurants in cities such as Cardiff are sadly a sign of the times. Wales, however, is no longer a gastronomic desert. Standards have improved dramatically in recent years.

Cardiff can boast an amazing selection of international cuisines with some of its Chinese and Indian restaurants comparing favourably with the best in Britain.

On your travels throughout Wales, look out for the *Blas ar Cymru*/Taste of Wales symbol. You'll find it at hotels, restaurants, farmhouses, guest houses and country inns which serve tempting Welsh foods prepared at their very best.

The Taste of Wales scheme embraces many styles of cooking. For the traditionalists, there are dishes such as succulent Welsh lamb and the Welsh speciality, laverbread, which is as distinctive to Wales as is haggis to Scotland. The more modern, lightly prepared style of cuisine is also very much a part of Taste of Wales – try some lightly poached sewin (sea-trout), for example.

Taste of Wales puts emphasis on fresh, high quality produce cooked with flair and imagination. The Welsh larder is a bountiful one, catering for all tastes. Southwest Wales is known as the cheese store of Wales. The green heartlands of central and North Wales give us the star of Welsh cuisine, lamb. And since Wales is surrounded by the sea on three of its four sides, seafood figures strongly. Try Gower oysters, Cardigan Bay lobsters, Menai mussels and Conwy salmon.

On cold days, try *cawl*, a traditional meat, root vegetable and leek soup – or perhaps *lobscows*, a warming lamb broth.

Morning coffee and afternoon tea may be accompanied by Welsh cakes (*Cacen Radell*). which are flat, round, fruited and spread with butter or castor sugar. Another teatime favourite is *Bara Brith*, an old-fashioned fruited tea bread whose equivalent is found in other Celtic countries: *Barm Brack* in Ireland, *Selkirk Bannock* in Scotland and *Morlais Brioche* in Brittany.

Where to Eat

The following is a selection of country house hotels, bistros, guest houses, country inns, farmhouses and tearooms noted for serving quality cuisine. Some display the "Taste of Wales" symbol, which denotes a commitment to using local produce and good service.

Aberdyfi

Penhelig Arms Hotel & Restaurant. Tel: (01654) 767215. Excellent country cooking in an 18th-century harbourside inn. Generous portions and good wine list.

Abergavenny

Greyhound Vaults, Market Street. Tel: (01873) 858549. Welsh and English dishes, including vegetarian specialities.

Walnut Tree Inn, Llandewi Skirrid. Tel: (01873) 852797. Italian gourmet fare, excellent but expensive.

Abersoch

Porth Tocyn Hotel. Tel: (01758) 713303. Family-run for 40 years. Good deal for children.

Aberystwyth

Gannets, 7 St James Square. Tel: (01970) 617164. Bistro making the most of fresh local produce.

Royal Pier Tandoori, The Pier. Tel: (01970 625719). Curry joint with great views from the end of the pier.

Bangor

Menai Court Hotel, Craig-y-Don Road. Tel: (01248) 354200. Traditional but finely cooked hotel food and extensive wine list.

Betws-y-Coed

Tŷ Gwyn, on the A5 to the east of town. Tel: (01690) 7103383. Delicious food in old coaching inn.

Brecon

Peterstone Court Hotel, Llanhamlach, near Brecon. Tel: (01874) 86387. Good food in elegant surroundings.

Broad Haven

Swan Inn, Little Haven, near Broad Haven. Tel: (01437) 781256. Very good seafood.

Caernarfon

Stone's, Hole in the Wall Street. Tel: (01286) 671152. Simple bistro-style meals.

Cardiff

Armless Dragon, 97 Wyevern Road, Cathays Tel: (029) 2038 2357. Offbeat restaurant with Welsh dishes plus fresh fish.

Blas ar Gymru, Crwys Road, Cathays. Tel: (029) 2038 2132. Wide range of traditional dishes from all over Wales.

Juboraj II, Mill Lane. Tel: (029) 2037 7668 or 2037 1381. Award winning Indian restaurant in Cardiff's vibrant café quarter.

Giovanni's, The Hayes. Tel: (029) 2022 0077. Reliable Italian menu and lively atmosphere.

The Noble House, Wood Street. Tel: (029) 2038 8317. Good-value Peking and Szechuan cuisine.

Tang's, Westgate Street. Tel: (029) 2022 7771. One of Cardiff's best Chinese restaurants.

Cardigan

Rose of India, Priory Street. Tel: (01239) 614891. Curries, etc.

Carmarthen

Farm Retreats, Capel Uchaf Farm, Capel Dewi, near Carmarthen. Tel: (01267) 290799. Good local fare.

Crickhowell

Bear Hotel. Tel: (01873) 810408. Interesting menus in characterful old coaching inn.

Dolgellau

Dylanwad Da. Tel: (01341) 422870. Colourful bistro offering vegetarian choice.

Harlech

Castle Cottage Hotel & Restaurant, Pen Llech. Tel: (01766) 780479. Oak-beamed hotel beneath castle's wing. Good value.

Haverfordwest

Celtic Corner, Nolton. Tel: (01437) 710254. Tasty food, energetic music-making.

Hay-on-Wye

Granary, Broad Street. Tel: (01497) 820790. Bistro with local fare and vetetarian dishes.

Old Black Lion, Lion Street. Tel: (01497) 820281. Best bar meals around, plus more expensive restaurant.

Llanberis

Y Bistro, 43-45 Stryd Fawr. Tel: (01286) 871278. Specialises in local Welish produce, including lamb, beef and mussels. Booking advisable.

Llandudno

Bodysgallen Hall. Tel: (01492) 584466. Imposing 17th-century fortified mansion set in large grounds. Extensive wine list.

Gwesty Leamore Hotel, 40 Lloyd Street. Tel: (01492) 875552. Good-value food in friendly guesthouse.

Llanfyllin

Seeds Restaurant, 5 Penybryn Cottages, High Street. Tel: (01691) 648604. Good vegetarian options.

Llangollen

Cedar Tree Restaurant, Bryn Howel Hotel, Trevor, near Llangollen. Tel: (01978) 860119. Award-winning food in beautiful setting.

Gales, 18 Bridge Street. Tel: (01978) 860089. Wine bar with church pews and bistro food.

Monmouth

French Horn, Church Street. Tel: (01600) 772733. Bistro food, including Welsh dishes.

Portmeirion

Hotel Portmeirion. Tel: (01766) 770000. Stunning setting. Contemporary Welsh dishes with Mediterranean influence reflecting Italianate surroundings.

St Davids

Morgan's Brasserie, Nun Street. Tel: (01437) 720508. Fresh fish, well prepared.

Ramsey House, Lawer Moor. Tel: (01437) 720321. Superb food in small hotel.

Swansea

Hwyrnos, Green Dragon Lane, Wind Street. Tel: (01792) 641437. Welsh menu. Live music in evenings.

The Schooner, Prospect Place. Tel: (01792) 649321. Good-value fish restaurant. Local catches.

Talsarnau

Maes-y-Neuadd. Tel: (01766) 780200. Peter Jackson leads Welsh Culinary Team. Collaborates with Ffestiniog Railway for "Steam and Cuisine" events.

Tenby

Plantagenate, Quay Hill. Tel: (01834) 842350. Local well-presented food in very old building.

Tywyn

Tynycornel Hotel, Talyllyn. Tel: (01654) 782282. Good, uncomplicated fare in anglers' hotel.

Welshpool

Royal Oak Hotel, The Cross. Tel: (01938) 552217. Good food in upmarket coaching inn.

Wrexham

The Stableyard, High Street, Bangor-on-Dee (SW of Wrexham). Tel: (01978) 780642. Fine food in converted village tavern.

Y Dafarn Newydd, Mountain Street, Rhosllanerchrugog, near Wrexham. Tel: (01978) 840471. Good-value local fare.

Banquets

Three Welsh castles stage medieval banquets – usually on as many as five or six evenings a week during the main summer months. Those with a taste for such fantasies can "join the Baron and Baroness in the romantic candlelit splendour" of Caldicot, Cardiff or Ruthin, being "welcomed and attended by the gracious and talented ladies of the Court in their colourful medieval gowns, and served with mead, wine and succulent dishes".

The banquets usually start at 7.30 or 8pm and last approximately two and half hours. The all-inclusive cost (meal, wine, entertainment) is in the region of £25 a person. Advance booking is advisable; dress is informal. Some main venues are:

Caldicot Castle, Caldicot, near Newport . Tel: (01291) 424447

Cardiff Castle, Cardiff . Tel: (029) 2037 2737

Ruthin Castle, Ruthin, Denbighshire. Tel: (01824) 702664.

If you are in Southwest Wales, traditional Welsh nights (gatherings where you enjoy food and song) are held in Nolton, near Haverfordwest (Celtic Corner). Tel: (01437) 710254/710239.

Drinking Notes

Pubs in Wales, as elsewhere in Britain, are evolving in many cases into wine bars or restaurants. Brewers are spending millions of pounds on refurbishment. Nowhere is this more apparent than in Cardiff, where the old established brewery company S.A. Brain turned many of the real pubs in the city centre into trendy bars.

New relaxed licensing laws now mean that many pubs in towns and cities are open on weekdays from 11am–11pm and usually from noon–3pm and 7–11pm on Sunday. But do not rely on these hours. The choice is left to the landlord, and in country areas most pubs will be closed between 3pm and 6pm in the afternoons.

Pubs in Wales are usually either brewery owned (or financed) or free houses. Free houses do not give their drinks away free – in these areas the pub owners are free to choose the type of beer and drinks they sell. They may buy from several breweries thus giving their clients greater freedom of choice. Free houses generally have greater character than brewery owned pubs.

Most pubs in Wales now serve at least one type of "real ale" – that is, beer brewed in the traditional method and cask-conditioned. The three largest Welsh breweries are all in the South: Brains (Cardiff) and Felinfoel and Buckleys (Llanelli). Brains has approximately 200 of its own pubs in Cardiff and the surrounding area whilst Felinfoel, brewers of Double Dragon ale in West Wales is justifiably proud of the fact that it is the oldest canner of beer in the world.

Wine bars and café-bars have become fashionable in recent years; but as with pubs and inns the food element is now in many cases as important as the drink.

For good Welsh company as well as good Welsh cheer, find out where the local male voice choir quench their thirst after their weekly rehearsal, or visit a cattle or sheep market when the farmers are in town.

Attractions

Culture

First and foremost, Wales is renowned for its castles. More than 100 are open to the public – everything from the powerful "showpiece" castles of Caernarfon, Harlech and Caerphilly to lesser known, but no less spectacular, fortresses hidden deep in the country.

It is also renowned for its narrow-gauge railways – the Ffestiniog, Talyllyn, Vale of Rheidol, Llanfair and Welshpool, Llanberis Lake and the Brecon Mountains Railway. And it's the only place where you can catch a train to the top of the highest mountain in England and Wales; then, within a few miles, go deep underground and explore old slate caverns.

Apart from its outstanding castles, narrow-gauge railways and museum, Wales offers a great variety of attractions. Comprehensive information, including details of current opening times and admission prices, is available from the Wales Tourist Board but here are 10 very different experiences that you shouldn't miss on your visit to Wales:

Portmeirion, near Porthmadog. An unique Italianate village and architectural work of art.

Caerleon Roman Fortress, near Newport. The only excavated Roman barracks building in Britain, together with amophitheatre and bath-house complex.

Big Pit Mining Museum, Blaenafon. An underground tour of a former working coalmine.

Carreg Cennen Castle, near Llandeilo. Romantic ruin perched spectaculary on a crag.

Dylan Thomas's Boathouse, Laugharne. The home and inspirational setting of Wales's most famous 20th-century Anglo-Welsh poet.

Llanfairpwllgwyngyllgogerychwyrnd robwllllantysiliogogogoch, Isle of Anglesey. The railway station with the world's most photographed placename.

Dolaucothi Gold Mines, near Llandovery. First exploited by the Romans and last worked in the 1930s.

Cardiff Castle. Fascinating three-in-one historic site - Roman fort, Norman keep and lavish 19th-century manion.

Centre for Alternative Technology, near Machynlleth. The world of "green living" explored at this innovative "village of the future".

Bodnant Gardens, Conwy Valley. Undoubtedly one of the best in Britain. 100 acres of trees, shrubs and flowers.

Castles

NORTH WALES

Most castles also house exhibitions on their own heritage and history.

Beaumaris Castle, Isle of Anglesey. Tel: (01248) 810361 Open all year. Begun in 1295 and on the World Heritage List as a site of outstanding universal value, it has the best example of concentric walls within walls in Britain.

Bodelwyddan Castle, 2 miles (3 km) west of St Asaph, off A55. Tel: (01745) 584060. Following an earlier building, this is another example of Victorian neo-Classicism on a heroic scale. Beautifully restored and used as a girls' school, it now houses some of the National Portrait Gallery's Victorian paintings.

Caernarfon Castle. Tel: (01286) 677617. Open all year. A medieval stronghold of immense significance, this majestic fortress with lofty towers was built by Edward I in the late 13th century. Another World Heritage Listed site.

Chirk Castle, 1 mile (2 km) west of Chirk, off A55, Clwyd. Tel: (01691) 777701. Magnificent medieval castle built in 13th century and occupied ever since as rich stately home. Also has a deep circular dungeon and acres of 18th-century parkland.

Conwy Castle. Tel: (01492) 592358. Open all year. An outstanding feat of medieval military construction; one of the great fortresses of Europe with wonderful views from its turrrets. A World Heritage Listed site.

Criccieth Castle. Tel: (01766) 522227. Open all year. Commanding superb views over Tremadog Bay, this castle was captured and burnt in 1404 and never rebuilt.

Denbigh Castle Tel: (01745) 813385. Most noted for its triple-towered gatehouse, this 14th-century castle has had a turbulent history and crowns a rocky outcrop in the delightful Vale of Clwyd.

Harlech Castle. Tel: (01766) 780552. Open all year. Built on a rocky crag high above the coastal flats, this is another World Heritage Listed site with aweseome defensive strength; it has great majesty and commands superb views.

Penrhyn Castle, 1 mile (2 km) east of Bangor, on A5122. Tel: (01248) 353084. Grand 19th-century castle built on a massive scale and elaborately decorated.

Powis Castle, 1 mile (2 km) south of Welshpool, on A483. Tel: (01938) 554336. Original medieval construction transformed into grand stately home but most noted for its beautiful and brilliantly designed gardens.

SOUTH WALES

Caerleon Roman Remains, Caerleon, 4 miles (7 km) northeast of Newport. Tel: (01633) 422518. Open all year. Remains of important fortress with modern exhibition and life-size figures. Well-preserved amphitheatre and excavated bath-house complex.

Cardiff Castle. Tel: (029) 2087 8100. Unique combination of Roman fort, Norman and medieval stronghold, and Victorian Gothic fantasy; perhaps the most bizarre building of the Victorian era.
Caerphilly Castle Tel: (029) 2088 3143. Open all year. One of the greatest surviving medieval fortresses, deriving its stunning impact from its vast size and distinctive water defences, it is an extraordinary sight with a great variety of things to see.
Carreg Cennen Castle, off A483, southeast of Llandeilo. Tel: (01588) 822291. Open all year. Commanding magnificent views of Brecon Beacons National Park, this 13th-century building stands on a great crag almost 300 ft (90 metres) above the River Cennen.
Castell Coch, 5 miles (8 km) northwest of Cardiff, off A470. Tel: (029) 2081 0101. Open all year. An astonishingly different construction, this 13th-century ruin was transformed in the 19th century by an opium-inspired architect, resulting in one of the most romantic buildings in Wales with pointed turrets adorning the steep hillside.
Chepstow Castle Tel: (01291) 624065. Guarding a major crossing from England to Wales high up on its cliff above the River Wye, this strategic construction mirrors the history of fortification from medieval times and also houses life-size models of the medieval lords.
Kidwelly Castle. Tel: (01554) 890104. Open all year. Remarkably complete, grand medieval castle with distinctive gatehouse.
Pembroke Castle. Tel: (01646) 681510. Impressive stronghold right in the middle of town. Also a well-preserved stretch of medieval town walls.
Raglan Castle, Raglan, off A40. Tel: (01291) 690228. Open all year. Situated in beautiful countryside, this 15th-century castle has distinctive French influences and a prominent Great Tower with water defences.
Tretower Castle and Court, Tretower, 3 miles (5 km) northwest of Crickhowell, off A40. Tel: (01874) 730279. Open all year. The glorious late medieval house replacing the earlier castle stronghold with its solid 13th-century keep creates vivid impressions of the life of the 15th and 16th-century gentry.

Museums

No visit to Wales is complete without a visit to one of its many museums.

The National Museums and Galleries of Wales has three oustanding museums in Cardiff alone, as well as the Museum of the Welsh Woollen Industry in the Teifi Valley in West Wales and the Welsh Slate Museum in Llanberis at the foot of Snowdon in North Wales.

Although many of the museums listed are small, the variety is considerable.

MID WALES

Ceredigion Museum, Aberystwyth. Tel: (01970) 617911.
Museum of the Welsh Woollen Industry, near Newcastle Emlyn. Tel: (01559) 370929.
Owain Glyndwr Centre, Machynlleth. Tel: (01654) 702827.
Powysland Museum and Canal Centre, Welshpool. Tel: (01938) 554656.
Robert Owen Museum, Newtown. Tel: (01686) 626345.

North Wales

Alice in Wonderland Visitor Centre, Llandudno. Tel: (01492) 860082.
Bersham Ironworks Heritage Centre, Wrexham. Tel: (01978) 261529.
Conwy Valley Railway Museum, Betws-y-Coed. Tel: (01690) 710568.
Doll Museum at Penrhyn Castle, Bangor. Tel: (01248) 353084.
Holyhead Maritime Museum, Holyhead. Tel: (01407) 762816.
Llangollen Motor Museum, Llangollen. Tel: (01978) 860324.
Museum of Childhood, Beaumaris. Tel: (01248) 712498.
Segontium Roman Fort Museum, Caernarfon. Tel: (01286) 675265.
Welsh Slate Museum. Llanberis. Tel: (01286) 870630.

South Wales

Afan Argoed Country Park & Welsh Miners Museum, Port Talbot. Tel: (01639) 850564.
Big Pit Mining Museum, Blaenavon. Tel: (01495) 790311.
Caldicot Castle, Museum & Country Park, Caldicot. Tel: (01291) 420241.
Cefn Coed Museum, Neath. Tel: (01639) 750556.
Cyfarthfa Castle Museum, Merthyr Tydfil. Tel: (01685) 723112.
Dylan Thomas's Boathouse, Laugharne. Tel: (01994) 427906.
Gwent Rural Life Museum, Usk. Tel: (01291) 673777.
Kidwelly Industrial Museum, Kidwelly. Tel: (01554) 891078.
Maritime & Industrial Museum, Swansea. Tel: (01792) 650351.
Museum of Welsh Life, St Fagans. Tel: (029) 2057 3500.
National Museum of Wales, Cardiff. Tel: (029) 2039 7951.
Stuart Crystal Visitor Centre, Chepstow. Tel: (01291) 620135.
Techniquest ("Hands On" Science Museum), Cardiff. Tel: (029) 2047 5475.
Welsh Regiment Military Museum at Cardiff Castle, Cardiff. Tel: (029) 2022 9367.

Arts Centres & Theatres

A number of modern purpose-built art centres throughout Wales attract leading companies and first-class productions throughout the year. In addition to their stage facilities, many of these centres have attractive exhibition areas, art galleries, cinemas, bars, coffee shops and restaurants.

Drop in at any time for a relaxing couple of hours. There's a theatre within easy driving distance of most holiday centres.

MID-WALES

Aberystwyth Arts Centre, Penglais, Aberystwyth, Cardiganshire SY23 3DE. Tel: (01970) 623232.
Theatr Ardudwy, Coleg Harlech, Harlech LL46 2PU. Tel: (01766) 780667.
Theatr Brycheiniog, Canal Wharf, Brecon LD3 7EW. Tel: (01874) 611622.
Theatr Felinfach, Felinfach, Llanbedr Pont Steffan, Lampeter, Cardiganshire SA48 8AF. Tel: (01570) 470697.
Theatr Hafren, Llanidloes Road, Newtown SY16 1BE. Tel: (01686) 625007.
Theatr Mwldan, Cardigan SA43 1JY. Tel: (01239) 621200.
Theatr y Castell/Castle Theatre, St Michael's Place, Aberystwyth, Cardiganshire SY23 2AU. Tel: (01970) 624606
Wyeside Arts Centre, Castle Street, Builth Wells. LD2 3BN. Tel: (01982) 552555
North Wales
The North Wales Theatre, Llandudno. Tel: (01492) 879771.
New Pavilion Theatre, East Promenade, Rhyl. Tel: (01745) 330000.
Theatr Clwyd, Mold. Tel: (01352) 756331.
Theatr Gwynedd, Ffordd Deiniol, Bangor. Tel: (01248) 351708.

SOUTH WALES

Berwyn Centre, Nantymoel, Bridgend. Tel: (01656) 840439.
Brangwyn Hall, Swansea, Tel: (01792) 635489.
Chapter Arts Centre, Market Road, Canton, Cardiff. Tel: (029) 2031 1050.
Congress Theatre, 50 Gwent Square, Cwmbran. Tel: (01633) 868239.
Dolman Theatre, 5 Kingsway, Newport . Tel: (01633) 263670.
Dylan Thomas Theatre, 7 Gloucester Place, Swansea. Tel: (01792) 473238.
Grand Theatre, Singleton Street, Swansea SA1 3QJ. Tel: (01792) 475715.
Llandovery Theatre, Stone Street, Llandovery. Tel: (01550) 720113.
Llantarnam Grange Arts Centre, Cwmbran. Tel: (01633) 4833321.
New Theatre, Park Place, Cardiff. Tel: (029) 2087 8889.
St David's Hall, The Hayes, Cardiff. Tel: (029) 2087 8500.
St Donat's Art Centre, St Donat's Castle, Llantwit Major. Tel: (01446) 799100.
Sherman Theatre, Senghennydd Road, Cardiff. Tel: (029) 2023 0451.
Tailiesin Arts Centre, University College, Singleton Park, Swansea. Tel: (01792) 296883.
Torch Theatre, St Peter's Road, Milford Haven. Tel: (01646) 695267.

Art Galleries

Few people realise that one of the best collections of French Impressionist paintings in the world, with works by such artists as Renoir, Cézanne, Monet and Manet is to be found in the National Museum of Wales in Cathays Park, Cardiff. The museum also has numerous sculptures by Rodin and Degas including Rodin's *The Earth* and *The Moon* and *The Kiss*.

Other art galleries in Wales include Turner House, Penarth (a small attractive gallery holding temporary exhibitions of pictures and objêts d'art from the National Museum of Wales and other sources); Glynn Vivian Art Gallery, Swansea; Oriel Plas Glyn y Weddw, Llanbedrog, near Pwllheli; Tegfryn Art Gallery, Cadnant Road, Menai Bridge, Isle of Anglesey; Oriel Ynys Mon, Llangefni, Isle of Anglesey (an outstanding collection of paintings by wildlife artist Charles Tunnicliffe, of special interest to ornithologists); Mostyn Art Gallery, Vaughan Street, Llandudno; National Portrait Gallery, Bodelwyddan Castle, near Bodelwyddan, St Asaph: Museum of Modern Art, Y Tabernacl, Machynlleth.

Concerts

The spectacular ultra-modern 2,000-seater St David's Hall in Cardiff is undoubtedly Wales's premier concert venue. World-class symphony orchestras, massed Welsh choirs, jazz bands, rock groups and international superstars perform here regularly. St David's Hall offers a tremendous variety of events, is open all year and offers an exciting programme on most nights of the week.

The North Wales Theatre at Llandudno is also an excellent modern venue with a wide-ranging programme of entertainments.

Music

Players of international repute are frequent visitors to Cardiff, and the *Jazz Cafe* on St Mary Street or *Sam's Bar* on Mill Lane can usually guarantee a live session on most nights of the week all year round.

Apart from the annual Welsh Jazz Festival, the success story of the 1980s and now acknowledged as one of the foremost in Europe, is the annual Brecon Jazz Festival (held in August). Another small town in North Wales, Llangollen, better known perhaps for its International Musical Eisteddfod, has also launched its very own annual Jazz Festival (May).

Welsh Choirs

Most towns and rural areas boast a choir of one kind or another, with male choirs by far the most numerous. Obtain a copy of *Events in Wales* from the Wales Tourist Board or call at your nearest Tourist Information Centre to find out details of concerts. If the dates do not correspond with your visit, then all is not lost.

The majority of choirs have no objection to visitors sitting quietly at the back of the hall during their weekly or twice weekly rehearsals. (August is usually a blank month). This is for many an experience of a lifetime. Some the the more thirsty choristers retire to a nearby pub after rehearsal. Try to join them and savour the best of Welsh fun and friendship. There are more than 100 male voice choirs in Wales.

Here are details of some of the best.

Aberystwyth Male Choir. Rehearsals: Thursday 7.45pm. Further details: Mr Mervyn Hughes. Tel: (01970) 828001.

Brythoniaid Male Choir (Blaenau Ffestiniog). Rehearsals: Thursday 7.45pm. Further details: Mr Huw Trefor Jones. Tel: (01766) 512863.

Caldicot Male Voice Choir (near Newport). Rehearsals: Monday and Thursday 7pm (except Christmas Holidays). Further details: Mr Roy Shuck. Tel: (01291) 423046.

Cor Meibion Llanelli. Rehearsals: Tuesday and Thursday 7pm (except Christmas and Easter). Further details: Mr M. Mason. Tel: (01554) 747206.

Cor Meibion Morlais (Rhondda). Rehearsals: Tuesday and Friday 7.30pm. Further details: Mr B. Young. Tel: (01443) 685095.

Cor Meibion Trelawnyd (near Rhyl). Rehearsals: Sunday and Tuesday 8pm (except August). Further details: Mr Vince Roberts. Tel: (01745) 710218.

Cor Meibion Y Traeth (Isle of Anglesey). Rehearsals: Monday 7.30pm (except August). Further details: Mr John Gwilym. Tel: (01248) 714196.

Cor Meibon Caerfyrddin (Carmarthen). Rehearsals: Tuesday 7pm (except August). Further details: Mr John James. Tel: (01267) 290537.

Dowlais Male Choir (near Merthyr Tydfil). Rehearsals: Wednesday and Sunday 7.15pm. Further details: Mr Mike Edwards. Tel: (01685) 389591.

Dunvant Male Choir (near Swansea). Rehearsals: Tuesday and Friday 7.30pm (except August and Christmas). Further details: Mr J.K. Jones. Tel: (01792) 203144.

The Morriston Orpheus Choir (near Swansea). Rehearsals: Sunday and Wednesday 7.30pm (except Christmas and New Year). Further details: Mr R. Pugh. Tel: (01639) 772370.

Pendyrus Male Choir (Rhondda). Rehearsals: Sunday 7pm; Wednesday 7.30pm (except August and Christmas). Further details: Mr J.H. Lewis. Tel: (01443) 730383.

Pontarddulais Male Choir (near Swansea). Rehearsals: Wednesday and Sunday 7pm (except August). Further details: Mr Winston Price. Tel: (01792) 865070.

Rhymney Silurian Male Choir (near Caerphilly). Rehearsals: Tuesday and Friday 7.30pm. Further details: Mr G.M. Morris. Tel: (01685) 841431.

Tredegar Orpheus Male Choir. Rehearsals: Wednesday and Friday 7pm (except August). Further details: Mr L. Neil Price. Tel: (01495) 724733.

Treorchy Male Choir. Rehearsals: Tuesday and Thursday 7.30pm (except August). Further details: Mr. I. Morgan. Tel: (01443) 435852.

Ystradgynlais Male Choir (Swansea Valley). Rehearsals: Wednesday 7pm; Friday 6.45pm. Further details: Mr Rhydian Griffiths. Tel: (01639) 843845.

Ballet

Britain's best touring ballet companies perform at the New Theatre in Cardiff, in the Grand Theatre in Swansea and occasionally in the smaller purpose-built theatres in West, Mid and North Wales.

Opera

The Welsh National Opera is now regarded as one of the world's leading opera companies. The company is based in Cardiff and does three or four "seasons" a year in the city (usually May and June, September and October).

These performances are held in the impressive New Theatre in the city centre. With over 80 years of entertainment behind it, the New Theatre has recently been refurbished but still retains its traditional design, ornate decor and red velvet and seats 1,100 people. The creation of a new opera house in Cardiff Bay has been a political hot potato for years; it now appears that opera may find a new home in the proposed Wales Millennium Centre, itself the subject of much heated debate.

The WNO also has at least one "season" at the Grand Theatre in Swansea (usually July) and since 1995 has also been performing at the new North Wales Theatre in Llandudno. In 1989, the orchestra performed for the first time in New York at the Brooklyn Academy before the Princess of Wales and a host of other VIPs and ardent opera followers.

Cinemas

Many conventional cinemas in Wales have closed, leaving probably no more than 20 throughout the country, and those mainly in the larger towns and cities. Cardiff once again offers the most exciting cinema viewing at its Chapter Arts Theatre, one of Britain's largest arts centres which includes among its studios and workshops, two cinemas, two galleries, a theatre, a restaurant and two bars. The Chapter offers a year-round programme for movie fans.

Nightlife

MID WALES

Barmouth

Sandancer Nightclub, Pavillion Buildings, Marine Parade. Tel: (01341) 280198.

Newtown

Crystles Night Club, Broad Street. Tel: (01686) 624275.
North Wales

Bangor

Octagon, Dean Street. Tel: (01248) 354977.

SOUTH WALES

Cardiff

Clwb Ifor Bach, Womanby Street. Tel: (029) 2023 2199.

Club Metropolitan, Baker's Row. Tel: (029) 2037 1549.
Evolution, UCI Building, Hemingway Road, Cardiff Bay. Tel: (029) 2046 4444.
Vision 2K, 43-45 Queen Street. Tel: (029) 2066 4469.

Swansea

Baron's, College Street. Tel: (01792) 650123.
The Palace, 156 High Street. Tel: (0802) 777274.
The Sanctuary, 85-86 Kingsway. Tel: (01792) 366511.

SOUTHWEST WALES

Carmarthen

Harveys Club, Queen Street. Tel: (01267) 234378

Saundersfoot

Sands Disco, Milford Street. Tel: (01834) 813728

Gambling

Cardiff

Les Croupiers, St Mary Street. Tel: (029) 2023 0652/2038 2810.
Tiberius Sporting Club Casino, Greyfriars Road. Tel: (029) 2034 2991.

Festivals

There are the festivals of song and dance known as *eisteddfodau*, country fairs and agricultural shows, sheepdog trials and market days, medieval pageants and Victorian weeks, theatre and music festivals, jazz in the streets and guided walks in the country. And in the cities and towns, you can enjoy everything from world-famous opera to performances by international artistes. The Wales Tourist Board publishes an annual Events booklet, usually available at the beginning of each year. Here is a small selection of important events held:

ALL YEAR

Festival of the Countryside, venues throughout rural Wales

MARCH

St David's Day Gala Concert, St David's Hall, Cardiff

APRIL

Antiques Fair, Brecon
Cambria Arts Festival, Llanddewi Brefi, Tregaron

MAY

Old May Day Fair, Museum of Welsh Life, Cardiff
Llantilio Crossenny Festival of Music and Drama, nr Abergavenny
Crafts in Action, St Donat's
Hay Festival of Literature, Hay-on-Wye (May/June)
Urdd National Eisteddfod (Welsh League of Youth National Eisteddfod), held at different venues each year (May/June)
Beaumaris Festival, Isle of Anglesey (May/June)
St David's Cathedral Festival, St David's (May/June)
Steam and Vintage Rally, Abergavenny
Llangollen International Jazz Festival, Llangollen

JUNE

Llanfyllin Festival, Llanfyllin
Criccieth Festival, Criccieth
Gregynog Festival, Gregynog, near Newtown
Gwyl Ifan (Welsh Folk Dancing Festival), Cardiff.
Gwyl Fawr Aberteifi (Eisteddfod), Cardigan (June/July)
Tregaron Music Festival, Tregaron (June/July)
Lower Machen Festival, near Newport (June/July)
Choral Festival, Llandudno
Three Peaks Yacht Race, Barmouth/Caernarfon

JULY

Llangollen International Musical Eisteddfod, Llangollen
Gwyl Werin y Cnapan (folk festival), near Llandysul
Welsh Proms, St David's Hall, Cardiff
The Snowdon Race (Fell Running), Llanberis
Royal Welsh Agricultural Show, Builth Wells
Gower Festival, Gower's Parish Churches
Fishguard International Music Festival, Fishguard
Musicfest Internaitonal Music Festival and Summer School, Aberystwyth
Cardiff Festival, venues all over Cardiff (July/August)
Abergavenny Festival, Abergavenny
Caernarfon Festival, Caernarfon (July/August)
Brecon County Show, Brecon
Beyond the Border Storytelling Festival, St Donat's

AUGUST

National Eisteddfod of Wales – alternate venue north/south each year
Brecon Jazz Festival, Brecon
Denbigh Festival, Denbigh
Pontardawe Festival, Pontardawe (contemporary world music and dance)
Llandrindod Wells Victorian Festival, Llandrindod Wells
Ruthin Festival, Ruthin
Machynlleth Festival, Machynlleth
Presteigne Festival of Music and the Arts, Presteigne
Gower Agricultural Show, Gower
Conwy Festival of Street Entertainment, Conwy
Menai Strait Regatta, Beaumaris and Caernarfon
Anglesey County Agricultural Show, near Llangefni
United Counties Agricultural Show, Carmarthen
Pembrokeshire County Show, near Haverfordwest
Cardigan Bay Regatta, New Quay
Merioneth Country Agricultural Show, Merioneth
Monmouthshire Agricultural Show, Monmouth

SEPTEMBER

Barmouth Arts Festival, Barmouth
Tenby Arts Festival, Tenby
Harvest Festival, Museum of Welsh Life, St Fagans
Conwy Honey Fair, Conwy
Vale of Glamorgan Festival, St Donat's
Welsh International Four Days Walk, Llanwrtyd Wells
North Wales Music Festival, St Asaph Cathedral

OCTOBER

Swansea Festival of Music and the Arts, Swansea
Swansea Cockles and Celts Week, Swansea
Llandudno October Festival, Llandudno
Anglesey Oyster and Shellfish Festival
Dylan Thomas Celebration, Swansea (October/November)
Experience the Mountains, Tregaron
Holyhead Arts Festival, Anglesey (October/November)
The National Trust Snowdonia Marathon, Llanberis

NOVEMBER

Internaitonal Film Festival of Wales (venue to be decided)
Mid Wales Beer Festival, Llanwrtyd Wells

DECEMBER

Royal Welsh Agricultural Winter Fair, Builth Wells
Christmas Tree Festival, Museum of Welsh Life, Cardiff

Outdoor Activities

Climbing

Snowdonia's great buttresses and gullies have attracted rock-climbers in ever greater numbers since before World War I when Colin Kirkus and John Menlove Edwards pioneered audacious new ascents. Later, in the 1950s, the likes of Joe Brown and Don Whillans immortalised such locations as the Llanberis Pass and Snowdon's Clogwyn Du'r Arddu. More recently interest has spread out from the inland crags to embrace the sea cliffs of Anglesey, the Lleyn Peninsula, Llandudno's Great Orme and the cliffs north of Tremadog. While it is feasible for confident hillwalkers to tackle scrambling routes (requiring the use of hands as well as feet), aid-climbing with ropes should only be attempted in the company of an experienced companion or a qualified instructor.

Courses in hillwalking, climbing, mountaineering and associated sports, including skiing, are provided at Wales's National Mountain Centre at Plas y Brenin, Capel Curig, tel: (01690) 720214.

Mountain Biking

Every kind of cycling terrain exists is the Snowdonia region, from meandering back-lanes to severe mountain gradients. Off-road riding is permitted on public bridleways, unclassified roads and on specially waymarked cycle tracks such as those provided in the Gwydir and Coed y Brenin forests. Cycling is not permitted on footpaths or over trackless countryside. Under the National Voluntary Cycling Agreement for Snowdonia, reached between the cycling organisations, the Sports Council for Wales, Gwynedd County Council and Snowdonia National Park Authority, cyclists are requested not to ride up to, or down from, the summit of Snowdon between 10am and 5pm from 1 June to 30 September. There is full access from October to the end of May. A leaflet available at cycle shops, Warden Centres and Tourist Information Centres outlines alternative routes through mountainous terrain in the Snowdon area. With careful use of an OS map, many itineraries "off the beaten track" can be devised to suit individual abilities.

Walking

Each mountain range enjoys its own distinctive character. In the north the Carneddau offer vast grassy whaleback ridges, while the adjacent Glyders and Tryfan are strewn with frost-shattered boulders. Behind Tremadog Bay rise the Rhinogs, unfrequented mountains of ankle-twisting rock and deep heather. Both the Cadair Idris and Snowdon massifs offer rugged walking, sustained gradients and wonderful views. By contrast, the featureless and often boggy Migneint between Bala and Ffestiniog is strictly for connoisseurs of solitude. The Aran ridge running north from Dinas Mawddwy to Bala Lake is regaining popularity after access problems. West and north of Blaenau Ffestiniog the Moelwyns are laced with the fascinating relics of slate mining.

For family groups and the less mobile there are miles of gentler footpaths and bridleways to explore. Good examples may be found in Gwydir Forest around Betws-y-Coed, in Coed y Brenin Forest near Dolgellau and around many of Snowdonia's more accessible lakes. The dismantled Welsh Highland Railway at Beddgelert gives an entertaining ramble through several tunnels and there is estuary-edge walking on the Penmaenpool to Morfa Mawddach Track west of Dolgellau.

Waymarked long-distance trails include the 108-mile (174-km) Dyfi Valley Way, the 60-mile (97-km) North Wales Path between Prestatyn and Bangor, and the circular 121-mile (194-km) Anglesey Coast Path. Of various challenge walks, the most famous is the Welsh 3000s, a gruelling 37-mile (60km) tramp over all 14 of Snowdonia's 3,000ft (914m)-plus summits within a 24-hour period.

Other Activities

You do not have to be an expert to enjoy pony-trekking. Trekking centres will match horses to individual riding ability; the pace is relaxed and younger children can go along too. Riding and hacking are for the more experienced, with trail riding, sometimes over several days, the most adventurous option. Welsh mountain ponies and the smaller Welsh cobs are used at most riding/trekking centres. Access to the countryside is virtually the same as for mountain biking. The main regional centres are situated at Penmaenpool, near Dolgellau, tel: (01341) 422377; Waunfawr, near Caernarfon, tel: (01286) 650342; Llanfairfechan, tel: (01248) 681143; Ty Coch Farm near Penmachno, tel: 01690 760248; and Dwyran on Anglesey, tel: (01248) 430977.

Snowdonia's long coastline bordering Cardigan Bay and the Irish Sea is a premier venue for dinghy sailing. There are excellent marinas at Conwy, Caernarfon and Pwllheli, as well as numerous sheltered moorings in fishing harbours and bays. Surfing, windsurfing and sea-kayaking are catered for by a coast offering exposure to, or protection from, all points of the compass. For more information contact the National Watersports Centre for Wales at Plas Menai. Tel: (01248) 670964.

Inland, canoeing is enjoyed on mountain lakes and challenging rivers. For suitable locations and prevailing conditions contact the National White Water Centre near Bala, tel: (01678) 521083.

Shopping

What to Buy

You are almost spoilt for choice in Wales, whether you find yourself in the cities of Cardiff or Swansea or in the coastal towns and mountain villages.

In recent years there has been a dramatic improvement in the quality of Welsh goods sold in craft shops throughout Wales – but look around, don't necessarily buy in the obvious shop. Much of the cheaper range of Welsh souvenirs are still imported. Insist on buying a Welsh product. Check it out in the shop and don't wait until you get home before discovering that the little Welsh doll you bought was made in Hong Kong.

Hand-carved love spoons, authentic maps and prints, cassettes of Welsh choirs, woolly sweaters, gloves, hats and scarves are good value and are easy to pack. Wales also has a wide range of excellent craft workshops where you can see the skills and buy the products of professional craft, gift and textile producers. The best of these are registered with the Wales Craft Council. For a free attractive and informative guide contact them at 20 Severn Street, Welshpool, Powys. Tel: (01938) 555313.

Shopping Areas

Cardiff's shopping centre is one of Britain's finest and most compact. One of its great attractions is that to go from any point of the centre to another is never more than a reasonable walking distance – a walk made simple and pleasant by the pedestrianised shopping streets and extensive system of charming

Victorian and Edwardian arcades.

Major department stores in Cardiff are part of, or are close to, an ultra-modern shopping precinct called the St David's Centre. The smaller shops in the arcades boast a wide range of speciality shops, boutiques, book and craft shops, soft furnishings, buttons, etc. Not to be missed is the covered market.

The market is also a highlight of any shopping visit to Swansea, Wales's second city. Here, as in Cardiff, most of Britain's many departmental stores rub shoulders with long-established family stores. In the old covered market here, you should still be able to buy cockles and laver bread (a Welsh delicacy prepared from seaweed) from the ladies of Penclawdd or some farmhouse cheese and home-grown vegetables from farmers' wives from Gower or Carmarthenshire. The market at nearby Carmarthen is also bustling with local produce.

The largest shopping town in Mid-Wales is Aberystwyth, although small market towns such as Machynlleth have an amazing choice of "speciality" shops. In North Wales, the elegant seaside resort of Llandudno boasts an excellent variety of shopping, whereas Bangor and Wrexham are also considered to be good centres. In the mountain resort of Betws-y-Coed, every shop seems to sell Welsh crafts, while almost every shop in the border town of Hay-on-Wye sells secondhand books.

Shopping Hours

Most shops are open between 9am and 5.30pm six days a week (Monday–Saturday). Some of the larger deparment stores in towns and cities stay open late on Thursday evenings, and, inreasingly, on Sundays. In country areas, smaller shops close for one afternoon a week (usually a Wednesday). Cardiff, Newport, Swansea and most of the larger towns have a good number of "corner" shops that seem to remain open until late at night on seven days of the week. And in tourist areas during the season many of the shops remain open until mid-evening.

Export Procedures

Many visitors will find it worthwhile to take advantage of the Retail Export Scheme whereby they can reclaim VAT (Value Added Tax) on goods purchased for export. Note that not all shops operate this scheme, and there is often a minimum purchase price (there are also minimum values which apply to travellers from European Union countries). Shops operating the scheme may ask to see your passport before completing the VAT form. This form must be presented with the goods to the Customs Office (at the point of departure from Britain or to customs at the point of importation into an EU country) within three months of purchase. After the Customs Officer has certified the form it should be returned to the shopkeeper, who will then send you the VAT refund, from which a small administration fee may be deducted.

Clothing and Shoe Sizes

Dresses/Knitwear/Lingerie

UK	10	12	14	16
USA	8	10	12	14
Europe	40/36N	42/38N	44/40N	46/42N

Shoes

UK	5	6	7	8	9	10	11
USA (ladies)	6½	7½	8½	9½	10½	11	12
USA (men)	–	6½	7½	8½	9½	10½	–
Europe	38	40	41	42	43	44	45

Sport

Walking

Walking is by far the most popular activity with visitors, although to the majority a two or three-mile stroll would be the ultimate. Much of the best walking or hiking is to be found in one of the three National Parks – Brecon Beacons, the Pembrokeshire Coast and Snowdonia – or in one of the areas of Wales especially designated for their outstanding natural beauty e.g. the Wye Valley and Gower Peninsula in South Wales and, in the north, the coastlines of the Llyn Peninsula and Isle of Anglesey together with the Clwydian Range of hills.

The serious walker will wish to tackle one of Wales's long-distance footpaths – the Offa's Dyke Walk from Chepstow to Prestatyn (170 miles/272 km) or the 180-mile (290-km) Pembrokeshire Coastal Footpath. Both offer spectacular scenery and everchanging light and landscapes. Another challenging walk it the Glyndwr Way, which runs for 132 miles (212 km) across some wild mountain scenery in Wales from Knighton to Welshpool via Machynlleth.

Golf

The 160-plus golf courses welcome visiting golfers. Only one club, the Royal Porthcawl, insists on a letter of introduction or a valid membership card from one's home club. The best courses are the links courses to be found around the Welsh coastline.

These are the top two dozen courses, listed by region:
Southeast Wales: St Pierre (tel: 01291 625261), Celtic Manor (tel:

01633 410295/410394), The Rolls of Monmouth (tel: 01600 715353), Bryn Meadows (tel: 01495 225590).
South Wales: Southerndown (tel: 01657 880476), Royal Porthcawl (tel: 01656 782251), Vale of Glamorgan (tel: 01443 222221), Langland Bay (tel: 01792 361721), Cradoc, Brecon (tel: 01874 623658).
West Wales: Ashburnham (tel: 01554 832269), Tenby (tel: 01834 842978), Carmarthen (tel: 01267 281588), Cardigan (tel: 01239 621775).
North Wales: Nefyn and District (tel: 01758 720966), Royal St David's, Harlech (tel: 01766 780361), Aberdyfi (tel: 01654 767493), Holyhead (tel: 01407 763279), Bull Bay (tel: 01407 830960), Conwy (tel: 01492 592423), Maesdu, Llandudno (tel: 01492 876450), Vale of Llangollen (tel: 01978 860906), Northup Country Park (tel: 01352 840440), Llanymynech (tel: 01691 830983),
Mid Wales. Aberystwyth (tel: 01970 615104), Llandrindod Wells (tel: 01597 823873).

Golf green fees in Wales must be as cheap as in almost any part of Britain. The average daily fee during the week ranges from £10 to £20; although this is higher on weekends or Bank Holidays.

Spectator

Wales's national sport is **Rugby Football**, played between September and May. The major first-class clubs are all located in South Wales, between Newport in the east and Llanelli in the west. Fixtures are usually on a Saturday, although many clubs play mid-week games – usually on a Tuesday or Wednesday evening. Almost every village and town in the south has a rugby team and the sport is gaining ground in north Wales.

International matches are all held in Cardiff at the spectacular new Millennium Stadium, still sometimes referred to as Cardiff Arms Park. Tickets for these matches are always extremely difficult to obtain as tickets are all allocated through member clubs.

Association Football (soccer) is the other main winter sport played throughout Wales. The three best teams who play in the English league are Cardiff, Swansea and Wrexham. As with rugby, most games take place on a Saturday.

The third major sport, this time played in summer (but as strange and foreign to most overseas visitors as are rugby and soccer), is **cricket**. Wales has one "championship" team (Glamorgan) which competes with the best counties in England. Most "home" matches are played in Cardiff or Swansea, although occasionally, the team will play in other towns e.g. Neath, Ebbw Vale, Abergavenny and Colwyn Bay in North Wales.

Athletics meetings are held regularly in the summer months. The two best stadia are in Cwmbran and Swansea.

Wales's newest spectator sport, **ice hockey**, attracts capacity crowds for all "home" fixtures in support of the "Cardiff Devils" at the National Ice Rink in Cardiff.

Details of major spectator sporting events taking place in Wales – from the Round Britain Cycle Race to the Network Q Car Rally through the forests of Mid-Wales – are included in *Events in Wales*, published annually by the Wales Tourist Board.

Leisure Centres

In the 1970s most local authorities (councils) in Wales built swimming pools, but since the mid-1980s leisure centres have been developed throughout the country. These centres are open to all and provide a wide range of leisure and health facilities. In almost all cases there are squash courts and a swimming pool, a health suite and a gymnasium. In Cardiff alone there are around half an dozen modern leisure centres with another three within 10 miles (16 km) of the city centre at Penarth, Barry and Cowbridge.

Language

English is spoken throughout Wales by practically all the population. There are various regional dialects, but most visitors to Wales find it easier to understand the Welsh when they speak English than to get to grips with most Scots or English regional dialects.

The most distinctive feature of Wales is its own Welsh language which has its origin in the cradle of European civilisation. It is still very much a living language for about 20 percent of the population and is spoken at home, studied at schools, colleges and universities and used on radio and television.

Welsh is a Celtic branch of the Indo-European family of languages and is related more closely to Breton than to Irish and Scots Gaelic. It has been used as a written language since AD 600 (300 years before French and German were first written) and has changed in few major respects since. The 400th anniversary of the first translation of the Bible into Welsh by Bishop William Morgan was celebrated in 1988.

Written Welsh is standard but spoken Welsh varies greatly in accent, particularly between north and south Wales. Interest in the language has gained ground especially in the more anglicised parts of south Wales, where there has been a remarkable growth in nursery groups, bilingual schools and adult language classes.

Channel 4 Wales (S4C) has its own showing of Welsh television programmes (22 hours per week) and Radio Cymru transmits for an average 12 hours per day. Some 400 books are published in Welsh each year.

Pronunciation

At first glance, many Welsh words look like a particularly unhelpful hand in Scrabble. In fact, once you've picked up the basics of pronunciation, Welsh is more straightforward than English (which is notoriously unphoenetical).

Welsh has 28 letters in its alphabet (English 26 letters) but has no j, k, q, v, x or z. Welsh is phonetic in all but one instance – the letter "y" has two sounds which the English ear can detect:
1. As the "u" sound in understand.
2. As the "ea" sound in the word lea.

There are some sounds in Welsh that are very different from their English equivalents. The following is a basic guide, with Welsh in italics, followed by English.

***c** cath = cat* **c**at
(never as in re**c**eive)
***ch** chwaer = sister* lo**ch**
***dd** yn **dd**a = good* **th**em
***f** y **f**am = the mother* o**f**
***ff** ffenstr = window* o**ff**
***g** gardd = garden* **g**arden
(never as in **G**eorge)
***h** het = hat* **h**at
(never silent as in **h**onest)
ll **ll**aw = hand
There is no equivalent sound. Place the tongue on the upper roof of the mouth near the upper teeth, ready to pronounce **l**; then blow rather than voice the **l**.
***th** by**th** = ever* **th**ree
(never as in English **th**e)

The vowels in Welsh are a e i o u w y; all except "y" can be long or short:

*long **a** tad = father* h**a**rd
*short **a** mam = mother* h**a**m
*long **e** hen = old* s**a**ne
*short **e** pen = head* t**e**n
*long **i** mis = month* g**ee**se
*short **i** prin = scarce* t**i**n
*long **o** mor = sea* m**o**re
*short **o** ffon = walking stick* f**o**nd
*long **w** swn = sound* m**oo**n
*short **w** gwn = gun* l**oo**k
y has two sounds:
1. *CLEAR*
dyn = man, a long "ee" sound almost like English g**ee**se
cyn = before, a short "i" sound almost like English t**i**n
2. *OBSCURE*
Sometimes like the sound in English r**u**n
Examples: ***y** = the*; ***yn** = in*; *d**y**nion = men.*
In Welsh the accent usually falls on the last-syllable-but-one of a word: e.g. c**a**dair = chair

A FEW GREETINGS

Good morning *Bore da*
Good day *Dydd da*
Good afternoon *Prynhawn da*
Good evening *Noswaith dda*
Good night *Nos da*
How are you? *Sut mae?*
Cheers *Hwyl*
Thanks *Diolch*
Thanks very much *Diolch yn fawr iawn*
Welcome *Croeso*
Welcome to Wales *Croeso i Cymru*
Good *Da*
Very good *Da Iawn*
Good health! *Iechyd da!*
Best wishes *Dymuniadau*
Happy birthday *Penblwydd hapus*

MEANINGS OF PLACE NAMES

Aber **mouth of river, joining of rivers**
Afon **river**
Bach **small, lesser**
Clwyd **gate, perch**
Du **black**
Fawr ***big***
Glas ***blue***
Glyn **valley**
Llan **clearing, early church**
Llyn **lake**
Maen **stone**
Maes **field**
Mawr **great**
Merthyr **saint's burial place**
Newydd **new**
Plas **hall, mansion**
Pont ***bridge***
Porth **port**
Taf **dark**
Tŷ **house**

Further Reading

History

A History of Modern Wales, by David Williams. John Murray.
When Was Wales?, by Gwyn A. Williams. Pelican.

Poetry & Literature

Dylan Thomas – Collected Poems 1934–1953, by Walford Davies and Ralph Maud (editors). Dent.
The Collected Poems of Idris Davies, by Islwyn Jenkins (editor). Gomer.
The Oxford Companion to the Literature of Wales, by Meic Stephens. Oxford.
Selected Short Stories, by Gwyn Thomas. Seren.
The Poetry of R. S. Thomas, by J.P. Ward. Poetry Wales Press.

Miscellaneous

Welsh Fever (Welsh Activities in the US and Canada Today), by David Greenslade. D. Brown & Sons.
The Mabinogion (11 stories regarded as a masterpiece of medieval European literature), by Gwyn Jones and Thomas Jones (translators). Everyman Classics.
Australians From Wales, by Lewis Lloyd. Gwynedd Archives & Museums.
The Matter of Wales, by Jan Morris. Penguin.
Welsh Folk Customs, by Trefor M. Owen. Gomer.
Wales (a photographic review of Welsh mountains), by W.A. Poucher. Constable.
The Textiles of Wales, by Ann Sutton. Bellew.
Castles in Wales, by Roger Thomas (editor). AA/Wales Tourist Board.
Complete Guides to North, Mid and South Wales, by Roger Thomas. Jarrold/Wales Tourist Board
Wynford Vaughan Thomas: *Wales*, Mermaid Books.

Biographies

The Autobiography of a Super-Tramp, by W.H. Davies. Oxford.
Rich (The Life of Richard Burton), by Melvyn Bragg. Hodder & Stoughton.
Dylan Thomas, by Paul Ferris. Penguin Library Biographies.
Richard Burton – My Brother, by Graham Jenkins. M. Joseph.
Laughter from the Dark (A Life of Gwyn Thomas), by Michael Parnell. John Murray.
George – An Early Autobiography, by Emlyn Williams. Hamish Hamilton.
Emlyn – A Sequel to George by Emlyn Williams. Penguin.

Learning Welsh

Catchphrase – A course in spoken Welsh, by Sain (two cassettes and/or book).
Welcome to Welsh, by Heini Gruffydd. Y Lolfa (book and cassette).
Welsh is Fun & Welsh is Fun-tastic, by Heini Gruffydd. Y Lolfa.
Teach Yourself Living Welsh, by T.J. Rhys Jones. Hodder & Stoughton.

Other Insight Guides

The 190-title ***Insight Guides*** series includes these titles: *Great Britain, England, London, Oxford, Scotland, Edinburgh, Glasgow, Ireland, Dublin,* and *The Channel Islands.*

In addition, ***Insight Pocket Guides*** to *London, Southeast England, Scotland,* and *Ireland* set out a series of carefully-timed itineraries together with the author's recommendations. The books are designed for the visitor with limited time and each includes a useful full-size fold-out map.

Insight Compact Guides (see panel below) are handy, on-the-spot reference books and include a guide to *Snowdonia & North Wales.*

Insight Flexi Maps cover various areas of Britain, including *London, Cornwall, Devon, The Cotswolds,* and the *Lake District.*

ART & PHOTO CREDITS

Charles Aithie/ffotograff 156, 157, 165, 177, 190, 266
Patricia Aithie/ffotograff 4L, 77, 136, 140, 162, 167, 178, 186R, 212, 218, 219
Allsport UK 74, 75, 76
Britain on View 22/23, 33, 34, 66/67, 68, 69, 71, 72, 104, 161, 163, 186L, 217, 229, 240, 247, 265, 271
Marcus Brooke 16, 120, 203, 233, 242, 251
ffotograff 1, 160, 115L, 192, 205, 259
Paul Gogarty 184
Tony Halliday 2/3, 224, 227L, 230, 231, 234, 238L, 238R, 239, 246, 249, 255, 257L, 257R
Dorothea Heath 111, 113, 115R
Hulton Getty 32, 36, 41, 47
Alain Le Garsmeur 8/9, 62, 63, 85, 88/89, 181, 204, 228, 241, 252/253, 254
Mike Mockler 207
Richard T. Nowitz 2B, 4B, 18, 21, 28, 31, 37, 42, 46L, 56, 57, 59, 70, 81, 82/83, 86, 87, 102, 103, 105, 107, 116, 118, 121, 124/125, 126, 127, 131, 133, 134R, 137, 139R, 138, 139L, 155, 182, 202L, 211, 213, 214, 216, 220/221, 237, 244/245, 258, 264, 267, 269, 272
Derek Pratt 270
Tony Stone Worldwide 19, 26, 40, 50, 52/53, 90/91, 94/95, 100, 134L, 168/169, 187, 202R, 236, 262/263
Topham Picturepoint 6/7, 10/11, 17, 24, 25, 27, 30, 35, 39, 43, 44, 45, 46R, 48, 49, 51, 55, 58, 59, 60, 61, 64, 73, 78, 79, 119, 141, 166, 185, 193, 198, 199, 206, 227R, 232, 235, 243
Wales Tourist Board 4/5, 20, 38, 80, 84, 98, 122, 130, 132L, 132R, 151, 164, 172, 173, 175, 176, 179, 183, 189, 201, 208, 209, 210, 215, 260, 268
Denis Waugh 92/93
Harry Williams 12/13, 29, 108/109, 110, 142/143, 144, 145, 148/149, 150, 153, 154, 194/195, 196, 220/221, 222, 225, 250, 256L, 261
George Wright 106, 117, 123, 135, 158/159, 170, 180, 188, 191

Maps Maria Donnelly/Apa

Editorial Director **Brian Bell**
Cartographic Editor **Zoë Goodwin**
Design Consultants
Carlotta Junger, Graham Mitchener
Picture Research
Hilary Genin, Britta Jaschinski

Index

Numbers in italics refer to photographs

a

b

d

e

n

“I was first drawn to the Insight Guides by the excellent “Nepal” volume. I can think of no book which so effectively captures the essencc of a country. Out of these pages leaped the Nepal I know – the captivating charm of a people and their culture. I’ve since discovered and enjoyed the entire Insight Guide series. Each volume deals with a country in the same sensitive depth, which is nowhere more evident than in the superb photography.”

Sir Edmund Hillary

INSIGHT GUIDE
NEW YORK CITY

INSIGHT GUIDE
DENMARK

INSIGHT GUIDE
SINGAPORE

BUDAPEST

COSTA DEL SOL

CORSICA

LONDON

HONG KONG

IRELAND

CHILE

NEW ORLEANS